MORAL VALUES

A STUDY OF THE PRINCIPLES OF CONDUCT

BY

WALTER GOODNOW EVERETT, Ph. D.

PROFESSOR OF PHILOSOPHY IN BROWN UNIVERSITY

NEW YORK

HENRY HOLT AND COMPANY

TO THE MEMORY
OF
HARRIET CLEAVELAND EVERETT

> Pour le philosophe . . . il ne doit
> pas y avoir dans la conduite un seul
> élément dont la pensée ne cherche à se
> rendre compte, une obligation qui ne
> s'explique pas, un devoir qui ne donne
> pas ses raisons.
>
> Guyau.

PREFACE

This volume, which is offered for the use of college and university classes, has grown out of the author's experience in trying to introduce students to the fundamental problems of ethics. It is hoped, however, that the book may make an appeal to a wider circle of readers—to men and women of various callings to whom neither convention nor authority seems to offer satisfactory answers to the insistent problems of the moral life. If such readers do not feel an interest in the more technical questions of philosophy, they are certainly concerned with those universal human problems that arise out of all genuine experience in the business of living. The titles and divisions of chapters will indicate the portions of the work best suited to individual readers. The attention of the general reader may, however, be called to Chapter VII, the World of Values, to Chapter VIII, Individual and Social Values, and also to the discussions of Moral Law, Freedom, and Morality and Religion. Several sections of this last chapter are devoted to the problem of evil. Contemporary events have served to make this problem keenly felt in many quarters where its significance has, in the past, been slighted or ignored.

The appearance of another book in the field of ethics may seem to demand justification by the presence of features that distinguish it from the many able works already extant. The most obvious characteristic of the present work is suggested by its title. All the problems of morality are here treated as problems of value. The principle of value is carried through from the first chapter to the last, where it is applied to the questions of religion. All human activities, it is shown, are judged to be good or bad, better or worse, according to the contribution which they are thought to make to the worth of human life as a whole. Man is indeed the only being we know that subjects his conduct to this test; he alone keeps accounts, and reckons the profit and loss of his transactions.

In making use of the concept of value I do not fail to remind myself that there is no magic in a word, and that no term must be allowed to conceal difficulties or to offer an escape from the task of rigorous thinking. But the choice of terms is not indifferent; and, quite apart from other advantages, the idea of value tends to bring ethics into more significant and helpful relations with the other sciences of value to which an increasing attention is now being given. I also recognize the inevitable abstractness which must mark every formulation of the moral ideal in terms of a single unifying principle. To avoid "vicious" abstractions, appeal has been made to the concrete interests of life, which alone furnish the specific content of value. The effort towards concreteness finds perhaps its most complete expression in the chapter on The World of Values, which is entirely devoted to the task of showing where this content must always be found.

In these days of the tragic conflict of warring human loyalties, when the supreme sacrifice has been unhesitatingly made by millions on both sides, it ought to become clear, even to the most ordinary intelligence, that no feeling of inner loyalty or conscientiousness can prove a sufficient principle of conduct. It has seemed worth while, therefore, to disentangle with care the inner and the outer, the subjective and the objective factors in moral judgment. Chapters II and X are devoted to this purpose. Chapter II offers a criticism not only of Kantian formalism but also of the more subtle forms of subjectivism, including Professor Royce's doctrine of Loyalty.

One conclusion at least will, it is hoped, be clear to every reader—that morality is nothing more or less than the business of living, with all the many-sided and complex interests which this business involves. Only confusion of thought and practical harm have resulted from the popular idea that morality is a special interest among other special and competing interests, and that "mere morality" can be satisfied by the observance of certain conventional virtues, as these are interpreted by current standards. What has been contended for is that morality is a regard for all human interests in just proportion and harmony. Wherever a narrower conception prevails there is sure to be, at essential points, a fatal divorce between morality and life. A solution of the pressing questions of the economic and social order, of political organization, and of international relations will never be found until they are recognized as of the very essence of morality.

In offering the book to teachers of ethics, two or three further remarks may not be out of place.

The text-book form has been deliberately avoided from a conviction that the elaborately subdivided and analyzed paragraphs of the traditional manual fail to tax adequately the powers of the student, and also tend to leave him with fragmentary ideas rather than to lead him to work through the meaning of fundamental principles.

For elementary classes whose work is limited to a single semester, it may prove desirable to make selections from the text. The topics into which the chapters are divided will in general provide a ready means of such selection.

Apart from the numerous references to the literature of the subject that appear in the foot-notes, no bibliography has been added. Useful bibliographies abound, and every teacher has his favorite selections of literature for the use of students.

I have endeavored to acknowledge, in the pages that follow, my chief obligations to various writers. But there are less tangible forms of indebtedness for which specific acknowledgment cannot so easily be made—the early guidance of teachers, the discussions with colleagues, and the almost unconscious influence of academic associations. I shall always feel deep gratitude to Dr. E. Benjamin Andrews for an initial impulse to the study of philosophy, and to Professor James Seth of Edinburgh University for valued instruction in the period of graduate study. The happy relations, continuing unbroken through many years, with President W. H. P. Faunce and Professor E. B. Delabarre in the department of Philosophy in Brown University have been full of encouragement. I am especially indebted to Dr. Alexander Meiklejohn, President of Amherst College, for discussions, often of almost daily occurrence, during a close comradeship of fifteen years at our *Alma Mater*.

During a year spent at Berkeley, California, in the final preparation of this volume, I received many kindnesses, and not a few helpful suggestions, from colleagues in the department of philosophy, and from former pupils now teaching in the University of California.

My thanks are due to my daughter, Mrs. C. D. Mercer, and to several friends for kindly assistance in proof-reading at a time when circumstances made it impossible for me to give undivided attention to this part of the work. To my colleague, Professor Alfred H. Jones, I am especially grateful for many valued criticisms made both in the manuscript and proof. But my chief indebtedness has been to my daughter Helen, whose untiring devotion, clear insight, and rare enthusiasm for these problems have made possible the completion of the work at this time.

WALTER GOODNOW EVERETT.

BROWN UNIVERSITY,
October 25, 1917.

CONTENTS

CHAPTER I

THE SCOPE AND AIM OF ETHICS

CHAPTER II

THE LOCUS OF MORAL VALUE; TELEOLOGICAL AND FORMAL THEORIES

CHAPTER III

THE DEVELOPMENT OF HEDONISTIC THEORIES

CHAPTER IV

HISTORICAL SKETCH OF SOME PERFECTION THEORIES

CHAPTER VIII

INDIVIDUAL AND SOCIAL VALUES

CHAPTER IX

DUTY AND CONSCIENCE

CHAPTER X

VIRTUE AS THE GOOD–WILL

CHAPTER XI

MORAL LAW

CHAPTER XII

THE ETHICAL INTERPRETATION OF FREEDOM

CHAPTER XIII

MORALITY AND RELIGION

CONTENTS

MORAL VALUES

CHAPTER I

THE SCOPE AND AIM OF ETHICS

I. THE FIELD OF ETHICS

WHAT is the field of ethics? What are the special facts which it undertakes to examine and explain? This is naturally the first inquiry raised by one entering upon the study of the problems of morality. The question may be answered in a preliminary way by the statement that the field of ethics is the field of conduct. But as all conduct is not commonly regarded as of moral significance, that portion of conduct with which ethics deals must be more exactly defined. First of all, ethical conduct may be distinguished from such activity as is seen in the processes of nature. To these we ascribe no moral quality. It is true that we call them good or bad according as they serve or oppose our interests, but it is obvious that these terms are not used here in their moral sense. It is, however, a striking fact that in the earlier stages of civilization men often treated the objects of nature as if they were morally responsible, and even inflicted legal punishments upon them. The Athenians had a special tribunal for the trial of inanimate things, and Plato in the *Laws* recognizes that a kind of guilt may attach to them. Even in modern civilization traces of the same idea have continued in legal codes to a very recent date.[1] Such primitive animism is still seen in the anger with which children, and occasionally older persons, treat the inanimate

[1] Cf. Westermarck, *The Origin and Development of the Moral Ideas*, Vol. I, pp. 260–264.

objects which have caused them pain or injury. Reflection, however, unhesitatingly excludes all activity of unconscious objects from the field of moral conduct.

There is also general agreement that the actions of animals are not properly moral. The mediæval practice of punishing animals, in the same manner in which human beings were punished for like offenses, has passed away as men have come to a clearer understanding of the differences between human and brute intelligence. Animals are believed to exhibit the germs of moral feeling, and their behavior doubtless throws some light upon certain problems in the evolution of conduct. But we know so little of the processes of animal consciousness, and those that bear resemblance to moral feeling in man are so rudimentary, that we are justified in excluding animal conduct from our investigation. The field of conduct to be examined is, therefore, at once narrowed to human conduct.

Not all human action, however, is of moral import, and the elimination of activities which are not significant for morality must be carried further. There are large classes of involuntary activities which are excluded from the sphere of moral judgment. These vary from unconscious reflex and automatic actions, like the beating of the heart or the movements of the eyelids, to conscious motor responses to external stimuli, as when one withdraws the hand from contact with a hot iron or starts at a sudden flash of light. Similarly the action of an epileptic in a fit, or of a patient under the influence of an anæsthetic, is no part of moral conduct. What is here excluded from the sphere of morality indicates by implication what is to be included within that sphere. Only voluntary action, action that is willed, is properly subject to moral judgment. But a still further requirement seems to be made in order that conduct may be judged as morally good or bad; it must be not merely voluntary, but intelligently so. Intellectual disability commonly excludes even voluntary action from the field of moral conduct. Children under a certain age, idiots, and the insane, are not held, in modern civilized communities, to be fully responsible. The history of jurisprudence, which in an important way reflects the moral sentiment of different peoples and periods, shows great diversity of opinion concerning the limits of responsibility as affected by intellectual disability.[1]

This is strikingly exhibited in the treatment of the insane. Among some peoples, the ancient Egyptians for example, these unfortunates were freed from responsibility for their acts, and even treated with a measure of religious veneration, whereas among other peoples they have been punished for misdemeanors or crimes with the greatest severity. The passing of the belief in possession by demons, and the recognition of insanity as pathological, have done away, among the more enlightened nations, with both of these extremes, and have placed the mentally diseased in the class of the morally irresponsible. The nicer questions that arise concerning degrees of responsibility under intellectual disability cannot here be discussed. Nor can we consider the still more difficult questions of the possible limitation of responsibility in cases of drunkenness and of temporary loss of mental balance due to other causes. The final conclusion reached is that ethical conduct is limited to the purposive, or willed, acts of normal and intelligent human beings.

But are all such acts of moral significance, or are some morally indifferent? At first glance it would seem that there is a relatively large class of indifferent acts, and this is certainly the popular view. It is also held by many students of morality. Herbert Spencer, while recognizing that "conduct with which morality is not concerned, passes into conduct which is moral or immoral, by small degrees and in countless ways," at the same time says that "from hour to

---

[1] See Westermarck, *The Origin and Development of the Moral Ideas*, Vol. I, Chap. X.

hour most of the things we do are not to be judged as either good or bad in respect of either ends or means."[1] In opposition to such a view it has been held that no conduct is strictly indifferent.[2] The attitude which one takes towards this problem will depend to a large extent upon the general theory of conduct which one finally accepts. A detailed discussion of the question hardly belongs to the initial step in ethical inquiry. But the difficulties which beset the limitation of morality to a narrow circle of rare or unusual acts can be appreciated at this point without undue refinement of analysis. To make the ordinary business of the day or hour morally indifferent is at once to remove the larger part of human activities from the field of morals. Very little reflection is needed to show that by far the greater part of these activities are related to ends from which they derive a clear moral value. Eating and drinking, amusement and recreation, expenditure and saving, work well-done or ill-done—these can all be seen to be of vital concern for morality. Carlyle's description of the slovenly carpenter at work upon his house, breaking "the whole decalogue at every stroke of his hammer," hardly exaggerates the immorality of careless work. It is clear, too, that no general group or class of acts can be regarded as indifferent, because all general types of action are intimately related to habits which are full of meaning for morality. No single act, however trivial, can be declared to be indifferent in the absence of a knowledge of the particular circumstances in which it finds its setting. While, for example, it is usually morally indifferent which chair in the drawing-room one chooses to occupy, even this choice may bear such relation to the comfort or pleasure of others, or possibly to one's own protection from a draught of cold air, that it is no longer indifferent. If we begin with the choices which are most momentous in their effect upon

---

[1] *Data of Ethics*, p. 6.
[2] Cf. Bradley, *Ethical Studies*, pp. 195 ff.

human life, and descend through all grades of importance to those which are trivial, we shall find it exceedingly hard to draw a sharp line at any point and say, "Here all moral significance ceases; here morality is at an end, and a non-moral taste, fancy, or whim, may determine action." Every act is potentially moral or immoral. In practice, however, the moral significance of our more trivial acts is largely disregarded, and theory follows of necessity the same course, fixing attention chiefly upon those parts of conduct which exhibit clear and indisputable moral value.

When we think of an act as expressing the purpose of a moral being, we pass from its outer to its inner side, from the external activity to the internal character that prompts and directs it. Conduct and character are only different aspects of the same fact, the two poles of the sphere of moral life. Conduct expresses character and in turn forms it. Character is a habit of will, the consciously organized system of one's desires and activities. This unity of conduct and character lies embedded in the life-history of the very words "ethics" and "morals." Ethics takes its name from the adjective derived from the Greek noun ἦθος, which came frequently to have the meaning of character. An allied form, ἔθος, denoted habitual action, manners, or customs. Similarly the word "moral" is derived from the Latin *mores* (customs, habits, character) through the adjective form *moralis*, a word introduced into the language by Cicero as an equivalent for the corresponding Greek adjective. In these etymologies [1] is seen the intimate relationship existing between conduct and character, between what one does and what one is.

It is clear, then, that whereas it is customary to define ethics in terms of conduct, this usage does not neglect character, but necessarily includes it. It may be added that character is to be distinguished from native disposition or

[1] Cf. the German *Sitte* and its derivatives.

temperament, which represents the active tendencies, aptitudes, or tastes of the individual, apart from the modifications effected by the play of external forces and the growth of an inner, organizing intelligence. Such original endowment is in many ways profoundly significant for the acquired character, but it is the material out of which the character is fashioned, not the character itself.

II. Ethics a Science of Value

Acts that are consciously purposive, or willed, have another very important aspect; they are directed towards ends. In this fact lies their meaning. The same is true even at the lower level of instinctive action. By unreflecting instinct the animal is guided to its appointed goal. But in man there supervenes upon this blind procedure the consciousness of ends, the debate over competing interests, and the possibility of error and long wandering in the search for his true goal. If we consider for a moment the immediate ends that we pursue from hour to hour, they appear almost numberless, so varied are human desires and interests. It is clear, however, that they are not equally important; some are less, others more, comprehensive and significant. The lesser ends are constantly referred to the greater, and become means in relation to them. There is, indeed, a hierarchy of ends in which can be seen an ascending gradation from the least to the most important. We count "the life more than meat, and the body than raiment." And we also recognize that even bodily life itself may be preserved at a price which we should be unwilling to pay.

Now the principle which determines the subordination of one end to another is always that of value. Estimates of value fix for us the place of each element in a system of human ends. And a system of human ends, too, necessarily implies a view of the interests of life as a whole, unified by the idea of value. Whether we consider the material factors of life such as wealth and bodily well-being, or the more ideal interests of science, art, and religion, or even the accepted principles of right conduct, like truthfulness, justice, and benevolence, each factor will be found to take its place at last in a system of ends according to the estimate of its worth. Here, in the idea of value, the appreciation of good, we have reached the most universal and significant element in conduct, the very nerve of moral thought and action.

The idea of value is, therefore, the basal conception of ethics. No other term, such as duty, law, or right, is final for thought; each logically demands the idea of value as the foundation upon which it finally rests. One may ask, when facing some apparent claim of morality, "Why is this my duty, why must I obey this law, or why regard this course of action as right?" The answer to any of these questions consists in showing that the requirements of duty, law, and right tend in each case to promote human welfare, to yield what men do actually find to be of value. If, as we here maintain, the idea of value occupies the primary position in moral thought and action, the definition of ethics should be constructed around this idea as a center. The task of science in any field may be described as the attempted unification of knowledge within that field. By the aid of a central concept science seeks to organize all its observed facts into a harmonious system. In accordance with this view of science, ethics attempts to unify the facts of conduct by means of the idea of value.

If a more formal definition is desired, it may be said that ethics is the science of values in their relation to the conduct of life as a whole. Ethics might be called the science of comparative values because every moral choice is a selection of a greater or a less value, positive or negative, according to the nature of the choice as good or bad, better or worse. Fearing to impair the absolute authority of morality, thinkers have often been unwilling to recognize the relative character of human values. But as we shall later see, the absoluteness of morality lies not so much in the values themselves as in the unconditional claim which relative values may have when they become objects of choice. Moral values are further regarded as elements in a totality of attainable value, an ideal system of worths; so that the final unity sought must comprehend all forms of value, not merely as they are successively experienced from moment to moment, but as elements in a completed span of life. Thus ethics is concerned with nothing less than the whole business of living.

The effort to secure a harmony of all values in the life of action is one of the features which distinguish ethics from the other sciences of value. The primacy of ethics consists in its right to settle the conflicting claims which various values may make upon us. Every science of value is of course supreme in its own sphere. Economics, for example, is the final authority in questions of market value, as is æsthetics in matters of beauty, and logic in matters of truth. But when values from these various spheres are found to be in conflict one with another, or when the limitations of practical life forbid—and they always do forbid—the equal realization of all valuable ends, the decision between them must be the task of ethical judgment. The ethical standard of value has in such decisions final authority.

Without prejudice to the definition just given, it may be admitted that no single definition of ethics can be made so complete and exact as to exclude all others. Of several definitions each may express some aspect of the subject with especial success. At best, any definition must at the outset appear largely formal, a mere skeleton that is to take on the substance of life from the entire discussion. But the idea of value which has here been made the central element of the definition is confidently believed to be the most significant, both for theory and for practice, of any that can be selected.

It helps to maintain a close relationship with other sciences of value, and to keep the discussion of necessarily abstract principles in fruitful contact with the concrete choices of daily life.

III. The Relation of Ethics to Philosophy

Ethics has been defined as a science. It is, however, commonly classified as one of the departments of philosophy, and many thinkers have insisted that the problems of human conduct are so bound up with the ultimate explanation of the universe in which morality has developed that ethical questions cannot be rightly studied independently of metaphysical theory. While the issues involved are too complex to be treated at length in an introductory chapter, a brief consideration of the question may shed some light upon the relation of ethics to general philosophical theory.

First of all, the distinction between science and philosophy is too sharply drawn. This is partly due to our unfortunate English terminology, which suggests that what is philosophical is not scientific, and that what is scientific cannot be philosophical. The misleading implication of such terminology is strengthened by the unfortunate tendency of many writers to limit science to the field of physical phenomena, and to ignore those sciences which deal with man as a conscious spiritual being.[1] Philosophers are also doubtless partly responsible for this unfortunate situation. They have often given to the world, under the name of knowledge, speculations that are not merely hypothetical, but highly questionable, without recognition of the fact that such "knowledge" has not the same status as the verified and verifiable results of science. But such an attitude is no less false to philosophy than to science. Surely philosophical

---

[1] There is no commonly accepted English equivalent for the *philosophische Wissenschaften* of the Germans.

investigations should be as scientific in method and spirit as investigations in physics or biology, although from the nature of the subject-matter the procedure cannot be identical, nor can philosophical inquiries attain the exactness of quantitative measurement. Philosophy, however, should not be less careful in observation of facts, less accurate in reasoning, or less disinterested in temper.

The effort of the present day to give to ethics a scientific character does not mean that it disregards its necessary relations to philosophy. Ethical reflection, if at all adequate, must issue in a philosophy of life, in a view of our relations both to society and to the world order. This will involve the recognition of all established truths of metaphysics and religion. There can be little doubt that the natural tendency of a study of moral experience is to cultivate a more wholesome temper of mind towards all fundamental problems. Neither dogmatism nor scepticism, partisanship nor indifference, finds encouragement in such a temper. A sense of the importance of intellectual beliefs grows in strength with increasing insight into moral relations. Our attitude towards questions that seem remote from daily choices takes on a new meaning. To disregard the limits of assured knowledge, to fail to distinguish between verified and unverified theory, between the certain and the uncertain, to refuse to acknowledge the mysteries of existence on the one hand, or on the other to be frightened by them, to deny that by the progress of knowledge more light may be given us—all these are seen to be ethically indefensible; they affect directly the conduct of life, and become habits of mind that block the wheels of progress.

True morality, then, involves a sane attitude towards the insights attained in the slow but unceasing struggle of mankind to solve the riddle of the universe. But we need not wait until the metaphysician has given a final verdict before a study of ethics is undertaken. Indeed, as matter of intellectual procedure, thought must advance from the more specific truths of science to the more universal concepts of philosophy, from the relatively known to the relatively unknown.

But there are those who, not content with the view that ethics and other sciences should prepare the way for a study of more ultimate problems, insist that ethics is dependent upon metaphysics. The acceptance of this programme would mean that one must determine the general nature of the universe in which morality has appeared, before discussing the nature of morality itself. After a theory of the universe had been established, it would be possible, upon this view of the matter, to pass by processes of deduction to the principle or principles that govern the moral life of man.

It is at once evident that grave difficulties attach to such a method. The disagreement among thinkers in their final interpretation of reality augurs ill for the success of ethical inquiry if it must wait until this far more difficult task is completed. It is a noteworthy fact that agreement in ethical theory and practice is far greater than that found in metaphysical theories. However much men differ in their theories of conduct, they differ here far less than in their philosophical views. Hedonism and self-realization, the chief theories of modern ethical thought, are never exclusive of each other. The representatives of the one are always found in the last resort to recognize an important element of truth in the other. Still more striking is this agreement if one turns from the theoretical questions of ethics to the field of concrete moral endeavor. Here idealist and materialist, agnostic and orthodox believer, Romanist and Protestant, Jew and Gentile, are often found working side by side for common moral ends. Implicit in this practical endeavor there is no small degree of theoretical agreement. This larger agreement in questions of conduct is natural and explicable. Our knowledge of human conduct is much more complete than our knowledge of that larger reality within which it exists. We understand even the most perplexing aspects of morality far better than the world-old riddles of the universe.

As already stated, the metaphysical method inverts the true order of procedure; it disregards the fact that ethics precedes and leads up to metaphysics rather than follows its completion. The central reason for believing in the logical priority of ethics is that all those values with which ethics has to do are developed in the historical life of man, and are disclosed to our knowledge by methods of observation and analysis that are essentially scientific. Metaphysics has never discovered a new type of moral value. From Plato to the modern idealist, who finds all possible values realized in the all-embracing consciousness of the Absolute, the types of value depicted are those, and those only, which are found in immediate experience and recognized by the scientific analysis of such experience. The same is true of theological systems. It is not the task of metaphysics and theology to discover new human values. Both, it is true, deal with values, but deal with the problem of their preservation and completion in a larger and more ideal order. In this relation values can, at most, be reinterpreted; they cannot be created or annulled.

A specific example may help to make clear the point under discussion. Among representatives of the metaphysical method the ideal of personality in some form is the most commonly accepted principle of value. The development of morality both in the individual and in the race is regarded as the temporal manifestation of an Eternal Self. [1] The effort of all finite selves to realize their complete development receives in this view the sanction and backing of the Eternal Self. Now while such a theory, if it can be established, is profoundly significant for metaphysics, it throws no ray of light upon the specific problems of morality or

[1] See especially T. H. Green, *Prolegomena to Ethics.*

upon the ways in which they have been, and are to be, solved. All this still remains for empirical determination. And further, a purely empirical judgment concerning the worth of personality always lies back of the attempt to justify such a use of the principle of personality in metaphysics. This empirical judgment is the spur that goads on reflection to an attempt to link what is precious to a universal and enduring order. But the same conviction with regard to the supreme value of personal life is held by large numbers of the most unmetaphysically minded, as also by many speculative thinkers who reject the form of idealism in question. In his upward flight from the field where he has observed and studied human conduct the metaphysical moralist takes with him only what he has there gathered, and when he returns from his long flight he brings back only the values he took with him. Moral values are never changed in their essence by projection into an unseen order. Whether they are high or low depends upon their own nature, not upon their temporal or even their eternal fortunes. The base and ignoble would not be rendered worthful by being made part of an eternal process, nor can that which is precious be denied all value because it may be transitory.

In pursuing the method of science ethics also accepts the limitations of science. It consciously restricts the scope of its inquiries in order that it may the better accomplish its chosen task. This task is the observation, analysis, and explanation of the facts of the moral life. The questions that lie outside of this field it does not attempt to answer, but leaves them to metaphysics and religion. Ethics accepts the existing moral order, but does not attempt to explain why there should be such a moral order in the world. The good and evil of human life are its high theme, but it does not push its inquiries beyond the region of actual experience. In other words, ethics does not attempt to determine the cosmic fortunes of our human values, or to discover whether or not they are so linked with reality as to be eternal.

It must be admitted, however, that while all the sciences reach results the implications of which they do not fully develop, the sciences which deal most intimately with our conscious life are more closely related to the fundamental problems of philosophy than are the sciences of external nature. It is more than an historical accident of the university curriculum that ethics, psychology, logic, and æsthetics are grouped with philosophy. The closeness of their relationship could well be indicated, if our English usage were amended, by designating them the philosophical sciences.

IV. Descriptive and Normative Sciences

The admission just made naturally leads to another problem. Although ethics is treated as a science, must it not be sharply distinguished in nature and method from the physical sciences? Indeed, are not all sciences of value to be separated from sciences of fact? Are there not two worlds which must be recognized in our quest for truth, a "world of description", and a "world of appreciation"? [1]

The familiar distinction between descriptive and normative sciences may serve as the point of departure for a brief discussion of this question. The former sciences, it is often said, describe existing facts, but remain wholly indifferent to their values; the latter seek a standard of value to serve as the measure of what ought to be, and the source of rules for its realization. The descriptive sciences, dealing with what actually exists, formulate all their results in so-called "is-judgments," or judgments of fact; the normative sciences, dealing with what ought to be, irrespective of whether the ideal is existent or not, present their results as "ought-judgments." Examples of the first class are found in such

[1] Cf. Royce, *The Spirit of Modern Philosophy*, Lecture XII.

sciences as geography, astronomy, physics, geology, biology, and psychology; of the second, in rhetoric, architecture, medicine, ethics, logic, and æsthetics.

Such a classification of the sciences, however, can serve only as a point of departure, for the sharp distinction between them at once breaks down when subjected to examination. Difficulties arise from the side of each group. All the normative sciences, in order to be sciences at all, must have as their data facts which are as real and indisputable as those of the so-called descriptive group. What, for example, could be said of a science of medicine as yielding the standards of health if it were not based upon observed facts of bodily structure and function? What of a rhetoric that should ignore the study of the established usages of speech, or of an architecture that disregarded the nature of building materials and the laws of mechanics? And what defense could be offered for a theory of conduct which was not, from first to last, faithful to the facts of human nature and practical life? No science can advance a single step without dealing descriptively with the phenomena which belong to its field of investigation. The norm which sciences of value seek, if it is to possess any degree of validity, must be found within the facts, not outside of them. The distinction also breaks down on the other side, since every fact of description is also in some aspect a fact for appreciation. All perceived facts stand in some relation to human interest, and thereby possess some degree of value. Even the most barren bit of earth-crust which geography or geology has to describe becomes, from the point of view of scientific interest, if from no other, a thing of value. Feelings of appreciation play in and out through the most prosaic facts of our experience. In fine, we appreciate the world of description, and we describe the world of appreciation.

Still another consideration makes the sharp distinction of descriptive and normative sciences untenable, the fact, namely, that the descriptive sciences all take on a normative phase in relation to practical interests. These sciences become the basis of the various arts for which they yield a standard, or norm, of action. Astronomy and geography stand in such a relation to navigation, geology and mineralogy to mining; botany by its descriptive method yields standards for agriculture and horticulture; and chemistry and physics furnish rules of procedure for the various industries.

We are compelled, therefore, to abandon the distinction between the descriptive and the normative sciences in the form in which it has often been held. This division of the sciences implies a difference in nature and method which does not exist. Especially is it false in its assumption that the sciences of value are not descriptive like the other sciences. But the distinction cannot be wholly disregarded, and it is necessary to attempt a different formulation of it. Instead of distinguishing the two groups of sciences by their methods, we must rather distinguish them by the character of the data with which they deal. Now the one group disregards the value aspect of its facts, while the other concerns itself solely with this aspect. The distinction, then, is no longer one between descriptive sciences of what is, and non-descriptive sciences of what is not, but what ought to be; it is a distinction between descriptive sciences of facts indifferent in value, and descriptive sciences of what may be called value-facts. This difference may be illustrated by a comparison of psychology and ethics. Psychology is concerned with the description and explanation of mental processes, and disregards the values involved in them, save as these values are significant merely for the explanation of the processes. The choice of evil illustrates the process of choice as well as does the choice of good, and for the purposes of psychology it is quite indifferent whether the one or the other is chosen. For psychology, one choice is worth as much as the other; for ethics, it is precisely the worth element that constitutes the whole problem. Other aspects of the facts are considered only in so far as they throw light on the value elements. Further illustrations of the difference between the two groups of sciences might be multiplied at will. To the science of geology, a Calabrian earthquake is neither good nor bad, but a fact of change in the earth's crust that requires explanation. From the point of view of economics, on the contrary, this same event is bad because it involves the destruction of a vast amount of wealth. We cannot satisfactorily explain the difference between the two points of view by saying that descriptive sciences like psychology and geology are abstractions that do not represent the "real" facts. Each view is equally real, and each, too, represents an abstraction of certain elements of the total reality.

What, then, is the relation of the "ought" to the "is" in morality, of the ideal to the real order? It is clear, first of all, that ethics deals primarily with what is, and finds all its data in the moral experience of the race. No ideal "ought" can have any meaning, either in theory or in practice, separated from what actually exists. If by the study of the moral experiences of men all moral judgments can be reduced to universal principles, then such principles will be valid for all future conduct. But this does not mean that ethics creates any new principle of value; at most it can only discover those that are implicit in moral experience. The types of value which it accepts must be those which human beings have realized, and are still realizing, in conduct; and if such values were not realized in the concrete acts of daily life, ethics would be helpless—as helpless as logic if it had the task of creating concrete reasoning. As in Locke's words, "God did not make men bipeds and leave it to Aristotle to make them logical," so, happily, it has not been left to the student of ethics to make men moral. He has the humbler task of interpreting morality, of making clear and explicit by description and explanation the moral values already existing in human experience.

An objection to such a statement of the task of moral reflection is likely to arise at this point. What has been said, it will be admitted, is true for the history of morality; and as long as ethics keeps to the firm ground of historical interpretation, it has a scientific task which can be executed with as much success as the perfection of the sciences of history and psychology will permit. But one of the most characteristic features of ethical theory, from the days when the Greeks depicted the character of the "wise man" down to the treatises of contemporary writers, has been the effort to point the way to a more perfect embodiment of moral values. Here at least, it is said, ethics parts company with all the descriptive sciences, and attempts to become a science of what ought to be. What relation does this aspect of ethical theory bear to scientific procedure? The answer, I believe, is that it bears essentially the same relation to scientific procedure that any hypothesis of physical science bears to the facts which it seeks to explain. Such an hypothesis, outrunning the power of full demonstration, is made in obedience to the demand for intellectual unity and completeness. The ethical ideal is similarly reached by a process of extension under the spur of the desire for consistency and completeness. The demand for an ideal completion of its task dominates every department of science, and ethics no less than the others. Thus it is that by this ever-present demand one is led to ask how we must picture the increasingly perfect embodiment of those principles of morality which have been the guides, conscious or unconscious, of the moral struggles of the past. But the facts of moral experience furnish the sole material out of which such an ideal is constructed. No new principle is invoked.

A misunderstanding with regard to the "ought" of a more perfect morality may easily arise. For such an "ought" can never be affirmed as a present obligation without reference to the actual capacities of men. It can be applied to the imperfect life of the present only in the same way in which the ideals of manhood can be applied to the boy, or the ideal of a high civilization to a people just emerging from barbarism. The boy ought, we say, to develop the qualities of the man, and the primitive society ought to realize the richer life of civilization. But here the " ought " is prospective, not immediate. Such an " ought " involves present obligation only for the first step of the long way; for the rest it is anticipatory of future situations. Both child and primitive people, if true to the " ought " of the present, will realize the more complete type of life. In no other sense than this can one speak of an ideal " ought " for humanity. Every ought-judgment is forever linked to an is-judgment, and by the same token ethics, like any other science, can deal only with existing facts when forming its theory of what ought and ought not to be.

Ethics, as we have maintained, does not differ from the so-called descriptive sciences in being non-descriptive. The difference in question is rather one of data, of the kind of facts to be described. Description, as applied to the sciences, it must be remembered, does not consist merely in analysis and classification, but also in explanation by general principles. All such explanation is necessarily abstract. From the concrete individual facts in all their variety, the scientist abstracts those aspects which are significant for his own purpose. The success of his undertaking depends upon the choice for abstraction of the really significant features, as well as upon the thoroughness, impartiality, and acuteness with which the work is done. This applies to ethics as fully as to the other sciences. From all our experiences of moral value, warm with the emotions and interests of life, ethics strives to select the essential elements of value, and to render them clear to reflective thought. To do this it must use abstract concepts. It is a pure illusion to suppose that logical procedure can do otherwise. By no process of "interpretation" can reflective thought escape "conceptual abstractions." [1] To reflect systematically upon the world of values is to move straight towards such abstraction. Ethics is of necessity just as abstract as psychology or physics. The difference is not in the degree of abstraction but in the nature of the elements abstracted. The only escape from the abstractions of description is in the rejection of the effort to think, in the complete surrender to immediate and unreflective experience. But this surrender leads, as the mystic has always taught, to the land of silence where the voice of science or philosophy is never heard. Science and philosophy exist only as the result of reflection upon experience; when they become non-descriptive, they become also "nondescript."

V. NATURE OF THE HUMANISTIC SCIENCES

We have so far considered the more familiar aspects of a scientific interpretation of ethics. But a number of important questions, less commonly discussed, at once present themselves whenever one touches the difficult problem of the relations existing between ethics and the allied sciences of human life. Let us approach these by a new path.

First of all, one must guard against the misleading implications of the departmental view of these sciences which would seem to represent human experience as a sphere split up into various segments, each one of which is handed over to a special science and regarded as its sole possession. In this familiar interpretation, psychology, economics, æsthetics, ethics, and religion, to mention no other departments, each takes a portion of human activity for examination, whereas the total life of man is considered as consisting of these parts pieced together. This view disregards the important

[1] For the view here criticized cf. Münsterberg, *Science and Idealism*, p. 15.

fact that each one of these sciences necessarily has to do with our experience as a whole; it is quite impossible to divide it between them in the customary fashion. On the contrary, the truth to be seized and held firmly in mind is that each of these disciplines is concerned with the whole of life, though always from its own point of view and for its own special purpose. The sphere, instead of being divided between the sciences, is surveyed as a whole by each one from a particular angle of vision. Each one of these human-istic sciences is inclusive of all the facts of the others just in so far as these others affect its special interest.

Psychology is indeed sometimes interpreted as the one universal science of human experience, because all experience of whatever kind is obviously psychical, an affair of mental processes. Statements of this fact often carry the implica-tion that sciences like logic, ethics, and æsthetics are mere branches of psychology or "elaborations of certain phases of psychology." [1] But this statement is in danger of obscur-ing the distinctive point of view of psychology. And it also loses sight of the fact that all conscious experience may be regarded as material for logic, æsthetics, ethics, religion, or any other of the anthropological sciences. The distinctive task of psychology is the explanation of the processes of experience, the events of the mental life in their interrela-tions. Psychology is indifferent to the values of our mental life save as it is interested in the clear understanding of the processes by which value is experienced.

Again, a too narrow interpretation of the task of political economy has been a limitation of the older classical econo-mists, and of those who have followed their methods. It has tended to prevent them from dealing adequately with the human valuation of economic effort, and from making needed studies in the field of applied economics. At all events, it is clear that a strictly scientific economics can permit no limi-

1 Cf. Ames, *The Psychology of Religious Experience*, p. 23.

tation of data within the complex whole of human ideas
and activities; they are all facts for economic study. Every
interest and ideal that men cherish exercises direct influence
upon the economic situation. There is no "economic man"
who without æsthetic, moral, and religious preferences en-
gages in the work of production, or seeks satisfaction in the
consumption of what is produced. Not a single article of
manufacture can be named to the making of which some consideration of æsthetic form has not been given. Moral
standards have condemned slavery and demanded the largest
possible freedom for the worker; they have limited the hours
of employment, especially of women and children, and have
otherwise changed the conditions of labor. These are only
outstanding examples of the way in which moral ideas have
affected directly the structure of industrial life. In fact
every subtle spiritual mood, whether inspired by art, morality, or religion, makes of man a different economic being.
Give a man a new idea, awaken in him a larger sympathy,
or kindle in his soul an ardor for the higher things of life, and
you have changed in some measure the existing economic
system. The production of things different from those
hitherto desired, and by methods different from those
hitherto employed, will be demanded. Economics, to be
sure, like every science that is in the making, cannot yet
deal with all the delicate phases of our complex life. It is
compelled to take the more obvious and significant phases
of experience for its scientific treatment. If we imagine
or assume an ideally complete science of economics, not a
single element would be left out of the account. Yet, from
beginning to end, all this varied and complex human experience would be expressed by economics in its own characteristic terms and principles.

The same truth applies to æsthetics. Although it is commonly associated with a somewhat limited field of objects,
in its wider ranges it may include all possible elements of

experience. Every object of the outer world and every idea or emotion within the mind of man may, in some aspect or relation, be subject to judgments of beauty or ugliness. How far the æsthetic judgment extends for any given individual depends upon the development of personal taste. No limit can be set to its possible scope. One may, for example, regard the economic life of a people as satisfying or failing to satisfy the demands of æsthetic taste. To men like Ruskin and William Morris the existing order of industry seemed to deserve condemnation, not merely because of conditions that they regarded as morally degrading, but also because of its sordid and ugly features. Moral character and conduct are similarly capable of æsthetic treatment, and are frequently so judged. The beauty and even the sublimity of character, when it rises to heroic or tragic heights, find expression in nearly all languages.[1] Religion has in an especial degree been the field of æsthetic appreciation, and has summoned to its service many arts: embroidery, sculpture, painting, music, and architecture.

All who reflect upon the nature of religion recognize that it seeks, from its own point of view, the unity of experience, striving to relate all its varied elements to a universal order. The conception of God is that of a Being who somehow embraces and unifies the manifold elements of experience, both inner and outer, in one organic life process. All the struggles of mankind, whether to develop economic wealth, to create beauty, or to realize perfection of personal life, are within, not outside of, a religious view of the world. Such an inter-

[1] Compare, for example, the Hebrew idea of the "beauty of holiness;" the Greek conception of the essential identity of beauty and goodness, expressed again and again in Greek literature; the "*schöne Seele*" of the German; the "*belle nature*" of the French; and similar phrases in other languages. For the more sublime aspects of character, sinister as well as noble, one may refer to such expressions as Renan's characterization of Caesar Borgia, "*beau comme une tempête, comme un abîme;*" and to Kant's association of morality with the wonder of the heavens, in the familiar words, "*der bestirnte Himmel über mir und das moralische Gesetz in mir.*"

pretation of religion involves no necessary conflict with any other human interest. If we regard each of the sciences representing these interests as inclusive of the facts with which the others deal, the rights of all are guaranteed, while at the same time their functions and limits are defined by their special tasks.

Coming now to ethics, we must regard its aim as that of attempting to appraise and organize our experience from the point of view of the worth of human life as a whole. It is the supreme effort at human valuation, the evaluation of all values for the life that we now know. Wealth, beauty, health, character, and religion are all included in its judgments of worth, and so in its scheme of duties. The defects and excellencies of the economic order in its relation to human welfare must here find ultimate appraisal. As far as art and other forms of æsthetic appreciation enrich life they will be approved by ethical judgment. If, on the contrary, the æsthetic impulse becomes perverse or degenerate, and so threatens the integrity of individual or social life, ethics will not hesitate to condemn it. The ethical criticism of religion is an unceasing process that is always going on before our eyes. Men rightly ask for the effect upon conduct of religious dogmas, rites, and ceremonies. By the steady operation of this criticism the crude and often destructive forces of primitive religions have been modified, and made to conform to higher standards of value. On the other hand, every true and worthful element of religion becomes a part of the system of values which ethics seeks to construct.

Finally, it might be shown that logic possesses a like universality. It aims to secure intellectual consistency throughout the whole of our experience. Every science in its procedure is subject to logical principles, and, to be valid, must possess internal consistency. Our thinking is not satisfied with the isolated sciences as independent systems of knowledge; it demands a world view in which the results achieved by all the sciences are brought into the harmony of a universal system. The goal of logic is the unity of experience in the interest of truth.

The reader who has followed this discussion will see how fundamentally the traditional departmental view of these sciences must be modified, not in the interest of any preconceived theory, but in recognition of their actual and necessary procedure. The one world of our experience is open to all inquiring minds. What aspect of this whole each student chooses to examine and to bring into ordered form depends upon the purpose of his investigation. How far any science can deal successfully with this whole for its own purpose depends upon its degree of completeness. But as life is an organic whole, in which every single element is in constant interaction with all the others, we need to beware of those processes of separation and of hasty abstraction which ignore the unity, and deal with the parts as if they were the whole.

VI. MORAL THEORY AND MORAL PRACTICE

A statement of the nature and aims of a scientific study of ethics may naturally raise various questions concerning the relation of moral theory to moral practice. For what end is moral reflection undertaken? Is it for the direct betterment of conduct, or has it an end of its own, independent of its application to practical life? Is the reflective moralist the pioneer who blazes the path of progress, or is he simply the painstaking maker of the map of life, the outlines of which have been drawn by others? And if the student of human conduct is successful in discovering the principles of moral value, is he thereby better equipped for the task of realizing these values? Or has he only won an insight that, like other knowledge, may yield satisfaction and contribute to culture, but has after all little more than an academic significance? May not one go further and maintain that the temper of scientific inquiry is often hostile to the interests of positive morality? Does not reflection upon the instincts which give to positive morality so much of its power, tend to destroy the instincts themselves?

It may be admitted, first of all, that the study of morality is not undertaken primarily in the interests of better morals, but in response to an intellectual demand. Man desires to understand the facts of the moral life just as he desires to understand other facts which are matter of scientific investigation. The same intellectual curiosity which impels the search for insight into the laws of nature also urges us to discover the principles of our spiritual life. As we seek to rationalize the one realm, so we seek to rationalize the other. But this intellectual demand for clear and systematic understanding of the moral life is not to be confused with the impulse to positive morality. It is one thing to understand right action, another to act rightly. So, too, it is one thing to teach men a rational system of ethics, and quite another to train them in ways of moral righteousness. The one requires serious study and reflection on the part of the individual in maturity, the other demands the constant operation from infancy of healthful influence and wise training. Positive morality is developed within one slowly in the process of life's unfolding. To be practically effective it must be wrought into the very fiber of one's being; it must be in a man as the instincts of the race are in him, as the blood of his father and the spirit of his country.

The effort to understand morality must therefore be clearly distinguished from the effort to produce morality, the task of the student from that of the preacher. Indeed, the very purpose of the preacher to exercise a controlling influence over the will of another, and the accompanying emotional tension, are obviously unfavorable to a scientific temper. The intrusion of such elements into the search for truth has always worked against scientific insight. Disinterested observation and analysis, the desire to discover and explain the facts, in a word, objectivity of temper, constitute the necessary condition of successful study, whether in the field of nature or of human conduct. Whenever the will hurries one on to a predetermined result, or dictates conclusions in behalf of immediate practical interests, the clarity of reflection is disturbed. Spinoza expressed the true spirit of the scientific study of conduct when he said, "I determined neither to laugh nor to weep over the actions of men, but simply to understand them."

The recognition of the disinterested temper of scientific inquiry, and the fear of its dissolving power upon the instinctive elements of morality, have often led to a kind of misology, a distrust of reason in its influence on the moral life. Students of ethics have themselves not infrequently recognized the danger, if not of reflection itself, at least of the undue hastening of the period of such reflection. They have seen that, once inquiry is started, the most cherished ideals will be challenged and made to yield answer to the persistent "Why" of investigation; that no principle of conduct is so sacred as to escape the demand for an explanation of its origin and validity. Plato long ago depicted with rare skill and humor the dangers of a too early appearance of "the questioning spirit." "You know that there are certain principles about justice and honor, which were taught us in childhood, and under their parental authority we have been brought up, obeying and honoring them. . . . Now, when a man is in this state, and the questioning spirit asks what is fair or honorable, and he answers as the legislator has taught him, and then arguments many and diverse refute his words, until he is driven into believing that nothing is honorable any more than dishonorable, or just and good any more than the reverse, and so of all the notions which he most valued, do you think that he will still honor and obey them as before? . . . For youngsters,

as you may have observed, when they first get the taste
in their mouths, argue for amusement, and are always
contradicting and refuting others in imitation of those
who refute them; like puppy-dogs, they rejoice in pulling
and tearing all who come near them. . . . And when they
have made many conquests and received defeats at the
hands of many, they violently and speedily get into a way
of not believing anything which they believed before, and
hence, not only they, but philosophy and all that relates to it
is apt to have a bad name with the rest of the world." [1]

Doubts of the practical advantages for conduct of the
scientific study of morality have sometimes included those
who have long passed beyond the period of youth. George
Eliot is credited with a saying to the effect that after long
study of ethics men succeed in conducting themselves almost as well as they did before. And I fear that some would
be inclined to apply to ethics Mr. Bradley's epigram concerning metaphysics, that it is "the finding of bad reasons
for what we believe upon instinct."

The feeling against the critical examination of current
morality is doubtless well-grounded as far as it concerns those
who are not sufficiently mature for the study. Most teachers of ethics would deprecate the attempt to introduce the
study of the theory of conduct into the earlier stages of education, a time when the child should be trained by precept
and example in positive morality. Such early study of
moral theory would be as ineffective for the purposes of
practical morality as the study by young children of dietetics
for the purpose of improving the digestion. Theoretical
instruction would also tend to make children priggish and to
destroy the charm of their spontaneity. Premature moralizing, like premature piety, is dangerous. Nature takes ample
revenge in later life for the production of such untimely fruit.

The time to make the nature and meaning of morality

[1] *Republic*, VII, 538–539 (Jowett's translation).

a matter of reflection may be said to have arrived when one cannot help reflecting upon it. And such a period is bound to come if normal intellectual development is unchecked. After thought has once been awakened one cannot act in unquestioning obedience to authority and tradition. If, as Socrates said, "the life which is unexamined is not worth living," it is also true that such a life is not possible for man. The growing mind, if it is to enter into the possession of full intellectual freedom, must experience a time of awakening, of transition from the unconscious and externally imposed morality of the child to the conscious and self-determining morality of the man. The question is not whether there shall be critical examination of conduct, but whether it shall be serious and systematic, and shall proceed under the guidance of the most enlightened reflection. If this reflection seems at first to inflict wounds upon the instinctive moral consciousness, the cure for them is not to be found in the abandonment of reflection, but in its more perfect work. For thought has the marvelous power of turning upon itself and of correcting by a process of repeated and unceasing self-criticism not only its positive errors, but its omissions as well. What is most to be feared for the youthful inquirer is the lack of thoroughness and patience in carrying the inquiry through to the end.

The careful student, however, learns that morality no more falls because he has been compelled to revise some of his ideas about it, than do the heavens fall because astronomy has forced him to change the crude conceptions of the universe which he formed as a child. He finds that the claims of duty are as real as life itself, and stand fast while life endures. At the same time, he understands that science does not create, but interprets morality—that the spring of all goodness is in those impulses of human nature which urge men on to fulness of life. He also understands that, like other sciences, ethics deals with general principles only, which the individual must apply to concrete cases as they arise. Even if science has succeeded in making clear to consciousness the principles of the moral life, there still remains the supreme art of living, an art in which each of us is compelled to try his skill. Ethics does indeed seek to discover the value to be realized in all the acts of the day, but it cannot tell in detail through what special tasks this value is to be won. The problem of filling the hours with worthful activities is our own. We cannot avoid the responsibility by appeal to any infallible authority; and our success in this undertaking will depend largely, as in all arts, upon fine perception and patient industry.

VII. Ethical Reflection Constructive

But when all these limitations are frankly acknowledged, do there not still remain certain services which a sound theory of conduct may render to the life of practice? It is not easy to determine the extent to which theoretical insights and convictions react upon conduct in special situations. Men do not always act with conscious reference to general principles, but they surely do not act in total disregard of them. If progress in the past has been largely the result of a kind of pervasive and untutored common sense, which has reflected in its own way on the lessons of experience, it is also true that the advance of European civilization owes something to the systems of thought which the moralists have developed. No one can lightly esteem the influence upon conduct of such thinkers as Socrates, Plato, and Aristotle among the classical Greeks, of the Stoic and Christian moralists of a later period, of Kant and Fichte in Germany, of Shaftesbury, Bentham, Mill, and others in England. A similar influence must be ascribed to Descartes, Pascal, Diderot, and their fellow-thinkers in France, where a clear-cut theory of life has always evoked a quick response. In the words of Fouillée: " Les pensées d'un Descartes, d'un

Voltaire, d'un Rousseau, d'un Kant, flottent pour ainsi dire dans l'air ambiant; une foule d'humbles, qui n'ont jamais entendu prononcer ces noms, subissent inconsciemment les influences philosophiques qui ont contribué à la civilization contemporaine. Il y a, grâce aux penseurs, quelque chose de changé sous le ciel et dans la conscience humaine. Rien ne se perd, tout se propage; les idées en apparence les plus abstraites, grâce à la force qui leur est immanent, finissent par prendre corps et par vivre chez tous les hommes: c'est là le véritable mystère de l'incarnation." [1]

Doubtless one important service of ethical theory to ethical practice may be seen in cases where a genuine perplexity has arisen as to the authority of conflicting claims. The perplexity, however, must be genuine; it must not be the hesitancy of a mind seeking means to justify itself for some departure from accepted standards for the sake of personal pleasure, nor the self-excusing temper of one who is unwilling to meet the demands of a call to special sacrifice. Whenever these attitudes are present, there will be found also means of justifying the desired solution. "The Devil can cite Scripture for his purpose." But cases of genuine perplexity do often arise. It may be the irreconcilable demands of freedom on the one hand and of the established order on the other, or the claims of affection against loyalty to truth. In such cases the solution will be found, not in the careful balancing of one rule against another, but in penetrating to the real source of the authority of both rules in such manner as to discover which one most fully expresses the standard of value.

Doubt and perplexity are inevitable incidents of moral progress. Among primitive peoples the path of duty is simple. It consists in following whole-heartedly the traditional order of established custom, the reasons for which are seldom asked or understood. Right conduct is for them

[1] *Humanitaires et Libertaires*, p. 203.

simply that which accords with existing custom, wrong
conduct that which violates it. But few would seriously
undertake the defense of mere tradition as the rule of conduct. The man who falls back upon it with the assertion
that what was good enough for his father is good enough for
him, must, by the same principle, allow others to follow
with like confidence in the footsteps of their fathers. Traditional right then often turns out to be contradictory,
for customs are exceedingly diverse. Under this principle
men will consent both to temperance and to intemperance,
to a stricter and a looser view of business morality, to the observance and non-observance of many social codes, appealing in each case to authority for their support. Reflective
morality seeks to make us aware of such contradictions;
to each individual it also sets the task of overcoming them
in his own conduct. In the precise measure in which life
develops into new and richer forms, the inadequacy of mere
custom as a principle of conduct is felt with increasing force.
Then ensues a struggle, often tragic in its intensity, between
reverence for the existing order and the impulse to realize
a larger life. In such situations the conscience which is at
war with itself can find peace and confidence only in some
standard of more ultimate valuation which gives to both the
existing order and the new impulse their respective values.
There can be no doubt that with the growing complexity
of modern life the need of intellectual clarity is ever more
keenly felt. The enrichment of the field of human values
makes necessary for every individual a constant sifting which
involves the rejection, not only of the bad in favor of the
good, but also of the relatively good in favor of the better.
With the wider diffusion of education there is an increasing
number of persons to whom the clear understanding of the
ultimate grounds of moral choice is a necessity. They can
move forward with confidence only when they discover the
goal towards which they are advancing. At the same time

there appears the possibility of a more rapid progress for society by substituting for an uncertain groping the purposeful struggle towards an end that is clearly seen and consciously approved.

Effort for moral progress by its very nature implies that ethical reflection must be constructive, not destructive, an extension of the area of moral action, not a limitation of it. If its work consists in part in the reconstruction of the existing order, it also consists in carrying the accepted principles of morality into new fields. The case could not be otherwise. Much human activity has never been moralized at all. It has been commonly assumed that many important interests may be left to the control of untutored instincts or to natural forces. Until recent times, wealth, poverty, population, physical and mental disease, have been so regarded. Yet nothing is clearer than the tragic failure of such uncontrolled procedure. Difficult as the conquest of this new territory is sure to be, the conquest must nevertheless be pushed forward. Ethics must be content to indicate existing defects in terms of human value, and to point the way in which progress lies; the detailed programme of reform, it must leave in each case to the science within whose domain the problem arises.

Those who believe that knowledge can illumine the path of life, where humanity seems at times to have lost its way in the prevailing darkness, will not believe that right conduct is arbitrary or merely traditional, but that it has its reasonable grounds and its adequate sanctions. To all such the understanding of conduct, both good and bad, will seem to increase rather than to diminish reverence for a deep and inward morality. For such an interpretation of morality the laws of right conduct are natural laws, in the sense that they are grounded in human nature and express the conditions of its highest development. One would no more expect, therefore, to escape the consequences of an immoral act than to escape the physical consequences of intemperance. Only the crudeness and shallowness of popular thinking prevent the clear perception that to foster evil thoughts or to cultivate selfishness is to condemn oneself to vexatious anxieties, and at the same time to lose the serene joys of the pure and generous spirit. Ignorance of the real nature of moral laws is in no small degree responsible for the false glamour of vice. To the same cause is due the idea that, were it not for the extra-ethical sanctions of some future order, there would be real profit in the ways of evil. There is always a probability that he who seeks to establish earthly morality by an appeal to something outside of it, needs both to enlarge his sympathy and to clarify his intellectual vision. If we should frankly surrender all those elements of morality which reflection upon experience is unable to justify, and at the same time should faithfully obey all that reflection can justify, who is prepared to say that practical morality would not gain thereby?

Finally, it may be urged that what reflection seeks to accomplish is to get the case for the moral life more clearly and completely before our eyes. This must be counted its chief contribution to positive morality. Everyone who has been in moral perplexity knows the help that comes from a statement of the case to another person. How often by this means the real issue is made clear and doubt dispelled! Such help is due in part to the greater objectivity which the problem assumes when it is frankly expressed. We view it more as a disinterested spectator and less as a partisan. But beyond this, there results a clarification of the problem itself by the intellectual process required for a statement of its full meaning. This experience of everyday life illustrates the essential purpose of the larger effort of a scientific study of conduct—the purpose to bring the issues more clearly before the mind, to present more adequately the case for morality. This done, the individual must be left to the desire inherent within him to reach the true goal of life. Such a desire is happily a part of the very will to live, for no man desires for himself real evil or ultimate defeat. So interpreted, the business of morality is not to create a totally new life, but to bring order into the life that now is; not to break the will or uproot the desires that pulse within us, but to reveal their true meaning and to bring them into more complete harmony. Ethical reflection comes not to destroy but to fulfill.

CHAPTER II

THE LOCUS OF MORAL VALUE; TELEOLOGICAL AND FORMAL THEORIES

I. MEANINGS OF THE TERM VALUE

ETHICS, as we have seen, is a science of values. But value is a word of wide and varied meaning. It may be used both in a positive and a negative sense; positive value will then be the good, negative value the evil.[1] Good, in the language of daily life, is everything that directly or indirectly ministers to our needs or advances our welfare; evil, everything that opposes and thwarts our true interests. A fertile plot of ground, a refreshing breeze, a beautiful sunset, ready tact, keen wit, an act of kindness or heroism, all these and innumerable other things, both trifling and important, we describe as good, thereby assigning to them some degree of positive value. A destructive earthquake, insect pests, extreme hunger or thirst, ennui, cowardice, stupidity, are among the many things we call evil, and which may accordingly be represented by degrees of negative value. It is further to be observed that only in relation to conscious beings is anything good or evil. The good presents itself to consciousness, in some aspect at least, as satisfying; it produces a feeling which we prize and seek to retain. Our attitude in the presence of evil is on the contrary just the opposite; evil is something we fear and resist. In the words of Professor Royce: "To shun, to flee, to resist, to destroy, these are our primary attitudes towards ill; the opposing

[1] Negation of value must not be confused with negation of existence. Evil is of course just as real as good. We assign to it negative value, however, as being an experience in itself undesirable in comparison with an experience in itself desirable.

acts are our primary attitudes towards the good; and whether you regard us as animals or as moralists, whether it is a sweet taste, a poem, a virtue, or God that we look to as good, and whether it is a burn or a temptation, an outward physical foe, or a stealthy, inward, ideal enemy, that we regard as evil." [1]

It is evident that not all values, or goods, are in themselves moral. Many things most essential to life do not depend on human choice, and by definition are excluded from the sphere of morality. This is true especially of the bounties of nature. Natural wealth, which is the basis of all the wealth that men produce by their labor, lies ready at hand awaiting use and development. So, too, a sound constitution, physical strength and beauty, rare mental endowments, and even a happy disposition, as far as these are merely inherited gifts, are for the individual possessing them natural, not ethical, goods. In the life of the race, however, these inherited traits are intimately related to moral values. Ancestors, near and remote, have helped to produce them by their moral choices. The child who inherits such gifts may be said to possess a kind of capitalized virtue which represents moral saving in the same way that inherited property represents economic saving.

Although many goods are not of our own making, but are the raw material of our inner and outer lives, the selection and use of them is to a large extent a matter of deliberate choice. Natural goods, constituting as they do the primary material of human activity, acquire moral significance when we purposely injure or improve them for human use, or when we have to do with their equitable distribution. All property has had ethical significance from the time primitive man fashioned implements for hunting or built his first rude shelter. Natural values, therefore, are constantly acquiring moral significance. Air and sunshine,

[1] *Studies of Good and Evil*, p. 18.

water and soil, even the depths of the sea and the heart of the mountain become instinct with moral meaning as soon as man enters upon the scene to claim use and ownership.

It is evident that an analysis of evil, or negative value, would show distinctions parallel to those found in the good, or positive value. All evil is not moral evil. A clear treatment of the problem requires discrimination between the evil which has its source in human conduct and the evil which seems inherent in the order of nature. Whether this distinction would disappear in a final analysis of good and of evil, is a question that cannot be considered here; it is rather a problem of metaphysics.

II. TELEOLOGY AND FORMALISM

Theories of ethics have usually sought for some one ultimate and universal value which would include the numberless particular goods that men daily seek. Moralists have endeavored to discover a final, comprehensive good, a *summum bonum*, which might stand as the goal of human effort. What, they have asked, is that which is desired, not as means to another end, but for its own sake? If the various ends which we pursue have value only as they minister to life, in what consists the value of life itself? When ethical reflection began among the Greeks it was this problem above all others which occupied their attention. Aristotle makes it the starting point of inquiry in the *Nicomachean Ethics*. "Every art and every scientific inquiry," he says, "and similarly every action and purpose, may be said to aim at some good. Hence the good has been well defined as that at which all things aim. As there are various actions, arts, and sciences, it follows that the ends are also various. Thus health is the end of medicine, a vessel of ship-building, victory of strategy, and wealth of domestic economy. But the highest good is clearly something final. Hence, if there is only one final end, this will be that object of which we are in search. . . . If it is true that in the sphere of action there is an end which we wish for its own sake, and for the sake of which we wish everything else, and that we do not desire all things for the sake of something else (for if that is so the process will go on *ad infinitum*, and our desire will be idle and futile) it is clear that this will be the good, or the supreme good. Does it not follow, then, that the knowledge of this supreme good is of great importance for the conduct of life, and that, if we know it, we shall be like archers having a mark at which to aim, and so a better chance of attaining what we want?" [1]

Were the Greeks justified in making the idea of some end to be attained, some final good, the fundamental principle of ethics? Or, as some moralists have claimed, is a still more primary element to be found in the idea of duty dictated by an unconditional law of right? The problem is to discover what makes an act right or wrong, to find the criterion of morality, the source of moral value.

One school of ethical thinkers affirms that the rightness of any act depends essentially upon the effects which it produces. Acts are right when they tend to promote human welfare, wrong when they tend to the opposite result. Thinkers who accept this general theory may differ as to what constitutes human welfare, or as to the particular acts that promote it, but they agree in believing that some end to be realized is the supreme principle of conduct and the foundation of morality. Such a theory is called teleological. Others have maintained that morality consists in an absolute quality of will, without regard to the results that may flow from it or the end that may be achieved. According to this view the moral value of an act is determined wholly by the rectitude of one's inner disposition, by the degree of one's loyalty to a command or law of unconditional authority. Inasmuch as a theory of this latter type regards the "how"

---

[1] Adapted from Chapters I and V, Bk. I, Welldon's translation.

rather than the "what" of conduct, the form rather than the content, it is called formal.

III. KANTIAN FORMALISM

The question in dispute between formalism and teleology requires further exposition before we can give a critical estimate of the significance and validity of each for ethical theory.[1] The classical statement of formal ethics is found in the works of Immanuel Kant. He attempts to define morality independently of any consequences, or ends, of action. Moral goodness, in his view, belongs to the will alone, apart from its relation to the objects willed. "Nothing," he says, "can possibly be conceived in the world, or even out of it, which can be called good without qualification, except a Good Will." [2] It is to be remembered that the will which Kant thus exalts is not good because it wills something good. Its worth does not consist in being fitted, like a well-made instrument, to bring about desirable results. By its unquestioning obedience to a law which it finds prescribed for it by the practical reason, it is good in itself, without reference to what it accomplishes. "Even if it should happen that, owing to special disfavour of fortune, or the niggardly provision of a step-motherly nature, this will should wholly lack power to accomplish its purpose, if with its greatest efforts it should yet achieve nothing, and there should remain only the good will (not, to be sure, a mere wish, but the summoning of all means in our power), then, like a jewel, it would

---

[1] The formalists have sometimes given a theological statement of their doctrine. God, it has been said, is the source of an absolute, unconditional law, which is good because He wills it. Even for Him it has no rational origin or ground in intelligence prior to its presence in His will. He does not will it because it is good; it is good simply because He wills it. A classical example of this doctrine is found in mediæval thought in the teaching of Duns Scotus and his disciples, who held to the primacy of the will against the Thomists, who affirmed that the intellect must be regarded as more fundamental than the will, since it dictates the end to be attained by the will.

[2] *Fundamental Principles of the Metaphysic of Morals*, Abbott's translation, p. 9.

still shine by its own light, as a thing which has its whole value in itself." [1] Kant goes still further and declares that no act which is prompted by inclination, or desire for an end, is morally good. This verdict is not changed even when the desired end is one which we fully approve. In such a case we can only say that it springs from the non-moral impulses of our life, and has natural, not moral, worth. In other words, a moral act is one performed not merely "as duty requires," but "because duty requires." When inclination and duty both happen to point to the same action we cannot know that our act is morally good, because we are not sure that it was reverence for the law, not inclination, which prompted the deed.

All moral requirements, to state Kant's formalism in other terms, are "categorical" imperatives; they express absolute and unconditional commands. In distinction from these, imperatives that are given with reference to some end are "hypothetical," since, if the end is rejected, the command no longer holds. "Thou shalt" and "thou shalt not" are the forms of every moral requirement, whereas all rules directed towards ends contain a condition, expressed or implied, as when we say, "Obey the rules of hygiene, if you would preserve your health;" "Be diligent, if you would prosper in business." Morality for Kant, therefore, was not primarily concerned with any end. "The end," he declares, "is conceived only negatively," and "not as an end to be effected." [2] And again to similar purpose he says that "the concept of good and evil must not be determined before the moral law (of which it seems as if it must be the foundation), but only after it and by means of it." [3]

This brief statement presents, it is true, only one side of Kant's ethical theory, and obviously cannot do justice to his

---

[1] *Fundamental Principles of the Metaphysic of Morals*, Abbott's translation, p. 10.
[2] *Ibid.*, p. 56.
[3] *Analytic of Pure Practical Reason*, Abbott's translation, p. 154.

system as a whole. It serves, however, to make clear his opposition to a teleological view, and suggests as well the rigorism of his morality, his sharp separation of the moral from the other elements of human nature. These latter features find expression in the well-known epigram of Schiller, in which he asks how one can morally do a service for a friend whom affection makes it a pleasure to serve.[1] This dilemma, if not a misrepresentation of Kant's theory of morals, at least does injustice to his humanity. Kant fully recognizes the beauty and excellence of such affection and service. He insists only that they belong to the non-moral qualities of human nature. For him all feelings are morally, not humanly, pathological, except the single feeling of reverence for the law. It was the inherent rigor of Kant's moral theory that dictated Fichte's saying: "I would not break my word even to save mankind."

The real meaning, for contemporary thought, of the problem with which we are here concerned may perhaps be made clearer by a different statement of it. Let us approach it by way of the distinction between the form and the content of the moral life. For purposes of correct judgment we must distinguish the inner, subjective disposition of a moral agent from his deeds, viewed as a system of ends, or values. We thus pass two judgments upon conduct, one upon the disposition and motive of the actor, the other upon the act itself in its total consequences. Such a judgment involves a distinction between the "how" and the "what"

---

[1] "The friends whom I love I gladly would serve,
But to this inclination incites me;
And so I am forced from virtue to swerve
Since my act, through affection, delights me—"

From Kant's standpoint the only answer can be:

"The friends whom thou lov'st, thou must first seek to scorn,
For to no other way can I guide thee;
'Tis alone with disgust thou canst rightly perform
The acts to which duty would lead thee."

of the moral life, between a universal formula for the spirit of moral action, and the endlessly varied material to which this spirit is applied.

The inner, subjective temper of moral conduct, its so-called form, has been expressed not merely by the good-will of Kant, but also by other terms which are instructive for our purpose. In Christian, and not infrequently in oriental thought, love, understood as active human sympathy, has embodied this ideal. Love, we are frequently told, is the one need of the moral life, and, were it present in due measure, its spirit alone would dispel all perplexities and cure all ills from which individuals and society suffer. In this case, as in Kant's good-will, one all-controlling temper of mind is made a principle of universal guidance in conduct, without appeal to any objective standards of value. A further instance is found in the use which Professor Royce makes of loyalty.[1] Loyalty, as inner devotion to a cause, will be able, we are told, to determine the causes which we should serve. Out of "the very spirit of loyalty itself" we may discover the answer to the most perplexing problems of conduct. We need only to be "loyal to loyalty" to know our duty in the world of action.

The distinction between form and content, as it appears in each case, is clear. It is the difference between the one good-will, forever obedient to the law of duty, and the many deeds in which this will embodies itself; between love as a single animating purpose, and the various outward acts that express the love; between loyalty as an attitude of personal devotion, and the causes of a conflicting moral order to which the loyal man should give his allegiance.

It will be seen that in these various expressions of a formal theory we have an element vital to morality.[2] All right

---

[1] *The Philosophy of Loyalty.*

[2] The reader need hardly be cautioned against the popular interpretation of the word formal which often identifies it with what is external or unimportant. It is

conduct, viewed from within, must express good-will, love, or loyalty. In this inner, subjective disposition of the agent we have a universal element of morality. As universal it is also *a priori;* that is, it is a principle which we can unhesitatingly apply to any possible moral act prior to all knowledge of its specific character. If any act of to-morrow or of next year is to be a completely good act, it will assume this form; it will be an act of good-will, love, or loyalty, not an act of perverse will, hatred, or disloyalty. Yes, if other planets are peopled by moral beings—beings of a morality that we can recognize—they, too, will be governed in all right deeds by such a principle of inner devotion. We can see at once that such a universal, *a priori* principle will be highly attractive to speculative thought. At a stroke it seems to unify our many-sided moral activities. It is a formula that can receive any content. Like a universal solvent it can be applied to the dispositions, tempers, attitudes of moral agents, from the Bushman, with his crude ideas of right and wrong, up to the most enlightened and prophetic spirit that labors for causes of world-wide import. Under the spell of such universality, however, thought is tempted to carry the principle still further, and to make it apply not merely to the subjective dispositions of moral agents, but also to the choice of objective acts, ends, and causes. Thus the principle would attain to an absolute universality, unifying both the subjective and objective sides of conduct.

The aim of such a speculative feat is to make the form of moral conduct dictate its own content by mere logical consistency, without appeal to any other principle. In practice this would mean that he who acts from a spirit of inner rectitude will, without other guidance, be directed to the

on the contrary, so important that it requires distinct emphasis, and in a later chapter we shall try to make clear its full significance. But for the moment we are concerned with the adequacy of formalism as an ethical theory.

choice of the right deeds. Thus Kant sought to develop his formal principle in such a way that it should of itself yield a criterion of moral distinctions, without appeal to the consequences of action. Likewise those who make love an all-sufficient principle fail to acknowledge its necessary dependence upon the hard-won experience of the race for the insights that must guide love in all its expressions. And Professor Royce, as long as he holds to his principle of "loyalty to loyalty" as the guide of conduct, is logically committed to a procedure that disregards the specific values to which one should be loyal.

IV. THE INADEQUACY OF FORMALISM. CRITICISM OF ROYCE'S LOYALTY

It is hardly necessary to record the failure of this type of ethical theory, attractive as is the unity which it seeks. We cannot so easily escape the humble path of the empirical method with its careful observation and study of the growing experience of mankind. Kant, in deciding the right or wrong of concrete acts, was himself obliged, as the critics have often shown, to abandon the principle of consistency for an appeal to ideals of personal and social welfare. Mere universality—Kant's test of consistency—affords no practical rule of conduct. The true reason for deciding that an act is immoral is found in its tendency to work in some manner or degree against human welfare. The "kingdom of ends" is the true source of the law which Kant vainly sought to establish independently of all ends. As for the principle of love, we ought indeed to love our neighbor; but love alone will not tell us what to do for our neighbor when we love him. The attempt to derive the details of right conduct from love alone would be as unreasonable as the choice of one's best friend as surgeon, irrespective of his knowledge and skill in surgery. Nor is loyalty in a better position to tell us what causes we should serve. The claim that the spirit of loyalty will itself be able to "furnish to us the unmistakable answer to this question," is itself essentially a repetition of Kant's claim that the good-will can yield us guidance in the specific choices of the moral life.[1]

Let us see more exactly the nature of the difficulty. To what causes should we be loyal? The answer of Royce's philosophy is that we must be loyal to those causes, and to those only, that will further loyalty among our fellows. So choose your causes, he tells us, that there will be more rather than less loyalty in the world. And obviously the good cause alone can accomplish this result. An evil cause can never permanently nourish and support the spirit of loyalty. This is all true. But how choose between competing causes? The cause of loyalty is defined in terms of the good cause, and the good cause in terms of loyalty. Thought here moves in a circle. We are helpless until we discover other principles of value. He who seeks to do the right, by his very quest, pledges his loyalty to the good cause; his only problem is to discover it.

A concrete case may help to make the issue clear. What, for example, shall be our attitude towards foot-ball as an intercollegiate sport? If the game is on the whole a good thing, we must give it our loyalty; if not, our loyalty must be withheld. Loyalty is here seeking its cause but cannot find the answer in itself; the circle remains closed until the

---

[1] *The Philosophy of Loyalty*, so stimulating to ethical reflection, is not, I am fully aware, professedly a formal system. Nor is it formal in the strict Kantian sense. It is saved from this extreme by its emphasis upon the causes of loyalty. My contention is that the doctrine tends to fall back into formalism by the overworking of the principle of loyalty to the neglect of other values. Contributing to this result is the too facile identification of the virtues as inner, subjective attitudes with a system of duties as objective causes to be served. Loyalty may well be used for the subjective temper, the inner spirit, of all right conduct, but it cannot prescribe or unify the objective causes to which this spirit must be loyal. One is bound to tell what it is in any cause that fits it to be a cause of loyalty. Precisely this is the most imperative need of morality. If ethics were to surrender this task it would lose its vitality and shrink to a statement of the obvious, viz: that one should be actively devoted to the good.

good cause is defined in terms of values other than loyalty. Accordingly we must try to evaluate the game in terms of its specific results. What must be said of its economic aspects, of the vast sums of money directly and indirectly expended? What of the probability of serious accidents, and, more important still, of the danger to the players of physical ills in later life? What of the influence of the sport on the intellectual interests of the students? Does it further the true ends of academic life? Does the game encourage success by low tricks and foul play, the winning of a victory at any cost? Or, on the other hand, are the evils incident to the game more than offset by positive good? What is the value of the recreation thus afforded, of the bodily discipline and clean living required? Is not the training in decisive action, self-control, and fair play a real gain? Does not the game cultivate unselfishness and a wholesome college spirit? By our estimate of such specific values, economic, bodily, intellectual, and social, we must make our decision. Once this decision is made, our waiting loyalty finds its cause.

Doubtless to men of good-will the path of duty is clearer, other things being equal. The loving and the loyal possess an impulse towards right choices. They at least desire to choose the best; but when they have to determine what the best is, they must consult something besides this desire. It is not the least of the tragedies we know, that loyal souls so often lose their way and miss the true goal of life.

But in spite of the fact that such a formal principle cannot give us adequate guidance in the choice of our many causes, we must not disregard its real value. It represents an element of all true morality. Its furtherance and increase among men is itself an important aim of moral effort, one of the causes which we should serve.[1] Thus the good-will,

[1] The relation of form and content, not only in ethics, but also in other fields of thought, is an important, though difficult, problem. The distinction between them should not be made absolute. Form is within, not outside, the content, and so in

as valuable, must will its own growth and triumph in the world; but it must also will the triumph of truth, beauty, justice, and every other good. Love, too, as a worthy spring of action, will seek its own increase. In this sense we should with St. Augustine "love love"; but we cannot love it alone. We ought likewise to be "loyal to loyalty"; yet we must be loyal to all other values as well. Not as untrue or unimportant, is the formal theory rejected. It is criticized rather for its inadequacy. It represents one human value; but it is only one among many which every human life ought to embody. To a completer end we must look for guidance.

We have been dealing with the distinction between form and content. But another statement of the difference between formalism and teleology may be made. The spirit of Kant's formal and rigoristic theory is well represented by the maxim, "duty for duty's sake." Duty is for Kant the feeling of reverence for the moral law. But this law, he holds, is, for us mortals at least, underived and ultimate; it has no end other than its own complete fulfillment. Reflection, therefore, cannot go beyond duty to ground it in any other principle. To this view teleology opposes its statement, duty for the sake of the good, that is, for the sake of a larger system of values. This larger system of values is for teleology the end from which duty derives its high

the last analysis is a part of the end which we seek to realize. A teleological theory must include all the truth of a formal theory. What is called the "form" of a player in any game may serve as an illustration. A player's form—his skill in plan and execution—influences each separate play and yet is coextensive with the game as a whole. Further, the cultivation of "form" may be an object of special attention apart from its immediate application. But such cultivation presupposes the game and derives all its meaning from it. So in life the cultivation of the good-will, or a keen sense of duty, has no significance apart from the actual tasks of life itself.

One other aspect of form deserves emphasis. Form has here been accepted in the historical meaning given to it by Kant and others. But the true "form" of the moral life, in a logical sense, is an adequate theory, or interpretation, of its meaning. If only we could fully understand this meaning, and so give to each element its rightful place in a rational plan, such a plan would be the true form of morality, since it would include and fashion the whole content of life.

authority. Duty is accordingly never the last word for reflection, and the formalist is found to rest his system upon an illusory appearance of ultimacy. Thus the issue is again drawn between the two theories.

V. Necessity of a Doctrine of Ends

At the first presentation of the problem in this form, sentiment not infrequently inclines towards the formal view. This view seems best to express the reverence which people feel for morality. "Duty for duty's sake!" What higher maxim can there be? What nobler ideal than unhesitating obedience to its requirements? But these questions betray a misunderstanding of the precise problem at issue. The teleologist admits that there is nothing higher than obedience to duty, when duty is known. The real question is as to the basis or *rationale* of duty. The teleologist contends only that the sense of obligation, or duty, stands logically as the representative of a higher authority from which it derives its sacredness. Another reason for the preference of unreflective sentiment for formalism may be found in the fact that, for the individual, right and wrong are, in the beginning, imposed by authority as binding rules of conduct. The child is taught to obey before it fully understands the reason for the rule to which obedience is required. The imperative which it hears is in truth a "categorical imperative," for the welfare of the child would be imperilled if it never obeyed until it comprehended the purpose of the command. One has, however, only to take the point of view of the parent, instead of the child, to see that the command is in no way arbitrary. Every requirement of a wise parent is justified by the end which it serves. Even if a somewhat heroic discipline is adopted, and strict obedience is required when no end of immediate importance is involved, it is for the purpose of cultivating the habit of obedience, which itself serves an important end in human life. Little by little the *rationale* of rules of conduct becomes clear to the growing intelligence, and from a purely formal view the child advances to a teleological interpretation of the rules of conduct. Thus the temporal priority of the formal view in the case of the individual does not constitute its logical priority.

The same principle applies to that larger body of rules and usages which make up the code of a people's customs and laws. These are at first received as an inheritance from the past, and a measure of obedience is exacted by society, whether or not the individual understands the ends which are thereby served. In the last resort, however, our critical reflection approves only that portion of the existing customs and laws, the purposes of which we can more or less clearly discern. We see that logically there is nothing ultimate or absolute about any system of laws regarded merely as requirements, or commands. We demand that they shall be translated into terms of value before we give them our unqualified approval. This teleological character becomes especially clear when we consider the slow process by which customs and laws, written and unwritten, are changed. The demand for change always rests on the conviction that the old order is in some way defective, that it does not adequately meet our human needs.

An unconditional rule of action, a "categorical imperative," is regarded by some as affording a special leverage over the conduct of men. They would wish to retain such an imperative as a popular doctrine, whatever the theoretical claims of teleology. But upon analysis, even the practical man quickly reaches the conclusion that a command, though "categorical" in form, is in effect "hypothetical." The door is always open to the transgressor if he chooses to accept the consequences of disobedience. A command given with the threatenings of Sinai is not a categorical imperative if one chooses to face the terrors of the broken law. Reflective minds can never be prevented from going beyond a command

and viewing the consequences of obedience and disobedience to it. One may ask not only, "Why is this my duty?" but also, "Why do my duty?" The answer to either question will take one beyond the command to the end for which the command was given.

The formalist often appeals to the sense of duty as the final and inexplicable fact of moral experience. The utterances of conscience, as revealing the requirements of duty, are regarded as ultimate. But mere presence in conscience of certain ideas and feelings does not mean that these are final for thought. It is the business of reflection to discover, if possible, their source and value, and at all events to distinguish carefully between what can be analyzed into simpler elements and what is truly ultimate. Otherwise we might without further ado accept the mere existence of any conscious experience as its own sufficient justification. But much which exists as indisputable fact is recognized as having no claim to be regarded as worthful or valid. We are constantly at war with the actual facts of experience in the interest of what we think ought to be. Conscience, with its painful reminders of duty to be done, or of duty neglected past the doing, in so far as it is mere matter of fact, might well be treated like a headache or any other physical pain; such pain is real enough as brute fact, but we seek to rid ourselves of it as quickly as possible in favor of some state of greater value. It is generally agreed, however, that one is not justified in getting rid of even the disagreeable monitions of conscience. We believe, on the contrary, that we should cultivate a considerable degree of sensitiveness to them. The ground for this lies in the fact that, in the economy of life, conscience is found to be purposive, to serve the ends of human welfare.[1]

In considering the function of conscience one should bear in mind the distinction between the habitual and quick de-

[1] For the nature and function of conscience see Chap. IX.

cisions of daily conduct, and the interpretation of these decisions in reflective thought. For the life of moral action a feeling of duty, when it represents a genuine conviction, not a passing sentiment or mood, is final and authoritative for the individual in his immediate choice. To disregard such a conviction is to imperil one's moral integrity. One must act upon it. This obligation holds even in cases where the conviction of duty proves to be a mistaken one; one is obviously limited to such moral insights as one possesses, and to act on them is better than to repudiate the moral task altogether. But for reflection the question, "Why is this act a duty," is vital. Reflection insists on weighing the value of the act in terms other than the feeling of duty itself; it interprets the single act as an element in a larger system of values. The end is doubtless implicit in ordinary practice, but such practice does not always make it explicit. We are all compelled to depend to a large extent upon habitual and customary standards, without in every case pressing back to the ground of their authority.

Conscience, we have said, is to be studied with reference to the ends which it serves in human life. An instructive parallel may be drawn between the explanation of conscience in ethical theory, and the explanation of bodily functions given by biology. In studying any bodily organ the biologist seeks to understand not only the mechanical processes by which it was developed, but also the function which it performs in the preservation and life purposes of the organism. Not content with an explanation of origin alone, the biologist also seeks an explanation in terms of value. So the student of man's moral nature strives not only to understand the forces, individual and social, that have made conscience what it is, but also to explain the validity and worth of conscience by the ends which it serves in the higher life of man. It is true that a point is soon reached beyond which teleological explanation cannot advance in its search for the principle of value, because an ultimate value is found. This ultimate value is the welfare of conscious beings. To ask why men prefer well-being to ill-being has the same meaning as to ask why man's native capacities are what they are. We have to recognize, as ultimate, the fact that we are so constituted as to be susceptible to weal and woe, and to prefer the one to the other. The task of reflection is to show in what type of experience well-being consists, and what conditions of life tend to further its realization. But the impossibility of carrying explanation beyond a certain point offers no excuse for stopping before this point is reached.

In determining the conditions of well-being our chief difficulty is not in discovering the right motive and spirit of conduct, but in choosing its content, the external acts and objective relations. If the claims of morality were fully satisfied by the formal correctness of acts, there would be no reason for preferring one kind of act to another, provided the spirit prompting them was equally good. To change the application of Bentham's phrase, "push-pin" would then indeed be "as good as poetry." "The recluses of the Thebaid, who tired themselves out in watering dead sticks, furnish us with a perfect illustration of a purely formal law freed from every material object." [1] The content of duty is also found to be particular and concrete. There is in reality no duty or goodness in general. Human beings can fulfill their duty only in concrete ways, as citizens, neighbors, members of families, students, artizans, etc. This fulfillment always takes place under definite conditions which require special forms of activity. The content of duty is, therefore, for each individual, highly specialized; indeed, for each it is unique. Reverence for moral law and loyalty to duty always mean the choice of a worthy content. In truth, the essential condition of the formal or inward right-

[1] Janet, *Theory of Morals*, p. 31.

ness of an act is the belief that the act will prove good in its consequences. What is not of such faith is of sin.

The prejudice against the moral criterion of consequences is largely due to the limiting of consequences to the external or even material results of action. The end is thought of as something outside of man which he is to win or to amass. The true end, on the contrary, is within. It is external only in so far as it involves the acquisition of certain objects which aid him in attaining to the highest expression of the capacities of his own nature. No external thing has any value save in relation to a consciousness in which it finds appreciation. The distinction, therefore, between inner and outer possessions, between what one is and what one has, loses none of its importance for the teleologist. Formalism has no advantage in spiritual worth; it esteems character no more highly. Good conduct is that which tends to develop the highest type of life; bad conduct, that which debases and cripples humanity.

VI. Teleological Character of the Virtues

Must we not further admit that those modes of conduct which we recognize as virtues and vices depend for their character upon the total effects connected with the practice of them? Truthfulness, justice, chastity, benevolence, and the other virtues are such, because they serve the true interests of life. For the sake of these they have been called into being, have been slowly developed and strengthened through long centuries of struggle. Truthfulness is prized because there are important truths to speak, because it makes a vast difference in human relations whether things are represented as they are, or are distorted out of all semblance to the reality. Were it not for this fact, truth-speaking would be indifferent, and one might always permit oneself the degree of license which is freely allowed in moments of gay banter and repartee. Were it not for the significant political, economic, and social interests of men, justice would be meaningless. Justice is important because there are important causes to be adjudicated. So, too, benevolence is a virtue because there is daily and hourly suffering which requires the ministrations of sympathy. In the same way every single virtue can be shown to draw its strength and sacredness from some primary need of life. They are all teleological, they serve ends of worth.

Imagine for a moment that these virtues were found to tend universally towards permanent unhappiness and the crippling of human powers. Should we not at once change our estimate of them? And if the acts now known as vices should chance, by some reversal of the existing order, steadily to serve the true interests of mankind, should we not come to approve them? The terms by which we now know them would cease to be condemnatory. We are not left to mere conjecture in support of this view. Actual transformation of virtues and vices is matter of historical knowledge. Polygamy has passed, in certain well-known cases, from a custom fully within the limits of virtue to a practice branded as immoral. A modern instance may be found in the matter of benevolence. The giving of alms to beggars, instead of being, as formerly, an approved act of charity, is now commonly condemned. It is profoundly significant, too, that those cases in which the judgment of good men tolerates and even requires exceptions to the accepted rules of morality, are precisely those, and only those, in which these rules are thought to produce evil instead of good results. The approved exceptions to the rule, "Thou shalt not kill," whether they are cases of self-defense, of capital punishment, or of justifiable warfare, we do not call murder. If men ever approve of an exception to the rule of truth-speaking, it is because they believe that the admitted evil of falsehood is, in a particular case, quite over-balanced by the good that is realized.

One is not justified, however, in assuming that the teleological view permits an easy disregard of established principles of conduct. This is not true even for the historical
forms of the most pronounced utilitarianism, to say nothing
of the theories which include consequences other than those
of happiness. It has often been remarked that the representatives of utilitarianism have been quite as strict as any class
of men in insisting upon the observance of the standards
of current morality. The late Henry Sidgwick, to cite a
single example, was far more rigorous in this respect than
most of the English clergymen who were his contemporaries.
The established and long-tried rules of conduct express the
general conditions of individual and social well-being, and
the evil results of breaking down, even in a single case, what
is so precious, would always demand a large balance of good
on the side of any exception, as well as clear proof that the
good aimed at could not be secured by obedience to the rule.
And it must also be remembered that any permissible exception is not an exception to moral principle, but only to some
special rule in which this principle finds expression. The
underlying principle which gives validity to the rule must, in
case of any exception, be better satisfied by its breach than
by its observance. Clearly the burden of proof always rests
upon one who would make an exception, and this burden
becomes especially heavy when the exception serves one's
personal interests.

It is by the skillful combination of all the elements in
favor of an exception that Victor Hugo wins, even from the
most scrupulous reader, approval of the lie uttered by Sister
Simplice to Inspector Javert. The purpose of truth-speaking to an officer of the law is to further the ends of justice,
but in the present instance the truth would almost surely
result in gross injustice to Jean Valjean. The case for the
exception is further strengthened by the fact that the saintly
nun abhors a lie, and has no personal advantage to gain;

rather will she be inclined to count the lie a stain upon her soul.

VII. Does the End Justify the Means?

Teleology, it may be noted in conclusion, is not to be confused with the maxim, "The end justifies the means." This maxim, as commonly interpreted, true teleology rejects. The abuses to which the maxim has given support in the course of history appear on analysis to be due either to a wrong end, assumed to be highly important, perhaps supremely important, or to a false separation of end and means. The teleologist, however, does not approve all ends. One great purpose of ethical inquiry is to discover the chief ends of life, which give value to all lesser ends and to all means. Religious persecution, for example, regarded conformity to a certain standard of theological belief as an end of the highest importance. If, with those who supported the Inquisition, we were to give supreme value to such conformity, we could hardly quarrel with their conviction that torture and death were none too high a price to pay for it. Happily the world has rejected this end, and with it the means which it was supposed to sanctify. Further, the separation of means and end suggested by the maxim is not valid. End and means form one concrete whole which must be estimated in its totality. No act is complete in its meaning until all its consequences are realized. We are, to be sure, unable to foresee the full meaning of any act, but the business of reflection is to bring us to an understanding of as much of this meaning as it is possible to grasp. The intelligent act, as distinguished from the unintelligent, is the one which appreciates in fuller measure its own meaning.

The means to a particular end, which in itself is desirable, may be so undesirable as entirely to over-balance the value of this end. The means to the preservation of life, for example, may be so objectionable as to destroy the value of a life thus preserved. Most would agree that a life preserved at the price of dishonor, or betrayal of one's country or friends, would not be worth living. Many would agree that a life which could be preserved only by a serious crippling of mental and bodily powers would not be desirable. In saving my life by an act of dishonor I not only save my life —I brand it with shame. It is no longer the same life, but a life that must forever bear the stain of its dishonor. There is a high degree of probability that any end which demands unworthy means for its realization is not worth the price. To grasp with too eager hands any good, even though it be from the table of the gods, is to court disappointment and disaster.

CHAPTER III

THE DEVELOPMENT OF HEDONISTIC THEORIES

THE result of the discussion of the preceding chapter has been to show that a formal theory of conduct, although containing an element of truth which cannot be neglected, is far from adequate, and furnishes no logical basis for our concrete ideas of duty. We are compelled, then, to accept a teleological view and to inquire after those goods, or values, which can serve as the end of all our striving, and give us a secure basis for the obligations which are commonly recognized in the moral judgments of mankind. Two opposing ideals at once present themselves. Whether we look to the history of ethical reflection or to contemporary discussion, we are met by the rival claims of happiness and perfection as ends of a reasonable theory of conduct. A purely formal theory must necessarily reject both, or at most give them only a subordinate place. Kant naturally repudiates as the foundation of morality not only the "empirical principle" of happiness, but also the "rational principle" of perfection. Indeed, as far as he is true to his principle—the principle of the "good-will," which is good in itself quite independently of the objects that may form its content—he is not concerned with any end to be achieved by the moral life.

A general history of ethics has no place in the present work. It may, however, be profitable to pass in rapid review some of the more significant forms which the history of ethical thought presents. Even a brief historical study will help to create a background for contemporary discussion, and thus will aid in understanding the significance of constructive criticism.

The theory of happiness and the theory of perfection both took their rise, like many other formulas of thought, among the Greeks; and both began as relatively simple interpretations of the meaning of life. Both, too, have undergone important transformations in the course of their historical growth, being modified by the various stages of culture in which they have appeared, as well as by the philosophical and religious systems in which they have found their setting. We shall first consider the origin and development of the happiness theory. The present undertaking will deal only with the principles which have guided its development, not with detailed views of individual representatives of the school.

I. Hedonism Among the Greeks

This theory first appeared among the Greeks as a simple doctrine of pleasure (ἡδονή), whence its name, hedonism. Aristippus,[1] who is commonly recognized as the first representative of hedonism, claimed for it the authority of his master, Socrates. And it is not difficult to see how, both by his life and his teaching, Socrates gave a measure of support to this claim. In practice he was no sour-faced ascetic who spurned the legitimate pleasures of life, but one who could, and on occasion did, enjoy them to the full. On the theoretical side, too, if we may trust Xenophon, he commonly identified the good with that which was useful and pleasant. To Aristippus it seemed that the pleasure of the individual was the only end for which things were ultimately useful, and accordingly he pronounced it to be the sole good and the sole end of life. In view of the uncertainty of the future, he emphasized the desirability of securing present pleasures as they offer themselves. He also regarded the pleasures of the body as more intense than those of the mind. All pleasure, whether physical or mental, was for him a positive

[1] *Circa* 435–356 B. C.

state of enjoyment springing from some particular activity. We have in the teaching of Aristippus a simple and by no means lofty doctrine of personal gratification as the guiding principle of conduct.   But we must not suppose that he taught a wholly uncalculating enjoyment of the moment, or a thoughtless abandonment to the lower pleasures.   Prudence is necessary even in gathering rose-buds.   And prudence especially dictates a self-control by which one remains master of his pleasures, possessing them but not possessed by them—ἔχω, ὀυκ ἔχομαι.   In fine, only the wise man knows how rightly to select and enjoy the good things of the world. His conduct is guided by insight and principle, not by circumstance or caprice, and no change would be made in his manner of life even if all existing laws were abrogated.

In the teachings of Epicurus,[1] the simple hedonistic theory of the Cyrenaics, as Aristippus and his followers were called, took on added elements of reflection, and assumed its final form for antiquity, a form which had an unbroken existence of six centuries or more.   With the passing of political life among the Greeks there was a decline in the buoyancy of the Greek spirit, and a lessening confidence in the possibility of securing positive satisfaction.   While Epicurus, equally with Aristippus, makes pleasure the only good and pain the only evil, he defines pleasure in negative rather than positive terms.   It is the "absence of pain from the body and of trouble from the soul," tranquillity and repose of spirit rather than the active pursuit of positive gratification.

The serenity so essential to the Epicurean ideal of life is secured by rational reflection, "which examines into the reasons for all choice and avoidance, and which puts to flight the vain opinions from which the great part of the confusion arises which troubles the soul." [2]   Especially did Epicurus feel

[1] 341–270 B. C.
[2] Diogenes Laertius, English translation, p. 471.

the need of some explanation of the world which would do away with the necessity of appealing to supernatural powers, and would consequently destroy the superstitious and terrifying beliefs of popular religion. For this purpose, the atomistic, mechanical system of Democritus was a ready instrument, and it was accordingly used to prepare the way for his moral régime. Every event in nature was explained as the result of forces inherent in matter. No deity interferes at any point in the system. Death, it is said, loses its terrors, since the wise man knows it to be the end of all consciousness. He at least does not fear the sad uncertainties of the world below, nor even the final meeting with the grim monster, death, since while he is living death is not present, and when death is present he is no more.

Prudence and insight were also needed to secure a proper distribution of pleasure throughout the whole of life, all parts of which are of equal moment. Epicurus sought according to his light to "see life steadily and see it whole." No pleasure should be hastily seized to-day for which one must pay too heavily on the morrow. And often pain will be endured in the present when necessary to secure a greater pleasure in the future.

Epicurus further regarded the pleasures of the mind as greater than those of the body, since they are often repeated through memory and imagination, whereas physical pleasure, as such, is of short duration. He felt, of course, no prejudice against physical pleasure; it was given a subordinate place simply as being quantitatively less. The teachings of Epicurus himself, however, give no support to that popular interpretation of his doctrine which identifies it with intemperate indulgence or a supreme regard for sensuous enjoyment. "When therefore we say that pleasure is a chief good," he writes, "we are not speaking of the pleasure of the debauched man, or those which lie in sensual enjoyment, as some think who are ignorant, and who do not en-

tertain our opinions, or else interpret them perversely." [1]
Most striking testimony on this point is furnished by Sen-
eca, who certainly held no brief for the Epicurean school.
"When the stranger comes to the gardens on which the words
are inscribed,—'Friend, here it will be well for thee to abide:
here pleasure is the highest good,' he will find the keeper of
that garden a kindly, hospitable man, who will set before
him a dish of barley porridge and water in plenty, and say,
'Hast thou not been well entertained? These gardens do
not whet hunger, but quench it: they do not cause a greater
thirst by the very drinks they afford, but soothe it by a
remedy which is natural and costs nothing. In pleasure like
this I have grown old.' " [2] One also naturally recalls the
familiar saying of Epicurus, "Give me barley-bread and
water and I will vie with Zeus in happiness." The virtues
of prudence, justice, and honor were made essential to pleasure. In the retired life of the old Athenian garden which
was long the home of the school, friendship was also exalted
as perhaps the chief source of human happiness, and remained a cherished ideal in the traditions of the school
throughout its entire history.

Epicureanism long outlived the creative period of Greek
thought. In the Roman empire it had a career of several
centuries before it passed, with other systems of ancient
philosophy, to its final decline; but it received here no fresh
elements of strength. It was ardently championed by Lu-
cretius, who cared less for its advocacy of pleasure than for
the atomistic philosophy of Democritus which served as its
theoretical support; it furnished a congenial philosophy
to a poet like Horace, who in early life reflected its spirit,
both in his verse and in his conduct, without a too violent contradiction of its exacting temperance; and it was
distorted by many who found it a convenient cloak that

----

[1] Diogenes Laertius, English translation, p. 471.
 Quoted by Wallace, *Epicureanism*, p. 48.

seemed to cover with philosophical decency their pursuit of vulgar pleasures.

II. Modern Development of Hedonism

In modern times, the most important contributions to hedonism are found in the works of the British moralists. Hobbes,[1] who launched the discussion of ethical problems in England, implicitly accepted the principle. Locke[2] explicitly avowed it, considering it "man's proper business to seek Happiness and avoid misery." These writers were followed by Hume,[3] Paley,[4] Bentham,[5] and Mill,[6] who, with other British thinkers, contribute to the development of the theory.[7] We are at present less concerned with the details of special systems than with the general principles which have changed the theory from the form in which it was held among the Greeks.

[1] Thomas Hobbes, 1588–1679.
[2] John Locke, 1632–1704.
[3] David Hume, 1711–1776.
[4] William Paley, 1743–1805.
[5] Jeremy Bentham, 1748–1832.
[6] John Stuart Mill, 1806–1873.
[7] To the above list must be added the name of Bishop Butler (Joseph Butler, 1692–1752), whose influence upon ethical thought has been wide-spread among the people of his own race. In spite of other elements in his system which have tended to obscure his adherence to a form of hedonism, he holds that the end cannot be conceived as other than happiness. "It is manifest," he says, "that nothing can be of consequence to mankind or any creature but happiness." (Sermon XII.) Man, to be sure, is not left to a calculating estimate of the pleasurable or painful results of acts in order to determine whether they are right or wrong; he is endowed with a conscience which serves him far better for moral guidance than would a prudential calculation of the effects of his acts upon happiness. He also maintains that the coincidence and harmony which he believes to exist between right acts and happiness-producing acts, is not always immediately discernible, perhaps is not discernible at all in the present life. But he none the less stoutly affirms that we cannot reflectively justify any supposed duty except on the assumption that it is perfectly coincident with our interests; and if sometimes temporal interests alone may not seem to justify such a claim, we must then take account of the interests of a future life as well. For while virtue does indeed consist in the pursuit of right and good as such, on reflection we do not feel warranted in following any course of action whatever until we are convinced that it will, at least, not be contrary to our happiness.

By far the most significant feature of this change is found in the emphasis upon universal, as distinguished from individual, happiness. The frankly egoistic view of Greek hedonism was gradually abandoned for an altruistic view, individualistic for universalistic hedonism. The forces that effected this change in ideals of social obligation were many and complex, and were active through centuries of European civilization. Among these forces was Stoicism, which in the post-classical period of Greek thought had worked effectively to break down the barriers of class and race prejudice in favor of a universal human brotherhood, and the social obligations which such brotherhood imposed. A still greater factor, operative far more widely both in time and in space, was the influence of Christianity with its cardinal principle of love of one's neighbor. But the change was due, not merely to the express inculcation of altruism ı moral and religious teaching, but even more, we may believe, to the slow growth of a pervasive feeling of social unity. The increasing contact of European peoples in videned intellectual, political, and industrial relations, prouced everywhere a more intimate feeling of mutual dependence than had been known to the ancient world. But a full recognition in ethical theory of the significance of the problem of the distribution of happiness was not reached at once. Let us note some of the stages in the process.

The problem had been raised by Hobbes, who represented man's nature as thoroughly selfish, but had nevertheless seen that the welfare of the individual was intimately dependent upon the social order. While he had abandoned a pure egoism as wholly impracticable, he had drawn a portrait of human nature which was far from pleasing. Man remained for him fundamentally selfish, and social organization was only a device for the satisfaction of egoistic impulses. The organic conception of society remained foreign to his thought. His libel of inherent selfishness later writers attempted to refute,

emphasizing the benevolent, other-regarding impulses, and
showing that these are just as truly a part of man's nature
as are the egoistic, self-regarding impulses. Shaftesbury[1]
and Butler[2] both impressively set forth this truth. Hume[3]
attempts to explain the origin of moral distinctions by reference to the tendency of qualities of character to serve the
good of mankind. Through sympathy we have a "feeling
for the happiness of mankind," which causes us to approve
whatever traits contribute to social happiness and to disapprove whatever produce social misery.

These important suggestions of an organic view of the
relation of the individual to society were largely lost sight of
by Paley and Bentham. Paley's egoism is less crude than
that of Hobbes, who, as we have seen, admits that the individual, in spite of his anti-social nature, is under necessity
—an almost painful necessity, it would seem—of living in
amicable relations with his fellows in order to escape the
evils of an existence that is "solitary, poor, nasty, brutish
and short." Paley, however, in the formal statement of his
system, still allows the chief weight to rest upon egoistic
motives. This appears in his well-known definition of virtue
as "the doing good to mankind, in obedience to the will of
God, and for the sake of everlasting happiness." [4] But in
spite of the fact that the "violent motive" by which one is
"urged" to right conduct is personal happiness, the content
of right conduct, and also of happiness, is for him largely
social. Bentham, starting with a similar view of the egoistic
nature of human motives, appeals to external "sanctions"
to bring due pressure to bear upon the individual in the
performance of those acts which make for general happiness.
These sanctions are pleasures and pains imposed from with-

[1] Anthony Ashley Cooper, third Earl of Shaftesbury, 1671–1713. See his *Inquiry Concerning Virtue, or Merit.*
[2] See especially Sermon XI.
[3] See his *Treatise on Human Nature*, Bk. III.
[4] *Principles of Moral and Political Philosophy*, p. 38.

out, and are four in number, the physical, the political, the moral, or popular, and the religious.   The physical sanction consists of those pleasures and pains which spring from the ordinary course of nature; the political, of those received at the hands of persons in authority; the popular, of those received at the hands of persons acting spontaneously and not from an established rule; the religious, of those received either in the present or in a future life "from the immediate hand of a superior being." [1]

III. Mill's Utilitarianism

But it is to John Stuart Mill that we owe the most forceful statement of universal as distinguished from egoistic hedonism.   Mill insists that "the happiness which forms the utilitarian standard of what is right in conduct is not the agent's own happiness, but that of all concerned; as between his own happiness and that of others, utilitarianism requires him to be as strictly impartial as a disinterested and benevolent spectator.   In the golden rule of Jesus of Nazareth, we read the complete spirit of the ethics of utility.   To do as you would be done by, and to love your neighbor as yourself, constitute the ideal perfection of utilitarian morality." [2] But upon what may we depend to secure such other-regarding action on the part of the individual? Mill here appeals to the combined influence of principles already recognized by his predecessors but not effectively united by them, and brings together the external and internal sanctions. On the external side, the forces of law, public opinion, and religious belief always tend to make it to the interest of the individual to consider the general happiness. It is not, however, to the external sanctions that we must look for the primal source of altruistic conduct, but to the "feeling of unity with our fellow-creatures." To this powerful natural sentiment Mill

[1] See *Principles of Morals and Legislation*, Chap. III.
[2] *Utilitarianism* (Dissertations and Discussions, Vol. III, p. 323).

appeals as the source of the real strength of the utilitarian morality. The social, sympathetic instincts of mankind constitute, in his view, a determining factor in moral conduct. And he even anticipates the evolutionary moralists in assigning to this factor a steady growth through a kind of natural selection, as he believes that it tends, even without "express inculcation," to become ever stronger with the advance of civilization. These statements show how completely Mill had escaped from eighteenth century individualism, and had reached the conception, so familiar in our own day, of the organic nature of society.

One new distinction in hedonistic theory appears in Mill, that of the quality of pleasure. From the beginnings of the theory among the Greeks, quantity had been the only criterion by which the value of different pleasures had been judged. Intensity and duration were the most obvious aspects of such quantitative measurement. But a much more minute and exact statement of the factors to be computed was attempted by Bentham, who holds that, in addition to the factors of intensity and duration, one must take account of those of "certainty," "propinquity," "fecundity," "purity," and "extent." [1] According to Mill, however, some pleasures are more valuable than others, even though not greater in quantity, since the quality of pleasure must also be considered in estimating its value. In his own words: "It would

---

[1] *Principles of Morals and Legislation*, Chap. IV.

The meaning of certainty and propinquity in the estimation of pleasures is obvious. Fecundity, Bentham defines as the chance a pleasure has of "being followed by sensations of the same kind"; purity, as "the chance it has of not being followed by sensations of the opposite kind"; and extent, as "the number of persons to whom it extends." Bentham expresses these criteria for the measurement of pleasure in the following lines:

> "*Intense, long, certain, speedy, fruitful, pure*—
> Such marks in *pleasures* and in *pains* endure.
> Such pleasures seek, if *private* be thy end:
> If it be *public*, let them wide *extend*.
> Such pains avoid, whichever be thy view:
> If pains *must* come, let them extend to few."

be absurd, that while, in estimating all other things, quality is considered as well as quantity, the estimation of pleasures should be supposed to depend on quantity alone." [1]   The test of quality is admittedly somewhat indefinite, but is expressed by Mill as the "preference" for one pleasure over another by those who, from experience and intelligence, are most competent to compare the values of the pleasures in question.   "Now, it is an unquestionable fact, that those who are equally acquainted with and equally capable of appreciating and enjoying both do give a most marked preference to the manner of existence which employs their higher faculties.   Few human creatures would consent to be changed into any of the lower animals, for a promise of the fullest allowance of a beast's pleasures: no intelligent human being would consent to be a fool, no instructed person would be an ignoramus, no person of feeling and conscience would be selfish and base, even though they should be persuaded that the fool, the dunce, or the rascal is better satisfied with his lot than they are with theirs." [2]   The ground for such preference of higher pleasures is, he thinks, best expressed by "a sense of dignity" which all possess in a greater or less degree. And if those in whom this sense is strong are often less satisfied, they are nevertheless unwilling to part with it.   "It is better to be a human being dissatisfied, than a pig satisfied; better to be Socrates dissatisfied, than a fool satisfied. And if the fool or the pig are of a different opinion, it is because they only know their own side of the question.   The other party to the comparison knows both sides." [3]

IV. SIDGWICK'S CONTRIBUTION TO HEDONISM

Henry Sidgwick,[4] in common with many critics of Mill, rejects this qualitative distinction as introducing an element

[1] *Utilitarianism* (Dissertations and Discussions, Vol. III, p. 310).
[2] *Ibid.*, p. 311.
[3] *Ibid.*, pp. 312–313.
[4] 1838–1900.

foreign to the principle of pleasure, and holds that "all qualitative comparison of pleasures must really resolve itself into quantitative. For all pleasures are understood to be so called because they have a common property of pleasantness, and may therefore be compared in respect of this common property. If, then, what we are seeking is pleasure as such, and pleasure alone, we must evidently always prefer the more pleasant pleasure to the less pleasant: no other choice seems reasonable, unless we are aiming at something besides pleasure." [1] But perhaps the most fundamental point in the system of Sidgwick, when it is compared with that of Mill, is found in his attempt to give a logical proof of universalistic as opposed to egoistic hedonism. Sidgwick seeks to discover a "rational basis" for utilitarianism which had been wanting in the systems of his predecessors. The chief principle of distribution to which he appeals is his so-called axiom of "Rational Benevolence." This demands that the individual shall have a regard for the happiness of another equal to the regard he has for his own.[2] Rational benevolence, Sidgwick maintains, is an intuitive principle and presents itself as self-evident as soon as it is clearly stated. It may be put as follows: in so far as anyone regards happiness as intrinsically good, good "not only *for him* but from the point of view of the Universe," he must admit that "*his* happiness cannot be a more important part of Good, taken universally, than the equal happiness of any other person." [3] Or, to state it in other terms, but still in the spirit of Sidgwick's thought, as far as I consider happiness to possess value whenever and wherever it may arise in the world, I must acknowledge that the value of a given quantum of it is not greater when it may chance to occur in my own ex-

[1] *The Methods of Ethics*, fifth edition, pp. 94–95.

[2] Equal, of course, when other things are equal, that is, when the good of any other individual is not judged "to be less, when impartially viewed, or less certainly knowable or attainable" by the agent. See *Methods of Ethics*, p. 382.

[3] *Ibid.*, p. 421. For a statement of the principle see especially Bk. III, Chap. xiii.

perience than when it occurs in the experience of another person, just as I cannot regard a coin of a given denomination in my own pocket as of intrinsically greater value than a coin of the same denomination in the pocket of my neighbor. If, then, I wish to act reasonably, that is, in accordance with principles the truth of which I am always compelled to admit, I must show impartiality between myself and my neighbor in the distribution of happiness.

Two other intuitive principles which have to do with the apportionment, or distribution, of the good are given by Sidgwick. These are the principles of "Prudence" and "Justice." The former dictates an "impartial concern for all parts of our conscious life," for the "Hereafter" equally with the "Now." [1] Mere difference in the time of the enjoyment of any good, provided all the elements remain the same, cannot affect its value. This is essentially a restatement in more exact form of the principle recognized by the Epicureans, that the aim of the wise man is the good of life as a whole and not the good of any particular part of it. The principle of "Justice" means that "whatever action any of us judges to be right for himself, he implicitly judges to be right for all similar persons in similar circumstances." [2] The mere fact that A and B are different individuals can never constitute a reasonable ground for treating them differently; such a ground could only be found in some discoverable difference in the "natures or circumstances" of the persons in question.

The implications of this principle of justice are important. It provides for a distribution of the means of happiness according to the discoverable differences of the "natures" and "circumstances" of individuals. It signifies that the means of happiness, if they are to produce the greatest good, are not to be equally distributed, because individuals are not

[1] *Methods of Ethics*, p. 381.
[2] *Ibid.*, p. 379.

equal in taste and capacity. If, for example, I have ten tickets of admission to a performance of a great opera, I do not hand them indiscriminately to the first ten persons I chance to meet. On the contrary I select, if possible, the ten persons most capable of receiving enjoyment and profit from the performance. Similarly, if I have a sum of money to give in charity, I do not give it where there is already abundance, but where the need is most pressing. This principle of justice therefore applies to the distribution of all means of satisfaction both material and spiritual. It implies distribution according to need, and is opposed to any communistic idea of a strictly equal division of goods.

V. Hedonism in Evolutionary Ethics

The most important development of ethical theory in the last half-century has undoubtedly been due to the influence of the doctrine of evolution. Although evolutionary ethics has not been committed exclusively to hedonism, there has usually been a close alliance between the two theories. Herbert Spencer,[1] perhaps the foremost representative of the evolutionary school, in his *Data of Ethics*, has dealt chiefly with the principles governing the growth of morality from its earliest stages—with the problems of its natural history. He has, however, accepted hedonism and made it an essential element of his system. Our judgments of conduct as good or bad, Spencer declares, can only be explained teleologically. The end by reference to which both terms receive their meaning may be defined in general as the preservation and enlargement of life. This statement holds true, however, only for the optimist, whereas the pessimist must accept the negation of such an end.

The radical pessimist, regarding life as a curse rather than a blessing, is logically committed to the view that the curtailment and ultimate destruction of life is the true goal of

[1] 1820–1903.

conduct. But there is a common postulate involved in the judgments of both optimists and pessimists, for both assume that "life is good or bad, according as it does, or does not, bring a surplus of agreeable feeling." [1] Conduct, in general, then, is good or bad "according as its total effects are pleasurable or painful." "Pleasure somewhere, at some time, to some being or beings," Spencer insists, "is an inexpugnable element" in any ultimate view of morality. Spencer also seeks to give biological support to hedonism by attempting to show that pains are the "correlatives" of acts injurious to the life of the organism, while those acts which further its welfare are normally accompanied by pleasure.

Of especial interest is Spencer's discussion of egoism and altruism, in which he exhibits the mutual interdependence of individual and social welfare. [2] Neither the one impulse nor the other has an exclusive right, but both are legitimate and necessary. In primitive life egoism seems to have supremacy over altruism, but this judgment must be modified by the consideration that egoism is, in a secondary way, dependent upon altruism. An instinctive and unconscious altruism is operative in the very lowest stages of physical life. Self-sacrifice is seen to be "no less primordial than self-preservation." As we trace the development of human society, not only does the mutual interdependence of egoism and altruism become clear, but it is also seen that in the course of evolution each has become more important for the other. Under the present imperfect conditions of life, however, the two impulses are in more or less open conflict, and in practice a compromise seems necessary. And yet such compromise is not the final stage of moral development, since a "conciliation has been, and is, taking place between the interests of each citizen and the interests of citizens at large; tending ever towards a state in which the two become

[1] For the argument see *Data of Ethics*, Chap. III.
[2] *Ibid.*, Chaps. XI–XIV.

merged in one, and in which the feelings answering to them respectively, fall into complete concord." [1] Parental altruism in its highest form is the best example of such conciliation. Although social altruism "can never attain the same level; yet it may be expected to attain a level at which it will be like parental altruism in spontaneity—a level such that ministration to others' happiness will become a daily need." [2] Progress towards such a state depends upon the growth of sympathy, the development of which is in turn dependent upon the pains and pleasures which its exercise yields. In the earlier stages of social evolution sympathy is largely painful, because there is so much maladjustment and so much consequent unhappiness, which sympathy must share. But with increasing adaptation to the conditions of social life, unhappiness from this source will diminish and the exercise of sympathy will become correspondingly more pleasurable.

Leslie Stephen,[3] another leading representative of the evolutionary school, presents, in his *Science of Ethics*,[4] a restatement of utilitarianism in harmony with the theory of evolution. He maintains that utilitarianism possesses "a core of inexpugnable truth," and that its fundamental error has been in accepting an atomistic rather than an organic view of society. He presents most effectively the conception of the social organism, the "tissue" of which is so modified in the process of evolution as to form the organs needed for the highest social efficiency. Health, rather than happiness, is the standard of morality. The two, however, always tend approximately to coincide, and the tendency of an action to produce happiness must be taken into account in judging its ethical quality. All moral conduct has this

---

[1] *Data of Ethics*, Collected Works, D. Appleton & Co., 1910, p. 243.
[2] *Ibid.*, p. 243.
[3] 1832–1904.
[4] See especially Chaps. III, IV, and IX.

tendency, and any conduct which can be proved to possess it is thereby shown to be moral.   It is a mistake, however, to press this general coincidence to the point of complete identity.   As society is at present constituted, we cannot affirm that in all cases moral conduct is productive of the greatest happiness to the individual agents.   "The attempt to establish an absolute coincidence between virtue and happiness is in ethics what the attempting to square the circle or to discover perpetual motion are in geometry and mechanics." [1]

This sketch of the development of hedonistic theories has been confined, in the modern period, to a statement of the contributions of British thinkers.   While hedonism has not been limited to British soil, it is nevertheless true that it has here had its chief growth, and that to this source it owes all its most essential features as a theory of moral conduct.[2]

One fact of importance in the development of hedonistic theory will be clear to every careful student of its history, the fact, namely, of the widening of its scope to include all the ideal satisfactions of human life.   This process of enrichment is indicated, in part at least, by the free use of the word happiness as well as pleasure.   The distinction which popular usage makes between these words is not recognized by the hedonist.   Pleasure, as used by the leading representatives of the school, includes all those states of spiritual satisfaction which attend the noblest and most unselfish activities.   Character is not disregarded or lightly valued. Mill tells us that he esteemed "the internal culture of the individual" to be of prime importance, and regarded "any considerable increase in human happiness through mere changes in outward circumstances" as hopeless.   No fairminded critic can be excused for following Carlyle in his

---

[1] *Science of Ethics*, p. 430.
[2] This fact gives point to Nietzsche's saying, "Man does not seek happiness; only the Englishman does so."

vehement denunciation of utilitarianism as a "pig philosophy." No quibbling over the terms pleasure and happiness should be allowed to obscure the significance of the doctrine. The hedonist may be judicious or injudicious in the use of terms, he may be right or wrong as to facts, but he should not be misinterpreted. Hedonism, if rejected, is to be rejected, not because it is low or unworthy, but because it is an inadequate interpretation of the facts of moral experience. Its inadequacy we shall examine in detail in the portion of the work devoted to a critical study of the theory. The real issue will there become clear: can the final good of which mankind is in quest be interpreted solely in terms of agreeable feeling, or does the conception of ultimate value contain other essential elements?

CHAPTER IV

HISTORICAL SKETCH OF SOME PERFECTION THEORIES

THE various theories of perfection, which have been offered as an interpretation of the moral end, do not display in their historical development the same steady progress that can be traced in the growth of the happiness theory. In the first place the ideal of perfection found a more adequate interpretation in ancient writers than did hedonism. In the teachings of Plato and Aristotle, as well as in those of the Stoics, there were expressions of the moral ideal which, at some points, have hardly been surpassed. The various perfection theories are also found to possess less logical unity than do the theories of hedonism; they show a greater wealth of originality and a correspondingly greater variety of form. This diversity does not readily lend itself to a brief outline. We can here simply indicate the leading features of some of the more typical forms which have appeared in the history of thought.

I. RISE OF THE PERFECTION THEORY AMONG THE GREEKS

As in the case of hedonism, so in that of the perfection theory, we turn for the earliest statements to the Greeks, and first to the Cynics, one of the so-called Socratic schools. Cynicism gave crude but vigorous expression to the claims of reason as the highest element in human nature, as that which constitutes the sole dignity and worth of man. Antisthenes,[1] the founder of the school, claimed for his doctrine the authority of Socrates. This authority he could invoke

[1] *Circa* 444–365 B. C.

only by an interpretation of the Socratic teaching as partial
and one-sided as that given by Aristippus, the Cyrenaic.
Although partial and one-sided, this interpretation contained
an element of truth. For there were aspects of Socrates'
teaching and practice which could not be reduced to the
simple formula of Cyrenaic hedonism. In asserting the
supreme importance of knowledge for the moral life, Socrates
had seemed to make reason the one distinctive and worthful
possession of man. No less in his conduct had he shown a
superiority to outward possessions, a disregard for conventional standards, and a fine scorn of consequences even to
the issue of life and death. Accordingly Antisthenes declares that only that which is within a man, his reason and
virtue, can give value to life. External possessions, beyond
absolute necessities, are not only worthless but tend to fetter
and enslave the possessor. The wise man will not compromise his independence by accepting them. The Cynic
regards the pleasure-loving Cyrenaic as the veriest slave,
dependent upon the uncertain favor of fortune. The simplest and surest way to secure true wealth and contentment
is to desire nothing. Rigorously carried out by such spirits
as Antisthenes and Diogenes, this principle involved the
reduction of all external possessions to the lowest terms. And
the same prudence which warned against the possession of
material goods also dictated abstinence from ties of family
and state. The life according to nature—for it is thus that
they describe the life of reason—is interpreted as a return to
the conditions of primitive existence, in comparison with
which the institutions of civilization all appear artificial.
On the other hand, whatever is necessary or natural to
man's physical life is right and honorable. The leading
Cynics were often charged with disregard not only of the
conventions but also of the decencies of life. This doctrine,
therefore, has on the one hand proved offensive to good taste,
while on the other it has excited admiration by its uncom-

promising assertion of the superiority of man's spirit to all merely external conditions.

The contrast frequently drawn between the Cynics and the Cyrenaics, which represents the former as anti-hedonistic, is in reality perhaps less justified than is commonly supposed. The Cynics repudiated the practice of the Cyrenaics as unsuccessful for its own professed end, and they stoutly asserted that their mode of life was the happier. There is not a little evidence that, as they prided themselves on their scorn of worldly pride, so they took pleasure in showing their contempt for pleasure.

II. PLATO

The Cynics have always been regarded as standing in close historical relation to the Stoics, who, however, reject the crudities and soften the harshness of their predecessors. But before Stoicism arose, Plato had developed an ethical system which, if it went far beyond the letter of Socrates' teaching, was still much truer to its spirit than was the interpretation of either the Cynics or the Cyrenaics. Plato's ethical theory is so interwoven with the total fabric of his philosophical thought as to render a brief exposition of it peculiarly difficult. It is necessary, however, in spite of inherent difficulties, to present some phases of his doctrine of ideas in its relation to the problems of human conduct.

In the first period of his literary activity, Plato was occupied with essentially the same problems as those which had constantly engaged the thought of his great teacher, Socrates. This thought had concerned the nature of the several virtues, and their unity as forms of that knowledge which constitutes man's highest good. But Plato's acceptance of his master's method soon carried him beyond the questions of morality to an all-embracing philosophical system. Socrates had held that there were universal and essential qualities common to all particular cases of moral action, and by analysis and criticism he had endeavored to discover them. Thus courage and temperance, if we understand them aright, express for our thought the qualities common to all possible acts of courage and temperance, of all men, under all circumstances. The general concept in which these common qualities are expressed would then represent the true and permanent nature of all the particular cases.

If this method of knowledge is valid for morality, why should it not hold good in all spheres? Must not the objects of the physical world be known in the same way? Are not all particulars of which we have knowledge similarly related to universals, the oak to oak-hood, man to manhood, and every plant or animal, or even inanimate object, to its appropriate class? A further step now seemed necessary. The object of true knowledge must be that which really exists; hence we are compelled to regard reality as consisting of universal and permanent elements, not of particular and changing individuals. This identification of the object of true knowledge with real existence was not peculiar to Plato, but was rather a presupposition deeply rooted in Greek reflection.

The philosophy which resulted from these movements of thought was an attempt at a thoroughgoing unity of all the objects of human experience. Plato still regarded "the good" as the highest principle of both knowledge and being; it is the end for which everything exists; it is the sun whose warmth vivifies, whose light illumines the whole universe.[1] And human life and conduct, as a part of the whole, must be referred to this central principle for explanation and guidance. It was thus that in the period of his constructive thinking Plato sought to lay the foundations of morality in his doctrine of ideas. He was not content until he had, as he believed, linked the temporal to the eternal order, and found the source of man's moral life at the very heart

[1] Cf. *Republic*, 508.

of reality. The connection between the two orders was effected within man's own nature. Reason, which is expressed objectively in the universe by the good, is also the guiding element in man's own spirit. Plato's psychology recognized three divisions in the mental life: first the reason, occupying the place of honor and authority; below it the active, or spirited, part; and lower still the appetitive element. Upon this division depends the Platonic scheme of virtues. Wisdom, courage, and temperance correspond respectively to the three divisions of the soul. Justice, the fourth virtue, is the harmonious activity of all three elements, and is possible only when there is strict subordination of the lower to the higher powers of man's nature.

From such a view of the individual life it was easy for Plato to pass to a parallel division of the classes in the state, the philosophical, or legislative, the military, and the industrial. To each class belongs the corresponding virtue, or excellence, and justice in the state is the same harmonious adjustment of functions that constitutes this virtue in the individual; on the wide stage of a people's life, however, it appears "writ large." In both the individual and the state reason is the source of all order and harmony. The ideal of moral perfection may then be regarded as the health of the soul. This ideal may also be expressed with equal truth in terms of beauty. With deep feeling for this central ideal of Greek thought, Plato does not hesitate to affirm the complete identity of the æsthetic and the moral, of beauty and goodness. Moral progress is at once a growing appreciation of the beautiful, an advance from the love of its lower to the love of its higher forms, culminating in the vision of the one absolute beauty of which all the fair forms of sense are but imperfect and fleeting expressions.[1] In this unification of æsthetics and morals Plato shows himself a true Greek.

[1] Cf. *Symposium*, 210–212.

From the possibility of a conflict between reason and sensuous impulse springs the dualism within man's nature.
This dualism largely determines man's earthly task, which
is to subordinate the appetites to the well-considered rule
of reason.   In the *Phaedrus*[1] this task is represented under
the figure of the charioteer who must guide aright two
winged steeds of opposite natures, the one low-bred and
unruly, the other of heavenly birth and noble instincts.
The familiar figure of the cave in the *Republic*[2] pictures this
same dualism as one of knowledge and ignorance, where
progress is represented as the process of enlightenment.
The dualism within man's nature is paralleled by that in
the world-order between the ideas, the realm of true being,
and the things of sense.   Thus Plato appears in the Greek
world as the herald of that doctrine, afterwards to receive
more emphatic utterance in Christianity, of two worlds
and of two opposing forces in human nature.   Though the
moral dualism is far less radical in Plato, it is still sufficiently
pronounced to give support to a measure of asceticism in his
ethical view.   Philosophical living is also a dying, a constant
negation of all those tendencies of our bodily life which hinder
the realization of truth, beauty, and goodness.   This negative, ascetic side of Plato's morality is often so strong as to
appear un-Greek.   It was due largely to Pythagorean, and
perhaps originally to oriental influences.

The place of happiness in this system is not altogether
clear and was not fully worked out by Plato himself, who
assumes towards the problem a somewhat different tone at
different periods.   Towards current hedonism his attitude
was naturally one of open hostility.   The Greek word for
pleasure ($\dot{\eta}\delta ov\dot{\eta}$) connoted gratification that was chiefly
sensuous and dependent upon external sources, leaving
almost untouched those elements of satisfaction which most

[1] 253–254.
[2] 514–517.

appealed to an idealistic temper. In the *Philebus* there are attempts at a scientific treatment of the problem, and insights of permanent value abound in the dialogue. But for various reasons, among them an inadequate psychology of feeling and the intrusion of other interests, a satisfactory statement of the place of happiness in the moral life was not reached. Yet there can be no doubt that on the whole Plato considers the life of completest virtue the happiest. We may believe that there was no ultimate conflict in his thought between true happiness and the highest ideal of conduct.

III. ARISTOTLE

In the *Nicomachean Ethics* of Aristotle we have the first systematic treatise on morals. In spirit and method the work offers a striking contrast to the dialogues of Plato. In place of the poetic and imaginative elements which mark the most characteristic of Plato's utterances, the reader finds here a prosaic, and in the main a scientific, interpretation of Greek morals as they appeared to a close observer of the life of the period. Yet these differences, heightened as they are by Aristotle's open criticism of Plato, do not prevent substantial agreement between these two great philosophers at many fundamental points.

Aristotle begins his treatise by an emphatic assertion of the necessity of a teleological view. All human interests and activities imply some end, or good. But all ends are not equally inclusive; one is desired as means to a still higher end, while another is desired for its own sake. What now is the supreme good which is desired for its own sake, and not for the sake of anything else? Aristotle answers that there is general agreement that this good is welfare, or happiness (εὐδαιμονία). But there is great diversity of opinion concerning that in which welfare consists. Some find it in pleasure or wealth, others in honor, and still others in intellectual pursuits. Aristotle rejects the dualism of Plato, and insists that the good must be something which can be realized in the earthly life of man, not a transcendent good outside of his immediate experience. A more precise definition of the nature of happiness must be sought. "The best way of arriving at such a definition will probably be to ascertain the function of Man. For, as with a flute-player, a statuary, or any artisan, or in fact anybody who has a definite function and action, his goodness, or excellence seems to lie in his function, so it would seem to be with Man, if indeed he has a definite function. Can it be said then that, while a carpenter and a cobbler have definite functions and actions, Man, unlike them, is naturally functionless? The reasonable view is that, as the eye, the hand, the foot, and similarly each several part of the body has a definite function, so Man may be regarded as having a definite function apart from all these." [1] This function, it is shown, can be found only in that which distinguishes man from all other forms of life, in the exercise of reason.

Man's true excellence, or virtue, thus consists in the proper functioning of the soul. The soul, however, displays itself in two spheres, a higher and a lower. The higher sphere is that of its reflective, speculative activity, its thinking and knowing in the interests of pure knowledge. The lower is that of the impulses and appetites in which practical activity is rooted. In the first sphere, reason constitutes by its activity the highest and most worthful human experience; in the second, reason regulates and controls the appetites, enforcing due measure and order. Thus man's rational nature has two divisions, "one possessing reason absolutely and in itself, the other listening to it as a child listens to its father." On this psychological division is founded Aristotle's classification of the virtues as intellectual, or dianoetic, such as prudence, wisdom, and insight; and practical,

---

[1] *Nicomachean Ethics*, Bk. I, Chap. vi, Welldon's translation, p. 15.

or moral, virtues such as temperance, courage, and liberality. In man's appetitive life virtue consists in the regulated, harmonious action of the various impulses which are appropriate to human nature. In other words, these elements of life, to be moral, must be rationalized. An impulse is rationalized, according to Aristotle, when it operates in just measure, being neither defective nor excessive in its action. The moral virtues may therefore well be described as means between two extremes. Thus courage is the mean between cowardice and rashness, liberality between stinginess and prodigality. The mean that constitutes virtue, however, is no absolute or mathematical mean, the same for all individuals, but is strictly relative to persons and circumstances. "That is the reason why it is so hard to be virtuous; . . . Anybody can get angry—that is an easy matter—and anybody can give or spend money, but to give it to the right persons, to give the right amount of it and to give it at the right time and for the right cause and in the right way, this is not what anybody can do, nor is it easy. That is the reason why it is rare and laudable and noble to do well." [1] This doctrine of the mean is an expression of the æsthetic element in Greek morality. It embodies the insight of the poets and wise men of earlier times who had seen in the observance of due measure and proportion the principle both of beauty and of virtue. As the perfection of Greek art consisted in its free, symmetrical form, in which no part showed excess or deficiency of matter, so the perfection of conduct appears in a like faultless proportion maintained in every act.

Aristotle's view of the organic relation between feeling and function shows clear insight and is of permanent value. By it he escapes the one-sidedness both of hedonism and of rationalism. All normal, healthful activity is attended with pleasure, and the more perfect the activity the greater the

[1] *Nicomachean Ethics*, Bk. II, Chap. ix, p. 55.

pleasure. As man's intellectual nature is the highest part of his being, the satisfaction that attends its activity is the highest of which he is capable. "It is the life which accords with reason then that will be best and pleasantest for Man, as a man's reason is in the highest sense himself. This will therefore be also the happiest life." [1]

In his theory of conduct Aristotle shows himself the "master of those who know" by taking account of the more homely needs of human nature. For the realization of happiness the gifts of fortune are also needed, such as health, wealth, beauty, friends, and length of days. In the place given by Aristotle to these relatively external goods, and also in his emphasis on the supreme value of knowledge, his view of life appears in striking contrast to that presented in primitive Christianity. An interesting picture of the Greek ideal of character, in the classical period, is given by Aristotle in the fourth book of the *Ethics*, in his description of the great-souled, or high-minded man. [2] It is one of the important passages in Greek literature for the comparative study of moral ideals.

IV. STOICISM

In the period of Greek thought following the death of Aristotle the chief constructive system was that of the Stoics. Indeed, of all systems developed in the pagan world, Stoicism has appealed most widely to the imagination of mankind. In its lofty devotion to a supreme law, in its exaltation of man's spirit above the material conditions of life, as also in its social and humanitarian teaching, it has had, in spite of its rigor and its paradoxes, a message for earnest minds in every age. Like all the post-Aristotelian philosophy, Stoicism was practical in its interests and aims. Theoretical elements served merely the interests of its practical

---

[1] *Nicomachean Ethics*, Bk. X, Chap. viii, p. 338.

[2] *Ibid.*, Bk. IV, Chaps. vii and viii.

teaching; logic and physics are subordinated to ethics. Philosophy, in its total content, the Stoics likened to a garden, the fence of which represents logic, the trees physics, and the fruits ethics. Nevertheless the moral teaching of the Stoics was so rooted in their general theory of the universe that the former cannot be understood without reference to the latter.

In the thought of the Stoics the whole scheme of things was unified and harmonized by an all-pervading law, a reason immanent in the material world.[1] On the religious side their philosophy was pantheistic. However men might designate the divine principle—and the Stoics themselves freely applied to it a variety of names—it was the source of all order, beauty, and worth. In nature it appeared as physical law. But man has no need to go to the outer world to discover its workings, for in his own breast he finds a spark of the same divine principle. His reason is identical in its essence with the world-reason. As the highest element in his nature it may rightfully claim authority over the lower elements. Hence the Stoic ethics appears as a pronounced rationalism, in which feeling and emotion have no adequate place. Indeed, man's moral business is the rooting out of the desires and passions that he may hear and obey the voice of his one true guide, and thereby attain to a serene, emotionless calm, the Stoic apathy. This rule of reason constitutes virtue, which is man's sole good. The Socratic doctrine that virtue is knowledge is thus reaffirmed and given fresh emphasis. The virtuous man is the wise man, the bad man the fool. Since passion is the result of false judgment, the wise man is necessarily free from it. It follows also that men are divided into two distinct classes, and are either wholly good or wholly bad. To possess one virtue is to possess all; to fail at a single point is to fall short of the whole law. The ideal of the Stoics culminated in the picture of the wise man,

[1] Cf. the expression of this idea in the *Hymn to Zeus* by Cleanthes.

who by his insight had risen superior to all human passions and had become complete master of himself, the happy possessor of all good. The paradoxes of the picture were often elaborated at length. Nowhere is this portrait of the sage more skillfully drawn than in the *De Finibus* of Cicero, who, though not a disciple of the Porch, was able sympathetically to interpret its teaching. "What dignity, nobility, and steadfastness," he exclaims, "does the character of the wise man display! And since reason has taught that what is honorable is also good, he is necessarily always happy, and to him truly belong all those epithets which the ignorant are wont to ridicule. For more justly will the wise man be called king than Tarquin, who could not rule himself or his own house; more justly master of the people—that is, dictator—than Sulla, who was the slave of three baneful vices, luxury, avarice, and cruelty; more justly rich than Crassus, who, had he not been in need, would never have crossed the Euphrates when there was no cause for war. Justly will he be said to possess all things who alone knows how to use all; justly even will he be called beautiful, for the features of the soul are more beautiful than those of the body; justly will he alone be called free, not obeying the dictates of any man nor yielding to the demands of appetite; justly will he be called invincible, for even though his body be bound, yet upon his spirit no chains can be fastened." [1]

Trust in the world-reason was the basis of the optimism of the Stoics, who declared all things beautiful and good. In their opinion evil is only relative to our limited, finite view, and would disappear for an intelligence embracing the entire universe. This optimism also gave to the existing social and political order, as a part of the whole, a value which it did not possess for the Cynics. Life according to nature meant for the Stoics the acceptance of all those institutions which appeared congruent with human nature. Their

---

[1] *De Finibus*, Bk. III, Chap. xxii.

attitude towards family life and the state was therefore professedly positive, although in practice many found excuses for refusing these reponsibilities. The practice of suicide, which was approved by the Stoics under certain exigencies, was not regarded as a contradiction of their professed optimism. The very stress of circumstances which justified one in taking his own life was construed as a part of a well-ordered plan; it indicated to the wise man that the hour had come to depart from life. Let him go, then, not unwillingly, but with submission and serenity.

In the common possession by men of a spark of the universal reason lay the foundation of Stoic cosmopolitanism. This cosmopolitanism asserted a universal brotherhood, and uttered vigorous protest against those divisions which differences of race, religion, and class had erected. Through the decisions of the *prætores peregrini* this conception of human kinship entered into Roman law, and worked effectively to lessen its inequalities and barbarities. Stoicism was thus one of the forces which made Roman law "written reason," "the pearl of Roman civilization."

In Roman Stoicism may be seen the sunset glory of pagan philosophy. The mellow light which it cast across the dark shadows of the age presaged the approaching twilight of classical civilization. If the Romans contributed little to the theory of Stoicism, they gave to the world the finest statement of its practical ideals and the fairest examples of devotion to them. Two figures of world-wide significance appear upon the stage, Epictetus, the Phrygian slave and freedman, and the emperor, Marcus Aurelius, in whom Plato's desire that a philosopher might be king was at last fulfilled. These moralists have had a message for men of every age and of every faith. The imagination of succeeding centuries has seen here the human embodiment of the ideal of the "wise man." History and literature testify to the profound impression which they have produced.

Long after the age of the Antonines had passed, busts of the emperor were cherished in private households throughout the Roman empire, not in flattery of a living ruler, but in genuine tribute to a dead hero. Many a monk in the middle ages kept the meditations of Marcus Aurelius with his copy of the gospels. A Roman cardinal translated them into Italian, that they might "quicken the faith of the faithful." Dedicating his translation to his own soul, he bade it "blush redder than the scarlet of his robe at the thought of the virtues of this pagan." [1] The literature of modern Europe bears testimony to the charm and power which the thoughts of the emperor have exercised over the minds and hearts of great men.

These Stoic philosophers have perhaps a special message to our own age. When luxury and pleasure-seeking abound; when physical pain has come to be regarded by many as the greatest of ills; when prudence and safety are exalted as the chief practical virtues, and often mean, alas! little more than rules for material success; when it is demanded that religion must above all else be comforting; when even philosophy, as interpreted by many, must be made to yield us reasons for what we desire to believe—in such an age we may well be reminded of their more heroic view of life. The message of both Epictetus and Marcus Aurelius is the message of a brave idealism. It declares that we must submit ourselves without reserve to the divine order as it appears in nature and in human society. This law is not to be found in our moods and impulses, in the feelings and emotions that come and go. It is a law of reason, to be discerned only by intelligence, a spark of which human beings all share as their birthright. Again and again we are urged "not to defile the divinity" within us, but to "keep it pure" and "preserve it tranquil, following it obediently as a god." Thus must a man ever keep faith with himself.

[1] Cf. Matthew Arnold, *Essays in Criticism, Marcus Aurelius.*

But these stern moralists also tell us that we need expect no reward of virtue, here or hereafter, except such inner joy as virtue itself can yield. To think that right conduct must have an external reward is wholly to misconceive its nature. To demand such reward is as absurd as to think that a precious stone is more beautiful because, forsooth, it has been praised. This profound inwardness determines at a stroke the place of all external things in the scheme of life. They can never be a part of man's true good. Woe to him who puts his trust in them and forgets to cultivate his own mind and soul! Our true fortune is within us, not without. The emperor on his throne and the slave in his hut are to be judged by the same standards.

This doctrine of the inwardness of life's true center escapes the anarchy of an extreme individualism. For Stoicism regards reason as a social principle, a common element, which binds men together in a universal brotherhood. "The prime principle of man's constitution," we are told, "is social." This social principle culminates in the ideal of a republic of reason, a veritable city of God, in which all men may claim citizenship. The Emperor had learned, he tells us, "the idea of a polity administered with regard to equal rights and equal freedom of speech," and of "a government which respects most of all the freedom of the governed," a platform that might have been framed for modern democracy.

Nothing is more impressive in this teaching than its note of fearlessness; fearlessness in doing right when to do right means to suffer blame; fearlessness, too, in the presence of death. Despite all this rigor, we are bidden to cultivate serenity and cheerfulness under all circumstances. Think not that a man could be a true Stoic and go sour-faced and snarling through the world. No, we are even admonished to take delight in the fair and goodly frame of nature and in the excellencies of our fellows. "When thou wishest to delight thyself, think of the virtues of those who live with thee; for instance, the activity of one, the modesty of another, and the liberality of a third, and some other good quality of a fourth."

It was a special merit of the Stoic teaching that it developed its view of life while steadily facing the complex tasks and limitations of earthly culture and civilization. Stoicism sought the regeneration and happiness of the individual while still holding him resolutely to the values of the present order. It refused to defer the realization of the worth of life to an uncertain future, whether conceived as a super-terrestrial state or as an earthly millennium.

The message of the Roman Stoics, marred by little that is local or temporary, is, in brief, to yield ourselves unreservedly to the laws of nature and of society; to subdue our passing moods and clamant passions to the rule of reason; to expect no reward in life except the joy of right living; to scorn the meanness of selfish ends; to shun evil thoughts as well as evil deeds; to be slow to take offense and quick to forgive; to cultivate dignity and sweetness; to be cheerful even in pain and sorrow; and to fear nothing in God's universe except cowardice and disloyalty to duty.

V. SPINOZA

From the Greek period to the time of Kant no philosopher developed an ethical system of equal interest to that of Spinoza.[1] His teaching is distinctive and important enough to merit a place among the typical forms of the perfection theory. It also stands in close relation both to classical ideals and to contemporary thought, and so may fittingly lead up to the modern doctrine of self-realization. Spinoza's view of human conduct, like that of the Stoics, is best approached from his general philosophy. This philosophy is monistic. One substance, nature, or God, is the only ultimate reality.

[1] Benedict Spinoza, 1632–1677.

All particular things are its expressions, or modes. These many particulars of experience appear to us under two attributes, thought and extension. Under the attribute of thought they appear as elements of consciousness, under that of extension as material existences. These attributes belong to all reality, and are strictly parallel throughout the entire universe. Spinoza does not regard thought as an aspect of human and animal life alone, but as present also, in lower degree, throughout the realm of inorganic nature. To the world as a whole, predicates of good and evil do not apply; these are purely relative and human. Nature is neither just nor unjust, but strictly non-moral. It is folly, then, for man to pronounce some parts of nature good and other parts evil, as if nature existed for the sake of man, the whole for the sake of the part! Perfection may indeed be asserted of the whole, but the term has no moral significance. In the sense which Spinoza gives to the word, things are perfect in precisely the degree to which they possess reality, which in turn is measured by their power or activity, and so by the extent to which they share in the being of the one divine substance. From Spinoza's view of man's place in the universe it follows that all events are causally determined. What any element of reality is and does, depends upon its own nature, and this in turn depends upon its place in the great system of things of which it forms a part. This determinism presents itself in Spinoza's psycho-physical parallelism as both physical and spiritual, or rational. The wise man is determined in action by his insight and reason, even as the stone is determined in its fall by its own peculiar properties. While this doctrine results in a complete rejection of the freedom of choice, it does not, in Spinoza's judgment, destroy the true freedom of man. Rather does it open the only path to such freedom, the only means for the realization of a holy and happy life, through the necessity of the agent's own rational nature.

Now all things tend, according to the measure of their reality, to maintain their own being; and we call things good or evil according as they aid or hinder man in this effort of self-preservation (*conatus sese conservandi*). All action which tends to this result is pleasant. Pleasure is a sign of the enlargement of the self, while pain accompanies the diminution and negation of the self. Although Spinoza promises no easy spiritual victory, but demands at the outset a complete renunciation of all the cheaper means of gratification, he is nevertheless no ascetic. "Assuredly nothing forbids man to enjoy himself," he says, "save grim and gloomy superstition. For why is it more lawful to satiate one's hunger and thirst than to drive away one's melancholy? I reason, and have convinced myself as follows: No deity, nor anyone else, save the envious, takes pleasure in my infirmity and discomfort, nor sets down to my virtue the tears, sobs, fear, and the like, which are signs of infirmity of spirit; on the contrary, the greater the pleasure wherewith we are affected, the greater the perfection whereto we pass; in other words, the more must we necessarily partake of the divine nature." [1]

As conscious beings, our essence is thought, or ideation. The content of thought, according to Spinoza, is two-fold in its nature, being partly active and partly passive. Active ideation has its ground or causes within the soul itself and expresses the soul's true nature, whereas passive ideation is due to causes which lie without, and expresses rather the nature of external things than the nature of the soul itself. Active ideation gives us adequate ideas; passive ideation inadequate, or confused, ideas. The meaning of this distinction will gain in clearness if we picture to ourselves in a concrete way the difference between two well-known aspects of our conscious experience. Consider for a moment the difference between a man's thought in such spheres as art,

[1] *Ethics*, Pt. IV, Prop. xlv, Note (Elwes translation).

and science, and literature, where he produces creatively
that which truly expresses his nature as a rational being, and
his thought when he reacts against forces outside of himself,
such as food and drink, heat and cold, storm and flood,
disease-bearing microbe and death-dealing earthquake. To
the passive side of our conscious life belong our sensations
and passions, and these it is which bring us into bondage,
since they depend upon external things and can satisfy but
a part, not the whole, of our nature. In their exercise man
does not determine himself, but is determined from without.
When they dominate our life they inevitably lead to weakness, to the impotency of our being. Thus, in an interesting
way, Spinoza is led to identify virtue with strength, and
vice with weakness.

The passion that brings men into bondage arises not only
from undue occupation with the external, but also from the
illusions of a partial and transient view of things. From this
source we all suffer our days and hours of bondage. For we
are all at times limited to partial views that distort the truth
of things. Passing episodes are made leading motives of
existence; transient hopes and fears, unworthy loves and
hates, fill for a time the whole field of vision; some petty
slight, some jealousy, or ambition, dominates our thought
till it leaves no place for the real interests of life; in short,
for the universal and permanent values, we substitute those
which are at best trivial and fleeting.

But how shall man escape the bondage of the passions?
His deliverance, Spinoza tells us, can only come through
the understanding, as it sees things in their true relations.
Freedom from the bondage of illusion is won by a widened,
clarified vision, which sees the whole instead of the part.
Disturbing emotions may be overcome through the insight
which, by revealing things in their true perspective, quickens
the appropriate emotion. The problem of our life is really
that of our loves and hates, the things we set our hearts

upon. If we are brought into bondage by the love of unworthy objects, we cannot free ourselves from their power by a fiat of the will. Only when we see their illusory, false character, and at the same time discern worthy objects of love and devotion, is our freedom won. The same principle applies in combatting evil in others. "He who chooses to avenge wrongs with hatred is assuredly wretched. But he, who strives to conquer hatred with love, fights his battle in joy and confidence; he withstands many as easily as one, and has very little need of fortune's aid. Those whom he vanquishes yield joyfully, not through failure, but through increase in their powers." [1]

Spinoza's ethics concludes with a profoundly religious view. The one object which never fails is God, the All-Real. "But love towards a thing eternal and infinite feeds the mind wholly with joy, and is itself unmingled with any sadness, wherefore it is greatly to be desired and sought for with all our strength." [2] But the love of man towards God, like that of God towards man, is not the natural love of the affections, such love as one human being bears to another. It is rather the emotion that accompanies clear insight and adequate knowledge, an intellectual love, *amor Dei intellectualis*, as Spinoza characteristically terms it. As in Greek ethics, so with Spinoza, it is the wise man who triumphs over evil and enjoys the blessedness of true freedom. We need not wonder that the victory is rarely won, for, in the closing words of his *Ethics*, "all things excellent are as difficult as they are rare." But that such a triumph was no idle dream for Spinoza, his own life, if we may trust his biographers, affords instructive evidence.

[1] *Ethics*, Pt. IV, Prop. xlvi, Note.
[2] *On the Improvement of the Understanding*, p. 5.

VI. Hegel

Idealistic systems, since the time of Kant, have developed with such variety of detail that an account of them would involve many chapters in the history of modern thought. Such an account is excluded by the purpose and limits of the present work. But the influence on contemporary ethical thought of Hegel,[1] the greatest of modern idealists, renders desirable a statement of some phases of his moral theory. Hegel's interest lay primarily in ethical institutions, in the concrete and objective expressions of morality, rather than in the intricate problems of moral psychology. Profoundly influenced by Greek ideals, he saw in the slow unfolding of social institutions, and particularly of the state, the ever larger realization of human freedom and perfection. The necessary condition of a worthy life, in his view, was that one should be the citizen of a state with good laws. He criticizes severely Kant's formalism as abstract and empty. While he recognizes Kant's merit in emphasizing the high claims of duty, he also finds that his principle of "duty for duty's sake" affords no clue to the particular duties. Apart from the concrete conditions of society, any kind of immoral act might be justified on Kant's maxim of universality. Immoral acts contradict this maxim only because they disregard our interests in life, property, and social order.

In his scheme of philosophy, Hegel passes from the Philosophy of Nature to the Philosophy of Spirit; in the latter he pictures the successive stages of the self-realization of the human spirit. Beginning with man in his natural condition, he traces his progress through the institutions of social morality, and rises finally to the perfection of his being in art, philosophy, and religion. The subject-matter of the entire movement thus described is the human will—and the will is the man—in its relations to the universal will of man

[1] George Wilhelm Friedrich Hegel, 1770–1831.

in society, and of this universal will to the Absolute, Divine Will.

If the will be conceived as existing in itself, outside of a world of possible relations into which it has not yet entered, it may be said to constitute, in legal terms, a person. Such personality may be regarded as the basis of abstract right. But to escape from abstraction and become truly real, the will must actualize itself in the objective world. This it accomplishes at first through the institution of property. Things themselves are will-less, and the person may rightfully subject them to himself. In doing this he makes them a part of his own person; by seizure, use, and alienation he constitutes them an attribute of the self. The institution of property, however, is possible only when it is recognized and respected by one's neighbors; it involves not one, but many, consenting wills, in fact a common will. We see, then, that the relation between things becomes a relation between wills. Persons are related to each other through their property. "Be a person and respect others as persons" is the formula of abstract rights.

The common will, objectified in the institution of property, is the basis of contract. Crime and punishment are conceptions that naturally flow from it. Crime is the violation or negation of the common will, and punishment the negation of the crime, hence a negation of a negation. Punishment is the natural completion of the crime; rightly viewed, it honors the criminal, since it is a recognition of his personality. It may even be said to be the criminal's right as truly as his desert.

External and abstract right needs to be internalized and transformed into ideals of personal will, in order that harmony may be established between the particular and the universal will, and inner freedom realized. This subjective phase of conduct is called by Hegel abstract Duty or Morality (*Moralität*). It is the stage of the dominance of conscience, of self-determination through personal ideals of duty. In the life of the individual it comes when he escapes from the control of merely external commands, and finds the law within himself, written in his own consciousness. The dictates of the inner voice now seem supreme and final. "Do right though the heavens fall," "My conscience against the world," represent the temper of this stage of moral experience. Subjective emotions, and even blind prejudices, may at this stage dictate the rule of conduct. The good as thus privately determined may not be the good at all. For subjective conviction, untaught by objective codes and institutions, may issue in positive evil. The conscience of the fanatic speaks with an authority no less absolute than does that of the wise man. Antinomianism, in all its forms, has been the result of this subjective attitude. "The striving for a morality of one's own is futile, and by its very nature impossible of attainment; in respect of morality the saying of the wisest men of antiquity is the only true one: 'To be moral is to live in accordance with the moral tradition of one's country.'" An objective social order with its concrete, living expressions of human needs and human welfare is required for the right guidance of the individual will.

Subjective morality is transformed into true ethical life (*Sittlichkeit*) when one enters the world of ethical relations, and accepts the obligations which these relations impose. The family, civil society, the state, and humanity as a whole, constitute an objective order which gives definite and enlightened aims for the guidance of the individual judgment. Abstract duty thus wins a specific content in one's "station and its duties." Here the individual escapes from all the capriciousness of subjective conscience and rises to the dignity of true freedom, a genuine realization of personality. The objective moral order offers a concrete union and harmony of the individual and universal will. Further, the conflict between egoism and altruism is now overcome; for the largest altruism is seen to be the largest possible self-realization. History, for Hegel, is the progressive unfolding and realization of man's true nature as rational and social. All customs and institutions which bind men together have been the work of an immanent Reason guiding the development of human freedom, which is possible only through human brotherhood. This is the high theme of his Philosophy of History. In some of Hegel's own statements it seems almost a glorification of the existing order, an acceptance of the *status quo*. The critics of Hegel have often represented his doctrine as the assertion that "Whatever is, is right," and it is true that he does not always do full justice to the protesting conscience in its constant task of criticism. Certainly he had little sympathy with the hasty and shallow reformer who would ruthlessly tear down all that the past has built with so much pain and labor. Indeed, in Hegel's view, he who fails heartily to accept the moral institutions of his age and race should be prepared to justify his action by proving himself a "heaven-born prophet." [1] But Hegel recognized that the present order of things, necessary and worthful as it is, is not final. It, in its turn, must be negated and give place to a higher order. He also freely admits that when a community or a state has fallen on evil days, the protesting conscience of the individual is abundantly justified in uttering its voice. From Hegel's final point of view the most perfect ethical institutions render possible only a partial realization of the human spirit. The ideal is never fully attained. Morality as such can never complete itself or attain its goal. From morality and all secular relations the spirit of man struggles upward towards the infinite ideal. Only in conscious relation with the Absolute Personality does it find its fullest realization. Ethics completes itself in religion; the secular task becomes a religious service.

[1] Cf. Bradley, *Ethical Studies*, p. 181.

VII. SELF-REALIZATION AND ENERGISM

The form of the perfection theory most frequently met with in contemporary thought is that known as the Ethics of Self-realization. Although expositions of the theory offer great variety in method, as also in emphasis upon different aspects of the ideal, they may all be described in general terms as Hegelian both in spirit and in historical relationship. Without attempting here a detailed exposition, we may indicate two or three leading features common to all statements of the theory.

The self to be realized is the total rational self, as opposed to the partial, fragmentary self of appetite and sensuous desire. In words of Mr. Mackenzie: "The true self is what is perhaps best described as the rational self. It is the universe that we occupy in our moments of deepest wisdom and insight. . . . To live completely in that universe would be to understand completely the world in which we live and our relations to it, and to act constantly in the light of that understanding. This we cannot hope to do. All that we can do is to endeavor to promote this understanding more and more in ourselves and others, and to act more and more in a way that is consistent with the promotion of this understanding. So to live is to be truly *ourselves*." [1] This rational self is also the social self, the self that finds realization in a community of selves and in a common good. All right acts are social acts, all moral values social values. "In the realization of individuality there is found also the needed realization of some community of persons of which the individual is a member; and, conversely, the agent who duly satisfies the community in which he shares, by that same conduct satisfies himself." [2] Wherever such a harmony of individual and social good is not matter of clear insight it still remains the postulate of ethics, the faith of our moral life.

[1] *Manual of Ethics*, pp. 251–252.
[2] Dewey, *Outlines of Ethics*, p. 131.

Further, it is freely admitted that the precise content of the moral ideal cannot be given in detail. The historical course of the development to the present point of attainment may be traced, but its possible future wealth cannot be fully described. "It must be once more admitted," says Green, "that our view of what the life would be, in which ultimate good was actually attained, can never be an adequate view. It consists of the idea that such a life must be possible, filled up as regards particulars, in some inadequate measure, by reflection on the habits and activities, on the modes of life and character, which through influence of that idea have been brought into being. If the idea, as it actuates us, carried with it a full consciousness of what its final realization would be, the distinction between idea and realization would be at an end." [1]

A different formulation of the moral ideal is offered in the Energism of Professor Paulsen.[2] This view is essentially Aristotelian. It finds the good of man in the exercise of his specific functions, the perfecting of his capacities. "We may say in a most general way that the goal at which the will of every living creature aims, is *the normal exercise of the vital functions which constitute its nature*. Every animal desires to live the life for which it is predisposed. Its natural disposition manifests itself in impulses, and determines its activity. The formula may also be applied to man. He desires to live a *human* life and all that is implied in it; that is, *a mental, historical life, in which there is room for the exercise of all human*, mental powers and virtues." [3] There is evidently no necessary conflict between this view and the doctrine of self-realization. The difference consists rather in method of exposition and in historical associations.

Even from such brief outlines of historical development

[1] *Prolegomena to Ethics*, pp. 310–311.
[2] *A System of Ethics*, See Bk. II, Chap. II.
[3] *Ibid.*, p. 270.

we can see that our intellectual inheritance in the field of ethics, as elsewhere, is highly complex and profoundly significant, and that to it every period and every school of thought has made its contribution. The scientific spirit is always eager to understand its material, be it rock or flower or spiritual ideal, and to know not only what it is, but how it came to be what it is. It is hoped that this brief sketch will lead the reader to seek fuller information from the sources. Our own task, however, is now to examine critically, in the interests of a constructive theory, the two leading interpretations of the moral end represented by happiness and perfection.

CHAPTER V

HAPPINESS AS ULTIMATE VALUE

HAVING passed briefly in review some of the more significant historical forms of the happiness and perfection theories, we must now seek to determine what place each theory occupies in a true interpretation of the end of human conduct. Can the good, as ultimate value, be defined in terms of either one of these ideals, or must it include both? If the latter alternative proves to be true, what is the precise rôle played by each? Are they independent and disconnected elements, or are they so related that their organic connection can be clearly seen?

One question naturally presents itself in view of the fact that these two opposing theories have permanently held a place in ethical thought. Is there not manifestly a strong presumption that each contains elements of truth? Otherwise would not criticism, working with a free hand, have overthrown the one or the other in the course of centuries? We have not to do here, as in some other controversies, with views authoritatively taught and supported by all the enginery of social institutions; scientific and philosophical criticism recognize no such external authority. The vitality of a doctrine is not, to be sure, always a safe criterion of its worth. But whenever two opposing views have both attracted to their support, through many centuries, equally able and disinterested thinkers, it is highly probable that neither one possesses a monopoly of the truth. In the age-long controversies between idealism and materialism, rationalism and empiricism, necessity and freedom, individualism and socialism, not to mention other examples, it can reasonably be maintained that each side in the dispute has represented elements of permanent truth, though not always that precise measure of truth which its defenders have supposed. It is furthermore significant, in the case of the ethical theories in question, that they have moved, not in parallel, but in slowly converging lines, and that they tend to approach still more closely. It is difficult to find a writer of the present day, who, however much he may inveigh against happiness as the ethical end, does not in the last resort admit its importance and give it some sort of recognition, however belated and unsystematic. On the other hand, it is easy to see that hedonism, in its historical development, has been forced more and more to recognize elements of truth in opposing theories. In this respect early Greek hedonism is separated by a wide gulf from any modern form of the theory. In its development moral experience proved too rich and varied to fit the simple formulas of early days. We shall be prepared, then, to find some element of truth in the theory that happiness is the final principle of human conduct. The present chapter will attempt to show that the happiness theory contains a kernel of truth which is essential to any adequate account of human good, and it will seek to make clear the part that happiness plays in the conception of value. In the very task of exhibiting its truth, however, we shall be led to see its inadequacy, and the defect of a theory which fails to provide any other principle. Only by comprehending the real function of happiness in determining our standards of value can the student appreciate the nature and source of its limitations. To see clearly what a principle of explanation does do, is at the same time to see what it does not do.

I. Psychological and Ethical Hedonism

If the element of truth in the happiness theory is to be clearly grasped, the theory must be freed from numerous errors and misconceptions which have persistently gathered about it and obscured its true meaning. One of these sources of confusion is so important as to call for consideration at the very outset of our inquiry. This initial misunderstanding consists in the failure to distinguish between motive and value in conduct, between the forces, whether instinctive or ideational, which impel us to the performance of an act, and the total value which we assign to an act when performed. It can be shown, I think, that the principles of motivation and of valuation are not always, perhaps are not often, precisely the same. Here, evidently, are two distinct questions. The one asks why we act as we do in any given case; the other, what is the ultimate value of our action. The one has to do with the act prior to its completion; the other is concerned with its complete and total results, and so with its rational justification. The difference may be illustrated by pointing out that the reason why we continue to live is not identical with the value which, in reflection upon experience, we discover in life. As we did not sit down "in a cool hour" at the dawn of our existence, and upon consideration of life's prospects conclude that "to be" was better than "not to be," so in most cases we do not continue to live because of a reflective estimate of the value of life, but because the instinctive desire for life, the "will to live," pulses strong within us. And this instinctive clinging to life is so powerful that it sometimes proves stronger in individuals than the reflective conviction that for them, under existing conditions, life is not worth living. Obviously the point of view is quite different and the question is shifted to another field of inquiry, when, instead of asking why we live, we ask how far life is satisfying, and what are the elements of value which it has been found actually to contain. A more concrete example of the distinction in question may be given. A normal, healthy-minded person does not engage in an athletic game from a calculating estimate of the pleasure to be enjoyed in the sport, but rather from an interest in its movements and situations. The game attracts because it affords expression to the play impulse. The impelling motive is within, and the sight or thought of the game is the stimulus which releases the spring of action. Quite different is a reflective judgment concerning the value of the game as actually experienced. This estimate may be favorable or unfavorable, but it does not change the motive which prompted one to engage in the sport. One may decide that the bruises are too many, that the fatigue is too great, or that the exertion is prejudicial to health. If this be the case, the result may be to inhibit or modify the impulse when it next appears. It is in this way that reflection upon experience actually modifies our playing of the game of life. As a result there is usually a growing identity between the moving forces in our activities and our reflective estimates of their value. If we could conceive a being of perfect intelligence, not driven by impulsive and appetitive forces, but moved to action by reflective estimates of value, we should regard these two aspects as entirely coincident, and the distinction which we are compelled to make in human conduct between impelling motive and judgment of value would disappear. But in the conduct of men we are not justified in disregarding this distinction.

It is interesting to observe in passing that in some cases we value conduct more highly when it is impulsive and spontaneous than when it is brought under the introspective estimates of value. We commonly esteem more highly a kindly deed that springs directly from unreflecting sympathy than one which results from reflection, or a decorous act that expresses innate good taste than one which is more consciously elaborated. Human beings best attain certain ends by the path of instinct and habit, though it is not to be supposed that instincts and habits can escape evaluation.

Now it has frequently been assumed that, in order to establish the truth of hedonism, the motive of every act must be proved to be the desire to secure pleasure or to avoid pain. And a refutation of this view has often been considered a refutation of the entire theory. Hedonism, however, has not always attached itself to the principle of motivation, but has also appeared in another form in which it has depended upon the principle of valuation. The theory that pleasure is the motive of every act is known as *psychological hedonism*, and must be distinguished from *ethical hedonism*, which holds that the value of conduct is ultimately measured by the production of pleasure. There is no justification for confusing a doctrine which makes pleasure the universal object of desire and regards it as the sole motive power in conduct, with a doctrine which finds the ultimate value of experience in feelings of pleasure, and so regards these as the final standard of moral judgment. We proceed first to the criticism of psychological hedonism.

II. Criticism of Psychological Hedonism

In studying the motives of conduct it is important, first of all, to recognize the influence of instincts and impulses which impel us to action by an inner constraint, and of whose meaning and power we are, at the beginning of their operation, only very imperfectly aware. In the case of instinctive and impulsive acts nature seeks expression, primarily without regard to the pleasure or pain attendant upon the act. Nature wills to live and does not reckon too nicely the cost to her countless creatures. And in man the "will to live" is a will to act in specific ways according to his propensities and endowments. If it is a will primarily to satisfy bodily wants and to gain possession of material things, it is also, as consciousness develops, a will to form family ties, to comprehend things intellectually, and to appreciate them æsthetically, in fine, to exercise all the various functions of body and mind. The general types of our activity are thus fixed for us by nature.

In a conscious being, palpitating with native desires, the mere presence of the idea of an object to be attained often issues in activity immediately, and without reflection upon its pleasantness or unpleasantness. The child thinks of its playthings and at once seeks them; it sees a flower and hastens to pluck it. The acts thus performed are, in the stricter sense of the term, ideo-motor, that is, they follow directly from the presence in consciousness of the idea of the act. Here the idea of the object which represents the goal of the inner impulse is clearly not the idea of pleasure as such, but is the idea of an object which, from its adaptation to some native propensity, is an object of desire. It is the same with acts which belong to the sphere of habit; the signal which summons us to the lecture-room, or the ringing of the telephone at one's desk, commonly results in immediate, unhesitating action. Evidently, in such cases, the act is not conditioned by the representation of it as pleasant or unpleasant.

But all these acts, it may be objected, are not instances of deliberate choice, and do not disprove the contention that pleasure is what we desire and seek in those cases in which we consciously choose between alternative courses of action, the cases of first importance for moral conduct. Yet here again it seems that normal human desires are objective and disinterested. By calling desires disinterested we simply mean that they are not primarily directed to the pleasure of their own satisfaction, but have some end, or goal, which is the center of conscious interest. If, for example, one goes to the relief of a suffering animal, it is not because one thinks of oneself as pleased by giving relief, but because one desires the animal to be rescued from its pain. The truth is, we find things pleasant because we desire them; we do not in the first instance conceive them to be pleasant and afterwards feel the desire. The appetite or desire for an object precedes and conditions the pleasure found in its attainment. Psychological hedonism inverts the true order; it puts the cart before the horse. Desire is the steed that bears pleasure in its train; until desire stirs, pleasure is motionless. New levels of pleasurable activity could never be attained on the principle of psychological hedonism. Men had first to hit upon the novel elements in experience before they could picture them as pleasant. Did they not produce works of art before they could desire the pleasures of artistic creation, first sing, and afterwards represent singing as agreeable?

Even in the case of the lower and more egoistic desires there is usually no conscious pursuit of pleasure as such, abstracted from the objects and activities upon which it is dependent. "A miser accumulates money, not deliberately saying to himself, 'I shall by doing this get the delight which possession gives.' He thinks only of the money and the means of getting it; and he experiences incidentally the pleasure that comes from possession. Owning property is that which he revels in imagining, and not the feeling which owning property will cause." [1] In the words of James: "I cannot help thinking that it is the confusion of *pursued pleasure with mere pleasure of achievement* which makes the pleasure-theory of action so plausible to the ordinary mind." [2] Only the voluptuary habitually abstracts from experience the feelings of pleasure, and centers attention upon these to the exclusion of other elements. And such pursuit of pleasure, we are constantly reminded, is certain to be disappointing. The objective, not the minutely introspective and calculating temper, yields the conditions favorable to enjoyment. How abnormal the attitude of the voluptuary becomes, is seen in the fact that, in the absence of natural desire, he seeks artificially to arouse the desire through the

---

[1] Spencer, *Data of Ethics*, p. 250.
[2] *The Principles of Psychology*, Vol. II, pp. 556-557.

gratification of which pleasure is secured.[1] Thus the gourmand by the use of stimulants whets his failing appetite for food; hence the restless search of the pleasure-seeker for satisfactions which are denied him because healthy desires have been killed. This empty and restless longing constitutes his true nemesis, his "fire that is not quenched." Healthy human consciousness is too much absorbed in the business of life to weigh with nice abstraction the probable pleasure to be derived from every detailed choice. Such a consciousness views the object which it desires as a whole, and the idea of it is much more than the idea of pleasure.[2]

To leave the question without further analysis, however, would do injustice to a hedonistic psychology of action, which, if not wholly true, is not wholly false. If we must insist that the object of desire is for our thought not the idea of pleasure, must we not admit that it is, normally at least, a pleasant idea? Even in the case of an arduous or heroic deed, is it not commonly true that, at the moment of choice, its performance seems more pleasant, or less unpleasant, than the alternative? To a brave soldier the thought of service in his country's cause, at the risk of suffering and death, may well seem pleasanter than the cowardice or desertion by which alone the chance of such a fate could be escaped. Many a noble spirit, we may believe, finds the way of renunciation less unpleasant than recreancy to cherished ideals. How far the choice made under such conditions seems pleasanter at the moment than the rejected alternative, is a difficult question. There is doubtless involved here the distinction

---

[1] Cf. the attitude of the laborer who "would not take fifty cents for his thirst."

[2] We are not concerned to deny that it is possible to desire pleasure as such. But the moment such a desire is in way of realization the object of choice becomes more than the idea of pleasure; it takes on specific content. If, after a period of monotonous work, we desire pleasure, we are compelled to cast about for some specific form of amusement. It may be golf or tennis, music or the theater; but in any case the object of our choice ceases to be merely the idea of pleasure. If the chosen content itself does not absorb our attention the pursuit of pleasure inevitably proves a failure.

between that which is pleasant in a superficial and transient sense, and that which is more deeply and permanently satisfying. But for psychology, as we shall later urge, this distinction is one between different kinds of pleasantness. The feeling of satisfying the demands of duty, or of striving to follow the requirements of an ideal self, may be in its own way truly pleasant. We are not, however, called upon to settle too nicely the account of pleasure in the act of choice, since we have shown that the choice does not present itself to us simply as a choice of the pleasant and unpleasant, but far more as the choice of an objective and disinterested content. It is probable that, in the choice of ideal ends, the hedonic element in feeling varies largely with different individuals, and with the same individual under different conditions.

But it is certainly true that the imagined pleasantness of an object does increase our desire for it, although we cannot by this means explain the origin of the desire itself. Moral education consists in no small degree, as Aristotle pointed out, in connecting pleasure with worthy objects. Its task is to enlarge experience and clarify insight, and thus to emancipate us from the domination of immediate desires. The quickened imagination is happily able to surround distant goals with warmth of feeling, and so to transform them into attractive and compelling ends. This power to rise above the stream of immediate impressions and to find abiding satisfaction in pursuits of universal and permanent value is the noblest endowment of human nature. Such capacity determines spiritual rank; at its highest, it is the gift of moral genius.

III. Ethical Hedonism and a Theory of Value

Thus far we have dealt with psychological hedonism, with the doctrine that pleasure is the sole object of desire and the determining motive of all conduct. This theory we have rejected as inadequate to explain the facts of experience. The existence of objective and disinterested desires is its essential refutation. We have now to consider a different and far more important theory, that of ethical hedonism. Whereas psychological hedonism maintains that pleasure is the only thing that we desire, ethical hedonism holds that pleasure is the only thing that is truly desirable, the one ultimate value of life. The ethical hedonist, it may be noted, is implicitly committed to the doctrine that, in so far as conduct is fully rationalized, a regard for pleasure will be the determining motive of conduct. At the same time, it is open to an ethical hedonist to maintain the objective quality of human desires. And he may consistently hold that a whole-hearted devotion, a generous abandon to ideal interests, as they present themselves in the social order, is for us mortals a far safer guide in conduct than a calculating regard for pleasure in detailed choices. In so far, however, as it can be shown that the existing order does not make for general happiness, he will seek to modify current standards by a more thorough application of his ultimate principle.

In order to appraise this claim of ethical hedonism, to determine how far it is true and how far false, we are compelled to pursue an inquiry concerning the general nature and conditions of the experience of value. This, for the present, is the central task of our study. Anticipating for a moment the result of what is to follow, we shall see that happiness is one essential element of all values, but is never the whole of any single value.

We have spoken of ultimate values and avoided "absolute" as a term for our human values because of the ambiguities and misleading suggestions of the latter word. If by absolute value is meant what is good in itself, the meaning is more clearly expressed by the word intrinsic, which we shall employ to distinguish certain final values from those which are instrumental in the production of other values.

In this sense knowledge is both an intrinsic and an instrumental value, because, while it is a means in the production of other values, it is also good in itself, one of the true ends of life, yielding immediate and high satisfaction. If, again, absolute means "unconditional," a challenge may at once be issued to point out a single value the actual existence of which in human experience is not subject to many conditions. The only unconditional moral value is obedience to the laws of value, and this means no more than that there is an unconditional obligation to do the best one can under existing conditions. A further objection to the use of the term absolute, as applied to moral values, is found in the fact that it suggests the problem of absolute idealism, the question of the existence of an all-embracing consciousness within which our human values are somehow contained. If one accepts the hypothesis of such an idealism and regards human experiences of worth as elements in the life of the Absolute, then, of course, all human values must stand in some relation to such a system of absolute values. But it is also clear that straightway to identify human values with these absolute values is a proceeding as unwarranted as the religious anthropomorphism which unblushingly identifies God with a magnified and exalted man. And still further, in order to make a system of absolute values serve as norms of human conduct, we should require nothing less than a specific and detailed revelation of these values, such as might be assumed to exist if we possessed an inspired philosophical bible or an infallible metaphysical pope. In the absence of both, we are compelled to limit ourselves to those values which our human experience has been able slowly but surely to win and to vindicate. Indeed, it is from human experience of value alone that any so-called system of absolute values is derived; deduction can never proceed in the opposite direction. The claim of such transcendent deduction may be likened to the descent of an aëronaut from the sky with the assertion that he never ascended from the earth. By rejecting the term absolute it is not intended to deny the existence of a world-order which determines the laws and the conditions of all our human values. Certainly the laws of value are not dependent upon our capricious personal desires, but stand authoritatively over and above them.

In limiting ourselves to the values discoverable in human experience we are not subjecting them to the whims of individual taste. All values are over-individual in the sense that the general conditions of experience are fixed primarily by a power transcending our wills. They are also over-individual in that they are universal. Like Socrates, we may find in them that which is valid because it transcends the here and now of individual experience and answers to common human needs. We may speak of these as ultimate, or fundamental, values, in precisely the sense that our analysis can never go beyond them.

We pass now to consider some further problems involved in a theory of values. First of all, value attaches alone to conscious experience. Nothing in the world can be conceived of as possessing any degree of worth save as it enters into, or forms an element of, experience. Whatever answer one may give to the idealist's contention that nothing in the universe exists outside of conscious experience, it is evident that no object can possess value outside of such experience. If we try to think a world which, in its earliest stages, was without consciousness—the world of the nebular hypothesis for example—all values that can be ascribed to it are strictly anticipatory of the time when conscious life appears. Until this time, "all the choir of heaven and furniture of earth" must be conceived as without the slightest value.

Assent to this view, it would appear, is not universal. It has been seriously asked whether, if we think of two worlds, the one the most beautiful and the other the most ugly that we can imagine, and both "quite apart from any possible contemplation by human beings," we should not think it better that the most beautiful rather than the most ugly should exist.[1] To make the case complete, however, it must be assumed that the beauty and ugliness in question do not enter into the experience of beings other than man in a way that would affect their satisfaction or dissatisfaction. With this proviso, we must, I think, unhesitatingly declare that it would make no difference which one of the two worlds should exist. Mr. Moore's opposite answer seems to owe all its plausibility to the fact that he illicitly assumes a certain relation of the two worlds to human consciousness after all, when he asks, "Would it not be well, in any case, to produce it (the beautiful world) rather than the other?" This obviously annuls the very condition essential to the problem. For certainly we should think it well to "do what we could to produce it," because, as beings who appreciate beauty, we find satisfaction both in contemplating and in trying to produce what is beautiful rather than what is ugly. Even the process of imagining a beautiful world is worth more than that of imagining an ugly one. As for a world which no conscious beings could ever try to produce, or could even contemplate when produced—a world sweeping forever through unconscious space—such a world would be wholly without value.

Just as certain as it is that there can be no value apart from experience, so certain is it that not all human experience possesses the same degree of value. Not only do we give widely varying positive values to different portions of our existence, but there is not a little human experience which, considered by itself, we agree in describing by purely negative terms of value. Such experience is like a bankrupt debtor; not merely is there absence of good, but the presence of positive evil. We should consider it better not to exist at all than to be burdened permanently with ex-

[1] G. E. Moore, *Principia Ethica*, pp. 83–85.

perience of this type. Few persons have reached maturity who have not passed through periods of such physical suffering or mental anguish that they would not instantly prefer complete annihilation to the permanent and unbroken continuance of these states of consciousness. If life were wholly made up of such experiences, the most pronounced pessimist would be more than justified in his judgment of life.[1]

IV. Feeling and the Value Experience

Is there any element common to all experiences which we regard as having positive value, and which we therefore designate as good? And similarly, in those experiences to which we deny value and which we call evil, is there some characteristic mark discoverable in all? There does appear to be a psychological factor common to all the experiences of each type, and changing its character whenever we pass from the one type to the other. For all experiences which we call good, however varied their content may be, ultimately affect us agreeably; all those which we call evil ultimately affect us disagreeably. More exactly stated, the principle would be as follows: all experiences which, considered by themselves, we call good, are accompanied by affective states that are agreeable, or pleasurable; those experiences which, considered by themselves, we call evil, are accompanied by affective states that are disagreeable, or displeasurable. This form of statement recognizes that there are numerous cases in which conscious states, not desirable in themselves, are considered desirable because they are believed to make possible future experiences of worth for the agent or for others. Here belong the familiar examples of painful operations, hard discipline,

[1] Whether there are experiences of a strictly neutral type to which neither a positive nor a negative value can be assigned, is a disputed psychological question. Logically such a neutral, or zero, point is required in passing through a complete series of possible values, extending both up and down the scale. But even if the existence of these neutral states be admitted, they are obviously rare, and are not significant for the present purpose.

costly self-sacrifice, etc. Conversely, there are experiences, considered desirable in themselves, to which reflection gives a negative value because they prevent the realization of other experiences of greater worth. Of many forms of gratification it must be admitted that they would be good if they did not prevent the realization of other and greater values. The warmth and cheer produced by alcohol would be good for the cold and tired workman returning from his day's labor, were it not for the reaction to follow, the formation of a dangerous habit, the neglect of wholesome food, and other ill effects.

Before attempting a further explanation of the relation of states of feeling to judgments of value, it is important to fix as exactly as possible the meaning of the terms employed. Although the psychology of feeling is admittedly in a less forward state than that of other phases of our mental life, some general positions may be outlined with tolerably complete agreement on the part of psychologists.

Feeling is a word which indicates the peculiarly personal and subjective aspect of our mental life, that with which "a stranger intermeddleth not." More than any other term it expresses our individual attitudes and reactions towards the objects of experience. Modes of feeling, or, as many would prefer to say, affective states, of varying degrees of intensity and quality, are an element in all our mental processes. These states are marked by a quality of agreeableness or disagreeableness. It has often been customary to refer to this series of affective states, in its hedonic aspects, as the "pleasure-pain" series. This, however, is not a correct designation, as pain is a special form of organic sensation, and is not the opposite of pleasure. It is better therefore to speak of the pleasure-displeasure series. Pain is in itself of course disagreeable; but one may have feelings of even acute pain, and still the total affective state may be agreeable. Unexpected good news, for example, may not cause the pain of a severe head-ache or of a wound to cease, but in spite of it the sufferer may find himself for a long time in a state of highly pleasurable feeling.[1]

Whether feelings can be reduced to the pleasure-displeasure series, or contain other and non-hedonic elements, is a question upon which psychologists are not agreed.[2] It is to a considerable degree a matter of terminology. Popular usage has given to the term feeling the most widely varied meanings. The "I feel" of daily speech includes almost every conceivable type of experience; impulses, desires, and emotions are all thus designated as feelings. But psychology must analyze this complex "I feel" into its various psychical components. Upon analysis, all the emotions, love, hate, fear, anger, etc., as well as all desires and impulses, are found to contain ideational and volitional, as well as feeling elements. It would be a great gain in clearness if, for psychological purposes, feeling were limited to the agreeable and disagreeable elements in consciousness. But whatever extension we give to the term feeling, it is in its pleasurable and displeasurable elements that we find the most immediate appreciation of the value of experience. It is important to give due emphasis to the word immediate, because it is the function of the reflective and imaginative powers so to represent for us the prospective and distant consequences of conduct as to enable us to disregard present gratification.

[1] One interesting example, among many, of the presence of pain in a state of pleasure has been observed in some cases of migraine, which, at a certain stage of the attack, are attended by a marked heightening of mental activity. There often result a clarity and vigor of the mental processes which yield a positive satisfaction in spite of the pain.

[2] Professor Wundt's tentative classification would make feeling vary in three directions, consisting of (1) the pleasure-displeasure series, (2) the "excitement-depression," or "excitement-tranquilization" series, and (3) the "tension-relief" series. Even if this analysis can be successfully established, it still remains to be shown that any sense of value can be discovered in feelings of excitement or depression, of tension or relief, apart from their pleasantness or unpleasantness. The same applies to Professor Royce's suggestion of the two series of feelings, "pleasure-displeasure," and "restlessness-quiescence."

This fact must not, however, lead us to forget that when such future consequences are actually realized their value will then become present to immediate feeling. He who resists the attraction of the pleasure of the moment, or heroically suffers in the interests of the remote good of his fellows, finds, if he thinks the matter out, that this remote good must always report itself somewhere, at some time, in the happiness of some conscious being.

For the sake of clearness we should also notice the relation of the term value to that of satisfaction, in which latter term there lurks a certain ambiguity. In discussing the motivation of conduct we have emphasized the fact that there are inherent in us various impulses and desires which push us on towards given ends and activities. Employing the term in a wide sense, we may call these impulsive elements will-attitudes. Their presence determines primarily the direction of all our activities, and conditions the experience of all our pleasures. The performance of the appropriate act constitutes the satisfaction of the given impulse, in the sense that that particular desire is stilled and no longer spurs us on to action. But it by no means follows that this satisfaction of desire is on the whole worthful; indeed, it may be quite the opposite. For our human desires are not only complex, but often conflicting. Many desires stir within us which demand their "satisfaction" just as urgently as do others, but the satisfaction of which, instead of bringing peace, content, and well-being, results in disappointment and disaster. The child may desire to put its fingers into the flame, or one may desire to eat unwholesome food, and although in each case the performance of the act satisfies the existing desire, the results are highly displeasurable. In other words, the "satisfaction" of a desire may ultimately prove to be either satisfying or dissatisfying. And if we are to employ the term satisfaction for the feeling of value, we must distinguish carefully between the mere fulfillment, or quietus, of an existing desire, and the enjoyment of relatively permanent and widely diffused states of agreeable consciousness that result from such fulfillment. Used in this latter sense, satisfaction is one of the best terms for the feeling of value, especially for popular use, since it is generally understood to mark those experiences of well-being that arise from the higher individual and social activities.

The so-called voluntaristic theories of value, which define the concept essentially in terms of desire, fail to observe the distinction which we have just stated. They overlook the necessity of distinguishing clearly between motive and value, between the desired and the desirable. The representatives of this view tend to define value in economic rather than in ethical terms.[1] The exchange value of any commodity, present in a given quantity, is determined quite directly by the existing desires for its possession. But exchange value and ultimate value do not coincide. Fakirs have always thriven by the possibility of arousing desire for goods which possess but little capacity to give satisfaction. And in the case of some goods which are permanently objects of desire, but which tend to be harmful, there is clearly no fixed relation between exchange value and ultimate value.

It is important to bear in mind the wide range of the pleasure-displeasure series. It extends from the humblest physical gratifications and discomforts up to the most refined and exalted intellectual, æsthetic, and religious experiences. The persistent disregard by many writers of the

---

[1] Cf. Ehrenfels, *Werththeorie und Ethik*, Vierteljahrschrift für Wissenschaftliche Philosophie, 1893. See also *System der Werththeorie*, I, p. 2. "Nicht deswegen begehren wir die Dinge, weil wir jene mystische, unfassbare 'Wert' in ihnen erkennen, sondern deswegen sprechen wir den Dingen 'Wert' zu, weil wir sie begehren." This statement expresses a most important truth, but it fails to take account of the fact that desires, although essential to the experience of value, do not accurately measure the final worth of their objects. The necessity of both elements is insisted upon by Professor Urban. "Worth experience," he says, " is always a feeling attitude which presupposes the actualization of some conative disposition." *Valuation: Its Nature and Laws*, p. 54.

higher ranges of feeling has greatly prejudiced the place of pleasure in ethical theory. Pleasure has sometimes been interpreted as "material welfare," or "animal contentment," as "fulfillment of desire for the things of the outer world"; feeling has been identified with "sensuous" feeling, with "impulse," with "instinctive desire," and even with the "flesh" as opposed to the "spirit," or rational life. Hegel suggests that feeling is the element common to the brute creation and man, and so naturally assigns it a relatively low place in human nature. It would be impossible to indicate in detail the number of misconceptions and perversions of the terms in question which have found currency in ethical and philosophical literature. Man *feels*, it would seem, according to these narrow views, when he eats and drinks, or when he smokes a cigar and basks in the sunshine, but not when he thinks, when he appreciates the beautiful, or when he worships goodness. The best contemporary psychology, however, recognizes that the affective states are only partly, often indeed only to a slight degree, determined by sensations referable to the special senses and to the organic processes. For human beings, those feelings which depend upon the ideational processes and whose source is "cerebral," [1] or "central," [2] rather than "sensuous," or "peripheral," become of first importance. As the child grows into the man, and the man advances in age, the higher feelings play an increasingly significant rôle. The same fact also holds true in the development of the race; pleasures and displeasures are more and more dependent upon complex mental processes. "Our life of feeling is conditioned to a larger and larger extent as we develop by processes of internal representation (recollection, imagination)." [3] The race, too, like the in-

---

[1] James, *The Principles of Psychology*, Vol. II, p. 468.

[2] Titchener, *An Outline of Psychology*, pp. 99, 100, 108. Cf. Külpe, *Outlines of Psychology*, pp. 226–227.

[3] Sully, *The Human Mind*, Vol. II, p. 13.

dividual, advances in the long process of civilization from a sensational to an ideational stage of mental life, attaining new universes of experience.

That feeling is thus increasingly dependent upon a rational or ideal content, and receives its special character from the nature of the content within which it arises, is of the highest import for ethics, and will receive attention further on. What we are here concerned to emphasize is the arbitrary and unpsychological limitation of feeling to the lower and narrower spheres of experience. Although in popular language the distinction between pleasure, as marking the more sensuous and special forms of gratification, and happiness, as representing the satisfactions of serenity and peace of mind, of harmony and permanent well-being, has gained currency in modern English usage,[1] there is no reason, on psychological grounds, for regarding this distinction as taking one outside of the pleasure-displeasure series. Within that series there is room for wide differences; within it, may be recognized the varied sources and types of both agreeable and disagreeable feelings, the special and the diffused, the transitory and the more permanent, the coarser and the more refined, according to the world of experience in which they arise. Interpreted in psychological, if not in popular language, the terms pleasure and displeasure may both claim the higher as well as the lower connotation.

With this psychological interpretation, which reduces the distinction between pleasure and happiness—a distinction of undoubted practical importance—to differences in the content of the pleasure-displeasure series, is linked the problem of differences of quality in pleasure. The answer to this must be, I think, an unequivocal assertion that pleasures do differ almost endlessly in quality, according to differences in the functions, physical and mental, upon which they de-

---

[1] In older English this distinction was not recognized, but pleasure was freely used even for the highest religious experiences.

pend. The types and shades of quality range from the most simple satisfactions of daily life to rare moments of supreme exaltation. How can one completely identify the kind of pleasantness experienced in eating and drinking, with that found in the presence of a great painting or a beautiful sunset, in noble friendship or the spectacle of moral heroism? But when we come to a comparison of the worth of different pleasures, it must be remembered that our judgment necessarily assumes a quantitative form. It has commonly been thought that any hedonistic calculus requires the elimination of all differences of quality in pleasures. But this, we hold, is by no means necessary. In every sphere we make quantitative estimates of the value of qualitative differences, although we recognize that these estimates are inexact. So, when a worshiper of old desired to express the superior worth of the service of Jehovah to all worldly pleasures, he exclaims, "A day in thy courts is better than a thousand." Although pictures are not valued according to their square surfaces, their qualitative differences are nevertheless given quantitative expression in price. In the sphere of moral endeavor, too, few would in practice fail to assent to the same principle. The raising of a single individual to a very high level of moral worth would not be regarded by most good men as of equal value with a small increase of spiritual quality in a large number of individuals. Somewhere in the quantitative scale, at ten, a hundred, a thousand, or, if not even at that point, then at hundreds of thousands, the balance would fall in favor of numbers. In cases of the quantitative estimates of qualitative differences, no matter to what sphere they belong, we must not assume an exactness that is unattainable. But we must none the less recognize that our judgment is one of more or less, of greater or smaller, in terms of value.

With this preliminary discussion of some problems in the psychology of feeling, we return to the exposition and defense of the thesis, that at least one element which is essential to the very idea of value, positive or negative, is found in the affective states as agreeable or disagreeable.

If we picture to ourselves a world of beings without any capacity for experiencing feelings of pleasure or displeasure, but with the cognitive and volitional activities unimpaired, we should have a world of indifferent fact, without any good or evil, any better or worse. The various relations of fact would be observed with perfect clearness, but no judgment of value could arise; the whole gamut of change would offer nothing to which a predicate of value could attach. To such a being, "one thing would be as important or as unimportant as the next, or rather not important or unimportant at all, but simply an existing fact. All predicates expressing relations of value would be wholly unintelligible to him." [1] And if we imagine such a being looking down upon the conduct of men, he would fail to understand all those exhibitions of admiration and disgust in which our judgments of value find their most characteristic expression; our vocabulary of approval and disapproval would indeed be an unknown tongue.

Although such a mental state is of course impossible of complete realization, since affective elements enter into all our mental life, it may be worth while to point out that there are certain experiences which approximate to it, and which enable us to understand its meaning. In carrying through a long and complicated process of computation, one seems to experience moments to which neither of the terms good or evil applies with any degree of force. Slight sensations of strain and pressure are all that can be recalled as determin-

---

[1] Paulsen, *Introduction to Philosophy*, p. 230. Cf. the following from his *System of Ethics:* "If there were no satisfaction and its opposite, all striving would cease, everything would be indifferent to us.—But what else does this mean than that feelings of pleasure ultimately determine all distinctions of value? Indeed of that there can be no doubt; if there were no feelings of satisfaction and their opposites, there would be no distinctions of value. Good and bad would be meaningless words, or rather we should never use them." Pp. 256–257.

ing the feeling element in the experience, and these are frequently so faint as to give it no decided tone. The affective state is at its minimum intensity. Could this be wholly eliminated, a mode of existence would be realized concerning which it would be meaningless to raise the question of value. But the duration of such a state is short. Immediately the affective element rises again into prominence. We perceive that our work is progressing well or ill, that the result is correct or incorrect, and we feel pleasure or displeasure accordingly. We note perhaps with a kind of æsthetic satisfaction the working of some formula, or we detect with all the pleasure of a fresh discovery some hitherto unobserved aspect of a mathematical principle. Some feature of the day's business, agreeable or disagreeable, may intrude itself upon us. Affective states, dependent upon these or other ideas, present themselves in consciousness and give value, positive or negative, to the experience. Illustrations of the reduction of the affective element in consciousness, with the accompanying reduction of the sense of value, can be given by anyone who has learned to watch his experiences with something of the temper of the psychologist. An example may frequently be found in the continuous performance of a mechanical task which requires a considerable degree of attention, but which is too monotonous or too stupid to be permanently interesting. The mark common to all such experiences, however induced, is the reduction of the sense of the value of existence; this value increases, whether for good or ill, only with an increase in the intensity of the affective states.

It is also instructive to attempt to reverse the process of abstraction which we have just sketched, by supposing the affective states to be retained, and the other elements of consciousness eliminated. A being so constituted, it would seem, would still be susceptible to good and evil. Feeling would of course be totally blind, but would nevertheless mean weal or woe to the subject of it. Life might thus consist of throbs of delight or throes of anguish, without any perception of their source or meaning. Doubtless, too, there are approximations to such types of experience, particularly in extreme physical pain, which often seems to benumb the other powers of the soul. The literature of torture offers numerous illustrations to the reader who cares to enter that forbidding field. As an example of the dependence of value upon feeling, one may call to mind Lotze's striking comparison of the crushed worm, writhing in pain, and the angel endowed with consummate intelligence, but without feeling.[1] Criteria of value would be applicable to the existence of the worm, but not to that of the angel. To the angel, devoid of feeling, the question as to the worth of life would have no meaning. It would be, in Nietzsche's striking phrase, "jenseits von Gut und Böse." Attention has already been called to the very wide range of feelings which enter into human experience, and to the significance of those attending the higher and more complex mental activities. But it may not be amiss, at this point, to insist upon the fact that the life of the scholar as well as that of the man of action, the artist, or the religious devotee, may be one of profound feeling. It is often assumed that the act of thought is normally unattended by strong and deep affective states, and is even antagonistic to them. The "passionless" life of some thinker like Spinoza is held up as an example of a life without feeling. What is quite overlooked is the fact that one may have a "passion" for other things than those which most men pursue, and that the currents of feeling may be fed by springs unknown to the multitude. Knowledge is part of the end of human life, as well as a means to other ends, just because it ministers directly to the delight of the knower and of those who share his interests. Many states of feeling are directly dependent upon the higher cognitive or ideational processes,

[1] *Microcosmus* (Eng. translation), Vol. I, p. 250; see also pp. 692–694. Cf. his *Practical Philosophy*, pp. 16–19.

and are made possible only by those processes. Everyone is familiar with the fact that our intelligence is often called upon to exercise control over the emotions. We need again and again to check one emotion and to arouse another by attention to the appropriate trains of thought. This function of our reason has been called "regulative." But the intellect is not merely regulative of feeling, exercising a measure of control over it; it is also constitutive of feeling, producing by its own activity new affective elements, both agreeable and disagreeable, which would not otherwise exist at all. Only on this view of the relation of thought and feeling does the life of the scholar, or Aristotle's ideal life of contemplation, appear tolerable. Otherwise it would be cold and colorless, mere "*graue Theorie.*"

It should not be forgotten that the value found in the affective states is not limited, in the case of any act, to the feelings which directly attend its performance, nor to those which immediately follow, nor to both of these together, but includes the total affective results of the act in the experience of all conscious beings in any wise influenced by it. Somewhere, and at some time, all acts must find their value in an inner world of satisfaction, which is expressible psychologically in feelings of the pleasure-displeasure series. Must we not say, too, that, prior to the production of such states of feeling, all values are strictly anticipatory?

V. Hedonistic Implications of Optimism and Pessimism

For the purpose of setting in still clearer light the place of feelings of pleasure and displeasure in any system of values, let us examine the attitude of both the optimist and the pessimist towards the worth of life. The question at issue between optimism and pessimism is fundamental for morality, and might even serve as the point of departure for the development of an ethical theory. For the answer which is given to the question. Is life worth living? will determine the goal of moral striving. A negative answer necessarily involves the judgment that conduct should have, as its ultimate aim, the decrease and even the final extinction of life, while an affirmative answer involves, with equal necessity, the judgment that conduct should aim to conserve and increase life. But optimism and pessimism not only determine, each in its own way, the final goal of conduct; they also contain implicitly the principle, or principles, for the valuation of life. The grounds on which the optimist justifies his assertion that life is desirable must express the elements of value which he finds in life. Similarly, the reasons which the pessimist assigns for his condemnation of life must also express, in a negative way, his own principle of valuation.

Such a procedure assumes the significance and legitimacy of the question, Has life any value? Perhaps the pertinency of this inquiry will not generally be doubted, although it has been challenged. One writer says: "If you can show me where living competes with non-living, and on which side the question is decided, I will allow that life itself can be tried by the standard of use or value. Till you do so I can attach no meaning to the question. The question to which I can attach a meaning is the question, What form of life has use or worth?" [1]

Although it may be admitted that ordinarily the question, "What form of life has worth," is the more pertinent, the other question cannot be excluded. To exclude it, would be to deny altogether the possibility of a radically pessimistic view. Against its exclusion it seems sufficient to say that "living competes with non-living," not only in the case of the suicide—where its competition is wholly unsuccessful—but also in the thought of no small portion of mankind, who at some time in the course of life ask with insistent earnestness whether life has any value at all. Mr. Alexander seems

[1] S. Alexander, *The Idea of Value*, *Mind*, N. S., Vol. I, p. 50.

forced to his statement by his own theory of value. The standard of value in his view is the "social equilibrium." He says: "Value is nothing but the efficiency of a conscious agent to promote the efficiency of society, to maintain the equilibrium of forces which that society represents." [1] One may, however, press the question beyond the individual agent, whose worth is here so completely merged in that of society, and may ask, What then is the value of society itself? Or, if this question, too, seems to have "no meaning," one may at least properly inquire for some principle by which the relative values of different periods or forms of society are determined; and if we answer this query according to the principle of the writer quoted, we shall be compelled to say that the value of any given period or form of society is measured by the contribution which it makes towards the efficiency of some other succeeding period or form of society, and so on *ad infinitum*. No ultimate criterion of value, either for the individual or for society, is attained by this process. Such a theory of value puts one in mind of the countryman, who, when asked the value of his herd of cattle, always computed it in terms of the prospective herd which it was capable of producing. The radical defect in Mr. Alexander's theory of value is the lack of any principle for the direct valuation of the experience of individuals, apart from whose consciousness society has no worth and no existence.

Pessimism has usually rested upon a frankly hedonistic basis. This is true whether one looks to the religious pessimism of the Orient or to the philosophical pessimism of the western world. It has not infrequently been urged, in recent discussions, that there may be other grounds for a pessimistic view of the world than those which are found in the conviction that life yields a clear balance of unhappiness. Thus Mr. F. C. S. Schiller, after repudiating the hedonistic basis

[1] S. Alexander, The *Idea of Value*, Mind, N. S., Vol. I, p. 54. Cf. also his *Moral Order and Progress*, p. 232.

of pessimism as in itself inadequate, suggests four grounds for a pessimistic theory of life.[1] Life may be condemned, he says, because it lacks happiness, beauty, truth, or goodness. Or, stating the same thought in negative terms, life may be a curse rather than a blessing, because of its unhappiness, ugliness, inscrutability, and badness. These are suggested, it is to be observed, as four coördinate grounds of pessimism. But this form of statement entirely disregards and obscures the fact that unhappiness, if it exists, depends upon the other factors mentioned, as well as upon others not here specified. For neither happiness nor unhappiness is an independent psychical fact that can spring from the ground or hang suspended in mid-air, without relation to the other aspects of human interest and activity. In unhappiness, the writer has given a general and inclusive statement of the pessimist's judgment on its subjective, affective side, and has then proceeded to state the same experience on its objective, ideational side. Clearness of thought would require that the statement should take one of the following forms, either of which, if standing alone, would be intelligible and consistent, though, as we shall attempt to show, neither alone would be complete: life is without value because of its unhappiness; or, life is without value because of its ugliness, inscrutability, and badness. One must admit, I think, on the one hand, that life would not be unhappy were it not ugly, inscrutable, bad, etc., and on the other, that we should not condemn it for any or all of these reasons, did they not report themselves in those affective states to which the term "unhappiness" is applied. Surely, if the recognition of ugliness, inscrutability, and badness were habitually attended by feelings of pleasure, they would never be presented as grounds of pessimism. Further, it is clear that, as mere intellectual insights or judgments of fact, these aspects

---

[1] "The Relation of Pessimism to Ultimate Philosophy," *International Journal of Ethics*, Vol. VIII, p. 48.

of life would never lead to that view. It is only when they are felt in experience that they become charged with despair. Indeed, there are conditions when these very judgments might be attended with affective states which would make them contributory to an optimistic view. Thus the sceptic who holds a brief for the impossibility of knowledge concerning ultimate problems, and who feels an absorbing interest in the defense of his position, would find a satisfaction in every fresh piece of evidence which tended to show that in their deepest nature things are beyond the reach of human knowledge. And such satisfaction might be so keen that no unprejudiced observer would hesitate to say that for the time, at least, our sceptic found life worth living precisely because of its inscrutability. The history of scepticism affords illustrations of this experience. One can hardly avoid the conclusion that, to men like Pyrrho and Sextus Empiricus, life had value at times very largely in proportion to their supposed ability to vindicate the agnostic position. But when one's heart is heavy with

> "The burden of the mystery
> of all this unintelligible world,"

then the same view becomes a source of pessimism. There are also many conditions under which the existence of ugliness affords pleasure. Consider the jealous artist or literary critic who finds this element in the work of his rival, or the caricaturist who fastens with keen delight upon what is ugly in the features of his victim. In these and similar moods the judgment that things are ugly will not tend to make one pessimistic. The ugly is, for the time being, just what is wanted to induce in the individual the opposite tone. The belief that beauty is unrealized will drive one to pessimism only when the longing for the beautiful and the abhorrence of the ugly produce suffering. It is not otherwise with moral badness. Despair never springs from the

mere intellectual recognition that such evil is widespread in
the world, but from the regret and pain and sorrow which it
produces.

It should be observed that this criticism is not directed
against the validity of an objective or ideational statement
of the grounds of pessimism. Indeed, such a form of statement seems indispensable to any adequate treatment of the
subject; and herein the contention that pessimism may be
stated otherwise than in terms of pure hedonism finds its
justification. The whole point of our criticism, however,
centers in a protest against setting down the peculiarly subjective and affective element, unhappiness, which must exist
in every conceivable ground of pessimism, as an element
coördinate with the objective, ideational elements, and thus
by implication excluding it from these. This is a procedure
which leads only to confusion, and obscures alike the truth
and the error of the happiness theory. Every experience of
good may properly be described in terms of the activities
which yield the feeling. Either description, taken alone,
tells only half the truth. This is evident from any statement of our most common experiences. If I say, "I had a
delightful day yesterday," the expression clearly indicates
that I ascribe to the experience of yesterday a positive
value, but it does not tell in the slightest degree what was
the objective content of the experience, or by what activities
the good which I enjoyed was constituted—whether the day
was given to an excursion into the country, or was devoted
to study, or was spent in social service. If my friend desires
to duplicate the delight that I have experienced, he is quite
in the dark as to the necessary procedure until my experience
is rendered, not simply in terms of feeling, but also in terms
of activity. Yet a description in terms of activity alone is
equally inadequate. If I say that I took such an excursion,
or read such a book, or performed such a service, without
any suggestion of the feeling that accompanied the experi-

ence, I have given no hint by this mode of description as to whether I regard the day as a failure or a success, whether I would advise my friend to take the excursion, to read the book, or to engage in such service. I might conceivably desire to warn him against any of these activities, but the mere description of the activities, as such, contains no suggestion either of approval or of disapproval. No good, then, is adequately described in terms of pleasure, though pleasure is an element in every good; and similarly, no good is adequately described in terms of objects or activities, though these constitute an essential element in every adequate description of the good.

VI. Happiness an Element in Every Value

The error of separating the two essential aspects of our judgments of value is seen in frequently occurring expressions. To speak of "pleasures and other goods," of "happiness and other values," is to abstract the element of feeling and set it up as an independent and complete thing. Such a procedure would be exactly paralleled by the absurdity of talking of leaves and other deciduous trees. For happiness never constitutes the whole of any good, but is an element of every possible good.

Precisely the same objection may be raised against the statement of the problem in the familiar formula: "Is happiness the *summum bonum?*" The question in its common interpretation implies that there are various *bona*, of which one, happiness, is distinct from the others and possessed of unique value. Whereas happiness, we repeat, is an aspect of all conceivable *bona;* nothing would be a *bonum* did it not somewhere, at some time, make contribution to the satisfaction of some conscious being. It is equally true, however, that this affective state can never be found alone, existing independently, but is necessarily linked to some function of the self, which function is capable of being viewed objectively, and without immediate reference to the satisfaction which it produces. Whenever, then, pleasure or happiness is set apart as separate from other goods, or values, there is a fundamental defect in analysis and description. As if happiness could ever be found apart from the various forms of economic, physical, æsthetic, intellectual, and religious activities! Or as if these interests would represent anything worthful, if, instead of resulting in states of positive satisfaction, they were attended ultimately either by perfectly neutral states of feeling or by those of positive dissatisfaction! Such abstraction of happiness from our concrete activities has been the error of hedonism, and, as we now see, a similar abstraction of other elements is the error of the anti-hedonist.

Certainly any thoroughgoing anti-hedonist who excludes happiness altogether from a theory of value is involved at once in difficulties and contradictions. For, if happiness is not an element in the goal of human endeavor, it may be disregarded as a negligible quantity. And being rejected from our ideal as non-essential, its increase or diminution cannot affect the integrity of that ideal. Let us assume that as this ideal—whether expressed by self-realization, perfection, or any other desired term—is progressively realized, happiness constantly diminishes; let its realization be attended even by unhappiness in ever increasing ratio. We should then have an ideal the realization of which would ultimately involve unspeakable misery. To this no objection can be offered by anyone who does not regard happiness as in some way essential to the good. But one has only to state such a conception to find it summarily rejected not merely by common sense, but by reflective thought as well. To reject this view, however, is to admit that happiness is an essential element in our ideal, and that it must have a recognized place. But what place? It is in the failure to answer this question that the defects of many ethical treatises are most strikingly exhibited. There is often, it is true, frank admission that happiness has always represented a measure of truth, and that it must have a place in ethical theory. What that place is, however, has often been left obscure. Happiness frequently fares at the hands of ethical writers like a guest whom the host has felt bound to invite, but for whom no place has been provided at table. Or it may be likened to an actor who is permitted to come upon the stage with the rest of the company, but who is assigned no rôle in the play. The relation of happiness to the moral life is far too important to be left thus vague.

It is sometimes said that the aim of morality is not to render men happy, but to make them worthy of happiness. But this statement only pushes the relationship one step further back and does not deny its ultimate validity. The worthiness aimed at is still worthiness of happiness. It is significant that the great rigorists, like Kant and the Stoics, have admitted this ultimate connection between virtue and happiness. The same is true also of Christian ethics. For while Christian thought has tended to find the ultimate sanction of morality in the bliss of a future, super-terrestrial order, this "change of venue does not alter the verdict." It is true that the first and chief concern of ethical training is to secure obedience to the laws of value. This often requires a disregard of immediate satisfaction; perhaps it even requires, as far as the individual is concerned, a permanent surrender of happiness in the interest of what is precious to the race. But this admission does not in the least impeach the principle. The real question concerns the ground-work of morality, the ultimate justification of the standards to which it requires obedience.

There are three possibilities of the general relation of morality to happiness. Morality may be regarded as tending to increase happiness; or it may be regarded as tending to decrease happiness; or its influence upon happiness may be regarded as quite indifferent and accidental, so that no general principle concerning the relationship of the two can be established. From these three possibilities the student of ethics may choose. Few, I think, would be willing to accept the view that no intelligible relationship whatever exists between morality and happiness; and still fewer, probably, would care to defend the thesis that the tendency of morality is to decrease happiness. This question of the relation of morality to happiness will meet us again in the next chapter. Here it is enough perhaps to point out that the view which we are developing finds in states of agreeable feeling an essential element of all positive values, and that morality forms no exception in this respect to other human values.

VII. Some Criticisms Considered

In order to show that happiness is an essential part of all ultimate good, it is not necessary to refute in detail the many traditional arguments urged against hedonism. The polemical literature of the subject has often confused ethical with psychological hedonism. This latter principle we have rejected, and with its rejection there at once fall away many of the arguments found in anti-hedonistic literature. Further, while it has been maintained that pleasure is an essential aspect or element of all values, it is not claimed that it forms the sole or adequate description of any value. It has been shown on the contrary that good and evil may both be stated in objective, ideational, or constitutive terms, as well as in those which we have described as subjective, affective, and evaluative. The two aspects are indeed both essential to an adequate description of any experience to which we assign a value, either positive or negative. Again, the method adopted, that of a critical study of the experience of value, cuts quite under the conventional approach to the problem. It rests its validity upon the analysis of experience in so far as it is recognized as possessing any worth, or value, at all.

Moral values are taken up into a larger category. And while problems of their relation to the total content of value in human life still remain for our consideration, they cannot, we may be sure, escape the general principles of value. In spite of these considerations, it seems desirable to examine some of the criticisms which are most frequently urged against hedonism in order to indicate more fully the significance of the view for which we are contending.

Some objections, more or less practical in motive, are often urged with considerable rhetorical warmth. The life of pleasure is held up to scorn as involving an unmanly avoidance of pain and suffering, a shrinking from all those heroic efforts and sacrifices which set the high-water mark of character. Self-indulgence and luxurious ease are accordingly represented as the only path to which a hedonistic view can lead. These criticisms will hardly seem to merit attention in any scientific theory, so obviously do they rest upon a false psychology and a superficial interpretation of experience. Pleasure is, in this view, identified solely with the more transient and limited states of agreeable consciousness, and the presence of pain and suffering is regarded as excluding the experience of pleasure. The criticism also wholly ignores the fact that many of the keenest and most enduring pleasures are habitually linked with struggle, with conquest of difficulties, and with victory over self. It is indeed almost a commonplace of worldly wisdom that the purest springs of satisfaction lie close to the more rugged heights of human endeavor. The representation of the happiness principle as a theory that makes morality identical with a régime of natural impulses or physical comfort, owes all its plausibility to the superficiality of its interpretation.

Equally misleading are those criticisms which rest upon the interpretation of happiness as an external product, "turned out" by the virtuous man, as a manufactured article is produced by a machine, or which in other forms represent happiness as a goal to be attained, where effort ceases and stagnation inevitably ensues. Both interpretations are unwarranted. The illustration of the machine altogether fails to illustrate. It could do so only provided the purpose of the machine were fully realized in its own activity, apart from any external product or result. The direct dependence of all feelings of value upon functions of the person who experiences and possesses the value, is a psychological truth which at once furnishes the corrective for all external views of happiness. And the same truth also stamps not merely as erroneous, but as wholly fantastic, the linkage of happiness with inactivity. The statement that, "A world of completed happiness might well be a world of quiescence, of stagnation, of automatism, of blankness," [1] could hold only for creatures wholly different in constitution from ourselves, or from any beings of which we have knowledge. There is no purely "passive" pleasure, for all our experiences of happiness are linked with activities, and cease when activity ceases.

Not a little dialectical skill has been expended in the effort to show that the conception of a "sum of pleasures," a phrase which has often been applied to a totality of agreeable states of consciousness, is inherently contradictory and impossible.[2] The expression cannot be defended as scientifically accurate, for no exact measurement and no mathematical summation can be applied to the problems of conduct under any theory of morality. It is a form of speech to be avoided. But it may nevertheless be contended that an intelligible meaning attaches to the words, "sum of pleasures," when an undue exactness is not insisted upon. The idea of the enjoyment of pleasures at successive periods and from various sources is certainly clear enough. It is also clear that the loss of any particular pleasure subtracts something

---

[1] Fiske, *Through Nature to God*, p. 114.

[2] See, for example, Green, *Prolegomena to Ethics*, pp. 235-246; Mackenzie, *Manual of Ethics*, pp. 229-230.

from the experience of such enjoyment, while its presence adds something thereto. Otherwise one might substitute for each pleasure some displeasure or disappointment, and still claim that the total hedonic effect remained the same. But nobody would care to maintain that there is no difference between a life of continuous and progressive satisfaction, and one of similarly continuous dissatisfaction.[1]

The critic of hedonism not infrequently makes claims at this point which are open to the very objections brought against the hedonistic position. The appeal to any "yard stick" of conduct, or to any exact unit of measurement, must be as summarily rejected as the notion of a mathematical "sum of pleasures." It is sometimes said that such a unit of measurement is found in the activity upon which the pleasure depends. But activities are as manifold and as difficult to reduce to a common denominator as the feelings of pleasure and displeasure which accompany them. The measure which is set up in opposition to the hedonistic standard is itself no exact measure at all, and the search for such a unit of measure is futile. Even the assumption here involved that feelings of satisfaction are measured by an objective standard, and that in and through the use of that standard some are rejected and others approved, is at most only a half truth. For one of the most obvious and persistent aspects of experience is the rejection of one activity in favor of another, because, when measured by the standard of feeling, the one is found wanting in the satisfaction which the other yields. The constant testing and sifting of activities by the feelings of pleasure and displeasure which they yield, is illustrated almost endlessly in both physical and mental life. In numberless cases the "yard stick" for the measure of the worth of activities is the subjective one of feeling. It may even be said that, if the evil-doer finally rejects his

---

[1] Cf. Taylor, *The Problem of Conduct*, p. 330; and Rashdall, *Theory of Good and Evil*, Vol. II, Book II, Chap. I.

course of conduct for one of right-doing, he does so because evil-doing is found to be deeply and permanently dissatisfying. As has already been stated, thought is compelled to take account of the objective, functional aspects of conduct, but this is not because we there find an accurate system of measurement which is wanting to the life of feeling.

Nor does the "unity" for which the doctrine of self-realization is claimed to provide, prove, on examination, to be any more exact in its meaning. At best it is an ideal of a very vague and elastic nature. As a matter of fact nobody is prepared to give an account of the moral life in terms which completely secure this unity. To give such an account would require one to show to what extent every function should be exercised in order to secure exactly the right degree of development of the individual and of society. Those who succeed most fully in realizing themselves would doubtless be the first to lament their failure in this respect, and would recognize that, if they are giants in some fields of activity, in others they are mere dwarfs with well-nigh atrophied organs. Who does not seem compelled by the very duties of his station to concentrate effort in such a way as to leave important sides of his nature only half-developed, perhaps hardly called into play at all? The unity of our moral life must be confessed to be an ideal which none can exactly define in theory or completely attain in practice.

Yet despite these obvious limitations, the conception of the full and harmonious realization of all our human capacities has great value as an ideal. It always keeps in advance of actual attainment, forever sounding the cry, "Excelsior." The criticism here intended is not directed against the doctrine when confined to its proper limits; it only concerns those claims which are made for it as yielding a degree of exactness that is sought in vain in a rival system, but which, from the very nature of the case, no system whatever can yield. The most precious things in life defy exact measurement.

VIII. The Hedonistic Paradox

The so-called paradox of hedonism is often urged as an objection to the happiness theory. The paradox consists in the fact that, while happiness is made the end of human action, it is generally admitted that it must not be directly aimed at, or in other words that "to get happiness one must forget it." The whole meaning of this mooted paradox when critically examined is that happiness, to be attained, must be sought in the right way, a statement that clearly applies to all objects of desire. More exactly, happiness must be sought through the appropriate objective interests and activities, and these must absorb one's attention. In truth, it may well be insisted that the paradox in question holds throughout the whole range of our practical aims, and that not only happiness, but also all other ends which men pursue, must in like manner be forgotten in order to be attained with success. The honor and respect of one's fellow men, wealth, and even the perfection of one's higher life, must in a very real sense be lost sight of if they are to be secured in any large measure. Honor and respect are won only when one forgets all about winning them, and becomes absorbed in those activities which develop and display the human qualities that secure approval and esteem. Wealth, too, is found equally coy to immediate approaches. Who has ever become possessed of wealth by thinking of gold? Who, rather, has not been compelled, in order to win it, to lose himself in those business and commercial activities which are the only means of financial success? The miserly instinct is fatal to large achievement in this field. And spiritual perfection is no exception to the paradox. "Who by taking thought can add a cubit to his stature?" The cubit of growth is only added to character in the current of the world's activities, in self-forgetful labor.

"Es bildet ein Talent sich in der Stille,
Sich ein Character in dem Strom der Welt."

In fine, it seems that out of all these paradoxes of our practical life, the paradox of hedonism has been chosen as scapegoat and sent forth into the wilderness of polemics burdened with the sins of all the others. Anyone who is still disturbed by it will do well to study the conduct of a well-trained child. For such a child has already learned that if it is to find happiness when the ordinary sources of gratification fail, as on a rainy day or when some expected pleasure has ended in disappointment, it can only be found in some absorbing pursuit or in devotion to the happiness of others. The child that has been wisely trained seeks happiness under these conditions and gets it, the hedonistic paradox notwithstanding.

This explanation was due to a much-abused paradox. The paradox, however, has lived because of the truth which it contains. And this truth is no other than that which has already been stated, the truth, namely, that every value must be viewed not merely as an agreeable feeling in some consciousness, but also as an activity by and through which the feeling is constituted. We are thus again led to recognize the dual aspect of every experience of value when subjected to analysis and description, as on the one hand subjective, affective, and evaluative, and on the other, objective, ideational, and constitutive.

IX. THE INADEQUACY OF HEDONISM

In the foregoing discussion we have been concerned to show as clearly as possible the place of happiness in an analysis of ultimate value. This discussion has shown, we trust, the reasons for the unbroken vitality of the happiness theory from the beginnings of reflection to the present day, as well as for the importance which in religion, in literature, and in daily life has always and everywhere been attached to the ideal. But after recognizing the significance of feelings of pleasure and displeasure in our immediate appreciation of value, one is inevitably brought face to face with the inquiry, How are they constituted? On what activities do they depend? What objective interests do they demand? What is the ideational content with which they are inseparably linked? And yet to attempt to transcend the happiness theory, without taking up into a constructive system the full measure of truth which it contains, is to rear an ethical view on an insecure foundation.

Now that we have reached the end of the discussion, it may be frankly admitted that the happiness principle, justly interpreted, is perhaps the most obvious of ethical principles. Although its truth, within the limits defined, is unimpeachable, the truth would seem to lie, at least for unprejudiced reflection, almost upon the surface of thought. As the truth that all objects must be perceived in space does not help in finding a lost article, so the truth that every good and ill of human life is a good and ill appreciated in feelings of satisfaction and dissatisfaction, will not tell us how we are to win the good and escape the ill. If we have gone too far by such a comparison, and have suggested a lack of utility that does injustice to the happiness principle, it is still true that its importance for practice is easily over-estimated. Happiness is too abstract, and also, if carelessly used, too liable to abuse, to be set up as a ready formula for guidance in the details of conduct. Despite these limitations, important considerations have seemed to justify a detailed criticism of the theory. The place it has held in ethical literature is such that it could not be disregarded in any discussion that aimed to be at all comprehensive. A further reason is found in the attractiveness of the doctrine to many students to whom, at the outset, it often appears as the solution of all difficulties. It is confidently believed that it is a great advantage to have mastered this theory, since the thorough comprehension of the principle is at the same time, of necessity, an understanding of its limitations. And, finally, one may perhaps be pardoned for a slight sentiment of chivalry impelling one to try to do something to set right an often misinterpreted and maligned theory. For it is hardly an exaggeration to say that no discussion of moral questions has been considered altogether respectable that did not hasten to give a speedy *coup de grâce* to hedonism.

It will be our task in the following chapters to exhibit more fully the limitations of happiness as an ethical principle, and to show how a theory of moral values may win that objectivity which reflective thought and practical needs unite in demanding. Such an objective principle is first presented in the theory of perfection, a theory which finds the goal of human effort in the enlargement of personality, the realization of all our human powers.

CHAPTER VI

PERFECTION AS ULTIMATE VALUE

WE have examined the merits and defects of one form of teleology, that which finds all ultimate value in agreeable states of feeling. But happiness is not the only interpretation of the moral end. Another interpretation appears under the various names of perfection, self-realization, energism, and personality. Still other designations have also been used, although they are less widely current. The reader need not, however, be disturbed or puzzled by this variety of terminology. With varying historical background and points of emphasis, these terms all express the same essential meaning; they all agree in affirming that the end of moral effort is the enlargement of life, the full and harmonious development of human capacities. The ground for the preference of one act to another, according to this interpretation, is that the one serves better than the other to express and to further such a life purpose. We may describe this type of theory as idealistic in that it finds the end of conduct implicit in the structure and meaning of the mind.

The division of teleological theories into two classes, the one finding the end in happiness and the other in perfection, has found general acceptance among students of ethics. Their verdict is well expressed by Sidgwick in his careful analysis of ethical principles. "I shall therefore confidently lay down," he says, "that if there be any Good other than Happiness to be sought by man as an ultimate practical end, it can only be the Goodness, Perfection, or Excellence of Human Existence." [1] Now, as has been already stated, we hold that both of these interpretations of the end con-

[1] *Methods of Ethics*, fifth edition, p. 115.

146

tain an important truth. And if our thought is to escape a permanent dualism and win real unity, happiness and perfection must be brought together in our conception of the end. It is in fact the purpose of the present chapter not only to show how a theory which finds the end in happiness must be supplemented by the ideal of perfection, but also to make clear the intimate and necessary correlation of these two principles. For happiness is meaningless apart from the life process, or activity, that yields it, as this activity is meaningless apart from the satisfaction which it directly or indirectly yields.

I. MEANING OF PERFECTION

What, let us next ask, is the essential meaning of perfection? It will be generally agreed that, when applied to any living being, perfection means the development of the capacities inherent within it. Thus it is a process of self-realization. But the capacities to be realized can be known only as they express themselves in activities, or functions. Perfection is perfection of function. There is no static or passive completeness of life that can satisfy our idea of perfection, for all life is a process, a becoming. The definition of perfection as perfection of function is equally true whether we apply a physical or a psychical standard. The biologist regards one form of animal life as higher than another when, through differentiation of organs, it is able to function in complex ways unknown to the lower form. In mental life the same is true; development is always estimated by the variety, range, and exactness of mental processes. Similarly, if it be asked what is that perfection of human nature as a whole which constitutes the moral ideal, the answer must be in terms of action, inner and outer. We mean that the good man is he who, in all the complex and endlessly shifting relations of life, responds with the activity of the appropriate kind and degree.

Such a preliminary statement of the ideal of perfection can convey no very definite or rich meaning. It is at present only a formula to which we must seek to give content in the course of the discussion. But even this brief formulation of the general meaning of perfection will perhaps serve to relieve the word of the forbidding character which, in popular usage at least, it often bears. The acceptance of this ideal of conduct does not of course imply that one expects to attain complete perfection, any more than one indulges the hope of attaining complete and unbroken happiness, health, or beauty.

Let us return for a moment to gather up the argument of the last chapter. It was there shown that an element essential to any experience of value, positive or negative, is found in the feelings as agreeable or disagreeable, and that wholly apart from such feelings, present or future, any and every content of experience would be completely indifferent in value. It was also seen that both good and evil, that is, both positive and negative value, are capable of a two-fold description, on the one side in terms of feeling, and on the other in terms of the objects or activities in connection with which the feelings arise. We must now consider more fully the importance of this latter factor of experience. To vindicate its place in a theory of ultimate values is to show the inadequacy of a purely hedonistic view of conduct.

But at this point the hedonist may be heard urging that we have found in the affective states of pleasure and displeasure, in their total range from the lowest to the highest phases of our conscious life, that element without which there could be no value at all; hence this is the one essential element which explains and unifies all judgments of worth; and hence, too, the various objects of desire and the activities which they involve are to be regarded merely as means to the end of happiness. To this we reply: it is true that there could be no value apart from these states of feeling, but it is equally true that there could be none apart from the objects and activities through which the feelings arise; one element is as essential to the experience of value as the other. Either alone is a one-sided abstraction. The hedonist and the anti-hedonist are both guilty of this partial and one-sided description. As against either one it is to be insisted that adequate description, for the purposes both of moral science and of moral practice, must include the two factors, which nature has indissolubly joined together. If experience is always appreciated in states of feeling as agreeable or disagreeable, it is likewise always constituted by objective interests and activities. Only if disembodied states of feeling could wander at large quite independent of all other mental content, and without relation to a psycho-physical organism, would the reverse be possible. In that case only, it may also be said, would the making of happiness a separate and independent end among other ends cease to be an error.

A distinction has been made between states of feeling and the objective interests and activities upon which these feelings are dependent. It may not be amiss here to offer a word of explanation with regard to the terms subjective and objective. Feeling is, as we found in the preceding chapter, a peculiarly individual and subjective element of experience; as such, it requires a more objective principle to which we must look both for its origin and control. Any use of the word objective applied to consciousness may at first seem confusing, since all consciousness is a process within the mind, and so, in contrast to the outer world, is termed subjective. But this conscious process within the mind presents two sides or aspects, one of which has to do with the objects of our attention and interest, the other with the way in which these objects affect us. To these two aspects of consciousness are applied the terms objective and subjective, ideational and affective. It is the importance of this objective principle for a theory of conduct that we wish now to consider.

In the first place, this objective factor lies embedded in the very nature of desire, which is the moving, dynamic principle of action. Desires, as we have seen, are normally objective and directed to ends other than the pleasure of their own gratification. While this fact admittedly is in itself a refutation only of psychological, not of ethical hedonism, it is significant in suggesting the lesson of· objectivity. The same may be said of the kernel of truth found in the paradox of hedonism, that the way to secure happiness is to surrender its too conscious and eager pursuit. This clearly indicates that a failure to regard objective interests would be fatal even from the point of view of strictly hedonistic standards.

The necessity for an objective principle or norm is further seen in the fact that one is unable to produce directly any desired state of feeling. By an act of will one cannot inaugurate immediately an agreeable tone of consciousness. Such a feeling is invariably dependent upon the activities of the self. It is to the right kind of activities, therefore, that the attention of human beings must be directed if they are to obtain happiness. As a principle of practice, then, hedonism is seen to be inadequate. And it is not to be forgotten that ethics must yield such a principle. However abstract its formulations may be, they must still be abstractions from real life; upon this depends all their validity. Adequate description of the general aspects of human conduct is precisely the task of the science of ethics. It is not, of course, the business of ethical science to lay down minute rules or to prescribe a list of detailed acts; these must always be the concern of the art of conduct, in which success depends largely upon fine sense and ready tact. And yet ethics must so state the principles of conduct that all specific acts can be seen, on reflection, to fall under the accepted principles. Is not the happiness theory found wanting when one makes this legitimate demand upon it? And is not the theoretical value of the ideal of perfection, or self-realization, vindicated, in part at least, by its service in this direction?

The point here in question may perhaps be illustrated in the limited sphere of the bodily life. As between the two precepts, (1) Seek the greatest bodily enjoyment, and (2) Seek the most perfect bodily development, one would scarcely hesitate which to recommend as a principle for practical guidance. At the same time no intelligent person will doubt that, other things being equal, physical satisfaction will depend upon, and keep even pace with, the perfection of the bodily organism. It is not, be it observed, that the hedonistic statement, here or elsewhere, is untrue, but rather that it is inadequate. Nor do we here urge the fact that the clamant demands of certain appetites, which press for immediate satisfaction, destroy the true perspective of the life of feeling, and cause one to put in hazard the greater and more enduring joys of life, or possibly to barter them irrevocably for transient pleasures. It is rather that a theory, in order to serve as a true principle for practice, must show how our feelings are objectively grounded, and what are their equivalents in human thought and action.

II. Value a Union of Objective and Subjective Factors

Further, a consideration of the meaning of value in other spheres than that of morality shows that the term must be construed objectively as well as subjectively. Value always involves a relationship between two factors, on the one side the feeling of appreciation in some subject, on the other the objective elements which yield the satisfaction. Indeed, in the case of economic values, it is the subjective reference that often escapes attention, since in common thought and speech we wholly objectify value, ascribing it to those objects upon which a price is set. Yet it is evident that the subjective element is never wanting. When goods of any kind are not desired and give no satisfaction, they possess no value. Many forms of wealth at present most highly prized would lie unnoted before the idle gaze of the savage. The same principle applies to æsthetic values. We freely assign the value of beauty to a landscape, a painting, a vase. Yet the existence of this value requires the presence of the spirit that can appreciate beauty, and until its coming the value is merely prospective. The Alps had no æsthetic value for the ancient world, which saw in them only hostile and terrifying barriers. The question here involved is similar to the old problem of the sense-qualities of bodies: do sounds, colors, odors, etc., exist apart from the perceiving subject? Any satisfactory answer must insist upon the necessity of both the objective conditions and the subjective process. Light and material objects, as well as the appropriate sense organs, are essential to the experience of color; and similarly both factors are necessary in the case of the other senses. Precisely the same is it, we hold, with every experience of value; there must be on the one side the feeling of appreciation, on the other the ideas and activities by which the value is constituted. We may illustrate this two-fold aspect by an example in the field of intellectual values. A scientific truth that integrates many facts hitherto wanting in a principle of unity will unquestionably give delight to the knower. But however keen the enjoyment, it is never apart from the process of understanding the facts and principles involved. Thus the value of knowledge includes the two factors within the mind which we have already described as relatively subjective and objective, affective and ideational, the one a form of enjoyment and appreciation, the other a content of ideas and ideals, of efforts and activities which, like economic goods and beautiful things, make the enjoyment and appreciation possible. To limit the application of value solely to one side of the relationship is arbitrary, and contrary to the requirements both of thought and of language. Herein is seen the essential defect of both hedonistic and anti-hedonistic theories of value. The hedonist has separated the subjective, affective factor of the process and given it exclusive recognition; whereas the anti-hedonist, disregarding this element, has emphasized the objective, ideational factor.

The psychology of value involved in the theory which aims to unify these two factors may seem to require supplementation at one point. It will be observed that the ideational and affective elements are both recognized, while no place is explicitly assigned to the will. But, as the whole personality expresses itself in the experience of value, all the psychical elements must be present in the process, the will no less than thought and feeling. What part does the will play in the value experience?   To this question, we should answer that the will is presupposed in every desire and impulse which expresses itself in conduct.   The will is nothing apart from the other elements of the conscious life, but is the thinking, feeling self in activity, or effort.

The objective factor in moral values, the necessity of which we have been seeking to justify, has been variously expressed as objective interests and activities, and this content has also been described as ideational. It will be simpler perhaps in the future to speak of this factor as activity, or function. Perfection of function as a moral ideal has played an important part in the history of ethical thought.   It is as old as Plato and Aristotle. Aristotle especially applies it to the problem of conduct with a skill which makes his statement at points almost final; and it is also prominent in the important modern school, the cardinal principle of which is usually known as self-realization. The primary justification for its use is found in the necessary interdependence of feeling and function. Every feeling, agreeable or disagreeable, is strictly dependent upon some function or activity. This is true throughout the whole range of life. Every

sensuous feeling of pleasure or pain is directly dependent
upon the function of the sense-organ to which it is referred.
The general and diffused feelings of physical well-being
and satisfaction, as well as states of pain and unrest, are
strictly conditioned upon the healthy or unhealthy functioning of the bodily organism. And if we bring under survey the
most exalted feelings of joy or happiness that human beings
know, we shall find them no exception to the rule. They
always depend upon those higher processes of thought which
constitute the ideal world of truth, beauty, and love.

It is clear, too, that pain, sorrow, and unhappiness, all
mean impeded or abnormal functioning. Disease, wrong-
doing or wrong thinking, and poverty of mental content,
are the fruitful sources out of which the warp and woof of
human misery are forever fashioned. True, a part of this
imperfection lies in the very nature of the psycho-physical
organism, which wearies, wears out, and finally breaks down
in death; a part, too, lies in the nature of the physical and
social environment in which we find ourselves, so that the
complete satisfaction for which men sigh must always remain a dream of fancy or a utopian ideal. But the prevent-
able portion of evil, which it is the business of moral effort
steadily to reduce, can only be eliminated by directing attention to the healthful, harmonious, and enlarged activity
of our human powers.

III. Organic Relation of Feeling and Function

The relation between the state of feeling and the character
of the function on which the state of feeling depends, is not
only close, but strictly organic, so that one can affirm a
general law of equivalence between capacity for feeling and
capacity for function. This principle is so important for the
theory of value that it deserves somewhat extended statement and illustration. It already suggests a question to
which attention will be given later, the question, namely,

whether or not we can affirm such a general equivalence between realized happiness and perfection in the moral world. How serious, from a theoretical view-point, must the cases of real or apparent conflict between the two be regarded? For the moment, however, the exposition of the relationship itself requires attention.

We have seen that all affective states appear in strict dependence upon the functions of an organism. Let us consider the principle of equivalence between these two factors, first of all as a biological law. Beginning with a low form of life, like the amœba, we observe that the organism is simply a mass of living matter with scarcely any differentiation of organs. Such processes as digestion and locomotion are processes of the whole mass; nourishment is absorbed by one part as readily as by another. The possible activities of such an organism are most narrowly limited. It is practically dependent upon its immediate environment; if this is hostile, it can not seek another more favorable. Judged by the biological standard of capacity for function, this organism must rank extremely low in the scale of life. At the same time it is possessed of a correspondingly low capacity for feeling. Possible pleasure and pain, if these terms can be used at all in such reference, are infinitesimal as compared with the pleasure and pain experienced by highly developed organisms. Ascending the scale of animal life, one finds an ever increasing differentiation and specialization of organs, and, by this physiological division of labor, the organism is rendered capable of a wider range of activity, a more varied diet, and a freer choice of environment. Keeping on the whole an even pace with this enlargement of function is a growing capacity for intenser affective experiences both of pleasure and of pain.

When we come to man, we observe that development takes the form of a high degree of specialization of the nervous system. As biologists have shown, nature, having ap-

parently exhausted the advantages of merely physical variation, turns to nervous, or psychical, variation to effect
further development. Morphologically, man is not, in all
respects, the most highly evolved of animal organisms. But,
through the unequalled development of his nervous system,
he possesses an advantage, functionally, over all animal
species. He is capable not only of adapting himself to very
different environments, but of constructing, to a large extent, his environment for himself out of the raw materials
which nature supplies. His food is varied to a degree without parallel among the lower animals, and he has become
master of so many means of locomotion as almost to transcend the limits of space and time. And as development,
measured in capacity for varied and complex function,
increases, the susceptibility to pleasure and pain also increases. Judged by capacity for merely physical enjoyment and physical suffering, man is at the apex of the animal kingdom.

The psychical development which accompanies the variation in nervous structure opens to man a new world of mental life, that of conceptions and ideals, in which he wins the
content of a truly human existence. In this sphere he exercises the functions distinctive of the human species. Aristotle's analysis has hardly been superseded at this point.
Every type of being, he tells us, has its distinctive function.
That of man cannot be found in the vegetative life of growth
and increase, nor in that of sensuous appetite, both of which
man shares with lower forms of life. His distinctive function,
and consequently his distinctive excellence, lies in his rational
nature. In this are found, according to Aristotle, all truly
human perfection and happiness; to accept anything less
would be to take the brute's portion, not the man's.[1]

The principle of equivalence, according to which an increased range of activities is accompanied by an increased

[1] Cf. *Nicomachean Ethics*, Bk. I, Chap. vi.

capacity for feeling, holds good of the psychical development of man in the process of civilization. At a thousand new points in this complex process man becomes susceptible to weal and woe, to agreeable and disagreeable experiences. The more complete his development, the more numerous and subtle do these become. Compare the satisfactions open to the mind which has many and varied resources with those of the mind which is limited to a narrow range of ideas. The realms of art, of science, and of literature, in all their departments, make possible for the cultivated mind a wealth of enjoyment, in comparison with which the possible pleasures of the narrow and untrained mind seem most meagre. The person whose interests are confined to a single field is capable of a mental life in only one environment, while the person of wide interests is at home in many. For the latter, all nature teems with possibilities of satisfaction; the world is his home, and he can live in any intellectual climate. As it is the function of the higher animals, and of man most of all, to create the conditions of their physical environment, so it is the task of humanity to create by its higher activities a spiritual environment, and to dwell in a world of truth and beauty of its own construction. This is one of the deeper aims of education—to build a home for the spirit which shall prove a retreat from the stress of material cares and the changes of worldly fortune. In the language of psychology, "Feeling becomes enlarged, spread out, as well as deepened and consolidated, by the development of representation (imagination and thought). The growth of ideation is thus a necessary condition of all the richer, more varied emotive experiences." [1] We thus find in the mental life the same general correlation of feeling and function which holds good throughout the stages of physical development.

[1] Sully, *The Human Mind*, Vol. II, p. 81.

IV. Progress and Happiness

At this point there presents itself an interesting problem for which we are chiefly indebted to the literature of pessimism. It may be objected that with the development of life there is no increase in its net satisfaction, but that susceptibility to both agreeable and disagreeable feelings simply increases, *pari passu*, with functional complexity. The net result of experience in the case of the more developed types, it is said, may not be more favorable as regards happiness. When the intenser sufferings of all kinds have been subtracted from the intenser enjoyments, the balance-sheet may be left practically unchanged. If the consciousness that looks out upon us so peacefully in the brute creation knows nothing of the intenser pleasures of a higher form of life, it is also free from the more poignant sufferings and deeper tragedies that are inseparable from human existence. Nay, may not the animal fare quite as well as his human fellow? And is not the same true of the more primitive races of men when compared with the more advanced? Does not the more sensitive organism offer to an indifferent environment more numerous and easy points of attack, without possessing any compensating advantage in positive satisfaction?

We can here offer no thorough treatment of the problem, which is incidental to the main purpose of the discussion. At best we can only indicate some lines of reflection that may lead to a more hopeful view of civilization. Obviously a full presentation of the case on either side would take one over wide tracts of the special sciences and of the history of human progress.

A consideration of first importance, for a belief in the progress of mankind towards a fuller realization of positive good, is the fact that one of the chief functions of increasing intelligence is to ward off evil, to protect both the individual organism and the social group from pain and suffering. Appearing in the animal kingdom as inherited instinct, this intelligence rises in man to the dignity of rational reflection with its understanding of causes and its subtle inventions. Considering the influence of this growing intelligence upon the fortunes of mankind, we observe certain acknowledged advantages of civilized over primitive races, in the escape from the more aggressive physical calamities. By the variety, regularity, and abundance of his food supply, civilized man has largely banished the terrors of famine; by adequate clothing and dwelling place he has mitigated the rigors of climate; by knowledge of hygiene he has escaped the horrors of pestilence. If disease has not been conquered, it has yielded much ground to sane therapeutics and skillful surgery, rendered relatively painless by anæsthetics. In modern times science has made universal among civilized peoples the recognition of insanity as a disease. It has rendered the treatment of the unfortunates thus afflicted humane and considerate, and thereby put an end to a long chapter of needless cruelty and suffering. The belief in witchcraft and similar cruel superstitions has likewise received a death blow. Indeed, while we are wont to dwell upon the achievements of science in conquering the forces of external nature, we cannot too often call to mind what it has contributed to the inner life of humanity, freeing the race from bondage to errors that have everywhere left their record written in tears and blood. Scientific knowledge has only begun to attack the problems of heredity, of mental hygiene, and of social organization. In these fields it gives promise of rendering inestimable service by striking directly at the sources of disease and crime. There is reason to believe that man has only just entered upon the exercise of conscious control over the forces which determine his earthly destiny. If it be urged that civilization produces, by the artificial conditions which it creates, some of the very evils

which it seeks to remedy, it may be answered that most of
these evils are not strictly necessary, but are remediable
through further enlightenment. And if it be insisted that,
wrought into the very structure of things, there are elements
of regret and sadness, of profound melancholy and even of
tragedy, from which human life will never be free, we may
hope that in time even here a larger triumph may be won by
a wise training of the spiritual energies. The belief that
human life can be made saner and happier should not be
identified with a shallow optimism which overlooks exist
ing evils, and declares that "all's well with the world." I
may even be said that no one who has not candidly fa?
the grim facts of evil has the right to an optimistic view.

But even more important than what has been suggeste?
as to the function of intelligence in avoiding pain and suffe?
ing, is the complementary truth, that intelligence has t?
power to create new sources of satisfaction which are rela
tively pure as well as intense. The production of these satisfactions belongs preëminently to the higher range of human
activities. The judgment of those whose experience is most
adequate undoubtedly assigns to the expression of these
higher powers, exercised creatively in art, literature, science,
and religion, a unique value in the production of human
happiness. In these spheres, the hostile competition which
still attends the production of material goods, and which
leads to so much suffering, both direct and incidental, largely
disappears. The enrichment of one person in these ideal
values is the enrichment of many; they tend to multiply
in diffusion, and to perpetuate themselves through successive generations. This fact is strikingly illustrated wherever
a unique degree of perfection is attained. The masterpieces
of genius remain permanent sources of delight to the race.
What the great artists have produced with inward joy en-
riches the lives of millions; the truths which have been the
quest of the great investigators are built into the abiding

structure of science; and not less do the insights of social and religious reformers, by which institutions have been transformed and ennobled, remain a perpetual blessing.

V. The Content of the Good Life

The objective aspect of value which has thus far been described in terms of activity, as a development and perfection of function, must in the end be rendered more concrete if it is to serve for guidance in the specific problems of conduct. This will be attempted in the chapter which follows. For the present, we may point out that the content of this activity found in civilization, in the existing social order. Here are the values which human experience in its long struggle has slowly discovered and vindicated; here each individual must find his moral task. Indeed, "There is no way of discovering the nature of the self except in terms of objective ends which fulfill its capacities." [1] It is an error, therefore, to think of the moral sphere as in any way remote; it lies close at hand in the actual station which each occupies. In this station must be discovered the values which found and determine all the obligations of the individual, who must organize these values into a system in which none even of the humbler goods can be neglected. The appropriate place must here be given to economic interests; the physical values of health, bodily well-being, and recreation must be recognized; and the ideal values of an intellectual, æsthetic, and religious order must receive their rightful emphasis. The task to which our human powers are called is that of winning the richest possible content for life; this is one with the task of the development and perfection of human nature.

The acceptance of the values found in the social order as the content of our activity, in this process of self-realization, does not mean that we are to consider those values which appear at any given stage of civilization as ideal or final.

[1] Dewey and Tufts, *Ethics*, pp. 391, 392.

The emphasis which a given generation places upon these values may be very faulty. Our own age, to offer a single example, is often charged with undue devotion to material aims, with a false estimate of the worth of the luxury which wealth can purchase. This criticism is doubltess justified. The evil, however, consists, not in the acquisition, but in the wrong use of wealth. A sound instinct has directed human energy to its production. The attempt to exclude wealth and even cultural interests from the field of moral obligation has frequently been made in the interest of ascetic ideals. Such a view has dominated centuries of religious life, and has cast its spell over many noble minds. Tolstoi, in our own day, as Rousseau in his, feeling keenly the evils of an ill-regulated society in the throes of transformation, has sought a solution in the rejection of many elements of culture. But the inevitable emptiness and tedium that result from the arbitrary limitation of activities hardly need emphasis. And the case is not bettered by giving such an ideal a religious or celestial setting. Visitors at the Campo Santo in Pisa will recall a mural painting which represents, in characteristic mediæval spirit, the fortunes of both saints and sinners. Hell is naturally pictured with all the torments which a vivid imagination could invent, but the prospect is not alluring when one turns to the other side of the picture, where the saints in paradise are seen sitting stiffly in idleness, while one of them, more fortunate than the rest, enjoys the solace of a lap-dog. A crippled humanity has never satisfied, and never can satisfy, our ideals. The impulses that have prompted to a realization of the fullest possible life have, in practice, been too strong to be permanently thwarted. Whenever, too, essential impulses are denied legitimate expression, they tend to break out in a perverted form, and to take costly revenge for their denial. To lose any of our human powers is to forfeit a part of our birthright. The only possible solution of life's perplexing problems is,

"Im Ganzen, Guten, Wahren,
    Resolut zu leben."

Looking back over the course of historical development
through which our system of values has been slowly discovered and won, it is clear that the logic of experience has
been stronger than any theory which has limited by preconceived ideas the range of earthly activities and interests.
The result is that life has often been richer than its creed.
The modern Christian world seeks fully to possess and enjoy the values of wealth, of bodily strength and beauty, of
recreation, of humor and mirth, of art in all its manifold
phases, of science in its countless fields of achievement, of
literature and philosophy in their widest sweep, although
these values lay beyond the horizon of the primitive Christian
society and beyond the vision of its founder. The attention
of primitive Christianity was centered upon a heavenly order.
The eager longing and intense expectancy with which the
early disciples looked to the speedy coming of this higher
kingdom made the concerns of earthly civilization seem of
trifling moment, the fashion of a world that passeth away.
He who tarries at an inn only for a night does not concern
himself too much with its accommodations. The kingdom
which was the goal of their desire was, in their thought, not
to be realized through the slow and painful struggle of
centuries of earthly life; it was not to be embodied in social
institutions nor to be maintained through human laws.

The doctrine of an incarnation, of a deity taking human
form, which appears in numerous religions, is an effort to
find a concrete and perfect embodiment of an ideal system
of values. But however precious the elements of value that
are thus more vividly impressed upon the consciousness of
a people, the embodiment of values in any historical character is never complete. The ideal must always be subject
to growth through the slow discovery of new values; and the

importance of one does not render the others unnecessary. While the principle of love, of effective human sympathy, is of universal value, this principle, as we have already seen, cannot itself supply the detailed values which form the content of a life of love. We may profitably change the application of St. Augustine's question and ask, "What do I love when I love my neighbor?" Obviously something more than his capacity to love; rather do I love in him all the elements that belong to a sound human nature, the free play not only of sympathy, but of strength, intelligence, and beauty, in endless variety of activity. If these are diminished, both his worthiness to be loved and the worth of his love are diminished; if they were wholly eliminated, love would be impossible.

If we inquire for the historical sources of our modern system of values, while recognizing the contributions of other peoples, we may describe these sources, for our western civilization, as chiefly Græco-Christian. To Christianity, the child of Hebraism, we owe the more important religious and humanitarian elements; but to Hellenic civilization, the chief elements of our intellectual and æsthetic ideals. The concept of culture, as it now exists for European and American peoples, can be traced back to the Renaissance. There it had its rebirth, when the humanists, breaking with the mediæval interpretation of life, sought to win again the full treasure of classical civilization. The aim of the greater humanists, it must be remembered, was not simply to revive the study of the classical languages, but to realize in their own lives the values for which Greece and Rome had stood in their best days. The goodly vision of truth and beauty, which the noblest of the Greeks had caught and immortalized in literature and art, again made its power felt. The modern world thus became heir to the classical ideals. Possessing as its heritage the insights of both Christian and pagan experience, it has striven to unite the two with its own new winnings, not always seeing that the elements have been profoundly modified in the long process of their fusion and growth.

Now the moral task of the individual is to appropriate the values which have been thus won in the historical life of the race, and to strive for their further enrichment and extension. If the effort to perfect the personal life by such activity be expressed by the familiar term self-realization, this term must be freed from misunderstanding. It cannot mean that all the impulses and capacities of the self are to be realized in equal degree. Such a realization of the self would be without any principle of law or valuation, and would result in disorganization and chaos. Nor does self-realization mean the realization of an individual self as against other selves. The lower and narrower self of egoistic desires must yield to the larger self whose interests are one with those of its fellows. Self-sacrifice in this sense is a necessary part of the process of self-development. The "nay" of morality is as real as its "yea." The old dictum, "*Omnis determinatio est negatio*," cannot be escaped. To affirm is to deny; to accept is to reject; to pursue is also to flee. Renunciation, always difficult, is always necessary. And although we are constantly compelled to renounce that which is in itself good, such sacrifice is not absolute. Unlike asceticism, it does not choose surrender for its own sake, nor count the sacrifice an end in itself. The smaller interest is sacrificed to the larger, the less, to the greater value.

VI. Some Conditions of Progress

No one, it must be confessed, is in a position to define or to describe with exactness the perfect human life. The stations which individuals occupy are so various, and their special powers and tasks so unique, that only the general features of moral life can be determined by the use of a concept as abstract as that of perfection. The more detailed problems of the good life can be profitably considered only in the light of an understanding of the more specific values which such a life must seek to embody. We can, however, form an idea of a life more perfect than that which is at present realized in human society, and we can discern some of those universal qualities which all good lives will progressively realize, as well as some of the conditions that they must all fulfill in the process. Three general conditions of progress may serve as universal aims of the moral life.

And first, to perfect our activities is to *humanize* them. This means that the pattern and standard of worth is to be found in man's own nature, not in beings higher or lower than himself. All spiritual aims are human. To pursue the ideal is not to attempt to walk the clouds or to climb the skies, but to seek the completest manhood or womanhood. The most ideal values must still serve as "human nature's daily food." But if our standard of human valuation cannot be found in any imagined beings higher than man, still less can it be found in lower types. To humanize our activities is therefore to lift them above the level of animal impulse and appetite. Man shares with the brute creation the bodily life and functions; like it, too, he is dependent upon external nature. But man, unlike the animal, cannot realize his perfection by following instinctive desires as they chance to arise. Subordination, control, and even repression of immediate impulses, are a constant necessity of his existence. The ethical process opposes, too, the pitiless struggle in which animal organisms are engaged, repudiating what Huxley called "the gladiatorial theory of existence",[1] in the interest of the higher human instincts and purposes. If this brute struggle still appears at times on the vast stage of international relations, it only shows that the ethical process is far from complete, and that great interests yet remain to be humanized.

[1] Cf. The Romanes Lecture, Evolution and Ethics.

Again, to perfect human nature is also to *rationalize* it. Reason, as the developed form of intelligence, is the guiding principle of human conduct. To it, we are compelled to look for harmony within the content of our activities, a harmony which the competing appetites and interests always tend to destroy. It is the function of this higher intelligence not only to assign to each interest its appropriate place, but also to subdue the impulsive life to the aims of a truly human purpose, and by its pervasive influence to transform the physical appetites so that they cease to be merely animal. Through the play of intelligence, the taking of food and drink becomes in human life a means of social delight, an opportunity even for the cultivation of æsthetic and intellectual interests, something wholly different from this process at the level of animal life.

If we are thus to describe the perfecting of human life, we must not misinterpret the work of reason. The narrow interpretation of rationalism identifies it with a one-sided view of life, in which reason, singled out from all the other elements, is exalted and made an end in itself. Little wonder that it has seemed poor and barren when compared with the life of action and of rich human experience! But a true rationalism does not call for the development of the intellect alone. Reason rather accompanies and molds the entire process of consciousness; it is interested in its own processes only that it may secure their integrity and thoroughness. For the rest, it finds its material beyond itself in the endless variety of being which the world presents, and in the impulses, emotions, and aspirations that stir within us. No human interest is alien to it, and nothing significant is lightly esteemed. Reason seeks to understand even the insignificant, in order that we may know it for what it really is, and may not be deceived by thinking it significant.

There remains a third essential condition of success in the effort to bring life to its noblest fulfillment. To perfect human activities means further to *socialize* them. As we shall later more fully show, no one can fulfill the moral task while remaining centered upon individual interests. Moral development is always a growth in devotion to more comprehensive causes, and our estimate of the worth of any individual is determined largely by his devotion to such causes. It is further true that the lower activities of men are relatively competitive and individual, the higher, coöperative and social. Thought itself is a social process, although carried on by individuals. It finds its problems set by common interests, and the solutions which it wins are social products. Science, art, and religion are thus impersonal in the sense that they are limited to no single individual, but include all individuals. It is a safe generalization that on the whole the most perfect character is found in those who lose themselves in the service of universal causes.

VII. Relation of Happiness and Perfection

We now glance back for a moment in order to gather up certain results of the discussion which are important for our theory of the moral end. In the examination of hedonism we saw that, to every experience of value, an element of feeling is essential. This feeling is dependent upon, and constituted by, the activities of the agent. There is, further, a general relation of equivalence between capacity for feeling and capacity for function in both the physical and the mental life. The more perfect the activity or realization of function, the greater the satisfaction normally felt. And we may also assume that, other things being equal, there is a correspondence between happiness and perfection in human life. As these two factors are interdependent, and as both are essential to the realization of value, we hold that any adequate account of that which human beings desire and pronounce to be ultimately worthful must present both of these aspects. In the preceding chapter, we have presented the doctrine of happiness; in the present chapter, we have considered perfection of function as a more objective statement of the ideal. Before concluding the exposition, it is desirable to consider certain objections that may be raised, especially with regard to the relation of the two elements recognized by our theory of moral values.

The correspondence between the subjective element of feeling and the objective factor of perfection of function involves the view that the enlargement and growth of healthful functioning is normally attended by increased satisfaction. Applied to historical development, it would mean that the advance of a people in civilization should be attended by increased happiness. This, it is sometimes said, is not the case; rather is the development of a people often attended by much discontent not felt before. In weighing the force of this objection, two facts are especially to be considered. One of these is that a whole people, or a class of society, may pass through a period of storm and stress, similar to that of the individual when in youth he awakens to the consciousness of new needs and untried powers, before entering upon the peaceful possession of the richer life which these make possible. Even this period of struggle and longing, accompanied by its inevitable measure of dissatisfaction, is not all suffering. The testing of strength, and even the hard struggle itself, are not without a joy of their own, which the pessimist is inclined to overlook. In the second place, any period of special advancement, and in fact all so-called progress, is subject to further criticism and revision. The choice of values is never perfect; now one set and now another is given undue emphasis, and not infrequently important ones are largely neglected. In an individual life, for example, intellectual development may be purchased at the price of physical health, and the result be necessarily disastrous to happiness. But in this case the progress is so one-sided that it could never receive deliberate approval or properly be called progress at all. Analogous conditions may be pointed out in general civilization. The rapid progress won in many directions within recent decades may be charged with failure in the production of that degree of happiness that might legitimately be expected to accompany it. But here again the undue preoccupation with material things, the neglect of a true culture that fits people to use and enjoy leisure, the haste and strain of competition in the commercial and social struggle—these and other defects in the spirit of the age have undoubtedly caused men often to miss the richer joy of life now made widely possible. To admit this is simply to admit that there has been a mistake in the choice of values; it is an arraignment of the proportion and harmony of the elements that form the general content of modern life, and is no impeachment of the principle of a general correlation of happiness and true progress in human activities. Finally, if one survey the general march of human development, it might be said that such gain as has been won is in the quality rather than in the quantity of happiness enjoyed. To this we would reply that an improvement in quality is itself an increase in value, and that it is precisely the qualitatively superior pleasures which are quantitatively the greatest, because they are permanent, productive, and universal.

There can be no doubt that the general verdict of mankind would always be against any so-called movement of progress, if it could be demonstrated that its ultimate and net result was a reduction in the amount of human happiness. Such a verdict is clear evidence of the value which is attached to happiness, even by the most idealistic thinkers. And, we may add, the presumption would be very strong that any movement of civilization which involved the destruction of happiness could not be one of real progress; somewhere the true path must have been lost. The dilemma of the sacrifice of either one of the aspects of ultimate value, humanity will not willingly accept. As an ideal, man will tolerate neither an unholy happiness nor an unhappy holiness. If either element fail, this failure will be referred to special causes, and will not be regarded as organic and normal. Further, both happiness and perfection are constantly used as norms of judgment. Conduct is approved when it directly or indirectly tends to the promotion of happiness, and condemned when it has the opposite tendency. Conduct is also approved when it expresses man's true nature as a spiritual being, when in its harmony, beauty, and strength it agrees with standards of perfection. Thought, both naïve and reflective, plays between these two poles, emphasizing now one and now the other, and assuming on the whole a general harmony between them.

The complete harmony of these two aspects of value, however, is not capable of strictly demonstrable proof, but is, in part, of the nature of a postulate of our moral struggle. By this is meant that it is a principle accepted on faith, or implicitly assumed, as the basis of action. It does not mean that there is no evidence in its favor. Were there absolutely no such evidence, still more were there clear evidence against it, it could not occupy the place even of a postulate. The necessity of regarding it in this light must not lead us to ignore the substantial evidence, physiological and psychological, in its favor. What is here admitted is the incompleteness of the evidence, if one asks for a complete demonstration. The necessity of making the assumption involved in the postulate appears, however, if we consider the three possibilities of relationship between perfection and happiness from which thought must choose. Reflective thought has never been content with the first possibility, namely, the denial of any rational tie between the two elements. And unless one be willing to pronounce for the out-and-out pessimism involved in the second possibility, that perfection makes for unhappiness, one is driven of necessity to accept the view that perfection tends in general to the promotion of happiness. As for such a pessimism, it would be logically pledged to an effort to annul the intolerable conflict by an extinction, if possible, of the forms of consciousness in which this tragedy of conflict appeared. Certainly all optimism or meliorism is pledged to a belief in the harmony of the two ideals. Those who believe that life is worth living cannot believe that to follow the call of the human spirit to a more abundant life means increased and hopeless suffering. This belief would strike at the very heart of moral endeavor.

The correlation of happiness and perfection has been denied on the ground that happiness is largely dependent upon natural forces, and is, in fact, an affair of the circulation and digestion quite as much as of right conduct. This statement contains an element of truth that no one is concerned to deny. But it is equally true that perfection of character is also largely a matter of native endowment, and that its highest attainment is impossible for the person who is naturally coarse, mentally deficient, or criminally inclined. And, in general, one must admit how largely, for most persons, the sphere of possible development is limited by forces that have determined the inner and outer life long before these became a matter of individual choice. Of how many lives must one say,

"Mortgaged too deep to Fate, alas,
To leave much scope for will."

A sound morality, quite undaunted, will accept these natural forces as setting for the moment the conditions and limits of its effort, but, knowing that even these forces are not wholly beyond its control, it will for the future seek to subdue them to its own ends.

Nothing is more misleading than comparisons instituted between the morality and happiness of individuals, for the reason that these comparisons assume that other things, temperament, natural advantages, environment, etc., are all equal. As matter of fact, the other things are never equal. Observation takes note of the unhappiness of many good, and the happiness of many bad men. But it is difficult to establish a causal connection between the two factors in each case, in such wise that A's unhappiness can be shown to be directly caused by his moral perfection, while B's happiness is similarly to be explained by his imperfection. The failure to secure happiness is often conspicuous, especially when it is measured by external standards. But anyone who is satirically inclined might easily make merry over the failure of perfection or any other end which moralists have fixed upon as the goal of conduct. If it seems at times that the wicked do really flourish while the righteous are afflicted, it is well to suspend judgment and await developments. Whenever prosperity proves permanent, it is found to be based on pretty substantial grounds. A too fervid proclamation of the combination of sins and prosperity in one's neighbor may justly arouse suspicion. The moral advantage may turn out to be not all on the side of David and the chosen people. Most of us perhaps are inclined to believe in the morality of our own conduct, and if it does not yield us happiness, we assert a disjunction between them. But there is always another possibility, the possibility, namely, that the morality in question needs revision, and that, if the revision were only thorough enough, the disjunction would tend to disappear. We cannot accept as ultimate the formulation of a code as it is made by any generation or by any individual, and we may be sure that, whenever a so-called moral maxim makes permanently against happiness, it needs critical examination. In Stevenson's words: "If your morals make you dreary, depend upon it they are wrong."

Yet it is impossible to deny or lightly to dismiss those

cases in which there does seem to be costly sacrifice and loss of happiness through adherence to the demands of a high morality. To be sure, what often passes for sacrifice is merely the rejection of an immediate or transient gratification for a future satisfaction that is more solid and enduring. The genuine cases of sacrifice are those where no such compensation can be detected, but where the loss seems complete and wholly unrequited. To everyone there will occur historical examples of those who have surrendered life, or perhaps what was dearer than life, for the sake of some cherished conviction or at the call of human service. Progress in civil and religious liberty, in scientific knowledge, and in general enlightenment, has in the past often been purchased at a great price of personal sacrifice. These cases constitute a surd which reflection is baffled in attempting to eliminate. This irreducible surd may be likened to the surd in other departments of thought. The various fields of science, as well as all departments of philosophy and religion, offer illustration of elements which thus far refuse to yield to accepted principles. The cases of genuine sacrifice in question constitute indeed one portion of the riddle of evil, and are no more and no less baffling than is the existence of evil itself.

Yet the difficulty of the problem just raised, as far at least as it concerns the principle of happiness, is greatly diminished when we pass from the individual to the social view, which will be considered in a later chapter. The very principle for the sake of which the sacrifice is made by the individual is deemed by him to be vital to the happiness of others. The reformer may suffer for his cause, the martyr perish for his conviction, but each deems his truth essential to the well-being and happiness of mankind; without it, the people will perish in blindness and ignorance.

A general correspondence between happiness and self-development would seem to many to imply a reduction of the moral life to the levels of prudential and egoistic calculation. On the contrary, it is precisely in the case of wise idealistic and altruistic endeavor that the harmony of the two elements appears most complete. The renunciation which such endeavor demands is commonly the sacrifice of the immediate impulses and desires. The death of these means, not less life, but a richer, more abundant life. Ideal and social aims tend more completely than anything else to lift the individual out of the circle of narrow interests which foster anxiety and *ennui*, and to free him from a swarm of petty emotions which are a veritable blight upon peace and happiness. There is a sound psychology underlying Goethe's picture of the restless and unsatisfying search for happiness in which Faust is engaged, and which never permits him to bid the hurrying moment of selfish pleasure to abide. He only finds the experience which has such value that he desires to make it permanent, when he enters upon a career of self-forgetful service. Poetry here is as true as biography; in the experiences of actual life the truth of the picture has again and again been exemplified. The more subtle psychological sanctions for ideal living operate unseen and are apt to escape notice, but they constitute a balance which cannot be disregarded. We do not here refer to the stings or remorse of conscience which are popularly supposed to constitute these sanctions. These may be as light and transient with most natures as the satirist represents. But even the coarsest nature cannot escape the sway of enslaving habit, or put to sleep appetites that by abuse have come to yield unrest and pain instead of pleasure. Nor can such a nature create at will, after long disregard, the interests that would yield peace and satisfaction. The wise man stands in greater fear of the searching nemesis of his own nature than of more loudly heralded judgments. The positive side of the matter cannot be neglected. Devotion and self-abandonment to ideal interest yield a joy unequaled by any other. In such service one finds duty transformed.

> "Stern lawgiver! Yet thou dost wear
> The God-head's most benignant grace,
> Nor know we anything so fair
> As is the smile upon thy face."

In the description which we have here given of the moral end, we have insisted upon the necessity of recognizing two essential aspects. If now the reader inquires for their underlying unity, we must point for answer to the personal life. The self which is their living unity no more falls asunder because we are compelled to think the moral ideal under two aspects than the self ceases to be one because we think of it as both mind and body, or as having a variety of functions. Historically, a unity has often been attempted through a one-sided abstraction, which has emphasized one factor to the neglect of the other. We have endeavored to maintain a just balance between them, and to give to each its due place. If it be said that the resulting view is too complex, failing in the simplicity of either of the rival theories when taken alone, it may be replied that it is no more complex than the facts of experience with which it attempts to deal. Simplicity is a merit in a theory only when it is warranted by the data to be explained.

But although we fall back upon the concept of personality to summarize in unitary form all that thought here discovers, we must not suppose that this or any other term can supply us with anything new, or can save us from the labor of analysis. It can at most refer us to the actual source of the material which it is the task of thought to unfold. As he who would describe a shield must represent its two sides, the one as concave and the other as convex, so in describing the moral ideal we have attempted to set forth its two essential and universal aspects, the subjective aspect of happiness, and the objective aspect of perfection. As the shield is the unity of its two sides, so the moral person offers the real unity of these two aspects. What we have here described in the abstractions of thought finds living embodiment in personal experience.

In conclusion, candor requires the frank acknowledgment that neither happiness nor perfection, nor both combined, can yield, for our practical conduct, a guidance which does not leave much to be desired. They are at best principles which only serve to point the way one is to go; they do not free one from perplexity where ways converge and cross. The traveler often requires more specific information even when he knows the general direction he is to take and can see beyond him the heights he would attain. Ethics, in striving for unity of thought, cannot neglect the manifold which it would unify. For it is the manifold which we always encounter in practical situations. Many voices call, many interests attract, many duties claim us. The abstract must be interpreted in terms of the concrete, the good must be translated into goods, value into values.

CHAPTER VII

THE WORLD OF VALUES

I. The Task of Morality Illustrated by Plato's Myth

In the closing pages of the *Republic*, Plato presents the problem of the moral life in the form of a vision. Er, the Pamphylian, so the myth relates, had been slain in battle, and ten days afterwards when the bodies of the dead were taken up, his body was found untouched by decay and was carried home for burial. On the twelfth day, while he was lying on the funeral pyre, he came to life again and described what he had seen in the other world. As the messenger who was to bring to mortals the report of mysteries hitherto unrevealed, he had been permitted to behold the meeting of those who were beginning and those who had completed their earthly pilgrimage. The souls meet in a meadow as for a festival, "some ascending out of the earth dusty and worn with travel, some descending out of heaven clean and bright." And when the spirits had tarried in the meadow for seven days, on the eighth, they were obliged to proceed on their journey and to go to a place where the spindle of Necessity determines the revolutions of all the heavenly bodies. Here, under the direction of the three Fates, the daughters of Necessity, the souls must choose their lots for a new cycle of life and destiny. "Let him who draws the first lot have the first choice, and the life which he chooses shall be his destiny. Virtue is free and as a man honours or dishonours her he will have more or less of her; the responsibility is with the chooser. . . . Even for the last comer if he chooses wisely and will live diligently, there is appointed a happy and not undesirable existence. Let not him who chooses first be careless and let not the last despair." "Most curious," we are told, was the spectacle of the choice, "sad and laughable and strange." The unhappy choices, it appears, were due to ignorance of their real meaning. Thus he who had the first choice came forward and at once chose the greatest tyranny; "his mind having been darkened by folly and sensuality, he had not thought out the whole matter before he chose; . . . his virtue was a matter of habit only and he had no philosophy." Only after reflection did he perceive his folly and lament his choice. But Odysseus, whose choice was last of all, taught by experience, and knowing the kind of lot he desired, went about for some time in search of the lot of a private man. Having found this at last, he was delighted and declared that he would have chosen the same had his lot been first instead of last.

In such poetic imagery Plato describes the moral task. Not indeed in a remote sphere or a preëxistent state, but here and now, he would remind us, is our lot slowly fashioned through continuous choices of good and evil. Interesting and profound are Plato's reflections upon the process. After pointing out the complexity of the problem, he adds: "And here, my dear Glaucon, is the supreme peril of our human state; and therefore the utmost care should be taken. Let each one of us leave every other kind of knowledge and seek and follow one thing only, if peradventure he may be able to learn and to discern between good and evil, and so to choose always and everywhere the better life as he has opportunity. He should consider the bearing of all these things which have been mentioned severally and collectively upon virtue; he should know what the effect of beauty is when combined with poverty and wealth in a particular soul, and what are the good and evil consequences of noble and humble birth, of private and public station, of strength and weakness, of cleverness and dulness and of all natural and acquired

gifts of the soul, and the operation of them when conjoined;
he will then look at the nature of the soul and from the
consideration of all these qualities he will be able to determine which is the better, and which is the worse;
and so he will choose, giving the name of evil to the life
which will make his soul more unjust, and good to the
life which will make his soul more just; all else he will
disregard." [1]

The meaning which Plato gives to the myth is clear. He
is telling us that to choose aright in this earthly life we must
know the values which it offers, and we must know them not
only singly, but in the relations which they sustain to each
other and to the purpose of life as a whole. Justice, which is
for him the crown of the virtues, is the true harmony of all
our human powers. Plato is also saying in effect that even
though the idea of the good, as universal and abstract,
is the highest principle of knowledge, "the master light of
all our seeing," it is inadequate unless it be translated into
terms of specific and concrete goods. And in like manner
the need of our moral life to-day is not the knowledge that
happiness is good, or that the perfecting of our human powers is good. This we surely know. But what we most lack,
not only when we set out upon the journey of life, but often
alas! when we are far on the way, is an understanding of
those interests by devotion to which happiness and perfection may be won. Without such knowledge, the quest for
happiness easily descends to the search for petty and vulgar
pleasures, and the longing for spiritual perfection remains an
unsubstantial vision, a vague desire without embodiment.
For us, too, as for Plato, who kept with rare steadiness the
ideal of unity, the specific goods must be viewed in relation
to the whole of existence. How many things good in themselves have to be rejected because they do not further, but
defeat, more inclusive ends! As the builder values the stones

[1] Jowett's translation.

from the quarry, not merely as individual specimens, but far more in their relation to each other and to the unified structure he would rear, so in fashioning a life we cannot disregard its totality, measured both extensively by the span of the years and intensively by the wealth of its experience. The moral effort to evaluate human interests becomes of necessity a re-valuation in the light of life's whole meaning and purpose.

Recalling the choice of the souls in Plato's myth, let us imagine ourselves as also choosing our lots. What do we want in life? Desiring, as we surely must, some measure of all good things, how shall we compound the lot?

"But this," it is objected, "is a strange way to state the moral problem. Are our wants a true criterion of value? So often the 'moral' is precisely what we do not seem to want, but rather feel that we ought to want." This is no doubt true. We all distinguish between the immediately desired and what we believe to be on the whole desirable, between the petty and transient wants of our nature and those wants which we discern in our hours of truest insight, of largest understanding. We thus require some standard for the testing of each desire. This can be found only in the ideal of what is desirable for life as a whole. Doubtless whatever we desire seems to us at the moment to be desirable, at least from some point of view. Yet in a deeper way we all desire the truly desirable; we want the good, not the ill. Outliving all our fickle moods and gusty passions is the desire to reach as nearly as may be the true goal. An ethics of value, which has as its aim the most complete welfare attainable, cannot be separated from an ethics of desire, which finds its task in the training and organization of the appetitive elements, higher and lower, of our nature. In practice they meet. For desires, conscious or unconscious, are a necessary condition of the realization of all values. Whether it is a question of bread or of righteousness, it is only as we "hunger and thirst" that we are filled. To be sure, an ideal good may outrun present desire. But happily our present system of desires is not finally and unalterably fixed; it is subject to growth and change. Unsuspected desires may lie beneath the surface, only awaiting a spark to kindle them into flame.

If we should make a detailed list of the numberless things which we desire and hold to be good, it would be found upon analysis that they would fall into classes, or groups, of values. Classification is a necessity of all scientific and philosophical method. And any classification, bringing together as it does many particulars, leads inevitably to a degree of abstraction. But the measure of abstraction involved in the classification of values is far less than that involved in a universal formula which seeks to express their final unity. The passage of thought from the countless details of conduct to a single unifying principle of ethical reflection is commonly far too hasty. In practical life we are confronted by the manifold, in theory by an abstract unity. The steps that lie between are often obscure. Ethics, no less than other departments of thought, has need to recall Kant's principle of specification: *Entium varietates non temere esse minuendas.*

II. A TABLE OF VALUES

Without further introduction we present a classification of human values in eight groups, as follows:

I. Economic Values.
II. Bodily Values.
III. Values of Recreation.
IV. Values of Association.
V. Character Values.
VI. Æsthetic Values.
VII. Intellectual Values.
VIII. Religious Values.

No finality or exclusive validity is claimed for this table, but it is believed that it offers a serviceable classification of the goods of human life. These are not, it is to be observed, separate and independent values; rather are they the aspects under which it is convenient, for purposes of evaluation, to survey the unity of life. How intimately these values are related, how deeply they interpenetrate in the organic structure of experience, is a fact of the first importance, to which we shall have occasion frequently to return. At present let us suggest this interdependence by a few illustrations. We must recognize, for example, the way in which, under the conditions of modern life, all the higher values have become dependent to a greater or less degree upon economic values. Education, art, and religion, all bear, in the present order of civilization, essential relations to the process of exchange and so to the exchange, or market, value, which is the standard of economic valuation. Similarly, it may be noted that if the bodily life is not properly maintained, all the other interests are insecure or even impossible of attainment. We are all aware, too, what a transforming influence every group of the higher values exercises upon the lower. Our use of material things is at once changed when touched by the spiritual forces of sympathy, intelligence, beauty, and religious aspiration. In their historical development the various interests have often been arbitrarily kept apart, and each has at times been pursued in disregard of the others. An example of such false separation of the elements of value is seen in many religions which have concentrated attention upon "the salvation of the soul." In this formula the soul stood for an abstract "something, we know not what," apart from actual bodily, intellectual, æsthetic, and even moral interests. But to-day all progressive religious institutions recognize the interdependence of these interests, and seek to provide the other values as essential to the integrity of the religious life.

But what, it may here be asked, is the concern of morality with any values, other than the character values? Do not the latter alone represent what is commonly understood by the moral life? The very terms by which other values are designated seem to place them outside of the sphere of morality. How is the domain of morals to cover the whole of life?

III. Narrower and Wider Interpretation of Morality

In answer it may be pointed out, first of all, that there is a narrower and a wider conception of morality. The narrower identifies morality with what we have designated as the character values, with the recognized virtues such as temperance, truthfulness, justice, benevolence, etc. Common sense defines the moral man as one who observes these principles. But the wider conception holds that morality is concerned with all the interests of life as these are found to further or to hinder the fulfillment of its purposes. Unquestionably the view which we have described as that of common sense is true as far as it goes. So important are the requirements contained in the common interpretation of the virtues that we may call them the daily bread of morality. They express some of the most essential conditions of human welfare. However limited a man's horizon or incomplete his life, we do not hesitate to call him moral if he fulfills to the best of his powers these primary requirements. And yet implicit in his assent to morality, as he understands it, is an assent to an ever-growing demand to extend it to new areas of activity. The logic of a partial morality inexorably carries him on to the whole of morality. Let us see how this is true. How far does the virtue of justice, for example, extend? Not merely, all would agree, to the rights of one's family and friends, or, in wider relations, to the formal requirements of law and convention. It also means by common consent the effort to make justice prevail in economic life, in political institutions, and even in international relations. Justice, if interpreted in its full significance, commits one, then, to a struggle against all the forces that oppose its realization. It envisages a programme so vast that our powers seem wholly inadequate to the task. And what, we may again ask, are the implications of the virtue of benevolence? Is it not a regard for the well-being of all mankind? Does it not mean the will that they shall have, as far as possible, all forms of human good? Benevolence, fully accepted, pledges one to the effort to develop and extend every form of the good. If we admit that ignorance is bad, we are thereby pledged to the extension of knowledge. If we believe that the appreciation of beauty enhances the worth of life, we acknowledge in the same way the duty to further its cultivation. And such is the logic of all the virtues; pursued whole-heartedly, they inevitably carry us on until together they encompass all the interests of human life.

This larger interpretation of the moral task is implicitly recognized by the average man. "Do you think it would be morally right," we ask him, "for you to neglect the economic support of your family?" His answer would assuredly be an emphatic "No." Perhaps he would reply in the words of St. Paul, who was not inclined to give undue weight to temporal interests, "But if any provide not for his own, and specially for those of his own house, he hath denied the faith, and is worse than an infidel." [1] "Would it be right," we further inquire, "to allow your children to grow up without education, recreation, and friendship, without any care for the cultivation of taste or for religious training?" The answer cannot be in doubt. At a single stroke any "plain" man will be found to commit himself to the entire table of values. If he would hesitate to pronounce the higher stages of scientific and intellectual activity a part

[1] I Tim. 5, 8.

of the moral task, he would entertain no doubt about elementary education. To neglect entirely the education of his children he would regard as a crime quite as serious as the infraction of one of the commonly recognized virtues. But where would he draw the line of the moral requirement in education? Admitting that his child should be taught common fractions, will he consider the knowledge of decimal fractions a matter of mere taste? If the child should know something of the history of his own country, is the boundary line which separates it from other countries to mark also the division between the moral and the non-moral requirements of historical information? Reflection cannot justify any such arbitrary line between the first steps of education and the most advanced stages of the intellectual life. Any arbitrary limitation is indefensible even on grounds of utility, for it is precisely the advanced researches of science that render the most conspicuous service to humanity. And on ideal grounds it is clear that the higher stages of the mental life are demanded as the fulfillment and fruitage of the lower. The cultivation of one's intellectual or artistic gifts is in principle as truly a matter of obligation as is the cultivation of truth-speaking or temperance. The loss, whether to the individual or to society, may be quite as great from the neglect of the former as of the latter. We rightly censure men for undue devotion to the insignificant, no matter how correctly the insignificant may be organized. To be good is to be good for something. The good life is, and always must be, the life that is devoted to good things, to true values. Poverty of content, the lack of worthy interests, often proves the chief source of disaster to the common virtues. This is a fact on which one cannot reflect too deeply. If it be true that, "Where your treasure is, there will your heart be also," it is well to consider what becomes of the heart when there is no treasure, or when the supposed treasure proves to be petty, sordid, or unworthy.

Each of the special groups of values, it may here be noted, constitutes an independent field for scientific investigation where the facts and principles are freely treated without interference. Ethics does not dictate the laws of physiology, of logic, of æsthetics, or of any other science; it accepts them. But the special values thus treated, while final within their respective fields, are not final for conduct because they are only parts, not the whole, of life. If man were simply an animal organism, physiological laws would yield sufficient guidance for his life; if he were merely an economic being, he would require no principle of conduct outside of economic standards; if he were only a knower, logic would be his sole concern; if he appreciated beauty, but had no other powers, "art for art's sake" would be a sound maxim, and ethics would reduce to æsthetics. But man is not merely any one of these, he is all these and more. So conflicts arise between the various values in which his welfare consists. And hence the necessity of a valuation of values, an appraisement and organization of all competing interests.

We thus see the justification of an examination for ethical purposes of all the various goods, or values, which form the content of life. Herein is found the vindication of the definition of ethics suggested in the introduction: "The science of values for the conduct of life as a whole." Conduct, rightly interpreted, is not three-fourths or even nine-tenths of life, but the whole of it. Nothing human is alien to the moral task. Morality is no special interest and no rival of any other interest. It is a just regard for all interests as they enter into the organic unity of life. If it be objected that reflection upon so vast and difficult a subject must always be inexact and often inconclusive, this may be freely admitted without the slightest prejudice either to the truth or the importance of the principle. The most precious things are the least susceptible of exact treatment, and yet are those which most urgently demand careful reflection.

We now proceed to deal briefly with the eight classes of values in order to indicate more exactly the relation of each to the moral task.

IV. ECONOMIC VALUES

Ethics, as we have already indicated, is not directly concerned with the solution of the special problems of economic theory. These problems it leaves to the science of economics, as it leaves to medicine and hygiene the special problems of the bodily life, or to æsthetics the discovery and formulation of its own principles. But ethics is vitally concerned that economic activities shall be ordered in the true interests of humanity, just as it is concerned that the bodily powers shall be rightly used, or that there shall be a just appreciation of æsthetic values. Each of these interests affects profoundly the quality and worth of human existence. The present economic order places a unique significance upon the power to secure, through the process of exchange, the satisfaction of needs which individuals are wholly unable to satisfy by isolated effort. We shall here treat economic value as exchange value, and wealth as power in exchange. So interpreted, wealth includes all purchasable things both material and immaterial. A universally acknowledged need of human beings is the possession of a portion of the world's exchangeable wealth. No individual produces more than an insignificant part of the numberless things necessary to his well-being. The gradual growth of exchange, from primitive conditions of society in which each group was dependent upon its own productive activities, to the highly specialized industrial methods of the present day, gauges the increasing moral significance of wealth. So rapid, in modern times, has been the increase in the processes of exchange that the readjustment of ideas on the subject of wealth has failed to keep pace with economic development. Students both of economics and of ethics have been slow to seize with clearness and vigor the new and intimate relations that must be recognized as existing between their respective fields.

Traditions concerning the conflict between lower and higher goods, between earthly and heavenly treasure, have long obscured the true place of wealth in civilization. Among many peoples and in widely distant lands the idea has prevailed that extreme poverty is a condition favorable to spiritual perfection. In Europe the sects and orders committed to this view have been numerous. In the Orient it has prevailed still more widely, and is there far more deeply rooted in moral and religious institutions. Primitive Christianity breathes not a little of this spirit. Without entering upon debatable ground, it is clear that in primitive Christianity the evils which spring from extreme poverty were not felt, and could not then be felt, as we are compelled to feel them to-day. In the second place, there had not dawned upon the consciousness of Jesus or of any of his followers an idea of the tremendous part which wealth was destined to play in civilization as an instrument of all the higher and more spiritual values. But the eager pulse of life proved too strong for tradition and bore men on, in spite of all contradictory theories, in the effort to win the treasures of this world.

We must here pause to make a distinction of importance between two aspects of value. Value is both intrinsic and instrumental. As intrinsic, it is good in itself; as instrumental, it is a means to the attainment of other goods. To illustrate this distinction between the intrinsic and the instrumental aspects of value, we may note that it is an intrinsic good to be fed, clothed, and sheltered. Even for the lower animals we desire animal comforts without regard to any further ends. But for man the greatest value of these bodily goods is that they contribute to higher goods, making possible an order of experience that transcends the worth of mere bodily well-being. Knowledge, too, is good in itself, but it is also good as an instrument in the pursuit of every other good. It is an immediate good to appreciate beauty, but its intrinsic worth does not exhaust the function of æsthetic experience, for it ministers in many ways to all other parts of life, even to the development of character and to the enrichment of religion.

Now it is a significant fact that economic values are the only ones which are purely instrumental. All the other groups, we shall find, possess both aspects; they are all in some measure good in themselves, and in some measure they all minister to other interests of life. Economic value alone does not yield direct satisfaction; only the miser regards wealth as an intrinsic good, and the miser, however shrewd, is a fool. The apparent exception to the statement that wealth is never an intrinsic good is found in the feeling of satisfaction, the sense of security and enlarged personality, which the possession of wealth yields. But this is, after all, only the satisfaction of possessing the means to other satisfactions; it is thus derivative, and wholly dependent, in the last resort, upon the instrumental power of wealth. Economic value, it must not be forgotten, expresses a relation between other values in the processes of exchange. The objects of economic valuation are sought primarily for the satisfaction of other desires than the desire for the possession of wealth.

Further, economic wealth, as instrumental, cannot directly, and of itself alone, secure to us the possession of any other values. The best food has no value to one without appetite or power of assimilation. Recreation affords no relaxation to a body so ill or a mind so harassed as to be unable to enjoy it. Knowledge cannot be bought outright; it must be won by the effort of the knower. Taste and social sympathy cannot be purchased in the market, but must be cultivated through years and even generations of life.

But in spite of the fact that the other values of life cannot be directly and immediately procured by wealth alone, it is none the less true that in modern civilization all other values are indirectly dependent upon it. This is the "hard saying" of the doctrine of wealth. But dislike it as we must, resist it as we may, it still remains and constitutes the growing moral problem of the economic order. Its truth is almost as obvious as the truth that we cannot live and move without a body. No one will question this dependence in the case of most goods. It is only too evident that bodily needs, the needs of recreation, and of social relationship, cannot be satisfied without a free use of this instrument. Equally clear is it that education costs money, that art and all forms of æsthetic good require large expenditure, direct or indirect, for their development. But this is not all. No one who has observed the effect of extreme poverty would hesitate to say that it is disastrous in its effects upon the development of spiritual qualities. Even religion requires vast economic outlay. "How shall they hear without a preacher? And how shall they preach except they be sent?" And how, we may ask, shall they be sent without means? The sting of the problem lies in the fact that we can no longer say of extreme poverty, as men have often said of it in the past, "It is inconvenient and burdensome, but it has great spiritual compensations." In the present economic order, on the contrary, we know that extreme and long-continued poverty means spiritual degradation.

The chief spiritual quality to which poverty has seemed favorable is the renunciation of luxury and ease in devotion to higher interests. But the full value of this can be realized only when poverty is voluntary. And, as we all see by countless examples, poverty is not an essential condition of such devotion. In general the struggle with extreme poverty is the crudest kind of materialism, unrelieved even by the elements of value that commonly accompany the materialism of riches. The man who is struggling for a bare subsistence is compelled to think more about the things of the flesh than one who is surrounded by all the material equipment that abundant resources can provide. Such equipment may be precisely the condition of entrance into the realm of higher values. But if used without moral insight, this equipment may, as we well know, only serve to enslave its possessor and to fasten more securely the shackles of materialism.

Morality demands an unceasing effort to secure the production of wealth in ways not destructive of the higher interests of those engaged in the work of production, and its distribution, not according to the unmoralized power of men to acquire wealth, but according to their varying human needs. If it be urged that when men are mentally and physically sound, and industrially well trained, they are sure to gain the economic wealth needed for a worthy life, the ready answer is that a large economic outlay is required to rear and train in this way. So easy to traditional modes of thought is an inversion of the real order! And if, finally, it be pointed out that economic resources alone will fail to accomplish the desired result, one may perhaps be pardoned for saying that no intelligent person has ever held such an absurd opinion. The absurdity of this opinion is only equaled by the opposite absurdity, expressed in the familiar saying, "He who steals my purse steals trash." He who steals a man's purse takes away the very means of life for himself, and, it may be, for those dearer than life.

Such a frank avowal of the rôle played by economic values, in providing the necessary means for the realization of the higher and intrinsic values, is simply a clear recognition of the hard fact of the industrial order. It is not a glorification of riches—the aggregation of great wealth in the hands of individuals—nor of luxury, nor of the passion for possession. Riches may prove a snare to the individual, luxury may work as an enervating influence, and possession may check the impulse to creation, the most precious of human powers.

You may develop the economic resources of a country to the utmost, you may attain an undreamt of equality of distribution, but the mass of mankind will not be happier than they are to-day, if you do not teach them what things are to be loved and what things are to be hated, if you do not show them that life will forever be barren unless it is dedicated to the things of the spirit. Once it is recognized that economic resources are purely instrumental, it follows that they can never be a part of the true end of human existence. Yet to admit that they are a necessary means to this end is to admit that they ought to be possessed in due measure by every human being. The ethical ideal with regard to the distribution of wealth is that it should be possessed by individuals according to their real needs, which obviously vary with capacity for the realization of life's intrinsic goods.

The ethical task, then, is to moralize wealth. And this means nothing less than its larger production, its wiser distribution, and its nobler use. All the processes of production, distribution, and consumption must be recognized as human tasks to be dominated throughout by an intelligent moral purpose, not left to the impulses of selfish acquisition or to the unchastened exercise of natural powers.

V. Bodily Values

When we speak of bodily values we do not mean that these are less an affair of consciousness than other values. They are simply those values which the mind refers to the body. They include everything which ministers to the health, efficiency, and beauty of the physical life.

The place of the bodily life in systems of morality has been a matter of very diverse judgments. Of these, two stand in sharp antithesis. The one has insisted upon the subjugation of the "flesh," and this has often been thought to require not merely its subordination, but its suppression. The result has been asceticism, chiefly the product of the

world-denying philosophy and religion of the East. In
opposition to this ideal, the classical Greeks appear in history as the leading champions of the dignity and worth of
the body. Its harmonious development seemed to them a
positive requirement of human perfection. They saw in the
body the outward symbol of the health and beauty of the
soul. The modern world has now returned in large measure
to the Greek valuation, again affirming the intrinsic worth
of the bodily life. Yet no ideal of the past reappears unchanged. Here, as elsewhere, the long tutelage of the centuries has left its impress. The influence of Christianity
especially has helped to produce a feeling of delicacy and
restraint unknown to the naturalism of the Greeks. A
deepened sense of what is required for the life of the spirit
has been reflected in our attitude towards the body.

The bodily values must be chiefly prized as instrumental
to higher interests, although we still regard them in their
own place as intrinsic goods. The familiar saying, "We
eat to live " and do not "live to eat," expresses, we feel, the
right relationship. Yet this saying does not state the whole
truth. Since eating is an essential part of life its enjoyment, within proper limits, is an intrinsic good. We do, in a
slight degree, live to eat, as we live to play, and still more to
learn, to enjoy social relations, to appreciate beauty, and to
develop character. We cannot completely reverse this order
and say, we play to live, we study to live, we form social
relations to live, and develop character to live. For the life
towards which these activities are directed would be empty,
a mere abstraction, apart from the content of such specific
interests.

The significance of the bodily life has received fresh emphasis in recent years from the results of various sciences,
especially of biology, physiology, psychology, and medicine.
Whatever final theory we may hold concerning the ultimate
relations of mind and body, their intimate interdependence

is one of the most certain facts of science, and has practical applications of the highest importance. Studies of mental and moral defectives show that the evils which in former times were often ascribed either to possession by evil spirits or to the perverse wills of the unfortunate victims, are the result of physical defects. In numberless cases, where the defect is in greater or less degree remediable, treatment has resulted in direct improvement. The child, thought by parents and teachers to be vicious, has often been found to be suffering from some positive defect or disease. The results of study and experience point clearly to the necessity of a careful examination of heredity and physical condition in all such cases. In more simple and popular ways the importance of the bodily condition is widely recognized. Men no longer consider a starved or mutilated body a fit temple of the higher life. Religion has learned to minister to pressing physical needs before attempting to preach the gospel. We look with rightful suspicion upon the mental states induced by protracted fasts, vigils, or other abnormal methods. As against these, we trust the judgments of men when in the soundest and most normal physical condition. No less important, on the other side, are the well-established effects upon the bodily states of mental habits. Ideas, emotions, and will-attitudes exercise here a power for good and evil so marked that control in the mental sphere is a recognized principle of therapeutics, and is destined to become a part of the fundamental education of the people.

But in recognizing the value of physical health and vigor, we must guard against an opposite error, which has proved fatal to the happiness and achievement of many individuals. Although the improvement of the bodily vigor of the race is of high importance, and is probably a condition of any great degree of intellectual progress, we cannot forget that not a little of the world's best work is always done by those who are handicapped by physical weakness and pain. To regard these as impassable barriers to a career of usefulness is a form of slavery from which one may well pray to be delivered. The intelligence and will must be summoned to vigorous combat against this dangerous error. The development of athletic exercise, with all its benefits, is sometimes in danger of giving a disproportionate place to bodily strength for its own sake. The purpose to keep "fit" finds full justification when the fitness in question is fitness for a worthy task. But to keep fit for a round of physical pleasures from which one returns again to become fit, inverts the place of bodily well-being, making it primarily intrinsic instead of instrumental to higher activities.

Here, then, as in the case of economic values, we have the task of more perfectly moralizing the life of the body, of so developing and controlling it that it shall be a thing of ordered excellence and beauty in itself, and a fit instrument in the service of higher values.

VI. Values of Recreation

Whatever might have been the reservation, secret or professed, of our ancestors a century ago, no one would to-day regard as complete a table of values which should omit play. In its numberless forms, whether of games and sports, of established amusements, or of the humor which may run through the most prosaic business, recreation is a good recognized even by the most earnest and serious-minded people. Physicians and moralists alike have learned the lesson so long ago taught by Spinoza—strange prophet of play, this poor, anathematized, and homeless Jew!—when he declared that we have need both for body and mind of every kind of relaxation that can be enjoyed "without injury to one's neighbor." Most people are willing also to acknowledge that play is an intrinsic good, an immediate enrichment of life. We do not feel compelled to resort to the "orthodox," "hyphenated" form, "re-creation," to use Dr.

Cabot's suggestion,[1] in order to give it respectability. We play not simply to work better, but for the sheer joy of playing. It is true, however, that the hyphenated form which suggests the instrumental value of recreation in restoring our powers for further labors, in giving exercise to unused energies, and in getting rid of troublesome inhibitions, does express the larger share of its meaning for most of those who carry the burden of the world's work. This instrumental value of recreation has attained in modern civilization a degree of importance unknown in more primitive societies. The reason for this change is chiefly to be found in the monotony incident to the division of labor, in the specialization of business and professional life, as also in the strain inseparable from the conditions of residence in large centers of population. Primitive peoples, to be sure, have their forms of play. But in the simpler life of pastoral and agricultural communities the need for organized recreation is far less. Work is carried on largely in the open air and is far more diversified.

Play may be defined as pleasurable activity for its own sake, whereas work is activity directed to an end other than the activity itself. But work, in all its more ideal forms, such as the creative activities of invention and commerce, of scholarship and art, is to a large extent pleasurable and so pays its own charges as it goes. It resembles play in that it is what we like to do; each moment is its own justification. Rising above the opposition of means and end, we reach here as nowhere else the goal of living. Such moments effect for us the happy union of immediate and ulterior aims, of intrinsic and instrumental good.

All work shares at times, and to a limited degree, the quality of play. The swinging of an axe or the pushing of a stevedore's truck may be a delight. But such tasks can be play only while the body is full of pent-up energy. To

[1] *What Men Live By*, p. 100.

those who must perform them for a livelihood these tasks
become, almost of necessity, monotonous and wearisome.
It is thus that all work, however ideal or delightful, tends
sooner or later to reach the point of drudgery. We may define drudgery as activity in which the end alone is desirable,
the activity itself having lost altogether the quality of play.
A measure of drudgery seems inevitable under present conditions; the business of life cannot be completed while the
workers are fresh and eager for the task. We pass by almost
insensible stages from play to work, and from work to drudgery. Industrial progress must be measured in large part by
the reduction of drudgery through shortened hours and
better conditions of labor. It is to be observed that, just as
work passes into drudgery, so play is in danger of degener-
ating into frivolity or dissipation whenever the other values
of life are not so developed as to furnish forces of control.
The best check here is less the conscious inhibition of the
play impulse than the unstudied limitation that comes
from the steadying power of larger interests.

It is always a great gain for human achievement when the
spirit of play can enter into and transform our work. Among
men of letters Stevenson has most fully presented this ideal
of work, as in the familiar lines:

> "This is the study; here a smiling God
> Beholds each day the path of duty trod;
> Approves and praises, and I hear him say,
> 'The time is brief; be diligent in play.'"

To a large extent this feat of transforming work into play
depends upon the attitude of mind which we cultivate
towards our work. We can spoil our job in advance by
calling it hard names, or we can learn to extract from it all
the possibilities of joy which it contains. Certainly we
can never bring to our work too much inward mirth and
gaiety.

As in the case of all the other values, so we have here the task of moralizing the life of recreation. This consists in cultivating it to precisely that degree which secures the free, joyous expansion of human nature, and the nice balance of our powers in the service of a life purpose. The same principle also dictates the choice of recreation in wholesome fields from which one returns with the least reaction and with the greatest zest for labor.

VII. VALUES OF ASSOCIATION

These values represent the satisfactions that spring from the association of individuals in groups of whatever kind or extent. If we begin with the most intensive form of association, which is found in family life, we find these values extending through friendship and acquaintance into the life of the community, taking form in political organization of various kinds, municipal, state, and national, and finally culminating at their widest extension in international and world-wide relations. These values are both intrinsic and instrumental. They offer immediate satisfactions of a high order, and they also make possible through coöperation many forms of good not otherwise capable of realization. Millions of human beings who are total strangers mutually contribute to and share in the values thus created.

It may not be superfluous again to insist upon the fact that we are here not concerned with anything separate from, or independent of, other values. Rather do we find here one of the significant aspects under which our complex life may be viewed for purposes of valuation. Every interest of human beings interpenetrates and in some measure transforms all the others. As, without the other values, association would have no significance, because it would be an empty relation lacking all content, so the other values would not arise apart from association, because they could not be produced by isolated individuals. But the social elements of our experience may, for purposes of more exact study, be segregated and subjected to examination, as is done in the social and political sciences.

The special problems that arise in this field of values cannot here be discussed, but simply indicated. On the one hand, there are certain questions which have been regarded as specifically ethical. Here belongs the much debated problem of egoism and altruism, and also that of the degree of harmony which can be affirmed to exist between the interests of the individual and of the society of which he is a part. These questions will find treatment in the next chapter. On the other hand, the subject reaches out into the foundations of institutions, law, and government. The discussion of all these would far transcend the limits of the present work. Some of their more distinctively ethical aspects will, however, be considered in later chapters.[1]

In the values of association we touch again the element of human sympathy, of love of one's kind, admittedly precious, which has often been exalted to a place of unique and supreme worth. This ideal has been held in one form or another by those who represent widely differing schools of thought. It has been the message of some of the greatest religious and ethical teachers, whereas others with a very different thesis have presented romantic love as a supreme good, justified in over-riding all the other interests of life. "Nothing matters but love," it has been said. To which it may be answered that, where nothing else matters, love itself does not matter, because all the content of personal life that makes love worthful or desirable is disregarded. Much more significant is the statement of an ethical writer, Mr. G. Lowes Dickinson, who suggests that "in the activity of love" or "in the life of the affections" we come "nearest to apprehending what perhaps we shall never wholly apprehend, but the quest of which alone, as I believe, gives

[1] See especially Chapters VIII and XI.

any significance to life." [1] Now in the "activity of love" or "the life of the affections" we have an element without which our human existence would, we also insist, be poor indeed. And yet precisely the same can be said of any other essential element such as knowledge or beauty, were it wholly disregarded. If we imagine for a moment those whom we love to be deprived, in ever increasing degree, of intelligence and æsthetic appreciation, they would soon cease to be lovable in any sense in which we now find them so. Love would sink to the level of animal affection, or be attended, as is the love for those who are defective, by a tragic sense of thwarted life. The play of intelligence, the understanding of life and the world, the passion for truth, the regard for all that is fair and beautiful—these are the things which, together with the other essential capacities of human nature, make the love of our kind possible and precious. The perfect good of which Mr. Dickinson's dialogue is in quest, or, to state the real problem, the greatest good possible of attainment—always something less than perfect—cannot be found in any single aspect of our nature, however exalted, but only in the integrity of all its parts, and the harmonious realization of them as a whole.

The practical corollary of this truth is important. No single reform or improvement offers a panacea for the evils from which society suffers. To proclaim any single principle as adequate to this task—unless it be the principle of a many-sided and thorough education of all the members of society —is to announce oneself a visionary or a charlatan. To make all social and political relations serve the interests of humanity is an undertaking so complex and vast that no one of sober intelligence will expect to see either its rapid or complete success. But no such person will, on this account, fail to recognize herein a genuinely moral task, or refuse to

[1] *Meaning of Good*, p. 231.

contribute what is possible because the contribution seems so insignificant.

VIII. Character Values

The term character values is used to designate the recognized virtues, temperance, truthfulness, justice, benevolence, and the like. Popular thought is inclined to see in these virtues the only distinctive moral values, and to limit somewhat narrowly their meaning and scope. Although "moral" values might seem here the most appropriate term for such virtues, I have purposely refrained from its use because I wish to insist upon the moral significance—a neglected significance—of all human values. It has been all too easy to satisfy the supposed claims of morality by an observance of the traditional, or even of the legal, interpretation of these virtues. Thus the legal claims of justice or the conventional practice of benevolence has left men morally satisfied without any adequate sense of responsibility for the use of wealth, or time, or talents. One recalls as characteristic of this traditional conception of morality certain remarks of Major Pendennis concerning Sir Hugh Trumpington's devotion to picquet. "'Did you see that dark blue brougham, with that tremendous stepping horse, waiting at the door of the club? You'll know it again. It is Sir Hugh Trumpington's; he was never known to walk in his life; never appears in the streets on foot—never. . . . He is now upstairs at Bay's, playing picquet with Count Punter; he is the second best player in England—as well he may be; for he plays every day of his life, except Sundays (for Sir Hugh is an uncommonly religious man), from half past three to half past seven when he dresses for dinner.'" "'A very pious manner of spending his time,' Pen said laughing." . . . "'Gad, Sir, that is not the question. A man of his estate may employ his time as he chooses.'" [1]

[1] Quoted by W. R. Sorley, *The Moral Life*, pp. 72–73.

As long as this false—I might even say vicious—limitation of morality prevails, the larger part of the business of life is left untouched by it. Without slight to the value of what the traditional observance of the virtues has rendered to morality, the verdict must be, "This ought ye to have done, and not to have left the other undone." Religious teachers were formerly accustomed to define morality in the narrower way, and often referred to "mere morality" in slighting terms as something falling far short of the demands of righteousness. To the truly moral man, however, every part of life will have spiritual meaning and purpose. He will never be inclined to say of the requirements of morality, "All these have I kept from my youth up; what lack I yet?" Pharisaical satisfaction in the fulfillment of the moral law can only be felt when that law is narrowly conceived or is misinterpreted.

The now familiar distinction between the intrinsic and instrumental aspects of value finds here also its application. The virtues are of intrinsic worth; they yield direct satisfaction not only to the possessor but to others as well. And like every other form of good they radiate through all human activities, giving form and order to what would otherwise be lawless and capricious. If their more primary influence is seen in the control of bodily appetites and social relations, they also extend to the highest achievements of science, art, and religion. Success in these spheres is conditioned in no small degree upon the fundamental virtues. The failure of gifted minds to achieve their full promise is often a failure at this point.

As Chapter X is devoted to a discussion of the doctrine of virtue, we pass at once to the next group of values.

IX. ÆSTHETIC VALUES

These are the values of beauty, in its countless forms, as it appears in nature and in art. It will be agreed that in the beautiful we have one of the purest forms of intrinsic value. Delight in the beauties of nature or in the creations of art lifts us above the struggle of life; our cares and preoccupations are forgotten, and we rest for the moment in serene and self-forgetful contemplation. This characteristic moment of æsthetic experience has found classical expression in Schopenhauer, when he contrasts its untroubled calm with the restless striving of the will: "At once the peace which we have been ever seeking, but which has ever fled from us on the path of the desires, comes of its own accord, and it is well with us. It is the painless state which Epicurus held to be the highest good, the blessed lot of the gods. For the moment we are set free from the miserable striving of the will; we enjoy the sabbath of rest from the servitude of willing; the wheel of Ixion stands still."[1] The same idea finds expression in the words of Dio Chrysostom concerning the Zeus of Phidias at Olympia: "Whoever among mankind is wholly weary in soul, whoever has experienced many misfortunes and sorrows in life, he, methinks, if he stood before this statue would forget all the calamities and griefs that come in the life of man." [2] Even though we cannot long dwell in this realm, our frequent excursions thither are among the best experiences we know. Art thus also serves the same ends as play, offering one of the best means of frequent, if temporary, detachment from the more monotonous and sordid aspects of life. From this insight came Goethe's advice to the effect that one should every day hear a little music, read a good poem, and look at a fine painting.[3]

The sense for beauty does not, however, work in isolation, but is assured a pervasive influence by the unity of our con-

---

[1] *Die Welt als Wille und Vorstellung*, Bk. III, 38.

[2] Quoted by C. H. Moore, *The Religious Thought of the Greeks*, p. 27.

[3] The passage runs as follows: "Man sollte alle Tage wenigstens ein kleines Lied hören, ein gutes Gedicht lesen, ein treffliches Gemälde sehen, und, wenn es möglich zu machen wäre, einige vernünftige Worte sprechen."

scious life. Like every other fundamental instinct it colors
and transforms all our activities. Herein lies its instrumental
value. It fashions the materials of industry, molds the
bodily life, elevates social relations, attends the labor of the
intellect, adorns religion, and profoundly modifies character itself. Ruskin's dictum, that "to teach taste is inevitably to form character", is fully justified by experience.
Many have found in the sense for beauty a barrier against
the allurements of evil. Happy the man whose feeling for
beauty supports the other forces that make for righteousness!

Although the æsthetic impulse may thus be an instrument
of high value, its moralization offers none the less its own
problem. Especially is this true of its creative activity in
the field of art, where its relation to the harmony of spiritual
forces is complex. The maxim, "Art for art's sake", cannot
be final. This maxim encounters the same difficulty that
we find in similar maxims drawn from other spheres of value:
business for business' sake, bodily health for the body's
sake, or even knowledge for its own sake. No one would
question of course that business should be conducted on
business principles, that bodily well-being must be guided by
physiological laws, or that knowledge should be pursued with
logical rigor and an eye single to the truth. But it is equally
clear that none of these activities is independent, self-con-
tained, and exclusive. Nor is art an exception to the principle. When working in his own field, the artist can have an
eye for nothing but the perfection of his art. Considerations of profit or popularity will inevitably work against
his creative power. So far, we may say "Art for art's sake";
but the place which art is to occupy among competing interests must be determined by the moral organization of
life.

Now art, of necessity, consents to deal with fragments of
experience. Some significant element is seized, and, unified

within itself by æsthetic principles, is presented as a whole
to our perception. So presented, it stands in isolation from
the rest of experience. The perfection of art, however, is
largely conditioned by just this limitation; it is inadequate
to a subject of too great range or complexity. A panorama
is interesting and useful, but it is not suited to artistic representation; it is better adapted to the purposes of a map
than of a painting. Similarly, should a sculptor attempt to
represent a great throng of people, his work would surely
fail of achieving artistic success. And a drama which should
attempt to reflect every phase of our many-sided existence
would lack, as we well know, the unity essential to its requirements. The works of art which in the judgment of the
centuries have attained the highest perfection—the works
which live in immortal youth—are notably those which
fully accepted this principle of limitation. By it, art attains
a finality of expression not attained in other spheres of effort.

Art itself provides no principle which determines its place
in a system of values. It evaluates the artistic significance
of its own products, but not their significance in wider relationships. Art, therefore, stimulates but does not regulate,
quickens but does not control our powers. One might go the
whole round of art in the manner of the æsthete, experiencing
in succession vivid and fascinating impressions. Each would
for the moment be engrossing and self-sufficient. These
impressions would, however, yield no principle of organization and harmony among themselves; still less would they
define their proper relation to other interests. This can
only come from the moral reason whose task it is to criti-
cize and arrange the many impressions of experience according to standards of truth and value. As long as one is
under the full sway of a drama or novel which has romantic
love as its theme, love is the sole object of interest and seems
indeed the whole of life. Similarly, a painting of Rubens
which presents the bodily life at high tide of joy and exulta-

tion represents a moment—and, we must admit, a real moment—of human experience. But such delight in the flesh needs strict subordination if it is not to override other and more enduring interests. It was Plato's charge against poetry that it allowed the passions to rule "instead of ruling them as they ought to be ruled with a view to the virtue and happiness of mankind." One cannot escape the conviction that the disorders often supposed to be inseparable from the artistic temperament are due less to a necessity of its nature than to a lack of broad and discriminating culture. A too narrow and exclusive devotion to any artistic interest may defeat its own ends. Such narrowness not only imperils the balance of the artist's powers, but it also impoverishes the content of his art. Even though the technical form of art might be maintained at a high level under these conditions, it could not have the richest meaning. Art is compelled to take its content from the other values, and defective understanding and appreciation of these must make its creations shallow and ephemeral. It was of the meaning, not of the mere form, of art that Plato was thinking when he prayed that our artists might be "gifted to discern the true nature of beauty and grace." The organization of life is moral and we cannot escape its laws. If our living fails at any point to recognize this fact, it is bad, and, in the end, unprofitable living. Equally true is it that if our reasoned morality fails to give rightful place to every legitimate interest, it will be an impoverished morality from which men will inevitably revolt. The sense for beauty cannot therefore remain apart from the sense for conduct; it must be taken up into the organized structure of life. Otherwise beauty is in danger of being lawless and life of being unlovely.

Art in its nobler forms is one of the great quickeners of moral endeavor. This power it owes in no small degree to the fact that it contains a transcendent element. The artistic impulse is not content until it has created something more perfect than yet finds embodiment in our experience; it strives to suggest what "eye hath not seen nor ear heard." Herein it is at one with the moral impulse, which is not satisfied to leave things as it finds them, but seeks to remold them into a more perfect order. Both the moral and artistic impulse are alike haunted by a vision of ideal perfection. Art, no less than reflection, may recall us to our better selves by suggesting in forms of beauty those ideals for which it is alike our duty and our joy to strive.

X. Intellectual Values

By intellectual values we mean the values of knowledge in its widest application. Knowledge is both an instrumental and an intrinsic good. It is an intrinsic good just in so far as the winning and possession of it directly yield legitimate and worthy satisfaction, a satisfaction provided for in the very structure and purpose of our nature. The intrinsic worth of knowledge hardly needs defense. Who, at happy moments of surrender to its uncompromising demands, has not felt the pure delight of intellectual effort? And who does not think better of his kind because there are men and women capable of finding the keenest delight in the disinterested pursuit of knowledge? But knowledge does more than enhance the moment of its immediate experience. All genuine understanding of the world and of human life has far-reaching consequences beyond itself; it is the master key to other values. By its light alone are we able to discover and appraise all the elements of experience.

There are never wanting detractors of the intellect who represent it as a poor thing, cold and barren in comparison with feeling and immediate experience. Such an interpretation of the intellect makes it a pauper in advance by isolating it and giving it no share in the production of the richer emotional experiences. But the opposition between reason

and the emotional elements of the mental life is artificial
and false. Feeling is always feeling about something; in
other words, it always has an ideational content in terms of
which its meaning and worth must be appraised. Whether
an intense and stirring emotional experience is significant
or petty, noble or ignoble, depends upon its meaning which
can only be determined by intellectual judgment. And it
must not be forgotten that all intellectual processes involve
feeling. " Be sure there is no process of reasoning which
fails of its throb of emotion in the exact degree of its depth
and clearness; no altitudes of the intellect where the fires
of feeling do not glow; and if it should ever seem to you that
that white light of truth which men say shines on the loftier
heights is a cold radiance, bethink you whether you might
not there find healing from the scorchings of the fires of
passion and of suffering which you chance upon below." [1]

Quite different from the disparagement of knowledge is
the error which declares all knowledge to be so good that
one bit is equal in value to any other, which finds no principles of subordination or superiority, and so none of ultimate valuation. Doubtless every bit of knowledge may be
good for something, at some time, to some person. But
thousands of known and knowable facts are relatively
worthless. One might conceivably spend a lifetime in acquiring and cataloguing such facts without being appreci-
ably wiser at the end of three score years and ten, and without having contributed anything to human welfare. I
might devote myself to counting the leaves on acacia trees,
or to determining the number of paradoxes in the writings
of Chesterton. I might commit to memory the dates of the
founding of all the post offices west of the Mississippi, or
try to discover through historical sources the daily changes
of temperature in the reign of Charles the First. All these
enterprises offer the possibility of acquiring certain exact

[1] J. M. Robertson, *Essays in Ethics*, p. 188.

knowledge and might yield satisfaction to curious minds, but they do not commend themselves to our judgment as valuable. The reason for our disapproval of time thus expended contains implicitly the principle for the evaluation of knowledge.

What determines the rank of any piece of knowledge? Unless we are prepared to maintain that all knowledge is of equal worth, that facts and principles do not in any degree differ in value, we inevitably face this question. We crave some objective criterion of the kind of knowledge that is most worth while, since the immediate satisfaction which knowledge may yield for any individual knower is too subjective to serve as a standard of judgment. All we can now hope to do in dealing with so complex a problem is to indicate the direction in which the answer must be sought.

In general, then, the rank of any portion of knowledge will be determined by its significance in the scheme of human interests as a whole. Knowledge is of all grades and of all degrees of value. Some portions of it are relatively insignificant, others of profoundest importance. In each case the rank is determined by its inclusiveness, its place in the whole of human meaning and purpose. The highest kind of knowledge, as Plato insisted, deals with the criticism of life itself, with the whole enterprise of civilization in which humanity is engaged. Such knowledge is primarily knowledge of inner needs, not outer equipment, of ends, not means; it is teleological, not mechanical; it ministers to our sense for conduct, to our deeper wants and aspirations; it tells us what to do with life when we have won the means of living. The parts of knowledge are all good, but they are good just in the degree in which they embody more or less of that total meaning which humanity is striving to discover and to express.

The knowledge required in constructing a heating plant or a traction system is valuable for purposes of heating or transportation. But if the life to which these minister were pitched at the level of merely sensuous gratification, we could not greatly applaud the achievement. Life has higher purposes than warmth and motion. When those who plan and create such mechanical systems are done with their task, they too must live their lives and fill them as best they can with a larger human meaning. "Apollo does not always bend the bow." Even a statesman who may devise financial or tariff legislation with rare skill is more than a legislator. He, like others, is building a personal life, noble or base, rich or poor in content; he too must be judged as a man by standards inclusive of far more than his special contribution to the mechanism of political life.

But insistence upon the valuation of knowledge according to the degree in which it ministers to the true needs of life, does not mean the disparagement of scientific knowledge. In fact scientific knowledge, even the most theoretical, does contribute to the guidance of conduct. Pure science wins from many faithful disciples a devotion which ennobles their own lives and at the same time exercises a tonic influence upon the standards of mankind. But science further serves, directly and indirectly, the criticism of life, yielding as it does knowledge of ourselves, our relations to our fellows, and to nature. If the physical sciences deal primarily with external mechanisms, the humanistic group deal with both the mechanism and meaning of inner experience. It must again be urged that the material conquests which are commonly regarded as the great achievement of science, are not its sole, perhaps not even its best, gift to the race. Science, by substituting ordered knowledge for disordered intuitions and conjectures, has delivered man from a maze of dangerous errors and cruel superstitions, and has thereby made a precious contribution to his spiritual life. A study of the history of medicine, of insanity, and of witchcraft, to mention no other fields of its influence, cannot fail to leave one profoundly grateful for the work of science. Transforming as it does the inner as well as the outer life, science must be recognized as a genuinely spiritual task.[1]

The significance of knowledge, in its widest range, for the moral life is not exhausted by its more dramatic achievements. What part, we now ask, does it play in the constant and repeated choices between good and evil made by every individual?

Is knowledge here necessary for right conduct, or is it a mere accessory, useful indeed, but not indispensable? What of the old dictum that virtue is knowledge? This ancient formulation of the problem is not the happiest. In fact, it is far less happy in our time than it was in the days of Socrates. For, at the present day, knowledge commonly suggests, not wisdom or personal insight, as it did for the Greeks, but rather the accumulation of vast stores of information in manuals, encyclopædias, and libraries. All this it certainly did not mean in any such degree for Socrates or Plato. If we change a little the form of the question we may get nearer to the heart of the problem. Does failure in conduct always imply something amiss in our intellectual processes, or do we err with eyes wide open, in clear and undimmed intellectual vision? That many of the worst acts of men are due to ignorance or to mental limitations no one will be inclined to deny. But that all wrong conduct means some limitation or disturbance in our thinking, we also hold to be true. If we are asked whether the man who yields to intemperance or to anger does not do so because of appetite or impulse that he knows to be evil, we unhesitatingly answer, "Yes."

---

[1] The temporary application of scientific knowledge to the construction of engines of death for use in war constitutes in no way a condemnation of science. As well condemn agriculture because incidentally it feeds vast armies! Long after the thunder of the great guns has ceased and the places of bloodshed have become again the scenes of peaceful industry, the same sciences will serve the interests of humanity by creating the instruments of conquest over nature. Principles do not cease to be valuable because they may be misapplied.

But at the same time we maintain that intemperance and anger mean that knowledge is, at the moment of the intemperate or angry deed, always defective. Let us take the case, for example, of the man tempted to anger. He knows in general that anger is bad and that it always recoils disastrously upon himself. To the proposition, "Anger is bad," he unhesitatingly assents. But when he is becoming angry he looks upon the present case as an exception. The insult or injury which is its occasion seems to him at the moment so outrageous that no man of spirit could fail to feel anger, and he does not hesitate to suspend the rule of self-control. Such is the subtle logic of self-sophistication! But if we could look into the mind of the angry man when he reviews the act in cool reflection, how different his intellectual processes! He then sees that his anger, in this case as in others, was foolish and wrong. He could now meet even that precise insult or injury and keep his temper. Why? Because his thinking is clear and undisturbed. Whenever we go wrong we go wrong in our thinking. If it be objected that the evil-doer is often clever and quick-witted, we freely grant the contention. We go further, and insist that he may be learned in some branch or branches of knowledge. He may be all this, and still lack that understanding of life in its wholeness, which, we have insisted, is the highest kind of knowledge. There is no necessary contradiction in affirming that a man may be a learned fool.

This is not, however, the whole case for knowledge in its relation to personal conduct. Its greatest service still remains in giving a new content to thought, new interests and points of attraction, so that, by a natural and inevitable process, unworthy ideas are driven from the foreground of consciousness, and so lose their power to determine conduct. To the empty mind, as to the swept and garnished house, the evil spirit returns to take up its dwelling. But if new and fascinating interests possess the mind, the disturbing forces may be overcome, as an armed enemy may be dislodged from a strong position when outflanked on all sides.

So important to the integrity of life is the increase and dissemination of knowledge, that it must be regarded as one of our chief and abiding moral obligations. Our stock of effective knowledge is forever unequal to the task of living. Through ignorance we are always in peril. Who in witnessing moral tragedies has not exclaimed with Meredith, "More brains, O Lord, more brains!" Although the great discoveries of science and the works of genius in literature, art, and religion cannot be produced at will by any moral imperative, but must come as the happy gifts of the gods, the vast majority of us, who are neither discoverers nor geniuses, may well be admonished to keep our souls alive by ever renewed devotion to the things of the mind. "Happy is the man that findeth wisdom, and the man that getteth understanding."

XI. Religious Values

The values of religion, like all the other values, are grounded in human nature. They are nothing superadded or adventitious. Man is a religious being just as truly as he is an economic, or social, or intellectual being. Placed in a world whose mysteries transcend our knowledge, dependent upon forces which we can only very partially control, drawing our very life from cosmic processes and rendering it up again to them after a few short years, it is not strange that we all feel a profound interest in the nature of the universe in which we play our little part. Such interest is of the very essence of religion.

Religion is throughout a problem of values. Neither its origin nor growth can be understood apart from the value-experience. Among primitive peoples, religion is, it is generally agreed, due chiefly to their concern for the primary needs of bodily life, which are dependent upon the processes of nature. And when, passing through the long course of its development, we reach the highest forms which religion has yet attained, we still find its theme to be the fortunes of good and evil in their cosmic relations.

The intrinsic values of religion are found in the immediate worth of the psychical states which it evokes. These values include a feeling of submission to the world order, a sense of harmony and coöperation with its purposes, faith and hope in the triumph of good, and delight in the divine law.

These must be recognized as at least the chief forms of value exhibited in the great historical religions, and especially in Christianity. We cannot, however, too narrowly limit the manifestations of the religious life, which is capable of expressing itself in a greater wealth of variety than is commonly assumed. Wherever we find the clear conviction that the physical universe, in which man holds such precarious tenancy, is indifferent or hostile to the highest values of man's inner life, religion is compelled with arms in its hands, as it were, to struggle for its very existence. In this case religious values are found in the exaltation of man above the world of nature, and in the winning by creative effort, even against heavy odds, of a home for the spirit. The spiritual life so achieved, although genuinely real, is not at one with reality as a whole. This belief frankly recognizes that the realization of values, which is the goal of religion, is always imperfect. The triumph of evil over good as well as of good over evil, the pangs of renunciation as well as the joys of divine creation, are permanent elements of the process. It sees that evil is wrought into the very structure of things, and no longer pronounces the universe wholly good. The world of worths is thus only an element of reality, and cannot be identified with reality as a whole.

Often, indeed, the intrinsic values of religion have been regarded as chiefly instrumental to the realization of still higher values of the same order in a future, transmundane sphere. But all deeper interpretations of religion reject such dualism, refusing to postpone in this way the realization of its purpose, and regarding the earthly life as an integral and indivisible part of the spiritual process with which religion is concerned. Religion has also an instrumental function which has been recognized by all ethical religions. These have held that religion does not stand apart from practical life. It has the task of transforming by its spirit all the activities in which men engage, and of furnishing the support and fulfillment of the moral ideal so imperfectly embodied in actual life. This function of religion, in giving support to the moral struggle, has been historically a great force in the lives of believers. The protesting and suffering champions of human right have, in evil times, turned to religion for solace and hope. They have been upheld by the faith that, if not here, then in the eternal order, good is triumphant.

But the sustaining power of such faith must not lead us to an uncritical acceptance of all its subjective hopes. The projection into some future order of what is ardently desired, but unrealized in the present, is a tendency easy to follow but hard to justify. We need to remind ourselves that religion cannot stand apart from the work of the intellect; it must not be merely an escape from the known order, an unregulated flight of the imagination into regions above the reach of reason. Religion, no less than other values, must be moralized in the interests of the harmony and completeness of the spiritual life. In the last resort the question of religious values, as of all others, is a question of fact and truth. Should the truest view of the world which we can win involve the necessity of a reconstruction of our hopes, we need not feel surprise or discouragement. Out of the seeming loss which such reconstruction brings may come that which will, in the long run, prove necessary to our spiritual progress

Certainly deep in us is the faith that it is best to know the truth and to adjust ourselves to its requirements.

As the relations of morality and religion will be discussed at length in the final chapter, we defer for the present further treatment of the problem of religion.

Concluding herewith our survey of the different groups of values, we may briefly consider a question as to the order in which the groups of values have been presented, and as to the possibility of establishing a strict hierarchy among them. To this question we reply: "For the order chosen no finality is claimed. It is possible that a somewhat different arrangement might serve equally well. The chosen order, however, is neither accidental nor arbitrary, but seems to represent a general estimate of the significance of the various groups." But we also hold that it would be impossible to demonstrate conclusively that any given order would constitute a strict hierarchy and be irreversible. To attempt this would be to ignore a fact of great weight to which we have frequently called attention. This is the fact that the values mutually interpenetrate and profoundly transform each other. Indeed, much could be said for the view that all the higher values stand, in the last analysis, upon essentially the same level, and that it is their harmonious and well-organized union which alone can claim an unchallenged primacy.

What we have proposed is no detailed treatment of these values. We have tried only to point out the place of each in the world of human worths, and thereby to indicate its meaning for the task of morality. The outstanding result of such a survey is clear. Morality is as wide as are the interests of life and must extend to the control of every part of its manifold content. It is no separate interest, but the principle of the order and harmony of all interests, the law of the whole. Ethics, thus interpreted, becomes in its widest meaning nothing less than a criticism of civilization.

XII. Definition of Civilization

Civilization may be defined as the effort progressively to embody in institutions, laws, customs, and ideals, all human values in just proportion. Such is the meaning given to the concept of civilization not only by the modern world, but by those of every age who have consciously grasped the problem. This certainly was the conception of the Greeks, who recognized the state as the embodiment of all essential human interests, the sphere within which alone the individual could come to fullness of life. This, too, was the ideal of the Roman *imperium* in the minds of those who conceived and built its world-embracing order. With mediævalism there came a change. Its characteristic feature was the renunciation of the tasks of earthly civilization for the sake of a transcendent order, which was at many points in open conflict with the true interests of this life. But when in the Renaissance men turned away in weariness from an interpretation of earthly existence which gave it no adequate meaning, they caught again the purpose of the Greek and Roman state, and sought to create a new civilization by a synthesis of the values both of paganism and of Christianity. We of the present day regard it as our task to mold all that has since been won by science, philosophy, and religion, by political, economic, and social reconstruction, into a still richer and more harmonious order. At no stage of the process are the various values complete in their development or perfect in their proportion. Now one group of values is enriched by new discoveries, now another. Here one value is slighted, there overestimated; witness, for example, the neglect of economic and bodily welfare inspired by the mysticism of India, or the other extreme of emphasis upon wealth and luxury among certain classes in the western world.

The ethical task, viewed from such a universal standpoint, is so vast that any critic will hasten to disavow the position of the specialist and claim that only of the amateur. Yet if there are no perfect seers, there are many, we may believe, in whom there stirs at times a prophetic sense of better things. Every insight is important; no criticism is impertinent. And as every individual shares in the responsibility for the progress of civilization, so even the humblest may rightly feel some measure of the dignity that belongs to the task.

Yet with all the imperfections of civilization, it offers at any moment a greater wealth of value than any individual can fully appropriate. Limitation of interests appears, then, as one of the first principles in dealing with the rich content of life. Indeed, to one whose eyes are open and whose spirit is alive, the problem of choice seems to be less the avoidance of positive evil than the selection of the good. On all sides the goods of life claim our allegiance and press upon us for acceptance. In contrast with this wealth of good, how sharply limited appear the capacities and opportunities of the individual! Within what narrow bounds our lives are set! To grasp at all is to lose all! "In der Beschränkung zeigt sich erst der Meister." Wise limitation is indeed the work of a master, and only comes with maturity of insight. But happily there is a measure of natural limitation provided by one's tastes and endowments as well as by the conditions into which one is born.

XIII. The Organization of Values

Such natural limitation, however, is not necessarily organization. Merely to exclude is not to unify. If life is to-be a well-ordered polity, a hierarchy of values, in which the less are subordinated to the greater, there must be within it a controlling purpose. This cannot be found in the desires alone just as they may chance to arise. Although the moral life is forever linked to desire, it must find its law in something above the separate and competing desires which are so often in conflict with each other. Desires, too, arise at different levels of worth. None are to be regarded as in themselves bad, none to be despised as common or unclean. But to obey merely "the law in the members" would be to live on the animal, not the human plane. From the dictation of uncriticized desire we must appeal to a more inclusive purpose, to an ideal of spiritual wholeness which comprehends and dominates all the interests of life. To such a unifying principle we must cling, in spite of the fact that its very comprehensiveness baffles a too exact formulation. All critics of human conduct have recognized that the demand for detailed principles of organization cannot be pressed beyond a certain point. The demand for exact prescription here is like the demand for infallible authority in law or religion. Life is too individual, too fluid, and too much in the making to allow such exact formulation. It is at best suited only to the lower stages of development, to the child or to the individual that remains in a childlike stage of tutelage. The organized scheme of family and social life provides this guidance for a time, but only for a time. Then each is set at the task for himself, and bidden to struggle forward even at the price of mistake or failure. Every individual is called upon to effect a unique but harmonious organization of values in a personal life—a creation which partakes of the nature of a work of art. Yet as the work of art, although a free creation, is not lawless but is governed in every part by principles of unity and order, so in life the choice of values must be dictated by the meaning of the whole.[1]

What can be said of the process of organization by which the end of the moral life is to be attained? Can ethics hope to give guidance in such a complex undertaking? Should we attempt the formulation of a single controlling principle, we must appeal to the recognized law that the less inclusive

[1] For a discussion of the problem of organization see Perry, *The Moral Economy*, Chaps. I, II.

must always be subordinated to the more inclusive interest. In the practical working of this principle it is doubtless easier to determine what is to be excluded than what is to be included. This need occasion no surprise. The plan of an inner life is always in the making, it is not a finished product. No one at the outset can see his life as a whole and dictate every part from the point of view of its final meaning. Rarely even does the outward scheme correspond with that which was pictured in youth. Often, too, the significance of a life is quite other than that which the individual assigns to it. Professor Palmer, in *The Nature of Goodness*,[1] has admirably unfolded the natural process of the development and integration of the moral life. In the course of the discussion he says: "We rarely have in mind the total plan of our unrealized being, and rarely ought we to have. Our work begins at a different point. We do not, like the architect, usually begin with a thought of completion. Rather we are first stirred by a sense of weakness. . . . I do not think a full plan of our ultimate goal is usually desirable. In small matters it is often possible and convenient. I plan my stay in Europe before going there. I figure my business prospects before forming a partnership. But in profounder affairs, I more wisely set out from the thought of the present, and the patent need of improving it, than from the future with its ideal perfection." [2] Such, I think, is essentially our procedure in daily life. We allow ourselves to follow the impulse to new activities, provided they do not conflict with already established purposes. The completed whole is achieved by excluding contradictory and discordant elements as we move forward in the direction of the largest meaning which, from day to day, we are able to discern.

Are there specific maxims which flow from the principle of the choice of the more inclusive end? Can we discover,

[1] See Chap. V.
[2] Pp. 134, 137.

in the lives of those who have best achieved an organization of values, the rules which have consciously or unconsciously guided in the process? Undoubtedly some of these rules can be formulated. And first, in all well-ordered lives we find the values which are chiefly instrumental subordinated to those which are chiefly intrinsic. Wealth, we have found to be a mere instrument, never to be exalted to the rank of an end. The same is true of all the material instruments of life. It is indeed the glory of man that his cunning brain and skillful hand have fashioned these for his service, but it is his shame that they should possess and master him instead of being his creatures. Although the bodily values have a degree of intrinsic worth, their chief function is to serve the higher levels of experience. The spectacle of bodily well-being, however perfect, if it does not promise something beyond itself, gives us a sense of inverted order and distorted value.

The rule which bids us place chief emphasis upon the more intrinsic values is one with the familiar maxim which counsels us to seek the goods of the inner rather than of the outer life. It has been an insight common to the masters of wisdom in all ages that the real center of life is within, not without, that true satisfaction is found in wealth of inner experience, not in abundance of outward possessions. Common prudence, as well as spiritual aspiration, dictates the setting of the affections upon those things of which fortune is not complete master and of which it cannot wholly deprive us.

Regard for the more inclusive interest dictates also the choice of the permanent, rather than the transient values. If we inquire where the more permanent values are to be found, there can be no doubt that we must seek them in the activities of the higher human powers. We are not without a measure of solid empirical evidence in this matter; we can appeal to laws which are firmly grounded in our physical and mental life. The senses soon weary and cease to respond with pleasure to repeated stimuli, whereas the ideational activities are capable of comparatively long and unwearied exercise. Unless life is filled with an ideal content, a sense of weariness and *ennui* follows in the long intervals between the more intense sensuous gratifications. This fact becomes of increasing importance to each individual with the passing of the years. One by one the cords that bind us to the world of sense are loosened; more and more we are compelled to find refuge and solace in the spiritual home which we have created.

The choice of the productive rather than the unproductive values constitutes still another maxim of organization. The unproductive values are "used up" in the process of yielding their immediate satisfaction. Not only do they fail to bring increase for the future, but often tend to be followed by experiences of negative value. In contrast to these, the productive values yield future increments of good both to the individual and to the community. It is in social relations that this principle of productivity finds its most striking illustration. Especially do the higher intrinsic goods escape the law of material things; they multiply in distribution and suffer no loss in division. To share these things with others is to increase one's own store. Everyone is the richer for such wealth possessed by his neighbor. As we shall see in the next chapter, it is through the increased devotion to such higher values that we may find hope of an increasing harmony among the interests of individuals.

The maxims given above are not to be thought of as separate, or exclusive of each other. They rather present different aspects of the larger and more inclusive good. For practical guidance appeal is made now to one, now to another. They all rest upon the axiom that, in a choice between two values, the one of greater worth is always to be chosen. More specific guidance than such general marks of the greater value cannot well be given. To do more, it would be necessary to consider individual cases with all their varying conditions, to enter, in brief, the field of casuistry in the wider sense of the term. General principles, however, are not to be rejected because one must use judgment in applying them.

Finally, the choices by which the less is subordinated to the more inclusive value are the work of reason. Although impulse and desire are the dynamic of conduct, driving it forward unceasingly, they cannot provide the principle of organization. This must be given by reason. If it be urged that the work of reason is imperfect, the answer to such criticism is that it offers the best guidance we know. Although the path it indicates may not always be clear, to reject its guidance is to wander in an untracked wilderness. Happily reason is constantly gaining fresh insight, and when at a loss has the power of turning back again and again upon its course to discover the point at which it went astray.

In the polity of the soul, then, we may picture reason as judge. It sits above the pressing throng of impulses and desires which, reckless of other interests, plead only their own special causes. As impartial arbiter it refuses to allow the lesser interests to prevail over the greater, or the greater wholly to over-ride the lesser. Rebuking the elements of discord in the soul, it seeks to secure an increasing harmony of interests and to establish ever more widely a true kingdom of values.

CHAPTER VIII

INDIVIDUAL AND SOCIAL VALUES

THUS far our discussion of ethical problems has proceeded without special consideration of the relations in which the individual stands to society. These relations have of necessity been assumed throughout, for they are so essential that, apart from them, human experience would not be what it now is, would in fact be nothing human or moral at all. The refusal to enter upon the problem hitherto can hardly have escaped attention, but the omission has been deliberate and intentional. It has seemed best that the task of description should thus far concern itself with certain universal and essential aspects of moral values. We have assumed that values are realized solely by individuals, and we have also assumed that no values can be realized by individuals in isolation. These assumptions, and the implications involved, must now be subjected to examination.

I. THE TRUTH OF INDIVIDUALISM

If, then, it be asked where good and evil are to be found, it may be answered that they are found in the lives of individuals. Our theory is an individualism, in the sense that the realization and appreciation of all value is ultimately always an affair of the individual consciousness. However one may exalt the social aspects of morality, it must inevitably be in this sense individualistic. Apart from individuals there is no morality, and no consciousness in which it could develop. The individual is thus, in the last resort, the home and center of all value. We often speak, to be sure, of the social organism, and even of the social consciousness, but these expressions are obviously figurative. While they are suggestive forms of speech, they are not to be taken literally or pressed beyond their legitimate symbolism. In the organism, biologically interpreted, the parts, or members, are not distinct centers of consciousness, and have in themselves no experience of value, whereas, in the social organism, it is only in the individual elements that this experience can be found. Society is, therefore, as Fouillée insists, "hyperorganic." [1] What is meant by the social consciousness is, in reality, the social elements in the consciousness of many individuals sharing in a common life and a common mental content. The term "over-individual" has been used for certain universal values. But this again is totally misleading if it is interpreted as something realized outside of the consciousness of individuals. The "over-individual" values are the universal values capable of realization by the individual. So far, any ethical theory is necessarily an individualism.

Such a doctrine of individualism does not mean a return to the atomic conception of society, which regarded individuals as independent and competing units. Nor is it to be identified with any of those forms of political individualism which have been the support of the economic doctrine of laissez-faire. Still less is it to be confused with that ruthless egoism which exalts selfish interests in the name of self-development, which pleads a divine right to live one's own life, and counts regard for the rights of others as a cramping of the personality. By the term individualism we mean only to express the truth that conscious selves are the many centers of experience and value in which life unfolds itself. To each one of these selves belongs an element of uniqueness—each in its own peculiar way mirrors the complex of physical and social relations.

If we attempt to evaluate this unique factor in individuality, we see that, whereas such uniqueness may be precious

[1] *Morale Des Idées-Forces*, p. 212.

because of its contribution to social values, it may be only
the conceit of a visionary and ill-balanced egotism. It is
easy to overestimate the worth for the individual of a refusal
to bear the yoke of common burdens, and to underestimate
the enrichment that comes from subjecting personal desires
to a law dictated by the needs of others. Individualism has
often misconceived the uniqueness of personality; it has
viewed the unique elements as alien to the interests of others,
and as remaining permanently apart from society. It is
true that new values come largely by a revolt of individuals
against the traditional order, but whether the uniqueness
which inspires revolt is subjective caprice and lawlessness
or a fresh addition to existing values, has to be determined in
the end by its over-individual worth. In the words of George
Eliot: "How far an individual may be justified in following
the dictates of his judgment in opposition to the customs of
his time and country, is a question no less delicate than
difficult to solve. And here is precisely the point where the
highest and lowest natures apparently meet. For opposition
to the customs may spring from the loftiest motives. It
may spring from the spiritual exaltation of the reformer,
braving social ostracism for the sake of an idea, or it may
spring, on the other hand, from the rebellious promptings
of an anti-social egoism which recognizes no law higher than
that of personal gratification." What we want is indeed
highly individualized persons who combine in original and
creative ways the over-individual elements in civilization,
and whose differences thus become sources of a common enrichment. True individualism is not mere queerness, nor the
exaggerated subjectivism that parades as genius in literature, art, or personal conduct.

II. THE INDIVIDUAL A SOCIAL BEING

We have insisted that the individual is the home and center of all value. But this avowal of an individualism, which

is inevitable to any theory of ethics, does not make against
the recognition of the full significance of the social character
of the individual. And no sooner does one turn to examine
the life of the individual than it is discovered how primary
and fundamental is this social character. Not only are all
values of the individual built up in coöperation with his
fellows, but his very consciousness, his innermost life, is
through and through social in its structure. Certainly
the individual self apart from social relations, if a human
being could exist in such complete isolation, would be so poor
and meagre a thing as to lack true meaning and worth.
Indeed, although the matter is for many reasons difficult
of experimental proof, and although observation can offer
only partial verification, it seems certain that, if a highly
endowed individual could be reared from earliest infancy in a
strictly non-human environment, the resulting consciousness would be nothing recognizable as distinctively human.
It is not necessary, however, to appeal to hypothetical cases
of isolation from society to establish the fact that the content of our consciousness is a social product. What would
be the mental content of our own age apart from the social-
historical life into which we have entered? Or what would
be the fate of any generation, were it to be completely sundered at infancy from the life of all previous generations,
so that it must begin its civilization anew? It would mean
nothing less than an immediate relapse into the lowest
savagery. All the values discussed in the last chapter are
social in their structure. From the simplest economic values
up to those of highest ideal meaning, all have been fashioned
by the contributions of unnumbered workers. If in each
field the names of only the most conspicuous contributors
are recorded by history, the labors of the many have been
no less necessary. At first thought it might seem that at
least the objects of the physical world by which we are surrounded remain an individual construction. But not even

this domain is left to the individual to interpret at will. The slowly-built systems of physical science and of philosophical interpretation, upon which past generations have toiled, determine our thought of our entire physical environment. Whether from childhood to old age one shall regard nature animistically, as everywhere peopled with spirits akin to our own, or as a mechanism of forces, depends upon the intellectual environment into which one is born. Whether also one shall regard particular objects in nature, as well as in art, as beautiful or ugly, is largely determined in the same way. From whatever side one approaches the subject, it is clear that, if the individual is the unit with which we always have to deal in moral theory, this same individual is in his deepest nature a social being.

We encounter at this point a seeming paradox of our practical life. The individual is, we say, the center and home of all values, and, apart from individuals, no values whatever exist. Yet with no less vigor we insist that the individual is nothing when sundered from his fellows, that if he is to realize his individuality he must transcend it, if he is to find his life he must lose it in the larger life of social relations. The paradox finds illustration in the work of charity. It is some neglected child, a sick laborer, or a social outcast, who arouses sympathy. Organized charity, ministering to such needs, then becomes one of the over-individual causes for the individual to serve. If, however, social service is made an end in itself, it negates itself by losing sight of the only reason for which it exists. In education the case is not different. We seek to educate individuals, A, B, C, and all the others whose names appear in the catalogue. But straightway the process of education must of necessity be carried on by inspiring in the student a devotion to universal interests, interests transcending each individual while ministering to all.

In whatever form this problem presents itself, it can find

solution only when we recognize that the relations of the individual and society are strictly reciprocal; neither one can be understood or can even exist apart from the other. The individual has no meaning apart from the community, and the community none apart from the individual. "The circles of the ego and the non-ego," we must acknowledge, "everywhere intersect." This is true of all human concerns, great and small, high and low. "If the glory of God is not also my glory and the salvation of society is not also my salvation, then God and society are necessarily strangers to me, and their good can be for me neither a moral obligation nor a psychologically conceivable motive." [1]

But this problem of the individual and society is after all only one aspect of a larger problem of general philosophy, the problem of the individual and the world in which the individual exists. If we begin at the level of material objects, we find that not one of them is an independent unit. No atom exists in isolation. The forces operative in inorganic nature bind together all elements in processes of action and interaction. A change at one point involves a change throughout the whole system. Still more clear appears this interaction of elements in the sphere of organic life. The individual plant is nothing apart from the earth, the sunshine and the rain, and, indeed, the entire cosmic order. The plant's existence is linked with the whole of things, and would be impossible apart from such over-individual relations. Ascending the scale to animal life, where consciousness appears, we find increasingly significant examples of the principle of interdependence. Thus the doctrine that the individual is not an independent being is a truth in no wise peculiar to the moral sphere.

In a world of interacting elements, adjustment is a universal and unceasing process. The adjustment of interests between persons may be viewed as the highest and most

[1] Fite, *Individualism*, p. 27.

complex case of adjustment. It is the task of moral reflection to comprehend the relations of individuals, just as the various sciences have the task of dealing with other problems of interaction in their respective spheres. Ethics here only parallels in its own domain the procedure of the other sciences.

If we seek in human nature for the psychological basis upon which social relations have been reared, we find in man an instinctive feeling for his kind. This instinctive element is perhaps best represented by the term sympathy. Although this social instinct has been recognized by thinkers in every age, it has received its most impressive statement at the hands of evolutionary writers, who have studied its manifestations in the lower animals as well as in man. The social, other-regarding impulses play an important part in the life of all gregarious animals, producing among them striking displays of instinctive sacrifice, as when the mother offers up her own life to protect the life of her offspring. It has been claimed that sympathy, appearing first as an instinctive form of conjugal and parental affection, has increased in proportion to the development of the animal organism; that it is accordingly least in the lower animal types, like fishes and reptiles, and greatest in the higher forms, the birds and mammals.[1] Precisely the same law, it is shown, applies to the various stages of human evolution. Among the lower savages, sympathy is limited in every case to the tribe; all outside it are enemies to be attacked and slain. In general, too, the tribe varies in size according to the degree of its development. With every increase of numbers in the tribe the circle in which sympathy operates becomes larger, while at the same time the manifestations of the sentiment tend to increase both in intensity and complexity. Numerical estimates, based upon the data available, are necessarily inexact, but at least serve to illustrate the principle. Among

[1] See, for example, Sutherland, *The Origin and Growth of the Moral Instinct*, Vol. I.

the lowest savages, like the Bushmen and the inhabitants of the Andaman Islands, the tribe has been estimated to consist on the average of about forty souls. The so-called middle savages, like the Tasmanians, Fuegians, and Hottentots, number about a hundred and fifty to the tribe, while the higher savages dwell in encampments of several hundred souls. In each case, the number may be regarded as marking approximately the extension of sympathy. With the advance from savage to so-called barbarous peoples the numbers increase to thousands, and the extensive operation of social sympathy is correspondingly enlarged. In the civilized nations of modern times we have the spectacle of millions of human beings linked together by bonds of cultural interests as well as of a common political life and destiny. But a still more striking fact is the way in which sympathy transcends all barriers of race and nation, and encircles the globe. As no individual can be defined apart from the community, so no nation can be defined apart from the community of nations. The extension of sympathy even to the animal kingdom, in systematic effort to secure kindly treatment of all forms of sensitive life, is an interesting phase of modern civilization. Only within a few decades has there been any widely organized movement for this purpose, and only within a still shorter period has it been a recognized factor in the education and training of the young. With the progress of civilization social coöperation everywhere displays both extensive and intensive growth.

III. Egoism and Altruism

Granting all that has been said of the social nature of man, and of the growing power of sympathy, are not all the motives that stir him to action strictly individualistic? Popular thought often interprets all social, and even so-called altruistic, conduct in terms of pure egoism. For, it asks, are not all acts which have social ends in view prompted by personal desire? Is not all altruism a concealed or un-conscious egoism? Does not one perform the act of social helpfulness, like any other, because it pleases one to perform it? And so, it is urged, we are all completely selfish in our conduct. The philanthropist is as selfish as the most vulgar pleasure-seeker, only he has learned to find his happiness in different ways, in ways, fortunately, that contribute to the well-being of others.

This view owes whatever of apparent force it possesses to the exaggeration and misstatement of a residuum of truth just sufficient to give countenance to the error. It is an example of the ways in which we are tricked by forms of speech. For the analysis of any altruistic, other-regarding act reveals a certain primary reference to the self as incon-testable. Whenever one performs such an act, one performs it because it pleases the self to do it. As Bishop Butler expressed it, "No one can act but from a desire or a choice or a preference of his own." [1] Any concrete case of altruistic action will serve to illustrate the principle. The mother who makes costly sacrifice for the welfare of her child does so because she finds satisfaction in maternal devotion. The man who leaps into the cold water to rescue a drowning person prefers, if he reflects upon the matter at all, the chill of the water, the struggle, and even the danger involved, to standing in cowardly inaction on the shore while the victim drowns. Similarly, in cases of more deliberate reflection, the act of altruism represents the personal pref-erence of the agent at the time the choice is made. This basal reference to an ego is essential and irreducible. It lies in the very mechanism of moral action that the act should express the desire and preference of some individual agent; for only in this way can acts be performed at all. But because all acts must be the choice and preference of a self, all are not therefore selfish; because they proceed

[1] *Sermons*, Preface.

from an ego, they are not necessarily egoistic. We must not allow ourselves to be fooled by a verbal puzzle. Whether an act is selfish or not depends upon the end in view. The selfish act, whatever its outward seeming, has as its object the satisfaction of the agent without due regard to the satisfaction of others; the unselfish act, although equally inspired by the personal interest of the agent, has as its aim the welfare of others. It is because the self is capable of including within its own interests the interests of others that altruism is possible. Some degree of it, indeed, may be said to be inevitable. Once it is seen that the self is a social self, the sharp opposition between egoism and altruism inevitably breaks down. The antithesis, if pressed too far, loses all meaning, since no individual can realize his personal interests without including more or less fully the interests of others. Further, the fact that the individual pleases himself and finds happiness in altruistic conduct, does not in the slightest degree lessen the beauty or worth of such conduct. In contrast with this harmony of individual and social interests, one may picture a moral order in which every altruistic act should be attended with displeasure, and should always mean ultimate loss to the doer. If such a world were possible, it would hardly commend itself as desirable.

Morality, then, is in no wise interested in lessening the satisfaction which the individual naturally obtains in unselfish, other-regarding action. Its interest lies rather in increasing the harmony between individuals, so that each may find his own good in the good of the many. No more is it the aim of social morality to make the self less of a self, to diminish the strength of desire or the ardor of pursuit of self-determined ends. For, if society is to be well served, there must be strong and capable individuals to undertake the service. Everywhere there is need of individuals who possess a wealth of personality, of self-hood, to offer. Self-assertion is not necessarily selfish or anti-social. It is true

indeed that "with only a little more rational self-love the
largest portion of human misery would disappear." The
proper assertion of personal honor and self-respect is better
in social influence than weak yielding to domination. The
entire process of education may be viewed as an assertion
of personality. But the long years given to such development and assertion of individual power are amply justified
socially by the larger and stronger self prepared for service.
The value of self-assertion, we must remember, depends
upon the kind of self that is asserted. Education aims to
develop the higher and larger self. The pleasure-seeker,
the miser, and the tyrant assert themselves in social relations; but in the case of these it is the lower, the partial,
and petty self that finds expression. The clash between individual desires and social interests always tends to disappear whenever the larger, more ideal interests of the self
become the object of desire.

IV. Conflict of Individual and Social Interests

It is impossible at this point to escape the question of
the degree of harmony which can be asserted to exist between the true interests of the individual and those of society.
Is this harmony complete, or are we left with an "ever not
quite" when dealing with the problem? It is a question
which no fully conscious individual can permanently escape.
There is within us a deep protest against a final dualism
between these interests. When I secure my own highest
good, must it be at the price of the good of my fellows?
And when, in turn, I serve my fellows, must I thereby
sacrifice my own highest good? Must the spirit be at war
with itself in these two deep impulses? Or, are we justified
in the belief of an ultimate harmony between the promptings
of social sympathy and the demand for the most complete
and satisfying life possible of attainment by the individual?

The question of the degree of harmony between individual

and social interests is analogous to that, already discussed, of the agreement between happiness and perfection. And a dogmatic assertion of complete coincidence seems as impossible in the one case as in the other. Again we doubtless have to do in the last resort with a postulate of harmony essential to the whole-heartedness and vigor of moral action. However convincing the evidence in favor of such harmony may be, and however hopeful the outlook for an ever-growing identity of interests, one cannot ignore the historical conflicts, or the cases of discord that present themselves in existing society. No thoughtful person would indulge in a dogmatic assertion of complete harmony.

The easy-going assumption which sometimes appears in the ethics of self-realization to the effect that, whereas from the point of view of hedonism there may be a conflict between individual and social interests, this conflict entirely disappears as soon as the standard of the development of personality is applied to conduct, is wholly unwarranted. It must not be forgotten that the development of personal power requires an adequate sphere of activity, a career suited to individual capacities. That everyone does find a career which gives the fullest stimulus and scope for development, is manifestly not capable of demonstration, but appears in many cases to be clearly contrary to the facts of experience.

But whatever conflict may exist between the spheres of individual and social welfare, there is historical evidence in support of the view that, with the advance of civilization, the conflict has on the whole diminished. Without entering again upon the question of progress, which we have discussed elsewhere,[1] a great gain in harmony is seen in the fact that it is now possible to make new contributions to society without the costly sacrifice which the past exacted of any pioneer who opposed existing traditions. Nowhere does this appear

[1] Cf. Chap. VI.

more clearly than in the careers of those who have discovered new truths in any field of thought. The most severe punishments which society inflicted were formerly visited upon those who criticized existing ideas and institutions, and suggested new ones in their place. The history of politics, science, and religion is replete with such examples. The only approximation in ancient society to the freedom of modern thought was in Greece, and in circles dominated by Hellenic culture. But at the present time almost all intelligent persons recognize the vital importance of the free expression of convictions, however these may be opposed to the existing order. Progress is seen to be dependent upon the infusion of new ideas. Even a frank and consistent expression of error may be better than unthinking acquiescence. Lord Bacon's dictum that "the truth emerges from error more quickly than from confusion of thought," is abundantly justified. In radical views, unflinchingly developed, society first becomes aware of the meaning of tendencies that have long been at work in its midst. However sinister certain of Nietzsche's views may appear, it is recognized that he has rendered a real service in developing, to their logical conclusions, ideas which had found practical, though largely unavowed and unconscious expression in the military and industrial life of the age. At the same time, elements of truth in his teaching add by so much to the stock of clear and consciously elaborated ideas. The modern pioneer in thought enjoys a freedom from all the harsher penalties which earlier ages inflicted. A certain degree of ostracism or of social reprobation is the only penalty that still remains in most civilized countries for the representative of radical or unacceptable views. This permitted freedom in holding diverse ideas, it may be added, is at once a mark and a condition of all progress. There is ample evidence to show that such diversity was unknown in primitive society. Among many tribes it has been observed that the only reason for the right or wrong of an act was the fact of its agreement or disagreement with existing customs.[1] Primitive men think and act in herds; the individual has yet attained little uniqueness.

As in the course of civilization men devote themselves increasingly to the things of the mind, the greater becomes the social value of the activities of the individual. This is strikingly exhibited in the discoveries of science, even in those fields which yield results of no immediate utility. No one can accurately forecast the value of highly theoretical investigations.[2] These can be abundantly justified against the spirit which demands immediate results, and estimates all intellectual activity by its contribution to material resources. The humanitarian spirit often short-sightedly joins with utilitarian interests in the cry, *cui bono?* But it would be disastrous to check arbitrarily any strong intellectual interest. Such a check would surely clip the wings of progress. And even apart from the enrichment of the content of civilization, the loss of any truth must in the end prove a bar to progress. One fact, clearly grasped, makes possible the understanding of another. The most recondite researches, in fields such as history and philology, help us to reconstruct the past. And to understand the past is at once to possess its truth and to be emancipated from its error. By such understanding alone do we escape the illusion which the unknown always creates. Too often a superficial knowledge of the past makes it appear as the golden age, bright with an imagined splendor.

The fact that the higher values, whether of knowledge, or beauty, or goodness, are in a unique degree social values, appears in no way more clearly than from a comparison of the conditions which govern the distribution of material and of spiritual goods. If we regard the economic wealth of the

[1] Cf. Westermark, *The Origin and Development of the Moral Ideas*, Vol. II, pp. 118–120.

[2] Cf., for example, the discovery of the Roentgen rays made in the prosecution of highly theoretical experiments.

world at any given moment as a fixed quantity, it is clear
that in case A possesses an undue share, B and C must have
less than a just portion.   If the loaf is of a given size, an increase in the number of shares decreases the size of each.
If I have a given amount of wealth, and distribute it, I am,
economically at least, the poorer for the distribution.   The
more one individual has, the less there is for the others to
share.   In our relation to things material it is often true,
in Dante's phrase, that "companionship is one with loss."
On the other hand, the increase of ideal values, in the possession of any individual, means an increase in the possession of these values by others.   No man can be intelligent,
courageous, or benevolent, without inevitably imparting
something of these qualities to his fellows.   Their very nature is to multiply in social relations.   The giving of these
things does not impoverish, nor the withholding them enrich.

We should not, then, think of the conflict between individual and social interests as unchangeably fixed, or as
wholly beyond our control.   The relations of individuals in
society are not determined by a law outside of man's nature,
but are largely subject to his own intelligence and will.   It
is possible, therefore, for mankind steadily to modify these
relations, and so to adjust them as to secure an increasingly
perfect reciprocity of interests.   The so-called "external
sanctions" of morality—political, social, and religious—have
always worked in some measure to secure a harmony between self-interest and the interests of others.   But these
sanctions are susceptible of development in many ways to
aid in securing a more perfect social order.

We must, however, be on our guard against placing too
largely in external sanctions what is, in the last resort, a profoundly inner experience.   And, from the point of view of
inner experience, there may be a deeper harmony than the
material fortunes of men indicate.   For the very temper,
the attitude towards life, of the individual in whom altruistic

interests are strong, is directly favorable to happiness. The spirit of love is in itself an experience of joy, directly enhancing the worth of life for him who cherishes it. On the contrary, hate, envy, jealousy, all of the anti-social sentiments, are in themselves a source of deep unhappiness. Even if we acknowledge that the unselfish temper may lead its possessor to acts that involve real sacrifice, is it not true that a liberal balance of satisfaction remains to his account as compared with the selfish spirit, a spirit which experience unanimously declares to be the foe of true happiness? Looked upon from without, the spirit of self-sacrifice may seem uninviting, but to those who, under whatever name or confession, have experienced it, it has been a source of joy and strength. It is further to be remembered that the activities open to the sympathetic and humanitarian temper constitute one of the great fields of objective interest. If biography and personal observation can be relied upon as trustworthy evidence, those who have most exercised themselves in these interests have found true satisfaction in them. Certain it is that the individuals who bemoan life as empty and unsatisfying are not found in the ranks of those who give themselves whole-heartedly to ideal causes.

The conflict between individual and social interests tends, then, to disappear in so far as the content of life consists of the more ideal values, and tends to increase whenever men set their hearts upon those material objects which cannot be shared without loss, at least in kind. The possibility of the production of economic wealth in such abundance that everyone should possess at least sufficient to furnish the basis of a life rich in ideal content, and to free the mass of mankind from the rôle of mere producers of material wealth, hewers of wood and drawers of water, so that time and strength would remain for the cultivation of intellectual, social, and æsthetic interests, lies doubtless far in the future. But the possibility cannot be rejected as wholly chimerical, when one considers the progress already made, as seen in the practically universal emancipation of slaves, the reduction in hours of labor, and the freedom from the severer forms of toil through the use of mechanical forces. The splendid development of Greek culture rested upon a broad basis of slavery. It is only the apex of the pyramid of Greek civilization which attracts attention. Its necessary economic foundation was laid in the toil of the masses, who never rose to a position of recognized human dignity. This order of things was perhaps inevitable, in the absence of scientific invention, if any portion of the race was to be free to follow the things of the mind. There was deep insight in Aristotle's jest that slavery would be abolished as soon as the shuttlecocks in the looms should begin to move themselves. How far the process of emancipation can go in the future is simply a question of intelligence. Nature does not appear so niggardly in her gift of raw materials and of physical energy as to exclude the possibility of the reduction of labor, involved in the production and distribution of the necessities of life, to a point which should no longer interfere with the highest possible development of the masses. However utopian this ideal may seem at present, it suggests principles of the highest importance for guidance in the slow progress towards such a goal. The necessity for an increasingly equitable distribution of wealth is obvious, whether the distribution be direct, or the wealth be held in such forms of public trust that it will yield to all the opportunity for the best training of the higher powers. The struggle of the proletariat for industrial emancipation has always been justified in principle, whatever the sharp limits of its possible realization at any given time.

V. SCIENCE AND SOCIAL ORGANIZATION

One of the most distinctive marks of twentieth century thought is its vision of the widening scope of social morality.

The goal towards which it looks is clear—the increasingly rich and harmonious life of individuals in organic union with the life of the community. But the principles which are to guide in the slow process of its attainment are often obscured by the complexity of the practical situation. In conclusion, we touch briefly upon a few of the fundamental problems involved.

In the economic life of the present day, perhaps more completely than anywhere else, the new tasks and the new renunciations to which men are called spring from new social contacts. The general fact of this changing situation is too familiar to require emphasis, but the primary cause of the new conditions is not always so clearly recognized. It is not always seen that the growth of what is called the social consciousness, with all its complex problems, is due chiefly to scientific discoveries. But of this fact there can be no doubt. Science is the magician that has transformed the conditions of life. It has brought the ends of the world close together. It has revolutionized industry and commerce, making every life in the great centers of population dependent for its very sustenance upon thousands of distant and unknown toilers. It has forced upon us new and baffling problems, and has made even the highest values of life dependent on industrial and economic forces. Science has become the chief agency in transforming both the material and the spiritual conditions of human existence.

How slow in comparison with the rapid strides made by physical science has been the progress in social and political organization! But the difference does not appear strange when one reflects upon the disinterested ardor with which scientific knowledge has been pursued, in contrast with the "interested" and partisan spirit of most who have played the rôle of statesman. Science glories in the forward-looking, creative mind, whereas politics and government have been dominated largely by the backward-looking and precedent-seeking mind. Loyalty to the traditions of the past is interpreted by science as an obligation to transcend all that it has achieved; loyalty in political life, on the contrary, has commonly been thought to require close adherence to forms satisfying the needs of an earlier generation.

VI. The Fallacy of Numbers

Progress towards a better social order must be extremely slow and precarious until truer standards of value are recognized, and constructive measures substituted for those which are merely palliative. One of the false standards of value, which has blinded men to some of the most important problems of social reconstruction, has been an undue estimate of the importance of numbers.

It is difficult to understand how intelligent men have so largely accepted this standard. The idea that numbers is the sole, or even the chief, criterion of social value will not bear examination. It is an estimate which takes no account of quality, and which is no more satisfactory when applied to society than when applied to an individual. In the case of the individual we all agree in rejecting it. We never admit that the value of a human life is measured by its length alone, apart from its quality. There are lives which would not greatly enrich the world if they were continued ten thousand years; and there are others, brief in time but great in achievement, for which the world forever counts itself the richer. No, numbers can never be a sound criterion of social value. The worst form of race suicide is that which, by undue multiplication at the lowest levels of intelligence and morality, strikes a fatal blow at the very quality of the race.

The chief sources of the undue worship of numbers among us are two, Hebraic tradition and the spirit of nationalism. Hebraic tradition discharged itself with almost unbroken force into the Christian centuries, where it appears chiefly as a sentiment regarding the sacredness of life. But traced back to its origin, this tradition was itself the manifestation of the spirit of nationalism. The command to "be fruitful and multiply" was in reality a maxim of prudence on the part of a people surrounded by implacable enemies. In modern times, the spirit of nationalism has exalted numbers chiefly from a military, and more recently also from an economic, point of view. To have abundant "food for cannon," to be able to present a strong fighting force against the enemy across the border, to show rapidly rising tables of industrial production, and a vast increase of national wealth —these are the popular standards by which national greatness is too often measured. But must we not confess that they are wholly inadequate? Numbers, to be sure, are not to be despised; only we have need to consider more seriously the question of what manner of people we are than the question of how many we are.

It may be worth while to point out a special form of the fallacy of valuation by numbers, which sometimes operates in political and economic thought. It is often assumed that a programme of imperialism or expansion, which has as its aim an increase in the size or aggregate wealth of a nation, is justified from the point of view of human values. But this is not necessarily the case. If, for example, an empire of fifty million people is increased to one of a hundred million by the incorporation of fifty million people who have hitherto been divided among relatively small states, we are never warranted in assuming, from the fact of such national increase in numbers, that an increase in values has been thereby secured. Such a change may indeed represent a gain, but it may also conceivably represent a serious loss. Both the original nation and the incorporated states may suffer in many ways by the consolidation. The only way of establishing the fact of gain or loss would be to take into account the effects of the change upon all the individuals concerned.

The result of the qualitative estimates so made would, as we have earlier insisted, take the form of a quantitative judgment of value. But this judgment would not coincide with a numerical computation of population, nor even with that of a majority of the population, although numbers and majorities would be important factors in the problem. It might be that a very great gain to a minority would outweigh a small loss to a majority. In the inexact estimates which are alone possible in such cases, however, the interest of the majority must always count heavily against that of the minority, and especially of any class or group representing but a small minority. Certainly the sense of added power and of enlarged personality which the ruler of an increased empire would naturally feel, a feeling which would also be shared by the ruling class, does not necessarily correspond with any actual realization of values. Similarly, although it is highly probable that an increase in the aggregate wealth of a nation, of any given population, means an increase in realized human values, this could never be asserted without careful consideration of the incidence of the increase, of the methods by which the wealth was produced, and of the way in which it was consumed.

VII. PROBLEMS OF SOCIAL BETTERMENT

The undue emphasis upon numbers as the criterion of value has led inevitably to the popular disregard of the responsibilities of parenthood. This is an evil which poisons life at its very source; it is an evil, too, which multiplies, affecting countless generations. It thwarts the production of a nobler race, stronger in body, clearer in intellect, and more generous in soul. All species of living beings are wellbred but man, and man for the most part very ill. The evil of irresponsible parenthood, not only in its economic but also in its other aspects, is one before which the evil of divorce shrinks into insignificance. Until those who are responsible for the education of the people deal with it seriously and vigorously, charity will be, as at present, helpless to touch a tithe of the actual needs of the poor, while the ever rising tide of population from the unfit, of whatever class, will continue to keep at a low point the average physical vigor and intellectual perfection of the race. Surely every child brought into the world has a moral right to decent food, clothing, and shelter, to proper recreation and physical development, and to an education that will fit it for some useful career, however humble. Where there is no reasonable prospect of such provision parenthood is irresponsible, and so far immoral; the child may have a right not to be born.

It was Kant's maxim that every human being should be treated as an end, never as a means. This expresses the essential idea of true democracy. But it is perfectly clear that in the social order this ideal has been very imperfectly realized. The lives of many men are used chiefly as means to the satisfaction of other lives; their personal development, their health and strength, are exploited for ends that are not their own. And it is a serious question whether this condition can ever be changed as long as there is such marked inferiority of birth and training. The nearer men approach the animal plane of existence, the more will their tasks resemble those of animals. When men cease to be of this type they will cease to be so used; their lives will be ends in themselves, and their tasks means of self-expression.

There is no greater anomaly in standards of social morality than the contrast between the sacredness which has been attached to the ending of life, and the thoughtless disregard of those forces which determine its primal character. Failure to deal with the problem, or rather blindness to the existence of the problem, has been one of the gravest defects of ecclesiastical morality. It is no longer possible to escape our human responsibility by referring the course of events to

the mysteries of nature or to the inscrutable decrees of a
Divine Providence. The social conscience of the future will
more and more emphasize the high responsibility of parenthood, and will condemn all irresponsibility, of whatever
kind, in this sacred relation. It will have scant respect for
the superstition that would hallow unworthy parentage, or
for the cowardice that would hesitate to brand it for what
it is.

But it is not enough for the future generations that they
be well-born and well-nourished; nor is it enough for the
present generation that it be freed from the unduly long
hours of labor, and the rigors of toil that exhaust the stores
of nervous energy which might else be turned into higher
channels. It is clear that without thorough education and
the cultivation of spiritual interests, nothing will avail for
the true self-realization of the race. The world's toilers
may be excused for judging the times to be out of joint
when they see so much wealth spent in needless luxury,
while "the poor have the gospel preached to them." And
yet, after all, the poor have far more need of a true gospel
than they have of the luxuries of the envied rich. It must
not be forgotten that the end of all moral effort is the production of a worthy type of personality, an inner life rich
and noble in content. It will never do to obscure this fact
by an undue emphasis upon the external conditions of civilization, important as these are. Without inner resources
those long accustomed to exhausting toil would find economic
emancipation a doubtful blessing. Nothing is more pathetic
than the use of unwonted leisure by the multitudes who
lack all taste for higher interests, unless it be the devices
of those among the rich who are wanting both in the traditions and in the personal possession of culture. With the
slow emancipation from the pressure of industrial need must
go hand in hand the process of education, both extensive
and intensive.

Much might be said of the necessity for social progress of a training which shall cultivate good taste and simplicity in the use of material resources. Without such taste and simplicity, there appears no limit to those desires for luxury and personal extravagance which are always anti-social. Indeed, with the present degree of inequality in the distribution of wealth maintained, it would be possible for production to be doubled, or even indefinitely multiplied, without yielding any substantial relief to the multitude, since the increased production might all be used to minister to the ever growing demands of the few for a multiplication of luxuries. The will to possess, unchastened and untrained, is insatiable. Of high social value is a restrained and tasteful use of wealth, which makes all material possessions subordinate to the life of the spirit. Such use presents a concrete example of what, ideally, should be the material equipment of all, an equipment ministering to the most perfect and beautiful living by lifting above sordid care and bondage to material things. Examples of such living are a continual blessing to mankind. It is a well-known fact that the standard of living which seems desirable to the masses is set by the few who are possessed of wealth. However long the distance which may separate the poor wage-earner from such a mode of life, it still forms the dream of what he would like to do, if wishes only passed as the current coin of exchange.

In concluding this brief study of the relations of individuals in society, it may be said that the institutions and legal arrangements, through which a more perfect adjustment of interests is to be realized, belong to the science of politics. This science is destined to undergo important changes, to become less an account of the mechanisms of administrative procedure, and far more an inquiry into the fundamental needs of human society. Government cannot be static. Its true logic must keep pace with the forces of life which move forward unceasingly, irresistibly. The present generation has proved the inadequacy of those methods of control that sufficed when the mutual interdependence of individuals was far less, and when means of communication, of travel, and of supply were far different. The inevitable result of this growth of relationship must be a corresponding growth, which no scruples can permanently check, of the extension of corporate control. The necessity for it lies in the changes already effected in the processes of daily life. If we substitute for paternalism the far more appropriate term, fraternalism, the prospect of tyranny does not seem menacing. Nor must we be misled by the view that a highly developed social order is artificial, whereas the ideal is found in some primitive mode of "life according to nature." The complex adjustments of the most advanced society of the future will be just as "natural" as the crude tribal adjustments of the savage, for they spring equally from the powers inherent in human nature, and answer equally to genuine needs.

Society is mankind, and mankind is living, creative energy, the most marvelous and fascinating force of which we have knowledge. The great minds of the past pictured the corporate life of humanity as finding embodiment at last in some ultimate ideal, some Utopia, or City of God. But we have learned that such a structure can never take final and unchanging form. It is always in the building, for its materials are not fixed and inert, like those of the architect, but are none other than pulsing, eager lives, which forever create, and forever re-fashion their own creations.

CHAPTER IX

DUTY AND CONSCIENCE

WE have found the end of conduct to be the realization of the richest possible system of values. This theory of conduct makes the idea of value the basal principle of ethics, the principle to which all others must ultimately be referred. The priority of the principle of value is, however, logical, not necessarily temporal. Other ideas may first win and hold the attention of the individual. The child associates morality with duty or law long before it clearly connects good and bad conduct with the idea of intrinsic worth, of that which has value in itself. But reflection is always forced back, sooner or later, to this most fundamental idea, which is, in fact, implicit in all moral experience from the very beginning.

I. DUTY DEPENDENT ON VALUE

Duty, then, derives all its strength and sacredness from the good. Value of some kind is inseparable from the very idea of duty. The specific duties, which are often presented in a table of duties, must necessarily be derived from specific goods. A system of duties could at best only reproduce, under a less fundamental concept, a system of values. The superior claim of one duty, as compared with another which may seem to compete with it, is found, by the same principle, in the superior value which it tends to realize. If the duty of cultivating rightness of heart, an inner devotion to what we deem highest and best, lays a stronger claim upon us than the duty of securing material goods, it is because this quality of character is of superior worth. While morality consists, in part, of the spirit with which acts are performed, it also includes the task of applying this spirit to valuable interests and activities. The devotion which duty demands cannot be blind, a fanatical or capricious surrender to any end that may chance to present itself; it must be a devotion to the true values of life. Any thoroughgoing study of morality, as we have seen, opens to inquiry the whole world of human worths. Popular thought does not always recognize the moral significance of all human interests, but this significance is acknowledged as soon as the issue appears in a concrete and vital form. Daily choices, struggles, and sacrifices are the expression of judgments of value, and these judgments of value may also be conscious judgments of obligation. To feel the value of any act is to admit it within the field of possible duties. Whenever, confronted by a real choice, I say of an act, "This is good," I say in effect that I ought to perform the act, unless some other, still more worthful, must thereby be left unperformed. The same principle applies even to material objects which serve the uses of life. To judge an object valuable for human use is implicitly to say that it ought to be secured, unless something still better must be sacrificed in obtaining it. Only on such an interpretation is it possible to give true moral significance to our daily and hourly business, and to prevent a fatal divorce between morality and life.

There is, to be sure, a wide-spread and comforting moral code which says: "Do not break the ten commandments, but for the rest use your time, strength, and means as you please. Whether one shall depend upon public conveyances or keep an automobile, eat a simple or a sumptuous dinner, dress in a more or less expensive way, strive to cultivate intellectual and æsthetic interests or rest content in a round of petty activities,—these and similar matters are in no sense moral questions. One's own pleasure, taste, or fancy may determine the choice. To place these acts in the category of morals would be to impose an intolerable burden upon conscience." So, at least, runs the theory of much popular thought and practice. We freely admit that it would be unwise to burden conscience with those details of conduct which, once decided, should be left to well-regulated habit, but there is no escape from the conclusion that all such questions are truly moral. Progress in morality consists, not in burdening conscience with the details of conduct, but in quickening a sense of responsibility for the use of time, money, and powers of body and mind. So quickened, conscience finds its task extended to the whole content of life.

Duty, then, we hold to be coextensive with the field of human values. It is true, however, that no coercive sense of obligation is commonly felt to realize those values which are the objects of natural desire. Regard for the beautiful, for example, is not ordinarily felt as a duty; the beautiful attracts and claims us by its own charm. Yet even here the spur of duty may sometimes be needed to secure to the æsthetic element its due place in the system of values. Certainly we should regard the absence of artistic creation and of its varied products as an immense loss to humanity. So essential is this element to man's higher life that it is a positive duty to labor for its cultivation wherever it is disregarded or lightly esteemed. In like manner the higher intellectual values are largely left to spontaneous interest. Knowledge grows from the desire for insight on the part of natures to whom the understanding of things is, in some way, an imperative need. And yet intellectual effort often requires to be quickened by the impelling force of duty, a force that can spring only from a conviction of the value of knowledge for the business of life. But if duty must sometimes reinforce natural desire for the realization of value, it is often called upon to limit and restrain desire. The physical appetites furnish a clear example of desires which commonly require, not the spur, but the rein, since these appetites have a powerful instinctive basis in our nature. This regulative function of duty, we must remember, extends on occasion to the whole conceivable system of values.[1]

II. CAN A MAN DO MORE THAN HIS DUTY?

But how far does obligation extend? Is it one's duty to realize all the values within one's power? Or may a man, by special effort, do more than his duty? May he, in the language of the church, perform works of supererogation, and thereby win special merit? If we affirm the first of these alternatives, as we are compelled to do, we must be prepared frankly to recognize that the same duties are not universally binding in all cases that may externally appear to be similar. For, although we can hold that it is always and everywhere the duty of men to be just and benevolent, it is clear that we should not say that it is the duty of every rich man to live with extreme frugality and to deny himself every luxury, that he may give his money to works of charity. We must recognize that the vocation of the individual and his special contribution to society are important factors in determining his specific duty. But when all the factors of the particular case are considered, if a man believes that such a course of self-denial is, for himself, in his circumstances, and with his nature and endowment, the best course, then the duty of this conduct for him would seem to be as clear as any moral obligation, no matter how unusual his action may be, or how little it could be required as a universal practice. Similarly, in a period of persecution, it may not be the duty of all who hold the views that are the object of attack to expose themselves to suffering in the cause of truth. But it may well be the duty of some persons to do so, and even to accept the rôle of martyr. When all the circumstances of particular

[1] Cf. Sidgwick, who defines duties as "those Right actions or abstinences for the adequate accomplishment of which a moral impulse is conceived to be at least occasionally necessary." *Method of Ethics*, p. 217.

cases are considered, therefore, we conclude that one cannot do more than one's duty.

This distinction between the spheres of duty and of meritorious action beyond the requirements of duty, represents the dual morality developed by the Roman church, which faced the difficult problem of adjusting the ethics of primitive Christianity to the tasks of existing civilization, and came quite naturally to recognize both a morality for the world of action, and the "counsels of perfection" for the cloister. Such a moral dualism, when taken seriously, always inclines on the one hand to an easy-going compromise with worldly standards, and on the other to an effort for an other-worldly perfection, which, trying to rise above existing morality, is in danger of falling far below it.

But the objections to the idea of doing more than duty requires go much deeper than is commonly recognized. It is questionable whether, from the point of view of enlightened morality, this conception of doing more than one's duty is not self-contradictory. In a world where so much needs to be done, and where the resources of time, strength, and means are so inadequate, it seems certain that an undue devotion in one direction must inevitably result in neglect in another, and that he who in some relation has done "more than his duty," will, in truth, be found not even to have done his whole duty.

There is an opposing conception of duty which is equally untenable, the idea that one's duty never is, and never can be, done; that at the end of life it stands like an unsatisfied creditor still demanding more. This view, which is essentially Kantian, has sometimes been made the basis of an argument for immortality. Duty, it is said, is "inherently endless," therefore the moral self is so.[1] But this statement is a complete inversion of the actual relationship. Duty is a function of life, life not a function of duty. Even though

[1] Cf. Calkins, *The Persistent Problems of Philosophy*, p. 455.

we freely admit that the best of men are, in the light of an ideal morality, but unprofitable servants, we are not justified in regarding duty as real beyond the specific and concrete life-needs that give it birth. Duty, appearing after life has begun its course, always exists for the sake of life. If the life of conscious experience is endless, duty is doubtless also endless. But we cannot reverse the order, and, asserting the endless existence of duty, deduce therefrom the endless existence of personal beings.

Our interpretation of the nature of duty, which relates it throughout to the field of values, enables one to bring all the business of life within the sphere of morality, and also to account for the widely varying content of duty in the course of historical development. This variety is the result of different needs and satisfactions, which produce in their turn different standards of value. In the development of social life new needs, physical and spiritual, have been felt, and new forms of activity have been required to satisfy them. Concurrently with the appreciation of new values, new duties have been recognized. If we could fix the point in any civilization at which the systematic pursuit of science and art was recognized as worthful for human life, we should discover the precise point at which the good citizen and parent began to feel the duty of providing an education rich enough to include these elements. The decadence of any form of duty depends upon the same principle. The value which was its necessary support ceases to be recognized as a value; what was a good is no longer so esteemed. The period at which, among any people, polygamy or slavery came to lose its character as a natural and beneficent institution, and to be looked upon as productive of evil, marks inevitably the decadence of one set of duties and the emergence of another. By the inherent logic of action our world of worths becomes our world of duties.

III. Theories of Conscience: Intuitionalism and Empiricism

Thus far we have considered only the teleology of duty, its meaning in relation to an end of value. The account may seem to have assumed a degree of harmony, not found in actual experience, between what is morally good and what we spontaneously desire. Although the morally good act must be thought of as that which, to a reasonable being, is the most satisfying—more satisfying than any alternative act possible under the existing conditions—it is still true that we have numberless desires which, temporarily at least, call for their own gratification, but which are in conflict with the completest and most enduring satisfaction. Certainly immediate inclination does not always prompt us to do what we recognize to be our duty. Hence the significance of duty as a coercive feeling, an imperative within us demanding that we shall do, or refrain from doing, certain acts. The question of the nature of this feeling of duty and its accompanying sentiments, of what, in other words, we commonly call conscience, has been in the past a much debated point in ethical theory. We shall attempt an outline of the main controversy concerning the nature of conscience. The account, however, will be brief because its interest is now so largely historical. The growth of knowledge in several departments of science, especially in biology, anthropology, and psychology, has led to an increasing unanimity of opinion on all the main issues involved.

Is man endowed with a native and inexplicable power of discerning right and wrong to serve as his guide in matters of conduct, or are his moral judgments and emotions explicable by reference to his total environment and education? Two leading theories, corresponding in general to these alternatives, have disputed the field. The one is the intuitional, the other the empirical, or historical, theory of conscience. The question at issue is, how do we form our standards of duty, how do we reach our judgments of right and wrong?

Intuitionalism, as commonly held, has maintained that men possess an innate and immediate insight with regard to the rightness and wrongness of acts. To discover the moral quality of a deed one needs, according to this view, only to look at the deed itself in its own nature, and without regard to its consequences. Certain acts are directly recognized to be universally and unconditionally right; others are seen to be universally and unconditionally wrong. Falsehood, for example, is known to be wrong, not from its incompatibility with social well-being, but from its own inherent nature. Honesty is seen to be right in itself, and not because of its beneficent economic and social results. It has further been held by thorough-going intuitionalists that moral insights have not been developed by education or long social experience, but have always been more or less clearly present as necessary constituents of human consciousness. The doctrine has been held in such a variety of forms that a general statement can scarcely do justice to them all. Some intuitionalists have implied that the moral quality of each particular act is immediately known, while others have held that we possess intuitive knowledge of the nature of general classes of acts only, and that reflection is needed to bring the particular act under the general rule.[1] In the latter view, although justice is immediately and universally known to be right, it might not at once be clear, in a case of conflicting property claims, what particular act would fulfill the conditions of justice. To discover this, a detailed examination of the facts in question and of the probable consequences might be necessary.

Still another difference among the intuitionalists concerns the psychological nature of an act of conscience. Some represent it as a self-evident truth of reason, others as an im-

[1] See, for example, Calderwood, *Handbook of Moral Philosophy*, p. 47.

mediate emotion or expression of taste, and still others as a
direct perception of moral values, not unlike any act of sense
perception.[1] The first of these views, that of rationalistic
intuitionalism, has been held by a large number of thinkers
who have given to the doctrine of intuitionalism what may be
called its classical form.[2] They all agree in making moral
judgments necessary and self-evident truths of reason.
According to the second interpretation, conscience utters
itself in certain emotions of approval and disapproval. Just
as we have an æsthetic taste, and approve or disapprove of a
work of art, so we have a sense of the good and evil in conduct. To this view belong the "moral sense" of Shaftesbury and Hutcheson, and the "moral taste" of Hume, who
distinguishes sharply between the function of reason and of
"taste"; the former, he says, "conveys the knowledge of
truth and falsehood," the latter, "the sentiment of beauty
and deformity, vice and virtue."[3] Martineau is the chief
modern representative of the theory that moral judgments
are a matter of direct perception. His theory is distinctive enough to merit a brief statement. All human beings,
according to Martineau, have an immediate perception of
the relative rank, or worth, of opposing impulses. When
"incompatible impulses" appear and struggle for mastery
over us, we are aware of the contrast between them. One
we see to be "higher or worthier than the other," and hence
to have "a clear right to us." This judgment, which assigns the superiority to one impulse over another, is not
"mediate," discovered by a chain of reasoning, but is an
"immediate revelation inseparable from their appearance
side by side." The moral valuation of the opposing impulses
is even instantaneous, decided "by a glance at the face of the

---

[1] Cf. Thilly, *Introduction to Ethics*, pp. 28-47.

[2] Cf. among other English moralists, Cudworth, Clarke, Price, Reid, and Calderwood.

[3] *Inquiry*, section 1.

alternatives," when they make their appearance. Conscience, Martineau defines as "this knowledge with myself of the better and the worse." [1]

It will avoid confusion to remember that the term intuition is sometimes applied to certain immediate, axiomatic judgments upon which ethical thought ultimately rests. This meaning is not to be confounded with the intuitionalism which claims that mankind is equipped with intuitions for the decision of the detailed problems of conduct. We have already pointed out that value, although describable in various ways as an immediate experience, is an ultimate term of ethical thought. And we hold that there is at least one intuitive, or immediate and axiomatic, judgment concerning it, which may be expressed as follows: "The good is worthy to be chosen." [2] No proof of this proposition can be given; it can only be stated in other words, as when we say that we are so constituted as to prefer good to ill. It is not the business of ethics to ask why man's original nature is as it is. The *what* and the *how*, not the *why*, are here significant.

It can be maintained, I think, that the axioms of Sidgwick to the effect that the greater good is always to be preferred to the lesser, and that the good of one man ought always to be treated as of equal importance with the like good of another, are deductions from the primary axiom given above. For if the good, as such, is worthy of choice, then to choose the lesser good, in any real alternative, is to choose something else than the good. And the same is true of the preference of the lesser good of one man to the greater good of another.

---

[1] *Types of Ethical Theory*, Vol. II, pp. 40–45. In criticism see Sidgwick, *Methods of Ethics*, pp. 367–372; and Sharp, *American Journal of Psychology*, 1898, p. 198. The article of Professor Sharp is an interesting attempt to refute intuitionalism by appeal to empirical evidence.

[2] This is, as I remember, a formula which I heard from my revered friend and teacher, Dr. E. Benjamin Andrews.

In the empirical, or historical, theory of conscience the sense of duty, with all its attendant elements, is held to be the product of experience on the part of the individual and the race, and to be explicable by the social-historical environment. Only in this way, it is believed, can the vast differences in the utterances of conscience be satisfactorily explained. Like intuitionalism, empiricism has been of various types. In its cruder form it has attempted to explain conscience as the result of individual interest under the control of the "two sovereign masters, pain and pleasure." [1] In its later and more adequate forms the theory has taken account of various instinctive tendencies, especially the social and sympathetic impulses, and the theory of evolution has been applied to show how these operate in the long course of racial development. [2]

Spencer's account of the origin and development of conscience is of recognized importance, and offers an interesting suggestion of a reconciliation of intuitional and empirical views. The essential feature in our moral consciousness he considers to be "the control of some feeling or feelings by some other feeling or feelings." It is, in brief, the control of those feelings which relate to more special and immediate gratifications by those which relate to more distant and general forms of good. "The simpler and less ideal feelings are consciously over-ruled by the more complex and ideal feelings." [3]

Three kinds of "control," the political, the religious, and

---

[1] This is the view of Hobbes, Paley, and Bentham, as well as of the French materialists. Hartley and James Mill introduce the principle of association of ideas to explain cases of apparent disregard of pleasure.

[2] See Darwin, *Descent of Man*, Chap. IV; also the development of Darwin's view by Sutherland, *The Origin and Growth of the Moral Instinct*, Vol. I.

[3] Compare with this statement the results reached by Henry Rutgers Marshall, who formulates the rule of morality as follows: "Act to restrain the impulses which demand immediate reaction, in order that the impulse order determined by the existence of impulses of less strength, but of wider significance, may have full weight in the guidance of your life." *Instinct and Reason*, p. 569.

the social, operate to check the gratification of immediate desires, and to secure the triumph of greater but more distant interests. These restraints work through the motive of fear—"fear of the visible ruler, of the invisible ruler, and of society at large." But these controls are not properly moral, for they are all external, restraining by extrinsic effects, not by those which flow from the nature of the deed itself. Moral control, on the contrary, operates by arousing thought of those natural consequences of acts which no external power can impose or can avert. In Spencer's own words: "The truly moral deterrent from murder, is not constituted by a representation of hanging as a consequence, or by a representation of tortures in hell as a consequence, or by a representation of the horror and hatred excited in fellow men; but by a representation of the necessary natural results—the infliction of death agony on the victim, the destruction of all his possibilities of happiness, the entailed sufferings to his belongings. Neither the thought of imprisonment, nor of divine anger, nor of social disgrace, is that which constitutes the moral check on theft; but the thought of injury to the person robbed, joined with a vague consciousness of the general evils caused by disregard of proprietary rights." [1] The feeling of obligation, Spencer explains as "an abstract sentiment generated in a manner analogous to that in which abstract ideas are generated." Through "accumulated experiences," the feeling is developed in consciousness that it is safer to be guided by feelings which represent remote consequences than by those which demand immediate gratification. The element of coerciveness in the feeling of obligation has been transferred by association from the dread inspired by the external sanctions, and finally becomes linked with the instrinsic effects as "a vague sense of moral compulsion." But with the clear emergence of the moral motive from those motives which have wrought in its origin

[1] *The Data of Ethics*, p. 120.

and development, the sense of duty as a "coercive feeling of ought" will cease to exist, and right conduct become spontaneous, a point of view also developed by other evolutionists.[1]

Spencer invokes his theory of heredity in explanation of the development of conscience. Experiences accumulated during the long life of the race become, according to his interpretation, the innate possession of the individual, who is thereby master of a moral capital which he could never win in his own brief life. The genesis of fundamental moral intuitions is thus described in his well-known letter to Mill: "Just in the same way that I believe the intuition of space, possessed by any living individual, to have arisen from organized and consolidated experiences of all antecedent individuals who bequeathed to him their slowly-developed nervous organizations—just as I believe that this intuition, requiring only to be made definite and complete by personal experiences, has practically become a form of thought, apparently quite independent of experience; so do I believe that the experiences of utility organized and consolidated through all past generations of the human race, have been producing corresponding nervous modifications, which, by continued transmission and accumulation, have become in us certain faculties of moral intuition—certain emotions responding to right and wrong conduct, which have no apparent basis in the individual experiences of utility."[2]

IV. Criticism of Intuitionalism

When we examine the two theories, the intuitionalistic and the historical, in order to discover their true place in a theory of conscience, it is at once clear that the various forms

[1] Cf. Guyau, *Morale Sans Obligation ni Sanction;* see also the discussion of Fouillée, *La Morale des Idées-Forces*, pp. 192 ff.

[2] *The Data of Ethics*, p. 123, note. For the full account of the genesis of the feeling of coercion see *The Data of Ethics*, Chap. VII.

of intuitionalism are open to serious objections. Perhaps the most obvious of these is found in the history of morality. Instead of the universal agreement in matters of conduct which is implied by the theory, the greatest diversity is seen to exist among different peoples. Ethnological investigations have shown that there are not even a few practices which have been everywhere accepted, that indeed no single maxim can be discovered to which there are not exceptions fatal to the claims of intuitionalism. Murder, unchastity, falsehood, revenge, and cruelty are found, not only uncondemned, but even approved. We cannot say that these deeds are known to be wrong, and are done with a bad conscience. If, to save the theory, we say that the principles are universally recognized, but that the diversity of standards is due to mistakes in applying them, the futility of appealing to intuitions as guides in conduct becomes evident. For if two persons, possessed of a common moral intuition, reach diametrically opposite judgments upon the same act, the intuition itself is clearly no criterion of right and wrong.

Even if the facts were other than they are, and it could be shown that there are universally accepted principles of conduct, intuitionalism would not thereby be established, since the universality would be susceptible of a different explanation. It might be shown that the universal rules were the necessary conditions of social welfare, and that the individual recognized them, not immediately or intuitively, but as the result of his experience in society. That such broad features of agreement as may be admitted to exist in moral standards are to be explained in this way, finds striking proof in a well-known fact of morality among primitive peoples. The tribal conscience, which disapproves of murder, theft, lying, etc., within the tribe, approves of the same acts when committed against aliens. Such a conscience is clearly not an intuitive judgment of universal or unconditional morality. The virtues which it enjoins within the tribe are precisely those

which condition its welfare and even its existence. Murder
and theft committed against members of other tribes are
virtues to this conscience, because these deeds help to ensure
the tribal existence in a state of things in which *bellum om-
nium contra omnes* expresses exactly the inter-tribal relations;
in this state, not to devour another is to be devoured oneself.
All the crude but effective mechanism of tribal education
is brought to bear in impressing upon the individual a reverence for these practices.

A similar explanation may be offered of certain facts
which often lend support to popular intuitionalism. The
facts are undeniable, but they may be very differently explained. There is no doubt, for instance, that in every community there are some moral judgments so widely recognized
and so steadily enforced that they have the appearance of
immediacy and complete universality. To a well-trained
child of ten or twelve years, truth-speaking and honesty
appear to be immediate and self-evident rules of conduct.
But the conclusion of intuitionalism does not necessarily
follow from these facts.[1] The judgments in question may be
the result of constant education, the "precept upon precept,"
and " line upon line" of early training. And there is little
doubt that the child who unhesitatingly obeys these rules
might have been so perversely trained from infancy as to
look with genuine approval upon the opposite modes of
conduct. This plastic character of conscience is shown
by the ease with which a person may be led to accept
an irrational content as readily as one that serves the
true ends of life. The most emphatic utterances of conscience in the child may, by the force of training, be connected with purely arbitrary and artificial principles. It

[1] Sidgwick thus enumerates some of the sources from which the illusion of moral
intuitions may arise: " . . . blind impulses to certain kinds of action or vague sentiments of preference for them, or conclusions from rapid and half unconscious
processes of reasoning, or current opinions to which familiarity has given an
illusory air of self-evidence." *Methods of Ethics*, p. 212.

would be possible to train a child to feel that it was quite as wrong to eat cherries, or to step on the threshold of the door when entering a room, as to lie or steal. The condition of success in such training would be a steady and united effort, on the part of all those who had to do with the child, to inspire it with a sense of the awful character of these acts. Let us suppose that tempting cherries were grown, but were never eaten by older people, and that cherry-eating were always spoken of as a most immoral act; and let us also suppose that when the budding intelligence demanded a reason for the fact, it were given a mythical but specious answer, as, for example, that the birds carried the cherries to the man in the moon, who was very angry if any of his cherries were eaten by others, and would consequently not give any light at night. Further, let all known cases of cherry-eating be severely punished, and the absence of light on dark nights studiously ascribed to these wicked deeds. The child of six or eight years who had eaten but a single cherry would feel a sense of moral guilt greater than if he had told a cowardly lie or had shown the most selfish and spiteful ill-will towards a playmate. At what age the child would escape from the bondage of such an idea, and whether it would ever wholly escape from it, would depend upon its intelligence, and the fortunes of its education and social environment in later years. Certainly, if the taboo were gravely maintained in good society, the eating of cherries would long remain an act with a fringe of unpleasant consciousness even for the person who had independently reached the firm conviction that the practice was harmless. Doubtless, too, in a society subject to the cherry-eating taboo there would be found moral philosophers who would gravely explain the belief as an intuition of universal and unconditional morality.[1]

[1] This hypothetical case of the perversion of conscience is no exaggeration; it is paralleled by numberless instances known to every student of ethnology. A single example may be cited from practices current among the natives of Western Australia.

The moral experience of the mature individual also seems to be in conflict with the intuitional theory. There are probably few persons who do not at times find themselves in serious perplexity as to what is morally right. Not only do different persons differ in their solution of the same moral problem, but the same person often reaches a different solution at different times, and in each case with full conviction of the rectitude of his choice. This perplexity does not consist, as some intuitionalists maintain, in the difficulty of discovering the relation of a particular act to a general rule; it often concerns a conflict of two principles, both of which are undeniably clear and obligatory in common practice. The difficulty is not to determine what particular act breaks the rule, "Thou shalt not lie," "Thou shalt not kill," "Thou shalt not steal," or "Thou shalt not injure thy neighbor." Sometimes under the pressure of exceptional conditions, for which one is in no degree responsible, one is called upon to decide between these alternatives. Should one utter a deliberate falsehood, or expose human life to grave danger? [1] Should one steal, or allow one's family to suffer, perhaps even to perish? The existence of such an issue, even in a single case, is fatal to the ultimacy of the so-called intuitions. The perplexity implies a principle, more ultimate than the

"Les Australiens attribuent la mort des leurs à un maléfice jeté par quelque tribu voisine; aussi considèrent-ils comme une obligation sacrée de venger la mort de tout parent en allant tuer un membre des tribus voisines. Le docteur Laudor, magistrat dans l'Australie occidentale, raconte qu'un indigène employé dans sa ferme perdit une de ses femmes à la suite d'une maladie; il annonça au docteur son intention de partir en voyage afin d'aller tuer une femme dans une tribu éloignée. 'Je lui répondis que, s'il commettait cet acte, je le mettrais en prison pour toute sa vie.' Il ne partit donc pas, et resta dans la ferme. Mais de mois en mois il dépérissait: le remords le rongeait; il ne pouvait manger ni dormir; l'esprit de sa femme le hantait, lui reprochait sa négligence. Un jour il disparut; au bout d'une année il revint en parfaite santé: il avait rempli son devoir."

Guyau, *Esquisse d'une Morale sans Obligation ni Sanction*, p. 55.

[1] Cf. the case of the Zürich theater manager who, in case of fire, gave a false reason for the suspension of the play, and cleared the theater without injury to anyone, when the real reason would almost certainly have produced a panic and fearful loss of life.

commonly accepted rule, by reference to which the problem
must be solved.[1]

V. THE HISTORICAL VIEW

If the explanation of conscience offered by intuitionalism
must be rejected, are we to suppose that the social environment is the sole factor, and that the individual mind brings
nothing with it, but comes in "utter nakedness" into the
world of moral relations? By no means. A crude empiricism is as untenable as intuitionalism. It is a trite saying that
the mind furnishes at least the indispensable condition of
morality, the capacity for developing moral ideas and sentiments. But this capacity must be regarded as something
quite different from a colorless receptivity, or registering of
stimuli and impressions received from the environment. The
mind is, on the contrary, charged congenitally with numerous
instincts which are sure, on occasion of the appropriate
stimulus, to manifest themselves in definite types of action.
Some of these, like the sexual and artistic instincts, are, in
the language of biology, deferred instincts, in that their
manifestation must longer await the development of the
bodily and mental powers. We must recognize that an instinctive appetite, or impulse, underlies all the various activities which yield our experiences of value.[2] Familiar
examples of instincts profoundly significant for the moral
life are found in love, sympathy, fear, and anger, as also
in the instinct for play, or for intellectual and æsthetic activity. Even religion is in this sense instinctive, for stimuli
from the surrounding forces of nature tend to produce in
the mind of primitive man certain specific manifestations of
dependence, fear, and worship. Of especial importance for

[1] See Chap. II, pp. 51–53.

[2] It is a popular error to assume a fixed form for certain instinctive reactions which
are capable of great variety of expression. Militarism often assumes an instinct
for war, as such, and asserts its perpetuity as a necessity of human nature. As well
talk of an unchanging instinct for settling disputes by personal combat, an instinct
for slave-holding, or for religious persecution!

the moral life are the social and sympathetic instincts, which are the basis of all altruistic conduct, and which are seen to be strong even in animal life. The full significance of the development of morality, in and through a social order objective to the individual, may be insisted upon, while at the same time we recognize the part played by the instinctive and impulsive elements of human nature. Without these factors inherent in the mind, the evolution of morality would be wholly inexplicable.

And further, however much we may view the conditions of social life and well-being as primarily external to the individual, these very conditions themselves, with all the modes of action to which they give rise, are the direct product of human nature. In this sense, all moral ideas have their origin in the human spirit, not in a source foreign to it. We are not to think of the individual as alien to society, but as possessing the very instincts, emotions, and ideas, whose play constitutes the entire drama of moral life in the history of the race.

The modification of the instinctive activities which underlie and condition moral conduct is the work of social forces. Moral progress is due far less to any change in the primary instincts than to the social control of their various expressions. It is probable that an exceedingly slow modification of nervous structure, with an accompanying change of moral susceptibilities, may attend the process of civilization. But it is clear that we must appeal to quite a different principle for the explanation of moral progress. It is mainly through the forces of organized society, through political, religious, and educational institutions, through literature, art, and science, that we become possessors of the wisdom slowly won by the race in its long moral experience. It is to this kind of inheritance, made effective through all the channels of education, rather than to an essential modification of human nature, that one must look for an explanation of

changes in the moral order. The child of the most highly
civilized parents, if reared from early infancy among savages, would, we may be sure, be able to play the rôle of the
savage with very considerable success.

If we regard consciousness as continuous in development—
and this hypothesis has a decided balance of evidence in its
favor—there was a point at which the germinal morality
of animal life passed into the conscious morality of the human species. If it is not possible to fix the exact point of this
transition, it is at least clear that the beginnings of historical
morality are connected with tribal customs. These customs
are the ways by which the tribe, more or less consciously,
seeks to preserve its common life, just as, at a lower stage,
the instinctive habits of gregarious animals are the ways by
which the species secures its preservation. Human morality
must have made its appearance in the transition from purely
instinctive habit to conscious custom. Primitive custom is
of course still largely instinctive and unconscious. But it
implies states of consciousness in which a better and a worse
are recognized, and it also implies the capacity so to reproduce these contrasted states in memory and imagination
as to make them the objects of future effort.

Before early custom could harden into any kind of code,
there must have been present the pressure of leadership
sufficiently strong to make its will authoritatively felt.
Physical prowess and mental sagacity would be the prime
conditions of such leadership. With increase in the size
and importance of the tribe would come of necessity the
crude beginnings of organized government, since only by
some kind of mechanism could tribal unity be effectively
maintained. Keeping pace with this development, there is
a growth in the force of social opinion as an expectation on
the part of one's fellows that one shall do, or shall refrain
from doing, certain acts.[1] He who disappoints this expec-

[1] Cf. Taylor, *The Problem of Conduct*, p. 140.

tation must reckon with disapproval, whereas he who fully satisfies it, or goes beyond its demands, will enjoy praise and popular favor. The tribesman who by cowardice has exposed others to danger, or who by selfish indulgence has deprived his fellows of what they regard as their portion of the common store, will become the object of general suspicion and dislike; he who, on the contrary, is courageous and self-denying will as surely win confidence and affection.

Added to these two factors of control—government and social expectation—is the force of religious belief. This is a powerful support of tribal customs, since it brings to bear the entire power of supernatural hopes and fears, which exercise such a strong influence upon primitive peoples. The tribal deities are also, it must be remembered, completely identified with the interests of the tribe; they demand of their worshippers what the tribal consciousness demands of its members. He who disregards established rights, or breaks faith with his fellows, is consigned to punishment in the nether world.

The factors just mentioned constitute the well-known "external sanctions" of morality. They have been criticized as operating only by force, and leaving the proper sense of obligation quite untouched. They would beget at most, it is said, a sense of "must," not of "ought." This criticism would be valid if we were to suppose, as it is quite impossible to do, that no sympathetic instincts were enlisted in behalf of the requirements, and that there was no belief on the part of those who feel their pressure that the rules to which obedience is required tend more or less directly to secure certain valuable ends. It is, however, such sympathy and conviction which save conduct from being merely an expression of "I must," and make it in part an expression of the judgment, "I ought." On the other hand, the beginnings of morality, both in the individual and in the race, are without question largely prudential. The "must" is, for long, quite as powerful as the " ought ". Prudential morality is the necessary school of a higher form of conduct, and is by no means to be despised or lightly esteemed.

We hold, then, that the development of conscience is not to be explained from one side alone. It is not wholly found in the external environment, nor is it present in the mind as a predetermined form, waiting only to be summoned into consciousness by the stimuli from without. It is not necessarily connected with a particular mode of conduct, but is fluid, capable of assuming a great variety of forms and expressing a widely diversified content, according to the nature of the training offered by the social environment. The conscience that, rightly trained, enforces the sound rules of truth-speaking and universal sympathy, may be so perverted as to approve deceit and national, religious, or class hatred. It may also be so darkened as to give its sanction to foolish scruples and hurtful practices. Although authority alone, apart from the growing consciousness of needs and values, could never produce the sense of obligation, the various forms of control, working upon a growing consciousness, have been a powerful factor in its genesis. The development of conscience does not, as is sometimes assumed, offer a unique difficulty, different in kind from that found in the development of other conscious powers of man. The problems of intellectual, æsthetic, and religious development are, each in its way, of similar range and seriousness. All these are but functions of the one growing intelligence operating in different spheres of interest. There is, I believe, no sufficient ground for the statement, so often made, that the moral cannot possibly have arisen out of the non-moral, that is, from natural instincts and impulses modified by intelligence. Logically this would commit one to the denial of anything new in the historical life of man. There is a sense, of course, in which all that ever appears is preëxistent in the realm of being. But why deny that the combination of existing elements may yield that which has never before appeared in actuality? The denial in question has doubtless been made in the supposed interests of the dignity of our moral nature, but it robs that nature of the higher dignity of the capacity for growth and for ceaseless readjustment to the needs of life.

The authority of morality is no whit impaired by accepting the historical interpretation of conscience. A knowledge of its origin and growth no more detracts from its value than the knowledge of the physiological origin of any bodily organ lessens the value of its function in the organism. The human eye is none the less precious for use when it is regarded as having developed from something which was originally not an eye at all, than under the old view that it was manufactured at a given moment of time. Language is of no less value when regarded as a product of slow natural growth than when viewed as a ready-made, heaven-sent means of communication. Morality, historically viewed, possesses all the authority which the interests of human life can give it, and greater authority than this no conceivable system of morality can possess. The moral imperative still holds, only it is not an unconditional imperative, sundered from the consequences of obedience and disobedience. Its sanctions are simply one with the total consequences of conduct. The principles of morality, considered as an historical development, come to us charged with the hard-won results of human experience. In them there speaks to us the accumulated wisdom, not only of our forefathers, but of ages and nations, long since past, with which our own life stands in relation through the unbroken chain of historical development. Moral ideals represent that for the lack of which the many have suffered, and for the winning of which the noblest have sacrificed. Such a view leaves the conscience free for needed changes. No considerations external to human life itself can fetter morality; the real interests of life must determine the modification of existing codes and ideals.

Far more clear than the beginnings of conscience in the race is the process by which, in each successive generation, the conscience of the individual receives its particular form and content, its concrete view of right and wrong; for this process is repeated at length in the education of every child, and is continually open to observation. From the beginning of life, tones, looks, and gestures of approval and disapproval, affect the plastic organism, and tend to reproduce themselves by imitation in the conduct of the child. All the language of the nursery, its rhymes and stories as well as its childish games, are charged with direct moral suggestion. Pleasure and pain following acts, either as the natural consequences of the acts themselves, or as imposed by parents or nurse, strengthen the inclination for some modes of conduct and the disinclination for others. The pain of burnt fingers that results from disregard of a warning or command, the suffering endured in punishment for disobedience, and the pleasure of reward for ready and cheerful obedience, are familiar examples of those external sanctions which attend the prudential stage of morality in the life of every child. Sympathy and love for others soon lend the weight of their influence in favor of those modes of action which find social approval. With growing intelligence the child perceives the value of acts in relation to ends. It then begins the life-long task of self-discipline, subordinating the impulses that call for immediate gratification to those wider and more permanent interests, the satisfactions from which may be long deferred. The process of education, begun in the home, is continued in school and in society. Religious teaching adds its sentiment in favor of the existing code. It is no wonder, then, that certain principles like truth-speaking, honesty, and chastity, often seem immediate judgments of right and wrong, inherent in the mind. Through the long process of education they have become a part of the self. All rules of conduct thus impressed gain such a hold on the individual that when he comes to examine for himself the questions of conduct, it is extremely difficult to escape from the spell of early training, even though an enlightened conscience demands certain modifications of the accepted régime. Almost everyone is familiar with the experience of uneasiness that attends the doing of acts contrary to early training, even though one is fully convinced that they are right, nay, even though one believes them to be obligatory. In some natures the struggle between early teaching and mature conviction is almost tragic in its intensity.

VI. The Authority of Conscience

It is often asked: "What is the authority of conscience, and how far may its utterances be trusted?" Before this question can be clearly answered, it is necessary to consider more exactly the psychological nature of conscience. The term conscience is commonly applied to a complex of mental states closely linked together in moral experience. So understood, conscience includes (1) a cognitive, or intellectual, element, (2) an emotional, and (3) a conative, or volitional, element. These three elements are not to be thought of as successive, following each other in consciousness as they follow in order of enumeration; the unitary moral experience rather contains them all as constituents. Any so-called act of conscience clearly involves the intellectual element, the perception of a moral issue and a judgment concerning it. We are compelled, let us say, to choose between a selfish deed and one which involves denial of private desires, but secures the welfare of several other persons. We think of these two acts, with their probable consequences, and pronounce one to be right and the other wrong. We say, "I ought to do this," "I ought not to do that." But this judgment is not a cold intellectual process. If it were, the distinctive sense of personal obligation would hardly be present in the form in which we experience it, since we may pronounce a similar judgment of right and wrong in the case of others, or as a matter of purely speculative interest, and feel no obligation of personal action. From the first, however, each of the alternative acts is colored by various sentiments and emotions. On the one side is the desire for personal gratification, for the delights of ease or enjoyment which promise to follow the self-regarding act. On the other are sympathetic feelings and the sense of approbation which we experience when we triumph over an egoistic, anti-social impulse. Both deeds have further, as we contemplate them, a deep background of emotional coloring, derived from all our past experiences and associations, extending far back into childhood, and, it may be, linked with hereditary forces that antedate the conscious life of the individual. But these mental states, just described, also imply an impulsive, conative element, a will to do or to refrain from doing. Indeed, to think and to feel about an act always and inevitably involves an inclination to do, or refrain from doing, the act, according to the nature of the thoughts and emotions in play. Such thinking and feeling would always issue in action were they not inhibited by opposing ideas and feelings. While usage tends to limit conscience to cognitive and emotional elements, it is important, not only for theoretical but also for practical reasons, to realize that volition is nothing independent of the other elements, but is determined by them. Those things which habitually command our thoughts and emotions become necessarily the objects of our choice.

Conscience, then, is not to be regarded as a separate faculty for the decision of moral questions. The "moral faculty" has gone the way of the other so-called faculties of the older psychology. They are no longer recognized, save as powers and processes of the one psychical life to which all conscious activities belong. The distinction between moral and other judgments lies in the objects or relations to which they are applied, not in the mental power exercised. When an act is judged to be right or wrong, the same mental power is called into play which, on other occasions, yields an economic, æsthetic, or religious judgment.

The kind and degree of guidance given by conscience now become clear. Obviously there can be no thought of conscience as an infallible guide. Its decisions possess the same degree of validity as belongs to other human judgments. My conscience is no more, and no less, fallible than my judgment of the values of life. Through the long course of history mistaken and perverted moral judgments have been honestly pronounced and faithfully obeyed, just as all kinds of grotesque æsthetic ideals and false scientific views have been seriously maintained. If a judgment concerning any matter of conduct is said to be final, this can only mean that no ground for a change of opinion will ever be discovered. Doubtless there are many moral decisions of which this statement is true. On the other hand, one cannot exclude the possibility of new light on the more complex problems of conduct; to do so is to put oneself beyond the reach of instruction. But the possibility that one may in the future gain further insight, and so change one's judgment of certain acts, cannot lessen the imperativeness of the claim of a present duty. One must act with the light one has.

The conscience of the day and hour is the best, indeed the only, guide we have. To abandon one's best judgment in favor of any external authority or internal impulse is to abandon the moral task. To trust blindly to external authority would be to revert to a stage of irresponsible tutelage; to surrender the control of conduct to mere impulse or caprice would result in moral anarchy. It is better to follow even a wrong judgment than to fail in loyalty to one's conviction. For the individual, therefore, at any given moment, conscience, though not infallible, is always authoritative. In this sense there is an absolute obligation in a relative and changing moral order.

VII. THE SOCIAL CONSCIENCE

We have seen that society furnishes the materials from which the individual mind constructs the moral ideal. At first the ideals of the social order are accepted uncritically, but gradually the individual conscience is more or less differentiated from the social conscience. The unique in the individual now voices itself. Tradition is questioned, criticized, and at certain points rejected as inadequate or wrong. The individual may now demand of himself acts which are more or less divergent from the social conscience; his conscience is at some points more exacting, at others less so. The rules of conduct are self-imposed in obedience to personal conviction. A richer and more varied life results from such assertion of the individual conscience. It is true, however, that although the individual conscience is essential to progress, there is no guarantee that it may not sometimes be powerful for evil as well as for good. The fanatic may champion views which, though honestly held, are opposed to social welfare.

This possibility of a conscientious choice of evil raises a problem which will be more fully considered in the next chapter. Here it may be remarked that such a possibility, once clearly discerned, enforces the duty of consulting all possible sources of light, and of keeping the mind open for new guidance. It also suggests the value to the individual of the social conscience, the conscience of one's day and race, as a corrective of the mistakes and vagaries of the individual conscience. This social conscience, which represents, in Burke's words, "the bank and capital of nations and of ages," gains especial significance when it is considered, not as a factor foreign to human nature, and imposed upon it from without, but as strictly organic to the needs of life, a necessary mode of its development. The social conscience offers a valuable counterweight both to the extravagant demands and to the dangerous omissions of the individual conscience, yielding a guidance in problems of conduct which no thoughtful person will neglect.

True, one may press too far the validity of existing standards, and fail to do justice to the conscience of the individual in its demands for a new and better order. One of the indispensable conditions of progress is that the reforming conscience shall make itself heard, and shall slowly modify the existing social conscience. In a much quoted passage, Mr. Bradley has gone so far as to make the desire to be better than one's fellows the beginning of immorality, unless it be in the case of a "heaven-born prophet." [1] Few care to profess the rôle of "heaven-born prophet;" but if there is not to be virtual stagnation, there must be many who are agreed in the desire to do better, at least in some particulars, than the majority of their fellows. There are, further, weighty reasons why acquiescence in the traditional order is not to be crowned as the highest virtue. Such acquiescence is, as a rule, only too easy. Almost every material and social advantage is on its side. There are few who do not find their immediate path made much easier by accepting without criticism the *status quo*. The young man who desires to enter upon a political career will usually find the difficulties of the initial steps wonderfully lightened if he is an uncritical advocate of party men and party measures. The aspirant for high position in the church will often advance most rapidly if he is known to be "sound" in his views, a man without doubts, who feels no need of theological reconstruction or ecclesiastical reform. The same is true of the servants of many corporations; unquestioning acceptance of "business methods" is a quality that, in many cases, has a high cash value. To material advantage is

[1] *Ethical Studies*, pp. 180–181.

also linked the tremendous force of intellectual and moral inertia. Not infrequently, therefore, the lower, not the nobler, impulses are leagued with the spirit of acquiescence. Traditional and prescriptive rights, even when they have ceased to be moral rights, always have the advantage of being so strongly intrenched as to make assault upon them difficult, if not dangerous.

The superior advantage on the side of the existing order tends to prevent rash changes and to preserve the equilibrium essential to progress. The reforming conscience and the traditional conscience may both be justified when viewed in the long process of their historical interaction. Their operation is perhaps most clearly seen in political history, where the struggle between vested rights and new needs is a persistent and significant phenomenon. Of this struggle, whether belonging to the past or the present, one may truly say that, if it is the duty of those in authority to control the elements of discontent, it is equally the duty of the discontented to see that the task does not become too easy. The lesson of history is less the need of conformity to the social conscience than the need of sane efforts to modify it through the slow but safe channels of education. Certainly the prophets and heralds of a new order ought to be wise with the best wisdom that can be gleaned from all past experience. If they are thus wise, they will not find the existing order wholly bad, nor seek to destroy where they cannot build. Realizing how slowly and painfully progress has been won, they will not hope to make an end in a day, or effect a reform without paying the price. Understanding the continuity of institutions and ideals, they will seek to link all efforts for the future with the present order, even as the present order is indissolubly linked with the past.

Progress is won through the influence of those who, possessing insight with regard to the essential and the non-essential in the requirements of the social conscience, have the courage to assert their disagreement. Some one appears, to use again our illustration, who says, "I will eat cherries, because they are good, and all the reasons against it are mere products of childish fancy; I will step on thresholds, if I please, because it can do no possible harm; but I must not lie, because lying is destructive of social relations and of my own integrity."

VIII. COERCIVE AND SPONTANEOUS ELEMENTS IN THE MORAL LIFE

Attention has been called to the fact that not all acts which are in full accord with the requirements of duty are performed from a sense of obligation. The circle within which the sense of duty may on occasion operate is much wider than that within which it is habitually felt. Many important forms of activity are, as we have seen, commonly determined by instinctive desires, spontaneous interests, and natural appetites. But even in these it is impossible to exclude the influence of the idea of duty, the pressure of which may sometimes be required. Appetite and interest sometimes fail even at points where we may usually trust them for the accomplishment of important ends. Physical appetites, like that of hunger, which are often in need of restraint, may, under exceptional conditions, need the spur of duty. Work which has been undertaken with keen desire may cease to yield its wonted pleasure, and require to be carried to completion solely from a sense of duty.

Morality, we have seen, is at first largely prudential. At this stage the right act is performed because it is the pleasure-giving act, and the bad act is avoided because it entails unpleasant consequences of some kind. In the infancy both of the race and of the individual the prudential factor is of the highest importance. At the higher stages of morality, however, both the prudential regard for consequences and the coercive sense of obligation are largely transcended.

Right choices are made because they are the only choices truly desired. Morality has now become an inner order, freely chosen, and obeyed because it is the expression of one's deepest nature, not an external force that binds and trammels the unwilling spirit. The primary and most universal factor in effecting this transformation is sympathy. But another important element that lends its support to the process of emancipation, in all finer natures, is the æsthetic sense, the feeling for what is fitting, harmonious, beautiful. If it does not extend over the entire field of conduct, its influence is very wide. The bad is now the ugly, the good is the fair and beautiful. As ugly, the evil act is in itself repugnant, irrespective of consequences. The view of prudential morality is thus completely reversed. For while, at the stage of prudential morality, one would like to do the evil deed, if it were not for the disagreeable results extrinsic to the act, one is now repelled by the deed itself, without regard to further consequences.

Nowhere has the æsthetic element played such an important part in the history of morality as among the Greeks. The beautiful was perhaps the highest category of their life. In the absence of the stern sense of duty, which was so strong among the Semitic races, the æsthetic sense served the Greek in a marvelous way for spiritual guidance. The earliest maxims for the conduct of life found in their literature are an expression of the æsthetic sense, demanding moderation, and warning against the fatal results of excess. Plato, in the *Symposium*, gave to the principle its consummate literary expression, as Aristotle its most adequate scientific statement in his doctrine of the mean. In the rigorous teaching of Stoicism its power was not wholly lost. The life of the wise man, even in the most tragic hour, is viewed as an element in a great harmony in which the whole creation unites. If this ideal failed at certain points to yield the highest morality, at others it wrought results of unequaled excellence. It tended to a many-sided and symmetrical development which saved its possessors from outbursts of fanatical extravagance, against which the sense of duty alone has been no protection, and to which it has even lent added violence when not balanced by a deep and rich mental life.

The sympathetic and æsthetic impulses are thus the chief means by which morality is taken out of the sphere of conscious obligation, and transformed into spontaneous, uncompelled choice of the good. Strong sympathy makes a pleasure of services to one's fellows which duty indeed requires, but which are now taken up by other and more willing hands. A true appreciation of the beautiful similarly attracts and draws one to the nobler side. Love and beauty furnish the inspiration by which, under the guidance of intelligence, the highest freedom is realized.

CHAPTER X

VIRTUE AS THE GOOD–WILL

THE necessity of a thoroughgoing teleology has been maintained in the preceding chapters. At the same time it has been admitted that what, according to Kant, is known as the "form" of morality is important, is in fact an essential part of the very end we seek. We must now attempt to make still clearer the nature of this element, and to show its relations to other parts of ethical doctrine. Virtue, more than any other term, expresses the good-will, which is the very center and heart of inward, subjective rectitude. It is this aspect of morality which formalism has always exalted. Such virtue may be described, in a preliminary way, as conscientiousness, as a whole-hearted devotion to one's interpretation of the claims of duty. But a more exact analysis of the relation between the inner spirit and the results of acts, between formalism and teleology, is required before the full meaning of the problem will be clear.

We have already seen that a person not infrequently feels under obligation to perform acts which later, from the vantage ground of wider experience and clearer insight, are seen to have been done under a mistaken view of what was morally required. As a result one would feel it obligatory to act in a different way if the same situation were again to be faced. A classical example, chosen from the career of St. Paul, may serve as an illustration. It was only after a complete revolution had taken place in his thought that he regarded his earlier acts of persecution with regret. From his own statement, his conduct had, at the time, the approval of his conscience; it was then his interpretation of his duty. Still more frequently, perhaps, men conscientiously pursue courses of conduct which others, with a more enlightened moral judgment, condemn as injurious to the agent or opposed to the interests of society. The reverse is also true. Deeds which, in all external features, we approve, cannot always be imputed to right motives; they often leave one in doubt as to the spirit which prompted them. If there is no "art to find the mind's construction in the face," it is also impossible always to discover the moral temper in an outward act.

I. THE TWO-FOLD JUDGMENT OF CONDUCT

We are compelled, therefore, to recognize that a two-fold judgment is passed upon conduct. On the one side, a judgment is pronounced upon the motive, disposition, or will of the actor; on the other, upon the act itself in its outward relations and consequences. This distinction between the subjective and objective rightness of conduct has long been familiar in ethical thought as that between the "formal" and "material" goodness of acts. Hutcheson[1] introduced the terms to English usage and defined them as follows: "An action is *formally good*, when it flowed from good affections in a just proportion." "An action is called *materially good* when in fact it tends to the interest of the system, as far as we can judge of its tendency; or to the good of some part consistent with that of the system, whatever were the affections of the agent." [2] It was Kant, however, whose influence gave wide currency to the distinction and made it familiar to every student of ethics. Resting the weight of his system upon the "formal" principle, he is justly regarded as the chief representative of the theory.

Based upon this distinction there are evidently four possible types of action, all of which are more or less frequently realized in daily conduct. In this analysis we substitute for

[1] 1694–1747.
[2] *Moral Philosophy*, Bk. II, Chap. III.

formal and material the more common terms subjective and objective. An act may be (1) both subjectively and objectively good, (2) subjectively good and objectively bad, (3) subjectively bad and objectively good, and (4) both subjectively and objectively bad. The first class of acts is the one to which we give unconditional approval—acts springing from a right temper and motive, and having beneficent consequences. The second class, of which an example has already been given in the career of St. Paul, may be further illustrated by the familiar case of misdirected charity, which, although it may spring from the purest desire to do good, often results in direct injury both to the recipient and to society. The same case, reversed, affords illustration of the third class; for a beneficent act of charity may be prompted by the desire to gain influence which the giver purposes to turn to account in purchasing immunity from wrong-doing, or in securing other selfish ends.[1] The last class is the typically immoral act. Acts which fully satisfy the conditions of the second and third classes are comparatively rare, so surely does the spirit in which an act is done tend to express itself in the results of the act. We may believe, therefore, that the subjective and the objective rightness of conduct tend largely to coincide. The best deeds are almost invariably those which are done with the purest motives. It is not often that the stream which rises from an evil source is so purified in its course through the world as to yield sweet water. It seems impossible, however, to accept the view of Green, who finally quite obliterates the distinction between the good in the motive and the good in the result of an act. "There is no real reason to doubt," he says, "that the good or evil in the motive of an action is exactly measured by the

[1] Hutcheson states the third and second cases, respectively, as follows: "Actions materially good may flow from motives void of all virtue. And actions truly virtuous or formally good may by accident, in the event, turn to the publick detriment."

good or evil in its consequences, as rightly estimated—estimated, that is, in their bearing on the production of a good will or the perfecting of mankind." [1] This complete fusion of motive and consequence disregards too much the limitations for good imposed upon conduct by the lack of insight, skill, and power. A "good will" so dowered as to be a perfect measure of beneficent consequences would be more than a "good will"; it would be not only a pure heart, but also a clear head, a skillful hand, and an unconquerable will.

II. VIRTUE AS SUBJECTIVE OR FORMAL GOODNESS

Leaving for the present the objective, or material, goodness of acts, and considering more closely their subjective, or formal, rectitude, we must recognize here a factor of great value for the moral life, and consequently for moral theory. To such subjective rectitude, regarded as an element of character, the term virtue, in its generic sense, may be fittingly applied. It may be described as a complete loyalty to one's conviction of duty, disinterested devotion to the good, and a steadfast purpose in its pursuit. The good at which such a virtuous will aims is variously interpreted according to the light of the individual intelligence. Its content is the world of values, the entire sphere of social activity, and all of worth that has been won in the course of civilization. Even the gifts of fortune are not excluded from this rich content, although all external goods are only instrumental for the enrichment and perfection of the inner life, and can never be the final objects of pursuit. But however manifold the content upon which such a will works, varying with age and race and individual lot, virtue is always essentially the same quality of character, an unswerving loyalty to one's conviction of duty. The value of the good-will is thus precisely the value of the submission of the whole personality to the laws of value. It involves

[1] *Prolegomena to Ethics*, pp. 320–321.

a steady response to the claims of these laws, and an unfailing readjustment of the conduct of life to meet every new imperative which the intelligence discovers in the world of values.

The use of the term virtue to mark this quality has at least the sanction of good use, and its employment in this sense serves the interests of a more exact terminology.[1] Viewed historically, it is a limitation of the original meaning of the term, as it is also a limitation of its loose, popular use. For among the Greeks the corresponding term, ἀρετή, was employed to mark any excellence whatever. Naturally among a people who so prized the things of the mind, purely intellectual and æsthetic excellences were given a prominent place. The intellectual element appears in the Platonic virtue of wisdom (φρόνησις or σοφία), and in a more developed form in the intellectual virtues of Aristotle (διανοητικαὶ ἀρεταί). The Roman *virtus* also received its content from the national character, but included all the essential excellences of Roman manhood, with a primary emphasis upon those of the citizen and soldier. Under the influence of Christianity certain virtues, which in the classical world had been highly prized, were disregarded or given a subordinate place. Christianity could recognize the military virtues only when they were completely transformed, and were turned from the sphere of physical warfare to the struggles of the spiritual life. To become the gospel of the multitude, Christianity of necessity remitted, as it were, the requirement of the intellectual and æsthetic excellences of the

---

[1] Kant defines virtue in essential agreement with this use as "the strength of the man's maxim in his obedience to duty." Abbott's translation, p. 305. See the excellent statement of Sidgwick, *Method of Ethics*, p. 394, where "the root and essence of virtue in general" is defined as "the determination of the will to do whatever is judged to be right and to aim at realizing whatever is judged to be best." Wundt says that "the virtue-concepts treat the facts of morality from the point of view of motives." *Ethics*, Part III, p. 143. Cf. also Mackenzie, *Manual of Ethics*, p. 88; Paulsen, *System of Ethics*, p. 478; and Muirhead, *Elements of Ethics*, p. 177, note.

Greeks. Its message was not adjusted to the immediate tasks of earthly civilization, but was primarily other-worldly; and its test of excellence was an inner spirit which the most unlettered might possess. Kant was influenced in his doctrine of the good-will both by the Christian ideal, as it came to him through the pietism of his early home, and also by that movement of thought, best represented by Rousseau, which found its ideal man in a state of nature, uncorrupted by the refinements and luxuries of civilization. While it is impossible to accept any ideal of human excellence which does not include the fullest possible development of all the powers of our nature, a virtuous will, as the corner-stone of character, is so precious that it may fittingly be marked by a special term.

The reason for the high estimate placed upon virtue, as we have defined it, is not difficult to understand. It is indeed easy to understand the sentiment which has led many to regard it as the sole good with which morality is concerned. The motive pervading all formal systems of morality is a deep sense of the value of simple rectitude of will, of what is familiarly known as conscientiousness. This motive appears even in Stoic rationalism, which, at least in its earlier form, tended to emphasize the goodness of the choice rather than that of the object chosen, "as an archer aims at the bull's eye, his end being not the mark itself, but the manifestation of his skill in hitting it." [1] And it is clearly the mainspring of all the formal systems of modern times, as far as they remain true to their avowed principle. Must it not be admitted that such virtue is fundamental, that in a sense it underlies all other excellences, and makes possible their fruitfulness for life? It alone supplies the guarantee that knowledge, skill, and power, as they are slowly acquired, shall be used according to one's best insight, not prostituted to an end that is even second best. Nothing but such a will

[1] Sidgwick, *History of Ethics*, p. 80.

can insure to the individual or to the race the full possession
of the beneficent results of man's growing mastery over
nature. Nothing else can make truly fruitful the ever-
widening experience in educational and social endeavor.
With such virtue the new insight, of whatever kind, does not
remain a merely intellectual possession, but becomes at
once a principle of action. That these beneficent results
may follow, the virtuous will must be, in the words of Kant,
"not, to be sure, a mere wish, but the summoning of all
means in our power." Virtue thus involves the training of
the will, its habituation to prompt obedience, that it may
overcome the moral inertia which would allow even the
clearest perception of duty to remain barren of good results.
Correct habit is the core of virtue.

It is the task of moral education to develop in the child
such reverence for the laws of value that the call of duty
shall have in practice the force of a categorical imperative.
This imperative is valid as an ideal in moral training, even
though the Kantian doctrine be rejected. For the categorical imperative, thus applied, does not mean that an act
can be judged to be right independently of its consequences,
but only that there shall be unquestioning obedience to
one's truest valuation of all the consequences involved in
an act.

For ethical theory it is not enough to recognize the value
of virtue as an element in conduct. It is necessary also to
show its relation to that larger good which has been presented as the goal of human effort; we must discover its
rightful place in a system of values. Without a clear understanding of this relation, the mere recognition of the value
of any element, however important, would be little better
than the eclectic procedure of selecting for enumeration
various ideas which are held to be true, and setting them
down as a system of ethics. System there could not be in
such a statement. The unity which, without losing the sig-

nificance of the part, sees the part in close relation to the whole, would be wanting. Now virtue as here defined is a part of that personal good which manifests itself in perfection of function and satisfaction of feeling. More specifically, virtue is perfection of the will, of the active self responsive to its ideals. As such, it is the essence of all the character values. It does not necessarily imply correctness of ideals, and so does not insure one from mistaken conceptions of value. But it does mean faithfulness to the ideals which one has, the holding fast of the good which has been made clear to the understanding. When this quality is wanting there is always a fundamental defect in character which no gift of fortune can supply, and no other endowment make good. Reverence for the laws of value is thus itself one of the chief values.

III. Place of Virtue in Ethical Theory

The place of virtue in any ethical system demands then careful definition in the interest of final unity. Self-realization makes it a part of the end, placing it among the powers of the self whose harmonious, well-regulated development constitutes, for self-realization, the moral goal. Hedonism of the stricter sort, which insists that value is interpretable solely in terms of pleasure or happiness, must logically make virtue an instrumental value. Those who accept neither self-realization nor happiness, nor an organic union of the two, will fail, I believe, to do full justice to the meaning of virtue in its relation to ultimate value. Mr. Rashdall, for example, interprets the good as consisting chiefly of virtue and happiness, although he does not exclude other elements.[1] This statement of the ultimate good contains too little or too much; too little by far to give the content of the good life, of which there are many essential elements besides the good-will, and too much to make clear the fact that happiness is

[1] *Theory of Good and Evil*, Vol. I, pp. 71 ff.

a constituent of every conceivable good, virtue no less than
the others. We can here only remind the reader that, from
our point of view, it is always misleading to speak of happiness and other goods, since every good is more than
happiness, but is ultimately meaningless apart from happiness.

Virtue is, we hold, both an instrumental and an intrinsic
good. It is instrumental as means in the production of
further good, and a part of the end in that it is an essential
element of that self whose development conditions all experiences of value. In both forms it is organically related to
the production of happiness, as truly as knowledge, beauty,
or love, is so related. In its intrinsic aspect it is an immediate
source of satisfaction. Courage, to illustrate by a single
virtue, is a direct and constant blessing to its possessor and
to others. We feel it good to be in the presence of a courageous soul even when we are in perfect security.

In its instrumental aspect virtue, as devotion to the laws
of value, is the representative and guardian of a thousand
precious interests not of the present. Habitual rectitude of
the will means that each one of these interests will be duly
guarded as it arises, not left to circumstance or capricious
mood. Virtue is, in this respect, precisely like a deputy,
who in a legislative assembly represents a large constit-
uency. His speech and vote have the weight, not of his individual interests alone, but of the interests of thousands who
are absent and cannot voice their own needs. So the virtue displayed in a single act of courage, truth-speaking, or
justice, is sponsor for the moral interests of a life-time. But
these interests are, it must be remembered, primarily other
forms of good than the virtue which guards them; they include all the values, from highest to lowest. What Mr.
Rashdall calls "the supreme value of the good-will" [1] can
only be rightly understood when so interpreted as to take

[1] *Theory of Good and Evil*, Vol. I, p. 76.

account of all the values which it wills to guard. If the popular moral consciousness does not recognize this larger meaning, it is, nevertheless, always implicit in that consciousness. Here, as elsewhere, it is the business of ethics to reinterpret popular thought, rather than to accept its unreflective utterances as final.

In an earlier chapter it has been shown that a relation of at least general validity exists between perfection of function and satisfaction of feeling. There should be, if this view is correct, a distinctive form of satisfaction attending the exercise of the virtuous will. And experience justifies this expectation. Virtue has its own joys. The sense of having fulfilled the claims of duty, of having done at least that which was sincerely believed to be duty, is one of the supreme satisfactions of life. The consciousness of having "kept the faith," one's own faith—that of others we cannot keep—is a source of peace and serenity which, judged merely as pleasurable feeling, far outweighs many more intense pleasures which are succeeded by the reaction of unrest and discontent. On the contrary, the infirm or disloyal will which is unable to realize in conduct the good which the intelligence demands, must always leave the spirit painfully divided against itself, the slave of circumstance and chance desire. There is, further, a direct æsthetic delight felt in the presence of the finer manifestations of virtue. The strength displayed by one who stands firm at the post of duty against the pressure of bitter opposition or the allurements of tempting reward, kindles an admiration akin to that which we feel in the presence of the great forces of nature. When this conflict reaches a tragic height, as in the most heroic figures of history, it arouses a sense of the sublime. The confidence with which we look for the performance of duty by those in whom virtue is highly developed is like our trust in the rising of the sun or the procession of the heavenly bodies. Such, one may believe, were the feelings which stirred in

Kant when he linked the moral order with that of the starry heavens.[1]

Our conclusion, then, is that the element upon which formalistic theories have rested their account of morality is a part, and a vital part, of a larger whole. The error of formalism is in accepting the part for the whole, and especially in ignoring the vast influence upon human well-being of other factors. The question at issue between the two views may be stated, like many another controversy, as one of adequacy of definition. If we consent to define moral conduct in terms merely of inner disposition, of the rectitude of the will of the actor, and rigorously exclude its more objective aspects, there is a clearly defined, though exceedingly narrow field, within which ethical thought can work. But such a limitation of definition is arbitrary and inevitably breaks down, even in professedly formal systems, before the demands of reflection, which cannot fail finally to admit all the varied content of value, all that our aspirations after richer and more abundant life demand. Although the grounds for rejecting the formalistic interpretation, in favor of a teleological theory, have already been given, there are certain aspects of the problem which may be seen to better advantage, now that the value of the formal element has been fully recognized.

The impossibility of excluding the objective results of conduct is evident from the fact that the very condition of the subjective rightness, or virtue, of an act, is the full conviction on the part of the doer that the deed is good in its consequences. Only on this condition can there be a truly conscientious act. To this principle there are no real exceptions. Even in the case of one who considers that the highest duty is obedience to an externally imposed command,

[1] "Two things fill the mind with ever new and increasing admiration and awe, the oftener and the more steadily we reflect on them: *the starry heavens above and the moral law within.*" Abbott's translation, p. 260.

the justification for obedience is found in the belief on the part of such a person that somehow, in his own life, or in the larger system of which he is a member, the requirement has a beneficent purpose. Only so can the agents of absolutism, whether political or ecclesiastical, give even the semblance of morality to their conduct. It is in this way only that Kant's imperative can be justified; its real authority is derived from his "kingdom of ends." The question, in fine, is whether one shall examine the separate items of a moral account, or, accepting as correct the final reckoning offered by some existing order, shall dismiss the details without scrutiny. But surely no reflective mind can steadily honor the drafts which morality makes upon it without seeking to discover the "material" [1] value which they represent. However high the place which we accord to the virtuous will, we cannot escape the ever-recurring question of the objective value of the various types of action in which this inner disposition expresses itself. It is further true that to the good-will alone, as loyalty to conscience, we can never give, as Kant asserts, an unqualified admiration or reverence. The good-will which can command this feeling has far transcended all subjective limits; it is no longer merely "good in itself," but is also good for something from its relation to the "kingdom of ends." If Kant is justified in denying unconditional worth to intelligence and "other talents of the mind" because they may be employed for evil ends, one is equally justified in denying unconditional worth to the good-will, independent of that which it wills, for, with erring intelligence, such a will may be prostituted to the service of evil. However loyally the fanatic may obey his convictions of duty, "though he give his body to be burned," we cannot regard his loyalty to duty as worthy of our full reverence. The mind does not "bow" before any conscientious-

[1] Material, of course, only in the technical sense, that is, having to do with content.

ness which works cruelty and death, or before any loyalty
that dwarfs and maims human life. And if we describe
fanaticism as consisting of an erring intelligence linked with
a strong will to do the right, it must be remembered that
such fanaticism is of all degrees and shades, from that exhibited by the great inquisitors of history, whose deeds fill
us with abhorrence, to that which works among us daily,
in narrow circles and in petty ways, to mar and sadden individual lives. "If therefore the light that is in thee be
darkness, how great is that darkness! "

IV. Knowledge and Virtue

We have here again reached a point at which the relation
of knowledge to the moral life becomes especially clear and
significant. The value of the good-will increases directly
with the growth of a true understanding of its ideal content,
in other words, with a true comprehension of individual and
social values. A just estimate of these values will, of course,
always include a just estimate of the values of the will itself,
and hence of the importance of its cultivation by all men.
But only when the good-will receives the stamp of intelligence does its precious ore become the current coin of good
deeds. If knowledge alone is a poor thing, as is sometimes
urged, the same may be said of the good-will, or of any
part of our nature taken by itself. An adequate criticism
of life always drives one from an undue estimate of any single
excellence to an insistence upon the rounded whole of our
nature. Especially does such a criticism, working either in
the field of history or of current life, make evident the numberless ills which spring from ignorance and error. If we exclude those misfortunes which are due to natural forces
beyond human control, the evils from which men suffer
are referable to two sources, a weak or perverse will, and ignorance. Otherwise expressed, they are the result of disloyalty to conscience, and of unenlightened conscience.

Popular thought lays especial emphasis upon the former of these sources of evil. "If to do were as easy as to know what were good to do, chapels had been churches and poor men's cottages princes' palaces." [1] This ready assumption that all know the right and fail simply in the doing of it, expresses the common view of proverbial philosophy. Reflection, however, is forced to recognize the power for evil of ignorance and error. With a clearer understanding of the psychological factors involved, it sees the relation of the impulsive to the intellectual processes, and recognizes that every evil tendency is also inevitably a wrong way of thinking. The only escape from wrong-doing is seen to be in an appeal to a better train of thought, a truer system of ideas. All evil passion is a literal blindness. It sees with partial and distorted vision. It is the intellect alone that can deal with the horde of evils that are directly due to stupidity and ignorance. When, therefore, the value of clear insight for the guidance of conduct is once made plain, we see that one important task of the good-will is to will to know.

Granting the limitations of our knowledge and the recognized duty of seeking enlightenment, is there any principle or maxim which may guard the will from the danger of losing such insight as we possess in our moments of truest understanding? That such a danger exists is evident if we consider the swarm of influences which spring from subjective moods, preferences, and prepossessions, from private interests and selfish aims. What an undue importance that which we have personally experienced tends to assume in comparison with other facts, equally significant, lying beyond our own experience! How indifferent to human needs distance in space, or time, or kinship often renders us! What a rôle is played in our choices by the impulses and emotions of the passing hour! Who does not find it difficult to make a can-

[1] *The Merchant of Venice,* Act I, Scene II.

did examination of views which are opposed to beliefs and
ideals deeply rooted in his past? And who at times is not
prone to make exceptions in his own favor, to excuse himself
from tasks or renunciations which he would impose upon
others? Kant laid down the principle of universality for
guidance. "Act only on that maxim whereby thou canst at
the same time will that it should become a universal law."
The difficulty with Kant's statement is that the only maxim
which we can will in accordance with it lacks all specific
character. One can always, of course, rightly act on the
maxim, "Will the good." But the moment the maxim is
applied to concrete moral situations, it loses its universality.
I cannot, for example, will as universal law the maxims to
rise at six o'clock, to abstain from wine, or to live the life of
a celibate. For while these may seem perfectly clear duties
for me, I am equally certain that there are many who ought
not to observe them. There is, nevertheless, great significance in the objectivity and disinterestedness which Kant's
formula demands. Reasonableness is preëminently shown in
the ability to transcend subjective tendencies in moral judgment. If objectivity, the power to see things as they are,
irrespective of their immediate practical value for the be-
holder, is justly regarded as a mark of intellectual genius,
it is no less a mark of the moral genius to view moral relations
with a like disinterestedness. It has been one of the chief
traits of those who have impressed the world by their moral
greatness. The Buddha views the suffering of the world as a
personal burden. Socrates, in prison and facing death,
decides the question of his escape as coolly as if he were
pronouncing judgment upon the fate of the veriest stranger.
While the Pharisees heaped upon men burdens which they
were not willing even to touch "with one of their fingers,"
Jesus held himself unswervingly to the fulfillment of all righteousness. The objective moral temper does not relax the
rule in favor of the self. It never shies at facts or shirks

its tasks. It seeks to recognize all the facts and scan their meaning with the same temper with which the scientist examines his problem. The judgment of a moral question should be as unbiased as any other intellectual judgment. If it is impossible to make objectivity consist in the universality of Kant's principle, it may be possible to accept a modified form of his maxim. We may say: Act only on the maxim which you can at the same time will should become a law for all persons in like circumstances. Such a rendering gives in effect the golden rule. It demands that I shall exact from others only what I, in like position, am willing to yield, and that I shall be willing to yield all that I exact.

Although such disinterestedness requires at times an examination of one's motives and temper, it does not dictate the habit of minute introspection. Virtue does not grow by habitually "taking thought" of its stature. The organs of our spiritual life, like those of the body, are usually most healthy when least obtrusive. When worthy ends—and such ends are directly or indirectly social ends—are the object of earnest pursuit, the moral nature almost unconsciously reaches up to the nobility of its task. On the negative side, too, evil impulse is not subdued by mere scrutiny. To sit still watching for its appearance is the surest way to invite its coming. It is best escaped by giving oneself whole-heartedly to opposing interests and activities, so that when it comes it may "find no place in us." A passionate and joyful devotion to the things of true value is the best antidote for all the baser passions. Of deep spiritual import is the saying of Spinoza: "Blessedness is not the reward of virtue, but virtue itself; neither do we rejoice therein, because we control our lusts, but, contrariwise, because we rejoice therein, we are able to control our lusts." [1] A simple list of the "deadly sins" recognized in mediaeval times, and taking their form from the experiences of monastic life,

[1] *Ethics*, Part V, Prop. XLII.

constitutes a profound commentary upon the perils of a "cloistered virtue." In a world of real moral conflict the noblest type of virtue must be won upon the highways of life, where "that immortal garland is to be run for, not without dust and heat."

V. The Unity of the Virtues

From the generic idea of virtue as the loyal and disinterested will obedient to one's moral insight, we pass to inquire as to the nature of the several virtues. It is no part of the present purposes to treat them in detail, as has so often been done; it is intended only to indicate their relation to the central quality of character which we have been studying. All the virtues may be regarded, on their inner side, as manifestations or forms of the good-will, for all derive their inner value from loyalty to the demands of conscience in the various spheres of conduct. Temperance, for example, as control of bodily appetite, has its excellence in steadfastness of will against the solicitations of present pleasure. Courage is the like quality in the presence of danger or pain. Justice is a determination of will to regard the rights of all persons according to an objective and impartial view of the facts, as against personal prejudice, preference, or interest. The question whether virtue is one or many, raised long ago by Plato in the Socratic dialogues, may accordingly receive the answer that it is one in essential nature, as a form of the good-will, though manifold in outward expression. The particular virtues have to do with the varying tasks and changing conditions of life, and so necessarily manifest themselves in a great variety of ways. On the other hand we think of the inner disposition as relatively permanent throughout all the variety of external manifestation.

This inner unity of the virtues has sometimes led men to suspect that he who fails at one point of conduct would fail at all others, if subjected to temptation. It was such an emphasis upon the unity of virtue that led to the paradoxes of New Testament and Stoic thought. But this unity must not be pressed too far. For we see that many factors such as temperament, education, age, sex, race, social class, and even profession, modify individual estimates of the relative value of different traits of character. The varying estimates of value made by persons living in the same community at the same time, according as they are educated or uneducated, young or old, rich or poor, men of affairs or scholars, members of an aristocratic or a democratic circle, are very striking.[1] We cannot say that because a man possesses any one of the several recognized virtues, he possesses all, or, because he is wanting in one, he is necessarily wanting in all the others. It has often been remarked that men of high integrity in personal relations have accepted bribes and employed scandalous political or business methods, while others of unquestioned honesty in all public transactions have had low standards of personal morality. A symmetrical development of character is conditioned by many factors; we often prize one virtue relatively too high, another too low. Not infrequently it is the virtue men are conscious of lacking that they most highly prize; by a natural process of psychological emphasis it comes to occupy a disproportionate place in their thought. But the doctrine of the unity of the virtues may well remind us that weakness in one moral relation does in fact tend to engender weakness in other relations. Once it is made clear to the understanding that there is disproportion or neglect in our estimates of the different virtues, it is of the very essence of the good-will to strive to remedy the defect.

The particular virtues correspond with the particular duties, as generic virtue with the generic sense of obligation. There is no sufficient reason for any differentiation between

[1] For some differences in the moral estimates of rich and poor, see Jane Addams, *Democracy and Social Ethics*, Chap. II.

the spheres covered by the two concepts. They represent different aspects of the same thing rather than different things in moral experience. Virtue stands for an inner quality or disposition of mind, whereas duty refers more directly to the sphere in which the character of a person finds expression. Popular thought, however, inclines to the view that virtue occupies a higher sphere than duty. "There is no virtue in doing that, it is simply my duty," is a sentiment often heard. Sidgwick, stating this point of view, says: "We should scarcely say that it was virtuous—under ordinary circumstances—to pay one's debts, to give one's children a decent education, or keep one's aged parents from starving; these being duties which most men perform, and only bad men neglect." [1] But can we deny virtue to the right performance of these acts? The only doubt, perhaps, arises from the form of Sidgwick's statement, which, in the case of the two last-named acts, suggests a grudging or imperfect performance of duty. But a grudging performance would by no means satisfy the claims of duty. Certainly, to discharge promptly one's debts, to give to one's children the best possible education, to care with faithfulness and devotion for aged parents, and to perform these duties steadily for years, requires in effect a constant exercise of the most fundamental virtues. And, further, for the discharge of just such homely duties, we commonly recognize a corresponding class of business and domestic virtues. On the other side, to affirm that there is a sphere of virtuous conduct beyond the requirements of duty is, as we saw in the last chapter, to limit duty by conventional and imperfect standards. Such a limitation would exclude from the sphere of duty all the finer and more aspiring utterances of the individual conscience to which the world so largely owes its moral progress. No effort which the reflective conscience of an individual may demand, however far it may be in

[1] *Methods of Ethics*, p. 219.

advance of popular standards, is for that individual more than duty. In the moral life there are no works of supererogation. There is no statute law or social requirement that one shall do an heroic deed, or give one's life to philanthropic work, or one's wealth to establish hospitals and universities. But if one is able to do these things, and believes them to represent the greatest good which he can accomplish in life, the good-will requires them at his hands, and he is morally recreant if he is disloyal to his cause.

VI. MILITANT AND SPONTANEOUS VIRTUE

The fact that struggle and discipline are so often necessary for the cultivation of the virtues should not obscure the fact that they are not in any sense artificial. All rest upon native aptitudes and impulses. These constitute the living root of virtue, and alone make possible its growth. It is not strange, therefore, that virtue, grounded as it is in human nature, should sometimes be spontaneous, running with our desires. But we must recognize that it is also often militant, involving a struggle with conflicting impulses; we have a "fight with ourselves," as we say, before the virtuous will is triumphant. What is the relation of virtue to these natural desires? Does the exercise of a virtue with a feeling of pleasure detract from or add to its excellence? What is to be said of the character in which the will is not moved by a sense of duty so much as by admiration and love of the good? Different answers have been given to these questions by ethical thinkers, and even popular moral judgment does not seem to be unanimous in the matter. The rigorism of Kant separates, as we have seen, the moral element from the rest of man's nature, and insists that the virtuous act is the act done, not merely in accordance with duty, but from a sense of duty. All inclination of feeling for an act he considers morally "pathological." The only distinctively moral feeling is that of respect for the imperative of the law. It would be an injustice to Kant, however, to suppose that he denied all value to other feelings. He declares that "it is a very beautiful thing to do good to men from love to them and from sympathetic good will, or to be just from love of order." [1] He only denies that such feelings have any place in morality. They are not the "true moral maxim of our conduct." This limitation of virtue to its militant type has been accepted to a greater or less degree by various thinkers.

Royce has well emphasized the fact that in the typical cases of moral choice, those of deliberate, conscious decision, an element of opposition is necessarily implied. He says: "A being possessed of but one motive could have no conscience. But if this be so, then the consciousness of every moment of moral choice involves, also, a consciousness— a confession, if you will—of the presence in the chooser of that which he himself regards as evil. He not only coldly knows, he includes, he possesses, he is beset with some evil motive. And nevertheless, he conquers it. This is involved in the very formal definition of a moral act. You might as well try to define the king without his subjects or the master without his servant, or the captor without his captive or his prize, as to define a moral deed without the presence in the agent of some evil motive." [2]

The view which, on the contrary, regards the highest virtue as of what we may call the spontaneous rather than the militant type, has been still more widely held. In an oft-quoted passage, Aristotle says that "a person is not good, if he does not take delight in noble actions, as nobody would call a person just if he did not take delight in just actions, or liberal if he did not take delight in liberal actions, and so on." [3] With this interpretation most writers are in accord. Wundt has somewhere said: "Whereas a moral law which de-

---

[1] *The Analytic of Pure Practical Reason*, Abbott's translation, p. 175.
[2] *Studies of Good and Evil*, p. 99.
[3] *Nicomachean Ethics*, Welldon's translation, p. 20.

mands that the good be done without inclination, i. e. without motive, asks more than can be accomplished, it is, on the contrary, the genuine mark of the mature character to perform the moral act without deliberation, from pure inclination." This spontaneity of the higher virtue is clearly expressed by another writer in the following passage: "It may further be said that, while the sense of duty implies a comparatively high development of the spirit, yet its presence also implies a certain difficulty in right doing. It shows a lack of freedom and spontaneity in the direction of the right. A man who performs a righteous act from a sense of duty stands much higher than one who does not perform it at all; but one who performs it because it seems the most natural thing in the world, simply because he wants to, stands still higher." [1]

This is also, with perhaps some limitations, the popular judgment. Certainly acts of benevolence, justice, and courtesy, are regarded as better when performed with pleasure than when done grudgingly. An act of charity loses its finest quality unless done with a degree of spontaneity. Such spontaneity, to indicate true moral worth, must not of course be the result of a transient emotion or a passing mood, but of a permanent sympathy which steadily prompts to deeds of helpfulness.

It would seem, however, that in some cases popular thought ascribes a greater worth to virtues which cost a distinct struggle. Self-control and temperance, in at least some of their forms, appear to be more highly esteemed when the opposing tendencies are so strong that they cost a battle with oneself. This disparity in the ordinary estimate of the value of spontaneity and struggle in the exercise of the virtues is not an opaque fact, but is, I think, capable of explanation. The explanation is to be sought in the values we assign to the various propensities and powers of human

[1] C. C. Everett, *Poetry, Comedy and Duty*, p. 223.

nature. We demand that an act of kindness, for example, shall be performed spontaneously, without inward reluctance, because if it is not so performed we necessarily infer that sympathy is weak and that the egoistic impulses are strong. Similarly, even-handed justice is relatively easy to a person of open mind and objective judgment. Hesitation or struggle in either of these cases argues, therefore, a defect in the endowments of personality. A virtue like self-control, on the contrary, when it costs a struggle, often indicates the possession of high spirit. And this quality is recognized as containing potentialities for good not found in a tamer nature. There mingles also, I suspect, in this popular estimate of militant virtue, something of that admiration which we instinctively render to a well-fought contest. But even in the cases in which the militant type of virtue is more highly esteemed, it is always recognized that the result of habitual effort at control should at length appear in well-poised self-mastery. The struggle for such mastery, which popular judgment approves as befitting the storm and stress of youth, excites suspicion of fundamental defect if carried into old age.

If we examine more closely the theory which limits virtue to its militant form, serious difficulties at once appear. As far as effort in the direction of right conduct is successful, it tends to become less and less difficult; but by the terms of the definition of militant virtue, such conduct would also become less and less virtuous. In seeking to enlarge its life, therefore, virtue inevitably commits suicide. Logically, too, high virtue would be conditioned by the presence of strong tendencies to evil, whereas moral progress in the race depends largely upon the production of types in whom virtuous tendencies are relatively strong and spontaneous. Virtue, thus limited, can never be the ideal goal of morality, which demands that all the forces of individual and social life shall be set free, as far as possible, in the service of worthy ends. As a country at war must suffer in its industries when its citizens are engaged in military service, so the strength of one who is compelled to wage an unceasing struggle with evil within himself is seriously dissipated. Such expenditure of force seems deplorable when we consider the inexhaustible spheres of worthy endeavor upon which it might be employed. If there were no want and suffering to be relieved, no truth to be discovered, no beauty to be created, no material and spiritual good to be carried to ever wider circles, the permanent presence of inner conflict might be viewed with approval as an antidote for stagnation. But as long as we suffer from an embarrassment of possible riches in the field of moral endeavor, such danger does not confront us. It is a tragic fact in the spiritual history of the race that men have often set up an artificial evil and then exhausted all their powers in the effort to overcome it. Thus the false standards of asceticism have not infrequently regarded as evil certain forces of human nature which, rightly directed, are a positive enrichment of the higher life. Noble spirits have, alas! not infrequently contended in such an arena only to win an empty victory, while causes of great moment were wholly neglected. St. Anthony's temptation typifies not only heroic struggle with human weakness, but also a pathetic spiritual illusion.

The struggle with evil is certainly a phase of the moral experience of everyone, and as long as goodness is esteemed among men this struggle will not cease to be approved and praised. It is impossible, of course, to define the limits of its operation in precise terms. In one nature for a longer time and at more numerous points, in another for a shorter period and over a more circumscribed area of the moral life, the conflict must be waged. But the normal course of moral development is to give over more and more of conduct to the sphere of regulated habit. Accompanying this process, there is a diminution of struggle and a growth of satisfaction in the practice of the virtues. This satisfaction is not so much a satisfaction with self and its fulfillment of the moral law, as a satisfaction in those worthy causes, devotion to which is the surest path to victory over evil. The term virtue might of course be arbitrarily limited to its militant type. But in this case its meaning would be greatly narrowed, and there would be need of another term to describe the highest form of virtue. Kant uses "holiness" for that obedience to the moral law which "apprehends no inward reluctance of the will." It seems more fitting, however, to use the term virtue for both militant and spontaneous goodness, for the fulfillment of the requirements of morality both from a sense of duty and from delight in what is good. We must recognize not only the character in which the victory over evil is won after long and hard conflict with opposing tendencies, but also those rare natures so finely attuned to the moral order that they seem instinctively to turn towards goodness. Schiller's words,

"Alles Höchste, es kommt frei von den Göttern herab," are as true of virtue as of other gifts. The flower of goodness is found in those whom Wordsworth describes in his *Ode to Duty:*

> " Glad hearts without reproach or blot,
> Who do thy will and know it not."

But whether the spontaneity of right conduct be the result of long discipline or the gift of nature, love of what is good and true and beautiful is the highest spring of action; it is indeed "the fulfilling of the law."

CHAPTER XI

MORAL LAW

THE ethical concepts with which we have dealt in the preceding chapters have all implied the existence of rules, or laws, of conduct. The concept of law in ethics we now desire to subject to examination.

I. MEANINGS OF THE WORD LAW

The word law does not primarily suggest moral relations; it rather puts one in mind of a statute enacted by some authority. This jural use of the word law was in fact its original use in all languages. When subjected to analysis it is seen to contain three elements: it expresses (1) a rule of action, (2) prescribed by some power in authority, (3) for the regulation of the conduct of subjects.[1] A study of the history of the word in the jural sense here indicated would lead one back to the unwritten tribal customs out of which positive codes slowly developed.

For the present purpose it is important also to consider another application of the word law which resulted from the development of science and philosophy. Succeeding its use in the jural sense, came its use in the sphere of nature. With the growth of observation and understanding of natural processes, it was seen that the physical world exhibits an order in some degree analogous to that which prevails in a well-ordered, law-abiding community. There slowly developed among the great thinkers of Greece the conception of a law of nature, embracing in its universal sweep both the physical world and man's own life. The idea of such a

---

[1] Cf. F. C. French, *The Concept of Law in Ethics*, p. 4.

unitary, world-wide law became a central element in ancient philosophy, especially in that of the Stoics.[1] In modern times, with the development of the special sciences, the term law has come into wide and familiar use as a statement of the uniformities of sequence observable in natural events. In this use of the word we are not concerned with the existence of a will in authority imposing its rules upon nature. Only the first of the three elements mentioned above is here present. For although religion and metaphysics have often ascribed the order observable in nature to a central will and intelligence, of which this order is the outward manifestation, the scientific view rightly limits itself to a study of empirically observed uniformities, and does not raise the question of their primal source or ultimate meaning. Scientific thought, as such, is neither religious nor irreligious, neither theistic nor atheistic.

The concept of law in ethics bears such important relations to law both in its jural and scientific uses that a brief examination of these relations may aid in understanding the nature of moral law. We first consider some differences between law in morals and in legislation.

II. Moral Law and Jural Law

A first point of difference is found in the fact that morality covers a larger field than the law. The written laws of a people clearly do not express with any degree of completeness their view of all that morality requires. Yet we must remember that all legal codes necessarily presuppose moral sentiment as their origin and support. They express convictions concerning what ought, or ought not, to be done. The principle underlying legal enactments in democratic governments seems to be that such enactments shall meet the requirements of a general sentiment as to what people

---

[1] Cf. the well-known Hymn of Cleanthes, and numerous statements in other Stoic writers.

shall be compelled, by use of force if necessary, to do or to abstain from doing. In an autocratic régime, the limit of requirement, within the will of the monarch, would seem to be what the people will tolerate. Morality obviously covers a vastly wider field. We cannot set sharp limits to its demands, whereas the law is always definite in the requirements which it imposes. To secure the performance of extra-legal acts required by morality, the community brings to bear a variety of forces, political, social, and religious, which supplement the law, and which operate more speedily and effectively upon the great majority of citizens than do the more tangible penalties imposed by courts of law. Although morality outruns the requirements of the law, the law always moves towards it as its limit. But this limit is not fixed; it, too, is always advancing. A growing moral sentiment, then, is a constant factor in the transformation and development of legal codes. Morality demands that statute law shall express as fully as possible its new insights. Thus, at the present time, one is compelled by law to do many things which in earlier centuries were either not required at all or were demanded only by a vague sentiment of propriety. In every community there are many rules of conduct now enforced which formerly were unknown. One has only to think of new sanitary regulations and of laws governing the conduct of business, to find illustrations of such extension of positive requirement. It is impossible to foresee how far, in the future, legislation may be extended to embody a growing moral sentiment. Many matters, which to-day are regarded as the sole concern of the individual, will to-morrow be seen to have such vital social consequences that they can no longer be left to the individual choice.

This growing demand of legislation in the interest of the well-being of society makes it clear that the distinction sometimes made between morality and the law, as one of positive and negative requirement, cannot be maintained. This distinction has only relative validity. The law makes many positive demands upon us, and morality imposes many prohibitions. Both are constructive in their aims, and in the case of both the negative element is only an instrument to further positive good.

Again, the statement that the law aims only at control of external acts, whereas morality makes its demands upon one's innermost purposes and feelings, contains only a relative truth. Jurisprudence is concerned with the motives as well as the consequences of acts, morality with consequences as well as motives. It is also true that the law is powerless to reach many forms of external conduct that are quite as injurious as those of which it takes cognizance. Thus the law offers protection against direct libel, but none at all against more subtle and malicious ways of "filching" from one one's good name. The law protects property rights and punishes theft, but it is often entirely powerless to prevent unfair business methods which may bring ruin to one's fortune more speedily and completely than the attempts of thief or burglar. Wife-beating is punishable by law, but the wife has no legal protection against the petty meannesses which may inflict greater pain and injury than an occasional beating. We observe also that technicalities frequently release one from the grasp of the law, but in no degree do they diminish the moral guilt of a wrong deed. Illustrations of the limitations of the law, even in the sphere of overt acts, can be multiplied by the reader at will. Such limitations are, to a large extent, inherent in any legal system. At its best, the law is a relatively crude instrument as compared with the niceties of moral requirement. Such must be the character of the law if it is to accomplish its work. It is a mechanism which must operate by fixed penalties, taking little account of the nature of the individual. Morality stands at this point in sharp contrast to the law:

its penalties are not arbitrarily fixed, but on the contrary are far-reaching and intangible.

Since legal enactments derive their authority from moral conviction, it will be generally agreed that, in case of conflict, morality has a higher authority than the law. It is not infrequently the case that intelligent and conscientious citizens regard certain laws under which they live as unjust or pernicious, and that they obey them only under protest, or from a conviction that obedience to law is in itself so important to the general welfare that it constitutes the more primary obligation. It is often the case, too, that instead of a protest against a law which does not accord with public sentiment, the law is allowed by common consent to become a dead letter. A familiar illustration of this is found in the "blue laws" dealing with Sunday observance and similar matters of conduct. But, given a system of laws sufficiently obnoxious to the moral sense, open revolt in obedience to conscientious convictions must result. The right of revolt and revolution rests upon an irreconcilable conflict between the legal requirement and the moral requirement.

III. MORAL LAW AND NATURAL LAW

Although moral law seems to bear the more obvious resemblance to law in its jural sense, it is none the less true that the concept of law in ethics has been greatly enriched through the contribution of the natural sciences. Moral laws must also be recognized as natural laws. This will appear more clearly if we ask for the source of our knowledge of moral law. In answering this question suggestive use may be made of the method by which natural laws are discovered in the various departments of science. All such laws, it is well known, are derived directly from a study of the phenomena of nature itself, and can never be discovered elsewhere. The so-called laws of nature—formulae of its uniform action—express the characteristic activities of the department of nature in question. The laws of chemistry are an expression of the nature of the various elements as they display themselves in action and interaction. The laws of plant life which botany discovers are a transcript of the nature of this life, a translation of it into scientific language. Let us now suppose that the chemist makes use of his chemical laws to secure certain desired results in medicine or industry, or that the botanist employs his knowledge to give rules to the horticulturist for the cultivation of fruits and flowers. The descriptive form of the law now becomes normative. The "is" becomes an "ought" in the service of a desired and chosen end. The rules which are observed in the care of any plant, the requirements of light, heat, moisture, richness of soil, etc., are a statement both of the nature of the plant and of the conditions of its fullest perfection. In a similar way all valid moral laws are derived from human nature, and are a statement of the conditions of its highest development.

The analogy between natural and moral law suggests again the question whether ethics deals with what is or with what ought to be. As we have already seen in the introductory chapter, it deals with both problems, but primarily with what is. How can any "ought" be considered apart from the qualities of human nature and the conditions of practical life? Certainly every question of duty is always, in the first instance, a concrete question of what "is," of certain special facts of individual and social life. If, for example, we ask what is the duty of a given citizen in time of war when the government calls for volunteers, it is clear that he cannot decide the question by reference to any ideal ought of arbitration or of perfect justice on the part of human governments. He is confronted with a great number of facts which are concrete to the core. Is the war, on the whole, just, and is it wise? If he cannot give an unqualifiedly affirmative answer to these questions, does the duty of patriotism still require him to serve as a soldier, in spite of his doubts and scruples? Is his family in immediate and pressing need of his aid? Is he fitted to bear arms, or can he render other services still more valuable than those of the soldier? These and similar specific questions of fact must furnish the data for the right answer to the question of duty. The same necessary reference to specific facts will be found true of any other moral situation. And if we pass from the question of what ought to be in a particular situation, to consider the more general and abstract ideal of personal life and character which we ought to realize, the answer must still be found in what human nature is, and what activities are capable of yielding permanent satisfaction to beings like ourselves. The law of morality, therefore, is a statement of what ought to be, in view of what actually is. The source of all known and knowable rules of conduct we are compelled to find in human nature as it reveals itself in the social-historical order. The test of any moral principle is its adaptation to the real needs of life. The attempt to discover moral laws elsewhere than in human experience must always prove futile. Even if we could conceive of moral laws as literally brought down from heaven, if they were written in fire on the sky above us, or were "revealed" in some other miraculous way, they could permanently win our allegiance only by answering to our human needs, and thus justifying themselves in the spiritual experience of the race. Laws of conduct which might be imagined to hold sway in a shadowy, angelic realm, would have no pertinency to the real problems of everyday human experience. This final test of fitness no moral code can escape; it must "find" men, if it is to command their reverence.

The good is, then, as Plato declared, the lawgiver. The world of values is the source of every principle and rule of conduct. The existence of a formulated law, or rule, is never an ultimate fact for reflection, but always points to an ideal of good rooted in the needs of our nature. The artificiality of any other kind of requirement must sooner or later appear and render it ineffective. But the needs which dictate the law of conduct must be the real and permanent needs, otherwise each passing impulse, every clamant physical desire, might impose its order upon the whole of our nature. As the whole, however, is more than the part, the larger and more enduring interest must control the lesser and more transient. The good of satisfied physical appetite, of whatever kind, might well give the law of conduct to man, if his nature were no more than such changing appetites. The law of his being would then dictate precisely such a rule of action as would bring these capacities into full play. By such action do animal organisms everywhere serve the ends of nature and fulfill their destiny. It is because these impulses are only elements in man's total life that "the law in the members" must yield to a higher law. The failure of moral requirement to correspond with one's immediate cravings is no reason for rejecting it. The fact that I may not feel inclined to exercise self-control, to improve my mind, to cultivate courage and self-sacrifice, or to render a social service, is not a sufficient ground for refusing to follow these courses of conduct. Asceticism has always embodied a relative truth. No life can realize a high degree of development without the strict subordination of many cravings which conflict with its central aim. One may go further and say that such development is not possible without the rigid exclusion of many things which, in themselves, are wholly legitimate. The limitations of time and strength do not permit the realization of all ends that are worthy. But the function of renunciation is negative. If it were made a principle of conduct and extended to the suppression of all particular desires and impulses, the result would be the entire lack of content, the loss of all interest in existence. The moral life would be suspended *in vacuo*. We are dependent upon our various particular impulses and desires for the realization of all good. This holds true for all planes of our life, from the humblest bodily appetite up to hunger and thirst of the spirit. Even this hunger and thirst must be translated into desire for concrete forms of righteousness. Otherwise it falls into the mystic mood which has for its object that which is at once "the all and the nothing."

One important characteristic of moral law is wanting in the laws of physical science. Moral law is consciously recognized and imposed by the self. There is, it is true, a stage antedating that of genuine morality, when the individual obeys rules dictated by external authority, without full consciousness of their meaning or value. For the majority of men, moral laws doubtless retain to the end something of this external character. But such an attitude must be regarded as provisional and educational. The goal is always the life of conscious self-direction. True morality is autonomy; it is self-control, not police control. The self is here, as Kant insisted, both "sovereign and subject," itself imposing the law and rendering obedience to it. This does not mean that one ceases to receive guidance from external sources, but that the external guidance, to be genuinely moral, must be consciously accepted, and reaffirmed by the self as its own freely chosen principle of conduct. The frequent impression of childhood that what is morally required is simply the decree of a stronger will, that the law is purely external and arbitrary, rapidly finds correction in the experience of life. The apparent arbitrariness is due to the fact that the claims of morality anticipate our development, and for a time outrun our power of interpretation. Later, however, there comes to every reflective mind a period of ferment and transition, when the yoke of external authority is thrown off, and the right of every rule to claim obedience is sharply

challenged. Nothing can escape this critical temper when
it is once fully aroused. No principle is so sacred, none so
deeply intrenched in long established tradition, as to be
beyond question. Those which seem to the fully awakened
conscience to be arbitrary or artificial will now be rejected.
Morality thus undergoes a process of immanent criticism,
more or less thorough, with each successive generation. But
when the process by which the law becomes internal has been
completed, it is reaffirmed as the expression of the individual's own conscious will. One no longer obeys like the bond-
man from the pressure of external authority, but with a deep
conviction of the "excellence" of the law. A new sense of
harmony and freedom is won. In all finer and deeper natures the law becomes a delight—it is truly "written upon the
heart."

This principle does not apply to the growing life of the
individual alone, but may be illustrated upon the larger
stage of historical life, where the process by which the moral
law becomes an inward power may be traced in national
development. Whether we turn to the Jews or to the Greeks,
the two peoples most influential in determining our own
moral ideals, the same increasing inwardness of morality is
clearly discernible. In the case of the Jews, the movement is
from obedience to laws externally imposed and "graven upon
tables of stone," to an obedience which is rendered from an
inner demand for rectitude, justice, and mercy. This culminates in the Christian law of love as an active principle
dominating the whole personality. The course of development among the Greeks led to a similar result. The method
of stating the moral problem was quite other than that which
prevailed among the Jews; it was always the ideal of an ultimate good to which the Greek appealed, rather than to
that of an authoritative law. But they, too, reached, in
the words of Green, "the conception of intrinsic value, as
lying not in anything that might happen to a man, in his

pleasure or his good fortune, but in what he might do and might become." [1]

IV. THE NATURAL SANCTIONS OF MORALITY

If it is true that moral laws are natural laws, in the sense of expressing the genuine needs of human nature and the conditions of its highest development, it follows that one cannot escape the consequences inseparable from their violation. An arbitrary law may be circumvented and its sanctions escaped, provided one is fortunate or shrewd enough to avoid detection by the authority imposing the law. This is not the case with a natural law, physical or psychical; the consequences are here bound up with the act, and are set in operation by it. This is a fact so familiar as hardly to require illustration. No one believes it possible to violate the normative rules of hygiene and escape physical ill. Intemperance always results in some degree of impairment of physical balance and vigor. In the same sense the violation of moral law brings with it inescapable consequences to the moral nature. The significant facts with which one has to reckon here are not those which popular moral and religious teaching has most frequently emphasized—the external sanctions of one kind or another which constitute an obvious prudential bar against evil-doing. They are found rather in an inescapable deterioration of personality.

Who that has closely observed moral phenomena, whether in himself or in others, can doubt that here is a region of determinately related events, and that one who yields to evil must pay the price in lowered moral tone and impaired moral development? Few thoughtful persons would question the existence of natural sanctions for acts of selfishness, of deceit, of sensual indulgence, sufficient to constitute a powerful motive against such conduct. The results of modern psychological study have rendered more impressive than

[1] *Prolegomena to Ethics*, p. 268.

ever the lesson of natural sanctions by exhibiting the effect of habit upon the psycho-physical organism. Acts of good and evil are seen to be "graven" upon the self with a literalness which had not been realized. A better understanding of the unfailing certainty of natural sanctions in both individual and social life would fortify against weak indulgence. The traditional postponement of the truly intimate sanctions of conduct to a future state has often been prejudicial to morality. If heaven and hell seem very real to some, to others they seem very distant. And when there is added to their remoteness the possibility of some kind of adjustment of offences through ecclesiastical favor or other external process, the view becomes morally dangerous. It may be urged that the less obvious natural consequences of conduct, of which we have been speaking, will appeal with power only to those who already possess a deep insight into moral values. This may be granted without the slightest prejudice to the truth or importance of the principle. Emphasis upon the more intimate sanctions of morality does not involve neglect of those external sanctions which constitute the only appeal to the thoughtless or hardened. For such there will always remain those more tangible penalties which affect men in their physical comfort, their reputation, and their fortune. But the moral rank of a man must always be determined by his sensitiveness to the more intimate inner sanctions of conduct.

Political and social forces can be trusted to inculcate by their own vigorous methods a regard for the more obvious and essential rules of social morality. In the operation of present tendencies to a closer organization of society, there is little danger that the anarchy of ultra-individualism will triumph. But I conceive it to be of the utmost importance for moral education that a juster emphasis be given to the more intimate natural sanctions of all our finer idealistic and altruistic strivings. What is needed is a more adequate psychology of moral experience which shall exhibit the scientific basis for the insights which at present exist in proverbial philosophy, and in that finer world-wisdom which speaks to us out of history, literature, and biography, as well as out of the living experience of the richest personalities. Such a psychology must establish for the modern world the value of spiritual aims—the transformation of consciousness wrought by devotion to a noble cause, the liberation of our petty, fearful selves from the tragedy of merely personal interests, the serenity and health of soul begotten by the ardor of passion in the pursuit of its ideal. The psychology of the last decades, operating in a limited field, has done much to exhibit the effects of certain mental states. It has shown the disastrous effects upon personal achievement and happiness of such vices as envy, jealousy, and self-seeking, and the beneficent results of the opposite virtues. It has been seen that states of *ennui*, despair, and pessimism are often the direct result of moral deficiencies; that purity of thought and life yields returns in serenity and cheerfulness of temper; and that lust and greed are the sure seeds of uneasiness and dissatisfaction.

V. Moral Scepticism; Historical Survey

We now approach one of the oldest and most persistent questions concerning the nature of moral laws. Are they universal? Are they the same for all times and places? Or, in the changing conditions of human history, are they also subject to change? And if this latter alternative be accepted, how does the admission affect their validity? Scepticism has almost invariably made its attack upon morality at this point. Finding evidence that moral standards are not universal and permanent, but relative and changing, it has proceeded to deny their validity. It has seen in the moral codes of different peoples and periods only more or less artificial conventions which had no foundation or fixed support in nature. The slowly but surely changing ideals of every race, and the varied and even contradictory standards of judgment accepted at the same time by different peoples, have furnished apparently powerful arguments to the moral sceptic.

The thesis of moral scepticism is, then, that all so-called moral laws are only a rough and artificial compromise which renders some sort of social life possible. Such was the position of the Sophists, the first European thinkers to reach a conscious moral scepticism. Moral laws, they said, are only conventions (νόμοι); they have no real existence in nature (ἐν φύσει). For they had seen how nature scorns external limitation and control. In the words of Euripides, "Nature knows no statute;" it follows the path of its own victorious might. It was easy for the Sophists, therefore, to transfer this view of natural forces from the external, physical world, to human nature, with the obvious result that the individual seemed to find warrant for the freest exercise of his native strength in any direction which his impulses or desires suggested. Thus might became right. To this thought of what was natural, and so presumably justifiable, there was further added, in the case of the Sophists, a powerful solvent of uncritical moral faith in the widened outlook which they had gained over the ideas and customs of different races. The opposition of religious and moral ideas, the clash of social customs, and withal the unquestioning confidence with which each race maintained its own system of beliefs and practices, dealt a staggering blow to the notion of absolute truth and absolute right. The later Greek scepticism developed this relativity with increasing fullness of detail, and drew the ready conclusion that it was impossible to reach any positive view on the subject. "Therefore the sceptic," says Sextus Empiricus, "seeing so great a difference of opinion concerning these matters, suspends judgment on the question whether there is anything good or bad by nature, and whether there is anything that ought to be done or not done." [1]

With the dawn of modern philosophy the same note is again heard. Montaigne declares: "Nothing in the world varies so greatly as law and custom. A thing is called abominable in one place and in another is praised, as in Lacedemonia clever thieving was admired. Marriages between near relatives are strictly forbidden among us; elsewhere they are regarded as honorable. Murder, parricide, adultery, traffic in stolen goods, licentiousness of every sort, there is no extreme which has not been accepted by some nation as common custom." [2] In a similar vein Pascal, who is a thorough sceptic in his distrust of reason, affirms that "there is hardly an idea of justice or injustice which does not change with the climate. Three degrees of latitude reverse all jurisprudence. The meridian decides the truth. Right has its epochs. The entrance of Saturn into the sign of the lion marks the origin of a certain crime. Wonderful justice which is bounded by a river! Truth on this side of the Pyrenees, error on that!" [3] Expressions of a similar satirical attitude concerning the variability of moral standards abound in the history of thought.[4] And they are not merely of the past. Thinkers like Nietzsche and Stirner have presented an extreme individualism equally destructive of the accepted principles of social morality. Especially has Nietzsche developed in the boldest and most vigorous form a doctrine of individual might as constituting ethical right, which reproduces many of the features of the Greek enlightenment of the fourth and fifth centuries B. C. "*Nichts ist wahr, alles ist erlaubt.*"

[1] *Pyrrhonic Hypotyposes*, iii, 232.

[2] *Essays*, An Apology for Raimond de Sebonde.

[3] *Thoughts*, Chap. IV.

[4] Cf. Leslie Stephen's account of Mandeville, who, as he says, "accepts the conclusion that the taste for chastity is as arbitrary as the taste for big buttons." *History of English Thought in the Eighteenth Century*, Vol. II. p. 92.

From quite another source one meets with doubts of the intrinsic validity of moral laws. The theologian and the devout religious believer often hold views which are equally sceptical as far as the rationality of moral laws in the field of our present human experience is concerned. They would make the moral order, viewed by itself, chaotic or irrational. Were it not for supernatural sanctions, evil would often be good, and good evil. The devil and his followers might, in such a view, have the best of this world. A young man of intense religious conviction, but of limited moral outlook, once remarked to me that, if he did not believe in a future life, he would "do the first thing that came into his head." [1] Such an attitude is clearly a radical scepticism as far as morality is concerned. It also involves a violent conflict between some of the most fundamental conceptions of morality and religion. For if, on grounds extrinsic to experience, one accepts as final and complete a code of morals supposedly "revealed" with absolute authority at a given period of history, the long-delayed appearance, and the limited extension of all such codes, must lead inevitably to the sorest pessimism concerning the actual moral career of the race. Were we to suppose, for example, that a true code of morality has been revealed to the Mohammedan world alone, or to any other single religion, how blind must seem the wanderings of the rest of humanity through the long ages of its moral struggle! Such partiality for a small portion of humanity would forbid the belief that the code in question represents the unchanging will of an all-powerful and beneficent Moral Governor. On practical grounds, too, the appeal away from immediate and verifiable experience to theologi-

[1] Cf. the case cited by Sutherland: "I have heard a religious man say: 'If I were to believe that there was no hereafter, I should start and have a good time. I should enjoy myself, I can tell you.' Thus he expressed a cynic selfishness, betraying that in all this universe there were no interests worth considering but his own pleasures, and, moreover, revealing but a gross idea of pleasure." *The Origin and Growth of the Moral Instinct*, Vol. II, p. 40.

cal or metaphysical hypotheses will always prove a source of weakness. For every doubt concerning the form or substance of such hypotheses, nay, every failure to establish them by positive proof, will by so much seem to involve in uncertainty the most fundamental requirements of practical morality. In quite other ways must we think of the moral order, whether we approach it from the point of view of ethics or of religion.

The difficulties involved in the question of the validity of moral laws are by no means those of a few isolated thinkers; they constantly recur in the growing intellectual life of the individual. A sense of the relative and changing character of moral codes is often one of the most powerful impressions of the student who, from the narrow region of human conduct to which his observation has hitherto been limited, comes to gain a larger understanding of the history of moral development in the race. How can we escape from the sea of doubt which seems at first to bear away all landmarks from the moral horizon? On what terms may one retain a living faith in moral standards?

VI. The Answer to Scepticism

It is clear that the answer cannot be found in a denial of the diversity which the historical facts present. Nor can we belittle the significance of such diversity. The results of all recent investigations only tend to make more evident the conflict of ethical standards, and the slow evolution of those ideals which are cherished to-day among the most advanced races. The evidence exhibited by ethnology and history is, as we have seen, destructive of any theory like the older intuitionalism, which sought to establish the existence, within the mind of the individual, of universal and unconditional rules of morality. The only rules of this kind which can be traced in the history of human conduct prove to be vague and general formulæ. As soon as they are filled with the content of actual moral behavior, this content is found to be extremely varied, and at times contradictory. Equally unsatisfactory would be the attempt to set up any detailed code of the present as final and perfect. We may certainly hope for continued change and growth. It requires no prophetic power to see that the moral order of the future will contain commands and prohibitions that are not dreamed of by most good people of our own day. Of humanity as a whole it may be said, "It doth not yet appear what we shall be." The standard of morality must be recognized as progressive.

We must be ready, then, to recognize, from the diversity and change in ideals, that moral principles cannot be universal in the sense in which mathematical truth is universal. The analogy of mathematics is indeed sometimes used to illustrate the universality of moral principles. As the science of mathematics is always of objective and universal application, so, it is urged, morality offers principles of equally necessary and universal validity.[1] Within certain limits such an analogy holds good, but these limits are soon reached. There are, it would seem, certain ideals which, if stated in sufficiently general terms, are capable of serving as principles of moral endeavor at all times and among all peoples. We may attempt to express the supreme command in such abstract terms as the following: cultivate a good will; realize the self; choose the highest good. Or we may affirm a wide recognition, as ideals of conduct, of certain of the virtues, such as truth-speaking, courage, temperance, and justice. Yet it still remains true that the moment we give to these formal principles any actual historical content, or seek to picture in detail that which they require at different stages of development, the universality at once disappears. What

---

[1] Cf. the statement of Martineau: "The supposition of subjective morals is no less absurd than the supposition of subjective mathematics." We, too, hold that morals are not subjective, but that mathematics offers no satisfactory analogy.

opposing conceptions of life, what diverse plans of action
have been brought under these formulæ! How differently
have they been interpreted, and still are interpreted! Compare, for example, the specific rules of conduct accepted in
good faith by the mediaeval monk and the modern man of
science or leader of industry, by the aggressive occidental and
the passive Hindu, by the savage Bushman and the representative of modern culture, by the imperial autocrat in-
voking the divine right of kings, and the socialistic reformer
to whom the inequalities of the existing order seem the essence of immorality. The difficulty is not disposed of by
saying that all "ought" to think and act in the same way.
A good Chinese citizen "ought," in this view, to act like an
American or European, only he is not aware of the fact!
Surely even the Chinaman ought to act, as he must if he is
to act at all, upon the knowledge and the ideals which he
actually possesses.

The analogy of mathematical principles cannot, then,
be pressed without doing violence to the facts of morality.
Neither the developing life of the individual nor that of
society can be treated in this way. A juster analogy, already
suggested, is found in the rules of hygiene as developed
from the principles of physiology. Although certain fundamental physiological processes remain the same at all stages
of life, there is a sufficient change to necessitate a radically
different regimen at different periods. What is hygienically
good for an infant is not required for an adult, nor are the
same rules of exercise and diet suited to youth and old age.
Following the suggestion afforded by the growing organism,
we may regard the changes in moral codes as the necessary
expressions of a developing human society which becomes
progressively aware of the true needs and values of life.
The crude, undeveloped life of a primitive people must
inevitably express itself in a very imperfect system of morality. Such a system may even be said to be the normal form

of its life.   To deny it this crude expression, would be to refuse it any form of life whatever.   Imperfect moral standards, as they appear in the course of history, are therefore justified, since higher ones would neither be comprehended nor in any way answer existing needs.   The extreme emphasis upon the war-like virtues in primitive society, for example, is justified in view of the fact that the absence of these qualities would have meant extermination or abject slavery.   So, at present, the chief moral justification, in the case of any given nation, for military equipment and service—an enormous drain upon civilization—is the impossibility of securing, thus far, a general consent to the principle of arbitration in any thorough-going form.

As a moral code is always a formulation of an ideal of human welfare, the code changes as the conception of human welfare changes.   A people which conceives its good to consist in the simple gratification of physical needs, or in military glory, or in the refinements of material comfort, will, in each case, frame its moral rules in harmony with its ideals of satisfaction.   And just as far as it is felt that these goods are unsatisfying, there will be a demand for a higher code, a code which more adequately expresses the ideal of that upon which man should set his heart.   It is necessary, therefore, to distinguish between the universality and the validity of moral codes.   As long as validity is made to rest upon universality, morality is always in danger.   Quite different is the validity which springs from the conception of a progressive standard.   This standard recognizes that morality is strictly organic to the needs of developing life, but it does not mean that a standard is wanting at any stage of the process.

The belief that the standard of morality is progressive is far more precious than the belief that it is universal in the form of its requirements.   Strict universality, even were it compatible with the facts, could be purchased only at the

price of a static moral life. This would destroy hope of a
better order, and would take away the high challenge, the
risk of endeavor, without which the moral struggle for causes
of worth would lose its savor. Growth is more to be
desired than fixity, the ardor of pursuit than passive possession. Why should we not cherish for the race the same
ideal of growth which we necessarily apply to the life of the
individual? One points the child to a noble character and
says: "Behold this man, so wise, so devoted to worthy ends,
so helpful to his fellows; this is what you ought to become."
At the same time the immediate realization of this higher
type of life is recognized as an utter impossibility. The
child must still think and feel and act as a child. But the
ideal is none the less one towards which, with growing knowledge and strength, it may progressively advance.

To infer from the historical progress of morality that all
codes are equally good, or that one may safely reject the conscience of one's own day and race, is a conclusion wholly
without warrant. The rejection of a higher type of morality
for a lower is a significant confession of one's place in the
moral scale. A man could not accept the code of a barbaric
people without thereby pronouncing himself essentially a
barbarian. And one cannot choose those standards which
the most enlightened experience has rejected, without a descent along the path up which the race has slowly strug-
gled. Every well-established moral convention embodies
the experience of the past, and has a right to our allegiance until a better way is discovered. The established rules
of conduct, being organic to the needs of life, are ways in
which men are able to live in social relations. That we can
live equally well by disregarding them requires, in each
case, thorough demonstration. The individual is, therefore,
happily not compelled to test by personal experience all ideals
of life and all modes of conduct. As we enter into the
inheritance of a vast body of scientific knowledge which has

been slowly won, and as we are content to accept its established results without personal test, so we also enter upon a heritage of moral wisdom, slowly and painfully won, which it were folly to disregard. No one, unless seeking death, takes active poisons or invites the presence of well-known germs of disease. Here the lessons of the past suffice. Common prudence dictates to the individual a similar caution in the moral sphere. The accumulated experiences of the past ought to count heavily against any impulsive desire to experiment in morality, or to test personally all forms of conduct.

There is a modern gospel the great commandment of which is, "Get experience." The apostles of this teaching make it clear that one need not be too particular about the kind of experience, provided it is varied and intense. Now it is doubtless true that the desirable kind of life involves wealth of experience. But what we insist upon is that the winning of experience must be governed by principle. To get experience without regard to the laws of value is no less unprofitable than to buy and sell commodities on the market without any knowledge of their price. The devotee of "experience" may also be reminded that there are inherent difficulties in the process. One cannot have all kinds of experience, simply because certain experiences are contradictory, the one of the other; in practice, as well as in logic, they exclude each other. I cannot have the experience of being a law-abiding citizen and a thief, a servant of ideal causes and a pander to vice, a lover of enlightenment and an obscurantist. And should I attempt to experience all these modes of life in succession, there are grave, not to say insuperable, obstacles in effecting a transition from one to the other. It is also to be remembered that the deliberate choice not to have a given experience, is itself an experience—an experience which, for the total meaning of life, may be one of the best and richest.

It cannot be denied, of course, that moral experiments must sometimes be tried. In this sense the laws which attempt to deal with intemperance and other forms of vice are experimental, and it is clear, from the very imperfect success of such legislation hitherto, that much more must be done in this direction. These experiments, however, should rest, like those of physical science, upon a basis of already acquired knowledge, and should be surrounded with all possible safe-guards. They are, in fact, commonly free from the danger, which exists in the case of the individual, of being the result of irrational impulse or prurient curiosity. But unhappily, in the sphere of individual life, any wide observation of men must lead the candid student to recognize that there are those with whom the experience of the past counts for little, those in whom evil desire is only checked by the bitter fruit of evil deeds. These are of the prodigal type, for whom "the tigers of wrath" are stronger than "the horses of instruction." But one must be prepared to pay a heavy price for the persistent, thorough-going folly that may lead at last to wisdom.[1]

VII. Objectivity of the Moral Law

The thesis of the sceptic assumes different forms. At one time he attacks the universality of moral law, and, from the fact that universality is wanting, he infers that validity is also wanting. But, as we have seen, such an inference is wholly unwarranted. As well affirm that, because the rules of health for the child are not the same as those for the adult, there are, therefore, no positive laws of health for the child whatever! A progressive standard has, at every stage, its positive requirements. But the sceptic, although driven from his first position, is not yet satisfied; he is inclined to return to the charge and to make his attack at another point. Morality, he tells us, is subjective; it exists in the

---

[1] Cf. Taylor, *The Problem of Conduct*, p. 247, and notes.

minds of individuals, and has no objective existence whatever. Let us consider the question in this form.

The attack of the sceptic at this point must be fairly
met. We admit the necessity of showing that morality is,
in a true sense, objective. Such genuine objectivity is essential to our reverence for it. We must think of moral law
as standing outside the immediate stream of consciousness
with its changing moods and passions. No one has felt
the meaning of morality who does not regard its laws as
august and supreme, having the right to command his whole
being. Such supremacy it could never have for one who
imagined that he could make or unmake it at will, that
"there's nothing good or ill but thinking makes it so."

In answering the sceptic, a possible confusion of thought
concerning the meaning of subjective and objective, as
applied to morality, must, first of all, be made clear. It is
obvious that our ideas about moral truth, as about all other
truth, are our own ideas; they exist in our minds, and are,
in this sense, subjective. Although they are social in their
origin and structure, they are always found in the minds of
individuals, just as are all ideas about the laws of the physical
world. But this does not affect their true objectivity any
more than it affects the objectivity of physical laws, whether
of our bodily life or of the external world. No one imagines
that these physical laws are merely subjective. They are
recognized as not depending upon our caprice, desire, or
taste. Rather do we think of them as having a real existence
outside of our minds. They "are what they are, and the
consequences of them will be what they will be."

Where, then, are we to look for the real existence of the
moral law? In what way is its objectivity to be established?
The answer which uncritical thought makes to this question
is familiar. Appealing to the analogy of jural law, it finds all
moral requirements in some code, more or less completely
formulated, which proceeds from a supreme Moral Governor.

If it rejects the cruder conception of a "table of laws" authoritatively revealed to man, it still refers the objective existence of morality to the mind of such a Law-giver. But even though we admit the existence of all moral principles in such a mind, we are obviously helpless to draw directly from this source a single precept or a single rule of conduct. On the contrary, we infer the existence in this mind of certain principles because we find them vindicated in human experience. Discovering here what is good, men ascribe it to a divine source, and complete the circle by bringing it back into human life.

We are not, however, thrown back upon subjectivity or scepticism because we are unable to discover moral law in an immediate knowledge of the Divine Mind. Moral law is just as real as human nature, within which it has its existence. Strange, indeed, if man alone of all living beings could realize his highest welfare in disregard of the principles of his own nature! And this nature, we must remember, is what it is—is always concrete and definite. Indeed the sceptic nowhere else assumes the absence of principles through obedience to which the highest form of life can be attained. He does not assume that a lily, which requires abundant moisture and rich soil, could grow on an arid rock, nor that a polar bear could flourish in a tropical jungle. No less certain than would be the failure of such attempts, must be the failure of man to realize, in disregard of the laws of his being, the values of which he is capable. The structure of man's nature, as conscious and spiritual, grounds laws just as real as those of his physical life, and just as truly objective. To use again the analogy we have suggested, whether or not I feel like obeying a law of hygiene makes no difference to its existence or validity. When thirsty, I may be tempted to drink water containing the germs of typhoid, and I may find immediate satisfaction in the cooling draught. But my desire and my satisfaction make no difference to the result. There remains the hard, inescapable fact of the danger of disease. As little can I escape the results of moral evil, which, with equal certainty, has inevitable consequences in my own nature.

If the sceptic finally asserts that his own nature is so unique as to require a moral regimen fundamentally different from that of his fellows, the fact of such a degree of uniqueness may be challenged. This is commonly the claim, not of maturity, but of youth, when, coming to consciousness of new desires and capacities, it imagines that no other being has had like experiences. But age has learned better; it knows that it would be impossible to attain the goal of life in disregard of social factors and psychological laws that are universal. In practice, however, the most extreme individualist does not assume that he could break completely with the *mores* of his people, and live in isolation. His revolt always reduces to the charge that, at some points, the existing order could be improved. If he has gained a deeper and clearer understanding of this order than his fellows, he may render the service of the reformer. If he be a prophet or seer, he may make the contribution of one of those great personalities who, at rare intervals, appear upon the stage of history.

What the youthful sceptic often demands is an infallible moral code. He asks for a degree of completeness and definiteness in knowledge that are not attainable. With something both of noble idealism and of rebellious unreason in his spirit, he revolts against the imperfect. Because he cannot have absolute certainty, he scorns all degrees of certainty; because he cannot have all he desires, he takes nothing; because an institution or code does not yield perfect results, it must be utterly destroyed. But one who is in such a mood may well be reminded that the fact that an institution or code does not work perfectly is no proof that it should be abolished, or that a different institution or code would yield better results. On what ground could we expect a perfect moral order among imperfect beings? Yet the revolt of youthful idealism may be turned to good account. "*Man sollte die Träume seiner Jugend behalten.*" Let youth only remember that each step forward must be bought at the price of a deeper understanding of life.

If, finally, it be asked what is to decide ultimately between conflicting ideals and codes of morality, our answer must be that the historical progress of civilization is doubtless the court of last appeal. "*Die Weltgeschichte ist das Weltgericht.*" The long course of racial experience, forever putting to test opposing ideals of life, must be left to sift the wheat from the chaff. Doubtless this slow grinding of the "mills of the gods" hardly suits our eager desire to discover a perfect moral order, and to see it immediately triumphant. But we must believe that by inherent strength the best will survive. This belief is not to be confused with the doctrine that "might makes right;" it is rather that, in the long run, morality is a life-preserving force. Those ideals which, in the light of the most adequate experience, fail to meet human needs will, we may hope, be slowly rejected. Those that beget in society weakness and decay will perish with their representatives. Those, too, which keep peoples in permanent stagnation will be forced to reconstruction, unless they are to be dominated by more progressive types. Constant readjustment is the condition of all life, which maintains itself and increases by the assimilation of new elements. This process, too, is the "fountain of youth" for man's spiritual life. In it each succeeding generation must bathe for renewal.

CHAPTER XII

THE ETHICAL INTERPRETATION OF FREEDOM

THE preceding discussions have implied the possibility of conformity, more or less complete, to an ideal of conduct and character. They have assumed that the claims of duty and the requirements of the moral law can, in some measure, be met in the daily life of men. The question of freedom, which logically might seem to claim precedence as being fundamental to any treatment of the problems of morality, must now receive attention. The postponement of its treatment may be justified in view of its complexity and the advantage of approaching it with some knowledge of the general field of ethical thought. No problem of ethics has been the centre of more fierce debate. And if modern discussions of the question show a growing tendency towards harmony of opinion, the harmony is far from complete; dissenting voices are still heard.

I. STATEMENT OF THE PROBLEM

The controversy concerning the problem of freedom, in modern times, lies chiefly between two opposing theories, commonly known as determinism and indeterminism. The deterministic view maintains that all events in man's mental life, equally with events in the physical world, must be conceived as antecedently conditioned, as having their origin in preceding events of which they are the necessary sequence. Applied to conduct, this means that any act, whether good or bad, is the necessary result of the inner nature and outward circumstances, in other words, of the total character and environment of the actor. One's character and environ-

ment are regarded, by the determinist, as the product of conditioning forces which reach back in an unending chain of
succession. This position also means that if we had a full
knowledge of the antecedents of any act, as in practice of
course we cannot have, we should understand the act, and
should see why the act is just what it is. Nothing in conduct
would then appear blind or a matter of chance.

The indeterminist opposes this view with the contention
that there are events in the mental and moral life which are
not explicable by reference to such a net-work of necessary
relations. These events spring immediately and spontaneously from the will, and appear in human experience as a
strictly new creation. On this theory, the will can form a
decision without reference to the strength of the competing
motives. It is possible that, given precisely the same antecedent psychical conditions and the same outward circumstances in two cases, the resulting choices will not be the
same.[1] Such acts of free will, in the words of Lotze, "could
just as well have been left unperformed." [2] As undetermined
and causeless, there was no sufficient reason why they were
performed. In the last analysis, therefore, there is an element in human conduct which, from its very nature, and not
merely from the limitations of our knowledge, must forever
baffle explanation and be declared not only inexplicable and
mysterious, but also strictly a matter of chance.[3]

The following discussion is an attempt to interpret freedom
and responsibility in harmony with the view that mental,
as well as physical events, are determinately related. Only
in this way, it is believed, can the interests of scientific

[1] Mr. Rashdall illustrates the situation by the hypothetical case of twin brothers,
"endowed originally with absolutely identical natures, and exposed from the moment of birth to exactly the same social and other influences." According to the
indeterminist, "one of them might have become a saint, and the other a scoundrel."
Theory of Good and Evil, Vol. II, p. 303.

[2] Lotze, *Outlines of Practical Philosophy*, p. 35.

[3] Cf. the statement of James, "The Dilemma of Determinism," *The Will to Believe and other Essays*, p. 145.

reflection and of practical morality both be secured. There can be no doubt that with the development of science and its successful extension to ever widening spheres, it more and more resists limitation to physical phenomena, and seeks to enter the domain of human conduct. Those sciences which deal with human activity, such as psychology, ethics, economics, and history, are all compelled to assume, as the condition of their existence and progress, that the actions of men, highly complex and varied as these are, lie within the series of necessary relations. As long as our thought deals with any series of events, it must conceive them as thus related. To cease to view them in this way is to cease to think them at all in any intelligible sense of the term. For the very idea of necessary relation in events, familiarly called the causal law, is a universal law of thought. Though the individual comes to the full consciousness of this law slowly through long experience, this law, when won, is of universal and necessary validity in the explanation of events. We cannot here discuss the problem of causality in metaphysics, but must limit ourselves to the statement that causality, in the sense in which we hold it to be a necessity of thought, means that we invariably seek the reason, or ground, for the occurrence of any new event in what has gone before. "An absolutely new beginning, unconnected with the past, is unthinkable." [1]

Granting the universality of this principle for most events, the indeterminist objects that there are events in human conduct, which, from their very nature, cannot be thought at all in relation to antecedent events. And, further, if the attempt to connect moral choices with their antecedents works havoc in morality, must not the attempt be abandoned? Life, it is urged, is more than science, and moral interests superior to the categories of thought. In answer to this objection it may be replied that, if we found any

[1] Rashdall, *The Theory of Good and Evil*, Vol. II, p. 337.

theoretical interest permanently at war with a moral interest, we should doubtless be compelled to sacrifice the one or the other. Either the scientific impulse or the moral impulse would be surrendered, according to the preponderance in the individual of the one interest or the other. But such a solution implies a permanent and intolerable dualism in our thinking, not to be accepted save as a last resort. Let us rather see if the two interests are not compatible—nay, if in the unity of our nature it may not be true that this theoretical impulse to think our conduct in a series of necessary relations also best serves our moral interests. The case may be stated as follows: theoretical interests seem to us clearly to demand the hypothesis of determinism; if moral interests are compatible with this hypothesis, we are reasonably bound to accept it; and if, further, moral interests should prove to be incompatible with indeterminism, the case for determinism becomes conclusive.

II. KANTIAN DUALISM

The attempt has frequently been made to hold both theories at the same time by a metaphysical doctrine which admits determination within the empirical sphere, and relegates freedom to a different sphere, to which the categories of science do not apply. The classic form of the doctrine is that of Kant, who distinguished between the "sensible" and "intelligible" worlds. In the phenomenal world of sense experience, the law of causality is of universal validity. Here freedom is impossible, for the "empirical character" follows with necessity the natural order. But man is, at the same time, a citizen of an "intelligible world," the world of "things-in-themselves." Through this higher citizenship he can escape the reign of natural law and necessity. Not here, then, in the empirical world, are we free; for here, all impulses, feelings, and ideas are strictly determined; but yonder, in the eternal world of reason, our freedom is exercised in a timeless, undetermined choice of character.[1]

Apart from the philosophical difficulties of such a dualism, which cannot be considered here, it is ethically unsatisfying. It identifies freedom in the last resort with indeterminism, and excludes any other interpretation of it. It also disregards the fact that our moral task lies primarily in the empirical world, the world of temporal choices and earthly experiences. That man is rational, and is not limited to mere sense impressions, is a fact of profound import for his freedom. But to found a doctrine of freedom upon this fact is quite different from creating an impassable gulf between different elements of human nature, or from denying that the higher, rational life has a mechanism through which alone the freedom which is possible for us can be attained. The attempt to rescue freedom by impeaching causal determination is an attempt to "climb up some other way," and to escape the ordered processes of the moral life.

III. The Natural History of Indeterminism

It is doubtless true that popular, uncritical thought is largely indeterministic, and that only slowly, with the growth of scientific reflection, has determinism won its present measure of recognition. What is the explanation of this fact? If an extended answer cannot be here at-

---

[1] It is from this latter point of view only that Kant can be called an indeterminist. There is another side to his thought, in which freedom appears as rational determination by the idea of duty. See, for example, the interesting note in the *Preface to the Metaphysical Elements of Ethics*, Abbott's trans., p. 292. Here it is clearly recognized that there are degrees of freedom, and that the highest degree is that at which one is completely determined, or "forced," by the idea of duty.

A similar dualism appears as an element in certain forms of modern idealism, according to which all mental processes are necessarily viewed by psychology as determined; but the interpretations of psychology are special constructions for scientific purposes, and have no validity for the moral life. See Münsterberg, *Psychology and Life*, pp. 7–9, and 221–222. For a different statement of this double-aspect theory see Royce, *The Spirit of Modern Philosophy*, pp. 428–434; also, *The World and the Individual*, 2nd Series, pp. 323–331.

tempted, there are still certain historical aspects of human thinking which enable one to understand why the inner life of man should long be regarded as an exception, perhaps the sole exception, to the principle of necessary determination. The attitude of primitive man towards nature is especially instructive, as is also the history of the development of scientific ideas.

It is well known that primitive thought is animistic. It peoples the world, animate and inanimate, with spirits akin to man's own. It regards all activities as due to a consciousness residing in the individual objects in connection with which these activities appear. The gushing forth of fountains and the flowing of streams, the restless movement of the ocean, the blowing of the wind, the life and growth of plants, are all conceived as due to the presence of living spirits analogous to that which man finds within himself. All events, therefore, occur with a kind of incalculable spontaneity and caprice. "The wind bloweth where it listeth." No idea of uniformities in nature has yet arisen. Just as the savage finds himself driven, now to this deed, now to that, by inner instincts and impulses of whose origin and meaning he is ignorant, so he conceives it to be in nature. Its processes are equally inexplicable, and equally wanting in any principle of unity which binds them all into a related and harmonious whole. Primitive religion is a monument in evidence of such a mode of thought. To appease the forces of nature and render them favorable is a central aim of early religious rites and worship. In the attainment of this end the worshipper uses the same means which he recognizes as effective in human relations, the same indeed by which another might win his own favor—gifts, entreaty, expressions of love and honor.

But with the growth of observation and reflection there slowly arises the idea of general processes and uniformities in nature. The countless objects of sense experience are grouped together. Classifications, which naturally precede logical explanation, are made. Winds and waters are no longer isolated and independent beings, but the expression of more universal beings or forces. The immobility and relative changelessness of inorganic nature made it easier to apply causal explanation first in this sphere. The stone moves only when force is applied; water does not run up hill, but forever seeks a lower level. The realms of plant and animal life, however, offer a greater mystery. In the plant, man confronts the mystery of life in its simplest form. And the plant that springs from the tiny seed and grows into forms of use and beauty, does not so obviously obey the rule of necessity, nor so clearly fall under the operation of general laws. Its growth takes place mysteriously, in ways he does not understand, not by mere aggregation, like the heap of sand or stones, but by an inner, hidden process of assimilation. It was not without a sense of this mystery that the ancient Roman invoked the many deities that he conceived as presiding over the life of the growing plant.

Still more mysterious and akin to his own nature was the animal kingdom. The beast with its sure instinct and great activity was man's nearest rival, often outwitting him by its cunning, or overpowering him by its strength. Here was a force that surely knew no law, but was a law unto itself, turning and changing subtly through invisible inner processes, not through external compulsions. This internalizing and complicating of the mechanism of action seemed completely to baffle explanation. The wide-spread phenomena of animal worship offer striking evidence that, for long centuries, man regarded animal conduct as a mystery to be revered rather than as a problem to be explained. Only with relatively ripe reflection did he come to regard all the wonders of animal life as lying completely within the realm of determined phenomena and offering no exception to the operation of the causal law.

Finally, man comes to himself. Though the race, like the

child, is long occupied with external things, it at last turns
to reflect upon itself. As man recognizes the wonders of his
own being, his growing mastery of nature, his relations with
his fellows, his appreciation of truth, beauty, and goodness,
he finds in himself the crowning marvel and mystery of the
universe. It is the one realm that defies explanation, the
fortress where blind, uncaused events have made their sure
retreat. But even here science has slowly penetrated.
Little by little it has extended its empire over this so complex and varied field, and has subjected its phenomena to
examination and explanation. The principle of necessary
connection has been the guiding thread by which man has
slowly escaped from many a fearsome labyrinth of error and
superstition. Consider, as a single example, the beneficent
results which have followed the application of causal explanation to the facts of mental pathology. Insanity in all its
forms has been taken from the realm of an inexplicable
demonology, with the saving of untold cruelty and suffering.
Witchcraft and other baneful delusions have been rendered
impossible among intelligent people by the march of scientific explanation, and even the higher spiritual life of man is
seen to unfold itself in no arbitrary and capricious way, but
to depend upon antecedent and conditioning events. The
last few decades have witnessed a most significant effort to
discover the laws which prevail in those profound religious
experiences which have seemed the peculiar realm of the
inexplicable. We must recognize, to be sure, that even if
the task of causal explanation were fully achieved, mystery
in a sense would still remain. Such mystery is seen in the
growth of the tiniest seed and even in the movement of every
atom, as well as in all the ranges of conscious life. But we
regard it as a mystery inviting inquiry, not a blank unknow-
able defying investigation. The clear comprehension of the
relations of all events in their ordered sequences would in
no wise destroy their marvel or their worth.

Thus briefly, and in broad outline, may be traced the growth of the realm of scientific knowledge, which is the realm of necessarily conditioned events. The history of this development exhibits at the same time the natural history of indeterminism. Indeterminism is the last stand made against the advance of scientific conceptions. In the words of Sidgwick: "The belief that events are determinately related to the state of things immediately preceding them, is now held by all competent thinkers in respect of all kinds of occurrences except human volitions. It has steadily grown both intensively and extensively, both in clearness and certainty of conviction and in universality of application, as the human mind has developed and human experience has been systematized and enlarged. Step by step in successive departments of fact conflicting modes of thought have receded and faded, until at length they have vanished everywhere, except from this mysterious citadel of Will Everywhere else the belief is so firmly established that some declare its opposite to be inconceivable: others even maintain that it always was so. Every scientific procedure assumes it: each success of science confirms it." [1] And is not the fear that the method of science, if admitted here, will work destructively, as groundless as the view that science destroys the wonder or beauty of nature?

IV. Points of Agreement between Determinists and Indeterminists

As has been already suggested, both determinism and indeterminism are attempts to interpret the facts of the moral life. We may even say that both recognize freedom, in some sense, as a factor in this life. The real difference is a difference in the explanation of a fact admitted by both. Both views of course agree at the outset in rejecting that crude and uncritical view which would make freedom con-

[1] *Methods of Ethics*, pp. 62-63.

sist in the power to do whatever one may desire, to work one's pleasure without let or hindrance both in nature and in society. Quite obviously such freedom exists nowhere outside of fairy-land. With all his mastery over nature how quickly man finds barriers which he cannot pass! Even though he is victorious for a little time, he is soon compelled to surrender life itself as a tribute to the might of her forces. No less certainly does society set sharp limits to the play of personal will. Most men are so thoroughly the creatures of their social environment that they never seem to transcend it sufficiently to rise into a genuinely individual existence. And when we look within, we clearly discern the limits of possible activity set by our own nature, a nature not of our choosing, but having its roots far back in the life of the family and of the race. Even the desire to become this or that type of personality is seen to have its source in inherited tendencies.

> "In vain our pent wills fret,
>   And would the world subdue.
> Limits we did not set
>   Condition all we do;
> Born into life we are, and life must be our mould.
>
> "Born into life! man grows
>   Forth from his parents' stem,
> And blends their bloods, as those
>   Of theirs are blent in them;
> So each new man strikes root into a far fore-time.
>
> "Born into life! we bring
>   A bias with us here,
> And, when here, each new thing
>   Affects us we come near;
> To tunes we did not call, our being must keep chime." [1]

These facts are so universally admitted that there may be said to be no controversy about them among intelligent

[1] Matthew Arnold, *Empedocles on Aetna.*

people. The indeterminist frankly admits that the field of undetermined choice is narrowly limited, and that determinism applies without reserve to the larger part of human conduct. His contention reduces, in the last analysis, to the claim that there are cases in which, of two alternative courses, he can choose either the one or the other, independently of that self which all the past has fashioned; consequently even a perfect knowledge of this self, prior to the moment of choice, would not give to an observer the key to the actual decision. The determinist insists, on the contrary, that just this choice here and now depends upon the character of the self, including all its potentialities, and that a full understanding of this self would also involve an understanding of every choice. To illustrate the narrowing of the problem, we may imagine the agent as standing at the center of a circle; radii extending to the circumference represent paths of action; through the influence of forces within and without, the general direction of the agent's movement is determined. The question is whether his choice of one special path rather than another is also determined. It is never a question of absolute freedom.

The fact of deliberation and choice is further admitted by both parties to the controversy. But this psychological process, with which everyone is familiar, is so significant for the problem in hand as to require some attention. As far as any so-called choice is not a matter of conscious deliberation, but springs from instincts or impulses that work within us blindly, there can of course be no difference of opinion. Acts having their source in the play of such instinctive forces are admitted to be determined by the nature of the inherited instincts in interaction with external stimuli.

V. THE MECHANISM OF CHOICE

Moral choice with which we are here concerned takes place only when there is conscious deliberation in the presence of two or more conflicting motives, that is, ideas of ends with their accompanying emotions. The motive of conscious choice properly includes both the idea of an end and the accompanying emotions, which are sometimes said to be the real motive, or "moving" element, in conduct. The separation of the two factors, however, is the result of a false abstraction. The ideational and affective elements vary in prominence; now one and now the other occupies the foremost place, but both are always present in a moral act. Even "blind" passion is never completely blind; its expression follows the path to some perceived end. And, on the other hand, the "coldest" idea that we entertain kindles feeling enough to secure for it some measure of interest and attention.[1] The larger portion of conduct is obviously given over to habit. One chooses a line of effort or an end to be attained, and, through a wise economy of nature, the details follow as a matter of course. But in any proper act of choice there is always a pause, longer or shorter, during which the possible choices are held in mind and compete for the mastery over us, each with the measure of attraction which it possesses for us. Strength of motive in this contest is not to be measured by any merely external standard, but always with reference to the self at the moment of choice. It is this self which gives to each motive its measure of strength. Or, more exactly, the given motive, which is one of the many activities constituting the total self, depends for its strength upon the nature of that total self.

Not a little of the prejudice against determinism is due to the impression that it makes the moral agent a "victim" of external and independent forces or ideas. A true determinism is, on the contrary, an auto-determinism, viewing all thoughts, sentiments, and preferences as activities of the self. The stronger motive which, as the determinist main-

[1] For an attempted separation of these elements see Taylor, *The Problem of Conduct*, p. 95.

tains, finally claims our allegiance is therefore the one which finds the most within us, or is thought by us with the most intensity, rather than the one which, to a disinterested, objective spectator, appears most attractive. What is an overwhelmingly powerful motive to one person may, as we well know, present no attraction whatever to another; it may even chill and repel him. The only meaning which can be given to the statement that in any particular case I have acted from the weaker motive, is that I have chosen that course which, in the view of others, has the least in its favor, or which, from my own subsequent experience, I condemn as ill-advised or foolish. No real exception to the triumph of the stronger motive is offered by those cases in which an action, attractive to one's sensuous desires or to any natural impulse, is rejected for a call of duty which, by contrast with the proposed satisfaction, seems at the first glance unattractive, and perhaps even forbidding. The superior strength of the moral demand in such a case lies sometimes in its congruity with an unanalyzed feeling of duty, deeply rooted in instinct and habit, and sometimes in its agreement with the manifest requirements of our nature as a whole, and our total life interests. But the idea that a weaker motive has triumphed over a stronger is corrected, upon reflection, by the consideration that, at the time of action, my judgment, taste, disposition, and character were such that the chosen act did in fact appeal to me more powerfully than any alternative act. And what can be said of this judgment, taste, disposition, and character which thus determined my choice? Are these factors the expression of a power of the self to affirm or deny in ways which introduce a strictly uncaused element into conduct? Rather, as we shall see, must we believe that these factors are nothing strictly self-created, evoked out of nothing at the summons of the will, but that they are the result of the total past life of the self.

The choice, in case of conscious deliberation, however it may fall, cannot be explained, or even thought, except as the result of the antecedent and determining motive. The "why" of an act necessarily implies this determinate relation. If there be no "why" of a human action, the action is confessedly given over to the realm of the inconceivable. "The determinist maintains that the question: 'Why did this man act in this particular manner?' is never a foolish question, although we may in any particular instance be ignorant of the answer. He assumes that there is always some cause or causes that can account for the result. The 'free-willist,' on the other hand, maintains that no complete answer to such a question can be given, not because we are ignorant, but because human actions are not necessarily the results of causes. If we ask him: 'Why did this man elect to put his hand in his pocket and take out a copper for the beggar on the street?' he is capable of answering: 'Just because he did.' . . . It amounts to asserting that, in so far as human actions are 'free,' they have no cause whatever, and the search for an explanation of their occurrence is wholly futile." [1]

Certainly a choice which has no ground, no determining motive, cannot be a reasonable choice. And are we not as surely compelled to regard a reasonable choice as determined by its motive as we are to consider the moving billiard-ball as the cause of the motion of the ball which it strikes? Unless we are willing to abandon the "why" of human conduct and give it over to chance and inconceivability, we must apply to it some principle of determination. That in all our practical judgments of the conduct of men we do actually regard their actions as thus caused, seems to me incontestable.

The indeterminist, however, at once replies: "Out of your own mouth is your determinism refuted. You speak of the

[1] Fullerton, "Free Will and the Credit for Good Actions," *Popular Science Monthly*, Oct. 1901, p. 529.

self as giving strength to its motives and as choosing in accordance with them. By indeterminism I do not mean that an act is uncaused, but that it is caused by the self, by its own 'causal energy.' " [1] Thus the question inevitably comes back to the self, its nature and its source.

VI. THE NATURE OF THE SELF

What, then, are we to think of the self whose "causal" energy is here in play? Does it come from no-whither? Has it no history that conditions its present activity? Does it possess an incalculable power to choose or to refuse courses of conduct in ways that break the continuity of its development? The indeterminist is compelled to affirm the discontinuity of the self. In his view, the self is a genuine *causa sui*. It, in the strictest sense, "originates" activity. Can such an interpretation of the self be accepted? Let us see. The self surely does not create itself, and it does not, as all would admit, "originate," in the early part of its existence, any activity whatever. Nor have we any evidence that the self sits down, as it were, at the beginning of its conscious life, or in the shadowy regions of a pre-existent state, to consider what sort of a self it shall be. When it first comes to consciousness it is a bundle of activities already moving swiftly along a definite track. It has, as far as we can judge, its beginning at a fixed point of time; it is endowed with a definite physical and psychical nature; it enters into a particular environment; it receives the stamp of a special training and education; and even the sources of those ideas and ideals, by which it afterwards modifies or transcends early conditions, are found in the social-historical life into which it enters. Let anyone seriously ask himself: "What sort of a self should I be if born in another age and country, the offspring of other parents, if of opposite sex, if endowed by nature with different physical and mental traits, and if

[1] Cf. Calderwood, *Handbook of Moral Philosophy*, p. 186.

subject to different training, intellectual, moral, and religious?" And if one further ask: "Why am I not this other self?" the only answer can be: "Because the self that I now am is the result of other conditions."

Doubtless the feeling against admitting this idea of determination in mental life is largely due to the transference to consciousness of the same kind of determination which holds in mechanical interaction. The self seems thereby reduced to a merely passive point for the transmission of external processes. But this view loses entirely the significance of all the complex inner processes and the constructive activities of the life of personality. The development of reflection and self-criticism, of self-direction and moral effort on the part of the self, are essential conditions of human freedom, a freedom in and through determination by rational insight. The self is active; it constitutes its experience, its ideas, its knowledge. We only contend that it does this in no arbitrary, lawless way. Indeed, it is just because the process of knowledge must be regarded as a conditioned, orderly, and necessary process, that our human freedom must be conceived in terms of determinism. Because we regard the tree as necessarily determined in its growth we never think of it as passive, as doing nothing, playing no part, or as the product of merely external forces. The tree is the organic unity of all the processes of its life and growth, and when it ceases to act constructively it ceases to live. Nor do we conceive the fate of the animal as determined apart from its own activity, but in and through its own marvelous instinctive processes. The self, too, is the organic unity of all its activities, vastly richer and more varied than those of animal life. And just as the mechanical formulae of inorganic nature are inadequate to plant life, and the formulae of plant life to the more complex life of the animal kingdom, so other and still more complex formulae, we hold, must be conceived as expressing the activities of the conscious, reasoning self, rising as it does above all these lower grades of being. If there is a "must" in the sequence of events within the self, it is not the "must" which expresses the uniformity of sequence with which one material body moves at the impact of another. It is not the resultant of merely mechanical forces. In its higher manifestations it is determined by ideals and ideas, a determination in which the final cause of action is also its efficient cause. Such determination by the attraction of ideas of value which challenge interest and claim obedience, is the one point in the universe where we are able to see clearly the identity of final and efficient causation.

VII. UNITY OF EFFICIENT AND FINAL CAUSATION

We are, then, capable of determination by the ideas of ends which are, at the same time, the driving motives for their own realization. Ideas are efficient forces. In this fact is to be found the true source of our freedom. Intelligence thus contains a genuine element of transcendence, by which we are delivered from subjection to the moment. This is indeed our human way of escape from bondage. The indeterminist, however, is prone to assume that whatever is within the sphere of such final causation is necessarily outside that of efficient causation. This assumption is doubtless one source of the dualism of thought concerning freedom and necessity which is so widely current. But the separation cannot be justified. It is never the future event, as such, and as separated from present and past events, that is causally effective, but the present representation of the future event. The end can never have the slightest influence save as a present idea which has been constructed out of antecedent elements. When, for example, does a man save for a possible "rainy day"? Obviously only when the idea of such a contingency stirs within him. And, with equal certainty, his present idea has grown out of the past. If I desire to arouse ambition in a young man by an ideal of future achievement, this ideal must be effectively related to his present state of mind. Antecedent process is as necessary in moral as in mechanical determination. As well try to drive an engine from Boston to New York by power generated in New York, and not present by transmission in Boston, as to expect a future event to influence conduct without first entering the mind as an idea antecedent to this event. At a lower level of consciousness this process is illustrated by the play of organic instincts. The rearing of young is said to be the cause of nest-building, but it operates causally only when represented in the organic processes which determine, step by step, the nest-building activities.

If, further, it be said that to insist upon the strict continuity of the life of the self from its earliest beginnings is, in effect, to reduce man to a part of nature, it may be answered that in this case one's thought of nature must be made rich enough to make room for spiritual processes. The self is not thereby beggared, but nature enriched.[1] Certainly the dignity and worth of man's self-directed life, of his control of impulse and appetite, of his aspirations after truth and goodness, are not one whit lessened by the view that all these processes are within the realm of law. It is a far greater menace to human dignity to regard our life as in any degree the sport of caprice or chance.

The problem of freedom, it should be noted, is often com-

[1] The problem of the relation of mental and physical processes deserves a word, although it cannot be discussed at length. I can simply state as briefly as possible my own view, to the effect that the self, mind and body, is a unity in a sense to which no dualistic theory can do justice. All conscious states are, at the same time, physical processes. Were our knowledge adequate, all mental experiences might conceivably be stated in physical formulae, and vice versa. But the knowledge that would make possible such a statement would clearly differentiate the physical formulae of our mental life from all those formulae which express the activities of other kinds of beings or things, and would at once interpret their significance and worth as lying wholly in the conscious experiences of which the physical processes are one expression.

plicated, at least in popular thinking, by a false view of the nature of the will. It is frequently assumed that the will is a power apart from the rest of the self, called into action in moments of choice, and for the rest inactive. It is regarded as a kind of special dynamo, held in reserve, to be used only on occasion. Such an idea of the nature and function of the will is altogether inadmissible. The will is not a distinct part of the self in the sense which the older psychology suggested. It is, as we have maintained, the thinking, feeling self in effort and action. My will of this moment is my total conscious self with all its predispositions, habits, feelings, desires, aims, and ideals, expressing itself here and now in concrete effort.

VIII. Indeterminism at Variance with Practice

Perhaps the severest arraignment of indeterminism is in its helplessness in the presence of the actual problems of conduct. If theoretical interests speak strongly for the explanation of the self in terms of continuity and necessary determination, practical interests seem equally to demand it. If the moral life be not a continuous development, if there be any break in the relation of its past and present, then indeed the good tree may bring forth evil fruit; in the moral world we may gather grapes from thorns and figs from thistles. Our sowing of the good seed to-day may count for naught to-morrow. Evil may be done with the hope that it will not matter. Expectation of the conduct of men is disturbed and confidence destroyed. Punishment and reward, the training of the young, education, government, social effort, responsibility—all rest upon an implicit determinism. As far as punishment has moral justification, it is inflicted upon the evil-doer either for his own betterment or for the deterrent influence which it will exert upon others. Its purpose is always to determine future conduct. But if, at the moment of the evil-doer's next choice between right and wrong, he may assert a sovereign freedom which breaks completely with his past, the experience of punishment may be wholly inoperative, and it then becomes a needless and wicked infliction of pain. The same ineffectiveness may extend to all those whom the punishment was intended to influence. It is quite true that punishment may be, and often is, ineffective. But this fact, the determinist insists, also has its cause. And it behooves us to bestir ourselves to discover it rather than to fold our arms and refer the failure to an arbitrary freak of human nature. Certainly all progress in dealing with evil-doers in the family, in the school, and in the state, has been due to the actual use of the deterministic principle, which assumes no fragment of conduct to be without its cause. The case stands precisely the same with the use of reward as with the use of punishment in influencing conduct. The effectiveness of reward is wholly conditioned upon the principle of determinism.

Why, we may ask, does the parent select the best possible environment for the child? Why is he so careful of example? Why does he attach such importance to education? Obviously because he believes that every influence is potent in fashioning the plastic life. But if freedom mean indeterminism, all this may count for nothing in the hour of most momentous decision. The theory underlying the entire mechanism of government is that men are determined by motives, and that adequate motives of hope and fear, of reward and punishment, must be supplied. Nothing would more certainly cut the nerve of all social endeavor than the general belief, accepted and acted upon, that men are capable of uncaused acts, acts which break the continuity of developing mental and moral life, and which stand out of all relation to the great web of social-historical events. Responsibility, for the sake of which indeterminism has so often been held, fares equally ill on that hypothesis.

As Hartmann has urged, if there were a human being burdened with a *liberum arbitrium indifferentiae*, the free will
of indeterminism, he would require the same treatment
from society as the madman, for his acts would be as little
reached by any kind of punishment or moral suasion.[1]
This statement is no exaggeration. Before the possibilities
of such a free will one might well stand in terror. Being, as
the indeterminist himself so strongly insists, the source of
unmotived and indeterminable acts which break in upon
the continuity of the mental life and appear as a strictly
new creation in it, there is absolutely no accounting for
them or controlling them. Who can say what strange re-
versals of conduct and character an undetermined will
may work? Your best friend, in whose integrity, honor, and
devotion you place unquestioning confidence, if seized with
a fit of such free will, may prove the veriest knave. Our
sole ground of confidence in our fellows is the assurance
that conduct is in no way arbitrary or the result of chance,
but flows with necessity from character. In fine, the indeterminist can save moral institutions and a moral order
only by limiting his view strictly to certain general proposi-
tions within the theoretical sphere. As soon as the theory
is called upon to explain the concrete facts of conduct it
becomes speechless and impotent. In practice, however,
the "free-willist" is often "the most determined of deter-
minists."

If we ask for the sources of moral help and progress, we
can represent them to ourselves as found only in the intensi-
fication of existing motives, or in the construction of new
and more effective ones to take the place of those already
existing. But neither the one process nor the other is regarded as unrelated to antecedents; we can only think a
change by either method as the result of adequately effective influences. In general we are able to refer our moral

[1] See his *Phänomenologie des sittlichen Bewusstseins*, pp. 467–468.

help and inspiration to certain specific causes. "Here and
here did England help me." It may be one's early training,
or the hard lessons of experience, or the influence of some
noble personality, which became the fruitful seed of a har-
vest that one still reaps with grateful heart. . Doubtless
there are instances of the access of moral power which are
not thus susceptible of clear reference to their sources. But
this by no means proves them to be uncaused. Often a
conviction which has been nourished by scarcely noted
experiences and fed by almost unconscious insights at last
breaks forth one day into clear resolve, and turns the whole
current of life. A close examination shows us that such
increments of moral power, though harder to analyze, are
not sundered from our past experience; rather are their
relations with that experience discernible at so many points
that we are impelled to regard them as completely continuous with it.

But if we reject the belief that the will in its choices is
free from determining conditions, does significance still
attach to the idea of freedom, or must we abandon this
ideal which has so often been the rallying call of the higher
interests of humanity?

IX. Freedom Consistent with Determinism

There remain certainly two important meanings of the
word freedom which require definition and explanation.
The first of these meanings represents what may be called
the negative aspect of freedom, the absence of alien restraint
over the will; the other is moral freedom, or true freedom of
life. In the first sense, an act is said to be free when it is
what we intend it to be, when through it we consciously
express our purpose, unhindered by physical interference or
by another's will. Thus I am free to cross the swiftly rushing
stream if the bridge has not been swept away by the flood;
I am free to follow the trail to the summit of the mountain

if my strength does not fail; and I am free to purchase a desired piece of property if I can induce the owner to sell. In this sense of the term the evil man is as free in his acts as the good man, provided he is no more restrained by society or by natural forces. When free in this sense, both the good man and the evil man can do as they please. The determinist only insists that there is always a sufficient reason why each pleases to do as he does.

If we designate the freedom just described as freedom from restraint, there remains to be considered the more important conception of moral freedom, or freedom of life. If the evildoer is as free from restraint as the virtuous man, he is not morally free, for his nature is in conflict with itself and with the moral order. Moral freedom as little means license, the doing simply what one may for the moment desire, as does civil freedom. And just as men are truly free in the state only when all are obedient to wise laws, so men are morally free only when they are completely determined in their conduct by the requirements of a true moral standard. To the extent even to which one hesitates between right and wrong, or coquets with evil, one is not morally free, for in this case the evil solicits, attracts, influences one. And to the degree that one feels the attractive power of evil one is subject to its sway. Moral freedom is properly to be contrasted with moral bondage. The experience of the good life is freedom, just as the experience of the evil life is slavery. On its negative side, moral freedom is freedom from the power of the lower impulses and desires, which destroy the harmony and hinder the development of personality. Moral freedom results in an inner harmony, a just expression of all the powers of the self, in contrast with the discord and strife which the competing appetites, if not organized and controlled, introduce into our nature. Such freedom is secured through the rule of reason, which seeks to subordinate to the central aim of life our partial, conflicting aims and desires. The morally free life is the life that has won its unity, and thereby gained harmony and peace. But this moral freedom might better be called freedom of life than freedom of will, for it involves a will steadily controlled by laws of value in the interest of a life purpose. This fact has long been implicitly recognized in popular religious thought. For God, according to the popular conception of His nature, is both completely determined and completely free. He is completely determined in His choices by the good; He cannot will the evil, nor of two alternatives choose the worse. To do this, would be for Him to deny His own nature, and to cease to be God. At the same time this determination by the ideally good is conceived as resulting in the perfect freedom, harmony, and peace of the Divine Life. And the ideal of human freedom is likewise not a free, that is, undetermined will, but rather a freedom of life won through a will determined by true insight. Our moral freedom is not emancipation from the empire of law. Though free, we still remain citizens, subject to all the exacting requirements of a well-ordered polity. But the allegiance of the moral freeman has been transferred from the rule of unorganized impulse and desire to the law of reason and truth. We are then no longer "children of the bond-woman, but of the free."

Such moral freedom is clearly not possessed in the same degree by all. Rather is it found in endlessly varied degrees according to the perfection of individual lives. One could scarcely construct a more erroneous view than that every human being is endowed at birth with the same "lump sum" of freedom, which remains an inalienable possession throughout life. Our freedom is not complete, it is in the making. He who, like the animal, obeys the changing impulses and appetites as they may chance to arise, without regard to their relation to his total life and its meaning, has small share in moral freedom. He is, as we have seen, in bondage. But in all growing personalities, in whom age or

habit has not finally fixed the course of conduct, freedom is a
developing process, a growing power. Little by little the
lessons of experience are coined into wisdom, little by little
mastery over the conflicting desires is gained, and all parts
of life are brought into harmony with its central aim.

We are now in a position to see the important relation of
knowledge to moral freedom. The process by which freedom is won is the process of enlightenment. It is the truth
that sets men free, the clear perception of moral relations
and moral laws, the understanding of human nature and its
true needs. Moral enfranchisement may also be described
as the escape from illusion and error. The reason that human freedom requires to be sharply differentiated from the
spontaneity of animal life, lies in the fact that man is capable in a higher degree of learning and of making his knowledge serve as an inner principle of guidance and self-direction.
"I am, for instance, more truly a self-determining agent
than a hemisphereless fish, because while the fish is so constituted that he cannot but snap at the bait that is dangled
before his nose, even though he has but this moment been
released from the hook that lies concealed behind it, I can
put down the glass that I am raising to my lips and consider the probable effect of the indulgence upon my health,
my work, and my reputation." [1] Through no chance event,
but through the ordered processes that hold in the mental
life, we can build conceptions of a larger and better self.
This higher personality, represented in our thought, is
capable of exercising an attractive, compelling power, of becoming indeed a determining force in the moral life. Thus
the end becomes, as we have already said, the efficient
cause. It is also to be remembered that our moral choices
are strictly limited by the circle of our ideas. One cannot
choose a good of which one is totally ignorant. That were
an act as impossible in the mental sphere as were Munchau-

[1] Taylor, *The Problem of Conduct*, p. 40.

sen's celebrated feats in the physical. The first need of the
enslaved and morally unfree spirit is to discern clearly a
better life which shall rebuke the life that now is. A change
of mind is the essential condition of a change of conduct.
It is significant that all religions and all systems of philosophy which have dealt seriously with the problem of the
moral life, have conditioned emancipation from evil upon a
process of enlightenment. "If the truth shall make you
free, ye shall be free indeed." It is, then, as learner that
man is free. Through knowledge alone can he progressively
transcend his past. Knowledge, not in any narrow or technical sense, but in the widest meaning of the term, is the
transcendent principle in human nature. Such transcendence, however, does not consist in escape from the determinately related processes of the mental life, but in development in and through those processes.

X. Objections to Determinism Answered

But certain difficulties and objections from the side of
indeterminism still remain to be considered. And first of all,
it may be urged: "Granted that such a determinism provides
for moral progress, does it not contradict that consciousness
of freedom of which we are all said to be immediately aware
in every act of choice?"

In answer it may be said that even if the feeling described
were a universal fact of consciousness, great significance could
not be attached to such an uncritical utterance. "Now,
if it were really true that we have a consciousness of being
free in the sense in which this term has been used, this feeling
would have as little weight as a scientific proof as the feeling that the sun moves round the earth has for astronomy." [1]
In the second place, the universality of such a consciousness
may be seriously questioned. [2] If it is common among peoples

[1] Thilly, *Introduction to Ethics*, p. 334.
[2] I have heard a child altogether innocent of any theory of conduct, give naïve

educated under the influence of certain theories which tend
to commit the mind to it in advance, the feeling is not generally found among peoples like the Mohammedans, who are
trained under the opposite teaching. And finally, this utterance of consciousness, wherever or to whatever degree it
does exist, is susceptible of a psychological explanation entirely consistent with determinism. In the absence of a
knowledge of the future we must naturally think of our
choice, up to the moment of decision, as still undetermined;
it may, as far as our present knowledge goes, coincide with
any one of the possibilities. Such ambiguity is inevitable
for beings not omniscient. By whatever delicate balance
our decision may have fallen to the one side or the other,
the self of the moment of choice must have been, in some
respect, a different self to have chosen differently. We are
not to think of a mere series of deeds as successively determining each other, but of a self as successively determining its deeds.

It is further objected that, on the deterministic theory,
one's past deeds, good and bad alike, could not have been
different from what they were. The evil deed of yesterday,
which I bitterly regret to-day, was necessary and inevitable.
Against such a necessity in past acts, the indeterminist
revolts, and appeals again to the consciousness of freedom,
which, he maintains, not only precedes but also follows the
performance of an act. We are conscious, he declares, that
we might have acted differently.

But when we carefully consider our past conduct, are we
ever conscious that an act might have been different, all
the conditions, inner and outer, being precisely what they
were? I think not. What we are conscious of when we
reflect upon the matter is that, if we were to act again under

expression to the most strongly deterministic sentiment. It seemed to be the result
of an immediate perception of the directness with which one's deeds flow from one's
nature. Certainly I believe that in all the deeper moral issues of life we feel as did
Luther when he declared: "*Ich kann nicht anders.*"

similar external conditions, our act might be different. And why? Because there has been an inner change. If one were to act again under the conditions, let us say, under which the regretted act of yesterday was done, the result would doubtless be different. For to-day, in the light of larger experience, of new thoughts and feelings which stir within us, the act is regretted. Nay, if the same situation could have been faced again five minutes after the choice was made, it might well have been different, and for the same reason. I believe that if we seriously ask ourselves whether we could have acted differently from what we did at any time in the past, if called again to face precisely the same situation, with precisely the same feeling and knowledge and point of view, with no gleam of the light that subsequent experience has shed upon our conduct, we must unhesitatingly answer that we could not, but that our choice must have been the same.

As regards the fact that people commonly say of past acts that "they might have been different," the case stands as follows. Prior to the decision with regard to any action, we think of either one of two competing courses as strictly possible. The thought of such two-fold possibility is the absolutely necessary condition of all doubt, debate, and suspense in the matter. Regard either alternative as antecedently impossible, and at once all debate ceases; certainty takes the place of uncertainty, decision of indecision; one course remains, and we consider ourselves necessitated to act in that direction. Now our indecision as to which of two alternatives we shall choose, stands in consciousness, antecedently to the act, as a genuine possibility of two courses of action. And when we view the case in retrospect, we reproduce the antecedent mental attitude in the familiar saying, "It might have been different." It is a significant fact that we use precisely the same form of expression concerning events which all intelligent persons agree in regarding as strictly necessitated. Thus, to give one example among many, after some dangerous feat of child or athlete we say: "You might have broken a limb." Clearly we do not mean that, all the conditions being precisely what they were in that particular case, this result was actually possible. If it had been possible in the order of nature, it would certainly have been realized. We mean that conditions were present, before the event, which made us, in our ignorance of the issue, uncertain and fearful. And we also mean that, if similar acts are continued, they will probably end in disaster, for one's control over the circumstances of action as well as over one's muscles is not always the same. But this form of speech, "It might have been different," means as much or as little in the one case as in the other. One must not be deceived by the *idola fori.*[1]

XI. FATALISM AND DETERMINISM

It is sometimes charged by those who have not grasped the full significance of determinism that it is only a milder term for fatalism, and that the two doctrines are equally destructive of moral effort. But there are two important points at which determinism may be differentiated from fatalism. In the first place, fatalism commonly suggests a hopeless view of morality by ignoring the fact that one's future deeds are not necessarily like one's past deeds, and that there is possibility of change. Although it is true that any given past act could not have been different, all conditions being what they were, the case is quite otherwise if we turn to the future. If we are obliged to discount heavily the saying, "It might have been different," and to regard it as an expression of our ignorance of events prior to their occurrence, quite another significance attaches to the resolution, "It shall be different." This means that there is already a new mental attitude on the part of the agent,

[1] Bacon's term for the errors which result from current forms of speech.

so that if exactly the same external conditions were to occur again, the internal would be different, and would make room for a new result. The good may be chosen, in the future, instead of the evil. We are not bound to a changeless order of conduct. The vast whole of events, linked together as we may believe in indissoluble bonds, is not a static world, but the scene of movement, change, and life. To hold that the mental sphere is through and through a determinately related sphere, no more excludes from it genuinely new experiences than a similar conception, which thinking men are agreed in applying to nature, excludes new events there.

Fatalism further ignores the part played by the self, and is inclined to represent human life as the helpless sport of external forces. The cosmic process is presented as the determining element in personal destiny, to the disregard of the inner world of consciousness. Fatalism regards human destiny as fixed independently of human action; determinism regards it as fixed only in and through individual choice. One's destiny is not determined apart from what one is and does. If, as is often said, the whole determines the part, it can also be said that this determination is not without the participation of the part. And the merely quantitative comparison of the world and the self, which represents the one as so great and the other as so small, is misleading. On any view, the individual is small in comparison with all persons and things set over against him. But as far as the destiny of any particular self is concerned, what that self is and does is the grand factor. Dependent upon a cosmic Power we all indeed are, but the fact that this Power accomplishes certain ends only in and through our thinking and willing, is disregarded by fatalism. It is often forgotten, too, that indeterminism itself runs into a fatalism of another kind. If there were really a power of unmotived choice, of blind, inexplicable willing, one might well complain that to precisely this extent life was given over to the worst kind of fate, that of caprice and chance.

If the belief in fatalism, with its thought of destiny as fixed by forces external to the self, would cut the nerve of moral endeavor and result in stagnation or in a hopeless surrender to circumstances, the same cannot be said of a determinism which recognizes the self as an active and potent factor in shaping human life. The spur to effort would be lost only if our knowledge of the future were complete and perfect. In that case, life would indeed lose its interest, for we should be able to wrest our experiences from the future and to possess them in advance. But for finite beings like ourselves, life will, in the deterministic view, always retain the curiosity of something yet unknown, the zest of something still to be striven for and experienced. When we set out to follow a trail our interest is not diminished by the fact that the path we are to take is already definite and fixed, or by the fact that it has been traversed by others. As we tread it for the first time it has all the charm of novelty. So, in life, what the future holds will prove at each stage a fresh experience. We do not even know our own capacities and powers with any degree of completeness. These, too, are among the things that remain to be discovered. How much we can achieve or how much of value we can win, we never know until we try. Desire and striving are, we may also remind ourselves, elemental and essential parts of our nature, never wholly quenched or exhausted until life itself is extinguished.

XII. Further Objections Answered

The feelings of penitence and self-condemnation are often regarded as inexplicable upon the deterministic theory. Some have even found in such feelings the chief argument against determinism.[1] But as far as such feelings are essen-

[1] Cf. Lotze, *Outlines of Practical Philosophy*, p. 35.

tial to morality, do they not still remain unimpaired? The
explanation of the method by which a certain form of life,
mental or physical, has developed does not affect its intrinsic worth. The human form has lost no line of beauty or
dignity by the theory of its slow evolution, and on the deterministic view the bad man is no less base, the good man
no less noble. Our judgments of value remain unchanged.
The evil doer cannot contemplate his conduct with any
more complacency. He must pronounce the same sentence
of condemnation upon his character. If morally enlightened, he will feel disapproval and dissatisfaction with his
evil past. And this feeling of dissatisfaction with the past
and present self is the condition of a change. As long
as it exists there is a principle of regeneration constantly
at work, making possible a genuine repentance, a forsaking
of the evil and a choosing of the good. But this feeling can
be operative only in and through the strict continuity of
our life, the dependence of the present upon the past, and
of the future upon the past and present. "If there were no
such dependence, if I could be something to-day irrespectively of what I was yesterday, or something to-morrow
irrespectively of what I am to-day, the motive to the self-
reforming effort furnished by regrets for a past of which I
reap the fruit, that growing success of the effort that comes
with habituation, and the assurance of a better future which
animates it, would alike be impossible." [1]

The problem of evil, it is also urged, assumes on the deterministic theory a form repugnant to our moral sense.
For we are compelled on this view to regard the most revolting of crimes as a necessary element in the world-order.[2]
A theodicy, therefore, it is said, must carry the burden of
all moral as well as physical evil. But is not this inevitable

[1] T. H. Green, *Prolegomena to Ethics*, p. 115.
[2] Cf. James, "The Dilemma of Determinism," *The Will to Believe and Other Essays*, pp. 160–161.

on any view of the nature of human volition? While, as
will appear, no man can escape the direct and immediate
responsibility for his own acts, the Creator of a world can
as little escape the ultimate responsibility for a world which
he has made. Accepting, for the sake of the argument,
that conception of an omnipotent Being which has found
most favor in the theologies of the past, and is still widely
accepted in popular thought, we cannot escape the conclusion that, if such a Being were to choose to create men with
the freedom of indifference, He could not escape responsibility for all the consequences of that act, save by divesting
Himself of the very attributes which religious thought has
made the essence of His nature. There is a flat contradiction between the notion of unlimited power and knowledge,
and that of limited responsibility. No theory has been able
satisfactorily to meet this dilemma. And what must one
say of a Being possessed of such attributes who should
create a world containing a real element of chance, which
might fall out well, but with equal likelihood might fall out
ill? It is, further, impossible in the complex web of human
experience to disentangle the threads of natural and moral
evil. To free the world from the weight of moral evil would
by no means solve the problem of evil, or make it easy.
Even the most revolting crimes which the indeterminist
ascribes to free will become insignificant when one considers
the extent and duration of the suffering and degradation
due to other sources. One cannot, for example, imagine a
human being so depraved as consciously and persistently
to impose upon humanity the evil wrought by painful and
revolting forms of disease. The evil that appears in human
choice is but a part of a far larger problem.

But it should not be forgotten that the indeterminist is
bound to apply his theory both ways. If on theological
grounds he takes refuge in indeterminism to free the Deity
from the burden of the evil choices of men, he can as little

ascribe to Him their good choices. And if one must choose
between the alternatives of ascribing to the Deity everything or nothing in human conduct, as long as one believ
in the preponderance of good over evil, one will, on religiou
grounds, choose the former alternative. That the source
of all good in us is ultimately a Power not ourselves, is a
fact which great and good men have in some way recognized in every age. If we consider the lot of those unfortunate beings who by hereditary tendency seem predestined
to evil, and who by an unfortunate environment have this
"calling and election made sure," what can we say of the
source of that light and help which has saved us from a like
fate? "Not unto us, not unto us," is the cry of our deepest
consciousness. This is the profound truth in the church's
doctrine of grace. As regards the religious question here
involved, we must learn to think of the nature of God and
of His relations to the world quite otherwise than in the
crude fashion which represents Him as making choices in
the presence of competing motives, or as standing before a
projected world like an artificer before his handiwork.

Determinism is not a doctrine of despair. As already seen,
it offers hope of deliverance from evil to every one who is
capable of learning, of gleaning wisdom from the experiences
of life. Discouragement and loss of moral power only follow
when the self is viewed in a fatalistic way. On the contrary,
determinism may furnish a stimulus to action by its emphasis upon certain important practical aspects of the moral
life. One result of applying the principle of necessary relation to conduct is to show that each successive act is linked
with those that have gone before, in such a way as to emphasize the importance of habit. Each successive choice
is made with all one's past upon one's head. A deeper significance, therefore, attaches to the present moral act.
What I this day think and do is fraught with grave consequences for to-morrow's thinking and doing. If it be true

that no effect is without its cause, it is also true that no cause is without its effect. By no magic, then, but in a strictly natural and necessary way, this thought may add its weight to the scale in which present choices are decided. The conviction that one is thus determined may itself help to determine one to resist present solicitations of evil, and to cling to the right. The social consequences of this teaching are no less significant. Each social act gains a new import. There is no escape from the responsibility of social relations. Our acts cannot return to us void. In the great complex of human history they all work with a power whose exact extent we cannot measure, but must recognize as inevitable.

XIII. Responsibility and Punishment

Our discussion of freedom has resulted in a reinterpretation of the meaning commonly given to the term. This was demanded not only by theoretical, but also by practical interests. For although popular thought is implicitly deterministic in all matters of education, punishment, government, social endeavor, etc., it is usually indeterministic in form, partly as the result of an uncritical estimate of the utterances of consciousness, and partly from the influence of certain theories long regnant in law and theology. It appears, therefore, that popular thought is not in harmony with itself. Ethical theory must either accept an intolerable discord or attempt reconstruction and reconciliation. Such reconstruction is its true function. It is not the business of ethical thought to leave the solid ground of experience and soar in mid-air. Nor is it its aim to refute the judgments of common sense in matters of practice. Its task is not primarily the creation of new forms of conduct, but the humbler work of explaining the already existing forms. Ethical theory does not destroy but interprets. In the question at issue it does not refute the central meaning of the indeterminism of common sense. That meaning is doubtless the preservation of a genuine moral significance for freedom and responsibility. And we have already seen that moral freedom is not, on the deterministic theory, a meaningless ideal, but an actual fact to which a clear meaning can be attached. Freedom does not consist in an undetermined will, but in a will determined by understanding and insight. It remains to consider briefly the problem of responsibility.

For the sake of clearness the discussion may begin with the idea of natural accountability, in distinction from moral accountability, or responsibility. Accountability, or imputability, in this sense is of universal application. It is thus that we speak of the impure water supply of a city as accountable for epidemics of disease, and of the climate of a country as accountable for certain characteristics of its inhabitants. In like manner, to the noxious plant is imputed the injury to the crop, and to the fox the depredations upon the poultry yard. The insane man is accountable for his deed of violence, and the idiot for his unseemly behavior. Thus applied, the term means simply that the person or thing in question is recognized as the immediate source of certain conditions or events. Obviously enough, moral beings are also in this sense accountable for their acts, that is, they are recognized as the sources of them. It is further to be observed that, in a world of necessarily related events, nothing can escape the consequences of its own nature, of being what it is. The impure water is not treated as if it were pure, or the unhealthful climate as if it were healthful; the weed is cut down, and the destructive fox ruthlessly slain; the insane man is confined, and the fool treated according to his folly. Those who fear that any reinterpretation of responsibility will undermine the moral order may be reassured, even from the point of view of natural accountability. Society will not cease to treat men according to their deeds. Those who work social evil will be recognized as the cause of evil, and will be held strictly accountable.

But moral responsibility, all will agree, involves something more than the mere imputability, or natural accountability, thus far considered. Otherwise, man would be responsible in no other way than the plant or animal. What is the further element required to constitute moral responsibility? We may here accept the answer of common sense, bearing in mind only that common sense must be pressed beyond a merely verbal statement to its underlying meaning. The answer of common sense doubtless would be that man is morally responsible because he is free. And this is certainly true, provided the appropriate meanings be attached to the terms. But we must ask again for some distinctive mark of a free being, some characteristic which differentiates man from other things and persons not thus free, from plant and animal, from madman, idiot, and infant. Here common sense will certainly not hesitate; it will point to man's intelligence, to his deliberative, rational nature, which makes him receptive to ideas and responsive to instruction, and which constitutes him a self-directive agent. But this means that man can act from ideas of ends, that is, from motives, and can determine his conduct by them. The infant, the insane, and the idiotic, we are told, are not responsible because they are not susceptible of instruction, not capable of receiving certain ideas and of being determined by motives. Further, this susceptibility to instruction and guidance by motive, it will be agreed, fixes the degree of responsibility. It clearly marks the stages of growing responsibility in childhood; it measures the degree of responsibility which we impute to various abnormal or defective types; and it is the criterion of responsibility in its legal aspects. To this principle there appears to be no exception. An interesting analogue of human responsibility

is found in our treatment of domestic animals. A kind of
quasi responsibility is ascribed to them precisely according
to their degree of intelligence and susceptibility to training.

But the crucial point, it will be said, still remains. Do
we hold persons responsible when we are compelled to view
their acts as necessitated? The answer cannot be in doubt
even in the view of common sense, whose judgments we are
here following. We do most certainly hold one fully responsible for a necessitated act, provided the necessity is
that of one's own nature, not of some alien power, and provided also that the nature is one susceptible of modification
through the determining influence of motives. And both
of these conditions we find present in the ordinary acts of
normal human beings. The father who sees his own too
hasty temper appearing in his son may recognize himself
as reincarnated, as it were, in his child's moments of anger.
He is compelled to regard this display of hot temper, when
it first appears, as the perfectly natural and inevitable expression of an inherited tendency, against which he himself
has had to wage a life-long battle. At the same time he holds
the child strictly responsible. By the hard discipline of experience the father has learned the evil and folly of yielding to a hasty temper, and he perhaps holds his child more
strictly responsible for this than for any other act, fully
assured that unremitting instruction and discipline will not
be without their effect. Responsibility for an act does not,
then, evaporate, as some suppose, when we regard it as in
the strictest sense necessarily determined, or as an act that,
under the given conditions, could not have been different.
Indeed, it is for those acts which we recognize as flowing
with the most direct necessity from our own nature, those
that we can trace to a determining ground in our character,
that we consider ourselves most fully responsible. In the
words of Green: "If a man's action did not represent his
character but an arbitrary freak of some unaccountable

power of unmotived willing, why should he be ashamed of it or reproach himself for it?" [1] The cases in which the measure of moral responsibility is held to be lessened, whether in popular judgment or in courts of justice, are those in which the agent's own character does not seem to be the determining factor, or in which that character, through some defect, cannot be normally influenced by motives. One of the strongest proofs in support of that view of freedom which reconciles it with self-determinism is found in the fact that it enables one to interpret the facts of moral responsibility in terms of the healthy moral judgments of daily life; for these judgments are right in practice, if sometimes wrong in the theory to which they are referred.

The moral aspects of punishment are sufficiently significant in their relation to our problem to require a brief statement. As far as punishment has moral value for the individual, and is not a means of social protection, its limits are clearly defined by the possibility of its entering as a determining factor into the complex of mental conditions from which the future acts of the agent are to issue. The justification of punishment and reward is found in the fact that they may bring new motives into operation. But on the indeterministic view, as we have already seen, they must both be ineffective to precisely that extent to which indeterminism is true. In fine, the only will of which use can be made in moral relations is a determined will.

One form of punishment, however, is obviously excluded; this is retributive punishment, which is inflicted as a supposed satisfaction for wrong-doing without regard to the consequences which will follow. As far as punishment cannot be effective for the improvement of the evil-doer or for the protection of society, it loses all *raison d'être* and becomes a needless and wicked infliction of pain. The growing exclusion of all vindictive elements from punish-

[1] *Prolegomena to Ethics*, p. 113.

ment has marked a great step in moral progress. Punishment containing the element of revenge is a dehumanizing process for all concerned, and may well be allowed to pass with other barbaric usages. One of the most beneficent effects of subjecting human conduct to deterministic explanation has been to beget a more sympathetic and kindly feeling toward one's fellow-men. The understanding of the deeper springs and sources of conduct is the necessary condition alike of all true compassion and of all just restraint. If this compassion embraces even the follies and vices of men, it is not a dangerous or indulgent compassion, since it understands all too clearly that in the social order there must be effective motives working to restrain evil. While it reaches out one hand in pity towards a frail and erring humanity, it extends the other in vigorous control.

XIV. The Determinist's Attitude Towards Life

In conclusion, we may still further inquire concerning the practical results of such an interpretation of freedom and responsibility as we have presented. It is doubtless true that no careful thinker will accept the immediate practical influence of any theory as a criterion of its ultimate validity. One need not feel concerned even to deny that, historically, intellectual error has sometimes seemed to work well. This does not mean, however, that error is as good as truth, but simply that, at a certain stage of human development, an error in belief concerning some matter has better harmonized with other current errors and with the total state of knowledge than the truth would have done. Often, too, error has appealed powerfully to men as a practical motive because of their very imperfections and limitations. With a higher type of personality such motives would become wholly ineffective. Certainly against any doctrine of the ultimate beneficence of error, our deepest conviction utters its protest. There is in us all a faith, supported by not a little evidence, that it is best to know and to act upon the truth. But the indeterminist has often attacked determinism because of its supposed practical consequences, and he may therefore properly be met on this ground. In ethics, moreover, we are dealing with a theory of conduct, and it would be a fatal defect in such a theory if it were found to be one by which men could not live, or if it tended to discourage the highest moral endeavor. What, then, are the proper fruits of such an interpretation of human conduct? How, in view of it, would the wise man seek to bear himself in daily life? Certainly he will feel no undue complacency or pride. If he finds anything of worth or goodness in himself, he will realize that its primal sources are not of his creating, but lie deep in the world-order. In any native power of insight, in any happy balance of character, in any aspiring impulses, he will recognize something which he has received, a veritable gift of grace. And the thousand forces of the environment in which he has wrought out his destiny, he will also recognize as a gift. So that if he compare his own lot with that of a fellow-being blinded by error and enslaved by evil, he will realize that, but for what he has received, he would be equally wretched. If he must regard in the same way the evil which he discovers in himself, this conviction cannot lessen his estimate of its gravity, or cause him to seek less earnestly after greater perfection. The painful discipline which comes from his own folly and wrong-doing he will consider the necessary condition of his betterment, and will count the price none too high for such gain. Towards his fellows he will feel the profoundest sympathy, knowing that they, too, are bearers of like natures, not of their own choosing. And if, because of this sympathy, he laughs and weeps at the alternating comedy and tragedy of life, his laughter will be without scorn and his weeping without bitterness. But a ready sympathy will not lead him to remit just demands or to cease to hold his fellows strictly responsible, for he knows that only through proper motives of hope and fear can they be held to their best endeavors. If he be called to administer justice or to inflict punishment, he will do it with compassion, but also without weakness. Least of all will he idly fold his hands and passively await for himself and others the decrees of an external fate, for he knows that not in vain stirs within him the will to action, and that, according to the measure of his strength and knowledge, he has an appointed part to play in the world-drama. And finally, such an one will not be without hope for the future of humanity, a hope founded upon the progress of the past. If from the humble beginnings of savage life, separated only a little from that of the brute, there has been slowly won so much of worth—of knowledge overcoming ignorance and superstition, of sympathy triumphant over selfishness and hate, of heroism unfaltering in the performance of duty, of aspiration untiring in the pursuit of higher ends—he may well cherish the faith that the Power which has thus wrought in and through humanity will yet bring its work to still nobler issues.

CHAPTER XIII

MORALITY AND RELIGION

THE departments of thought which deal with the values of human life may, as we saw in the first chapter, each rightly claim the totality of experience as the field of its activity. But each of these disciplines has a unique purpose, and this purpose dictates alike the method and the goal of its work. Ethics, in the pursuit of its own aim, will deal with the values of religion as constituting a part of the world of values which it seeks to organize. And a study of religion must no less, for its own purposes, embrace ethics as a part of its content. Each therefore includes, and at the same time reinterprets, the facts of the other. But the reciprocal relations of morality and religion are so important as to demand special consideration in a study of human values. We must now attempt to bring their relations under careful scrutiny. To be seen aright, this border-land must be viewed from both sides. We shall be compelled, therefore, to go beyond the boundary itself and to enter the field of religion in order to examine its nature.

I. THE SCIENTIFIC TEMPER IN THE STUDY OF RELIGION

The necessity of conducting this further inquiry in a scientific temper will at once be recognized by every student. Indeed, the study of the problem of the relations of morality and religion can mean nothing less than the effort to bring them under an analysis as candid and searching as that which is brought to bear upon any other problem of science. To popular thought, the extension of scientific inquiry into the field of religious experience has sometimes seemed strange and even menacing. But the objection that religion is too sacred for investigation falsely assumes that the understanding of the facts of the religious life will destroy that life itself. Such a fear would be justified only in case religion were an illusion, to be dispelled by the clear understanding of its nature and sources. One who believes that religion is an integral factor in human life can have no fear of such a result. It is true that one cannot actually have a significant religious experience and at the same moment reflect upon it. But one may have a most vital experience of any kind, and may at another moment reflect upon the nature of this experience. Scientific procedure does not exclude the possibility of appreciation. The surgeon who performs his work with a coolness and absorption which forbid any emotion of sympathy for his patient, may yet, at another time, feel most keenly the human pathos of all that passes under his eye. So, too, the astronomer who makes his observations with a scientific attention as rigorous and prosaic as that of the engineer who surveys a barren sand hill or desolate marsh, may, at other times, thrill with the wonder and beauty of the starry heavens. It is also clear that to urge the sacredness of religion as a ground of refusal to examine it critically, is to present a reason which would have been equally applicable in the case of the most crude of primitive religions. To its devotees every religion is sacred. Such an attitude would doubtless have fixed a low form of animism as the permanent religion of the race. Any departure from this faith must have been regarded with a deep and fearsome distrust by all timid souls.

Nor can it rightly be claimed that religious phenomena offer an insuperable obstacle to investigation because they lie in unclear depths of the spiritual life, or because the experience of each individual is unique. When one enters the precinct of religion one does not leave the realm of law and order. The notion of miraculous happenings, long ago abandoned as a principle of explanation in the physical world, is equally untenable in the psychical. Even the most wonderful of our human experiences, we now believe, occur in accordance with definite laws of the mental life. As regards the claim of the uniqueness of religious experience, it may be said that every fact in the universe is in some respect unique. No two objects or events in the physical world are alike in every particular; and no two conscious states are completely identical. If identity were a prerequisite of scientific treatment, there could be no science at all; nor, for that matter, could there be any philosophy. Both science and philosophy deal with the significant elements common to many differing individuals. Religious experiences, like all others, differ widely in different persons, but they also present common features. Hence one may speak not only of religions, but also of religion in its universal, generic sense.

It is not our purpose to investigate in detail the relations which have existed historically between codes of positive morality and the religious systems with which they have been linked. It is rather to discover the general principles by which the relations of ethics to religion may be explained by one who desires to understand these elements of our spiritual life. In the history of the race, morality and religion have grown up together in close union, and they still constitute, for most people, a single whole within which the two factors are not regarded as distinct or separable. For the practical life, such merging of the forces of morality and religion is natural and wholesome. But for the purposes of thought, it is necessary to separate and distinguish between them. However closely the threads of the one are interwoven with those of the other, clear thinking demands that they should be disentangled. Otherwise we could never be sure to which field any given fact of the complex whole is to be referred for explanation. And instead of attaining to a clear understanding of the part played by each, there would remain simply the original mass of undifferentiated experience.

II. Distinction between Morality and Religion

First of all, then, we have to define the generic character of these two types of experience, the moral and the religious. The nature of morality, it may be assumed, will be sufficiently clear from the previous discussion. As we have insisted, morality is concerned with the discovery and development of the richest possible content of value that can be realized in human life. Its task is to evaluate all forms of spiritual activity that appear in the course of civilization, and also to determine the importance of the material factors that make possible their realization. We shall, perhaps, best discover the nature and function of religion by considering some differences between its point of view and that of morality. In this way we may hope to arrive at a tenable definition of the essential nature of religion.

One striking difference between morality and religion lies in the fact that religion involves a wider outlook. It scans a more distant horizon. It is concerned with the cosmic fortunes of good and evil. While morality springs chiefly from man's relation to his fellows, religion has its source primarily in the relation which man sustains to nature, to the totality of those forces by which he is surrounded. If men attained by their own efforts a perfectly satisfactory life and felt no dependence upon outside forces, the need for religion would never be felt. The origin of religion thus implies the existence of other and more immediate values than those of religion itself. Were it not for the primary values of comfort of body and peace of mind, religion would never have developed in the life of primitive man. Religious values are, in this sense, as Höffding points out, secondary in origin.[1] They presuppose the existence of still more primary forms

---

[1] Cf. *The Philosophy of Religion*, p. 107.

of good. Faith or hope, for example, can never be a value unless there is something of worth which is its object, something for which we hope and for the sake of which faith is precious. It is because these primary values were constantly threatened by powers beyond human control, that the sense of dependence, which is of the essence of religion, arose. The picture that we are able to form of primitive life presents to us the spectacle of a constant struggle on the part of man to secure the satisfaction of even his most simple bodily needs. His supply of food is often uncertain; the fruits of the earth are threatened by drought and frost and blight; he has no store laid up for the lean years that are sure to come upon him; the springs from which he drinks may dry up under the burning sun; tornado or flood may bring destruction to his rude hut; the terrors of the darkness oppress his mind; in every movement and sound of the forest there seems to lurk a shadowy foe; sickness comes upon him and takes away the bodily strength which is his best defence; and, finally, death with its supreme tragedy threatens the destruction of all his hopes. Thus the humblest values are dependent upon a power beyond man's control. Students of religion are agreed that primitive religions are largely religions of fear. But at higher levels of intelligence other elements arise. The mysterious unknown, stretching limitless on every hand, challenges the understanding for an explanation, and spurs the imagination to supply what the understanding is unable to give. Awe is awakened by the sublimity of natural forces; admiration is kindled by their order and beauty. At every step, too, appears the impulse to objectify and to project upon the universe with poetic freedom the ideals of the human heart—the strength, the intelligence, the beauty, and the love for which men long. This impulse also leads to the picturing of some super-human personality in whom these values may find their embodiment. Gratitude and love are the natural sentiments of those who have received blessing and happiness from the higher powers, while a desire to propitiate them and win again their favor is strong in those who are suffering loss and disaster. Such, in general, are the psychological experiences which make man a religious being. And they may be distinguished with considerable exactness from those which lie at the root of morality. For morality springs chiefly from those human relationships in which the individual finds himself compelled to live and act. Morality has its deepest roots in the physical and spiritual needs which other human beings can satisfy, and in the sympathies which answer to these needs. "By the impressions made on him by nature, his reason was incited, we conceive, towards religion,—by social life towards morality." [1]

III. THE NATURE OF RELIGION

Any definition of religion must necessarily be general and abstract. It can be little more than a skeleton-form which the mind of the reader must clothe out of its own experience and reflection with the flesh and blood of living reality. A definition may nevertheless be of service in stimulating and guiding the reader's thought. The definition here given expresses the conception of religion which will determine the discussion of the following pages. Religion is the experience constituted by those thoughts, feelings, and actions which spring from man's sense of dependence upon the power or powers controlling the universe, and which have as their centre of interest the cosmic fortune of values.

It is often said that religion is a matter of feeling, and it is doubtless true that this is a prominent element of religion. It is also true that the intellectual grasp of the object of religious experience, the vast and relatively unknown cosmic power, is necessarily imperfect and vague. This inevitable vagueness gives rise to more or less indefinite ideas which,

---

[1] Pfleiderer, *The Philosophy of Religion*, Vol. IV, p. 227.

in colloquial use, are expressed by the term feeling. But such use of feeling is altogether inexact. Feeling, in any proper use of the term, cannot adequately express the nature of religion. Indeed, a little scrutiny of those experiences which are loosely described as feeling makes it clear that the other psychical activities are always present in them. A feeling is always a feeling of something; it has an object or content. This object of feeling is more or less clearly represented in terms of ideas. Further, the existence of certain ideas and of the emotions which gather about them involves volitional activity, the play of the will; we respond inevitably with answering effort to the ideas that interest us. Thus all the elements of the psychical life are involved in religious as well as in all other experience. In short, men have ideas about the universe in which they exist; they feel emotions when these ideas are present; and they act, practically, in response to them. A vindication of this view is found in the historical religions, all of which have attempted to offer an intellectual interpretation of the world, a cosmology of some kind. They have sought to claim the attention and respect of men by saying: "We offer you here the truth about the universe; take this truth to your minds and hearts and lives; believe it, feel it, and act upon it."

The fundamental error involved in the definition of religion which would limit it to feeling only, is a far-reaching one. There is here a very fog-bank of obscure thinking, from which error and misunderstanding constantly issue. We hear and read much in religious discussions of the "reasons of the heart," and we are often warned that the other sides of our nature require satisfaction as well as the intellect. The confusion involved in such utterances is little less than an intellectual scandal. As if every genuine reason were not an affair both of the heart and of the head! As if, too, there were an intellectual satisfaction which is not, by the very necessity of our natures, also a matter of feeling!

Or as if the will had some special form of satisfaction of its own! It can hardly be too often repeated that any satisfaction is of necessity, in one aspect, always a state of feeling. It is the function of feeling to yield that direct personal appreciation of things which we call satisfaction or happiness. In this sense there are no "satisfactions" of the intellect or of the will, for without feeling all value would vanish from the world. But this fact must not lead one to forget that there is no satisfaction of feeling which is not, of necessity, at the same time an affair of the intellect and of the will. All satisfactions have their ideational side; they are represented in thought. They also have their active side; they involve effort, they are volitional processes. Every end, or value, is thus at one and the same time an idea, a mode of feeling, and a process of effort. Those who speak of "reasons of the heart" doubtless mean that there are deep longings of human nature, the satisfaction of which seems necessary to happiness, but which is not assured by direct knowledge. Yet no yearning or longing is in itself a "reason" in the sense intended. All cravings of human nature for a good not present must be critically examined with the purpose of determining their significance in the scheme of things, and also the hope of their fulfillment. Otherwise we might at once find in all our longings not only reasons for the belief that they will be gratified, but also reasons for gratifying them whenever gratification is in our power. But there are numerous desires which, in our best moments, we recognize should not be gratified, and there are also many worthy desires which, alas! are not gratified at all in the lives of millions of human beings. Another error, closely allied to that which finds expression in "reasons of the heart," appears in the frequent assumption that what is in the sphere of value is thereby removed from the sphere of reason and of intellectual scrutiny. This entirely overlooks the fact that value, as much as any other thing in the world, may be the object of thought, of scientific observation and analysis, and of a genuinely reflective appraisal. Religious teachers have often assumed that, in the presence of certain experiences of worth, the critical faculty must sleep, or at least keep silent. But it is precisely in such experiences that the human reason finds its highest exercise, its noblest expression. It is the glory of man to know good and evil. For the guidance of his life he must grasp these in reflective thought, not merely in immediate experience as they are known to the brute creation. Such reflective knowledge means sorrow as well as joy, but we cannot escape it save by ceasing to be human.

The definition of religion given above expresses, as we have already seen, the psychological root of religion, the experience that makes man a religious being. This is the inevitable sense of dependence for his weal and woe upon the vast and largely unknown power which both stirs within him and encompasses him from without. This sense of dependence owes all its vitality to the fact that there are values for the securing and preservation of which man is profoundly concerned, and at the same time largely helpless. The cosmic favor and disfavor, the good and ill that transcend alike the individual will and the social order, constitute forever the high theme of religion; all historical faiths are variations upon this one theme; and to the end of time the developing forms of religious thought and life will centre about it. Men will never cease to ask the meaning of their relations to the World-power that encompasses them and determines the fortunes of their destiny.

The ideal form of religion, which men are always seeking, must involve that interpretation of the world which is truest, and that adjustment of conduct which, in view of this interpretation, will yield to humanity the richest values. This conception of religion doubtless means an enlargement of the conventional ideas of its nature. But such enlargement is both inevitable and desirable. Nor can we arbitrarily determine in advance the limits of such growth and transformation. The inability to picture new forms of religious life is due largely to a failure to interpret sympathetically the deeper spiritual experiences of the race in the course it has already traversed. As long as it be admitted that religion derives its essential character from man's interpretation of the whole of being, we cannot refuse the name of religion to any life-moving experience that springs from this source. It may even be maintained, to put the case in an extreme form, that if a distant posterity should be forced to the deliberate and firm conviction that the world is, on the whole, bad instead of good, as the radical pessimists have taught, a candid acceptance of the bitter truth, and an unswerving devotion to the task of diminishing the misery of existence in all possible ways, would then constitute a religious attitude.

Other questions concerning the definition of religion naturally arise. Is religion instinctive? Are all men necessarily religious? And how broad should be our interpretation of what constitutes to-day a religious attitude? To the first question, it may be replied that religion is certainly instinctive in the sense that man is endowed with tendencies which inevitably lead him to respond in his relations to the world-order with those special ideas, emotions, and activities that constitute historically the religious life of man. The universality of religion also follows from this fact. All men are religious. But this answer requires explanation. Not infrequently we speak of certain people as irreligious, and it is obvious that all men do not respond in the same way to religious stimuli. But these stimuli are everywhere operative. Every man at times has experiences which can be referred only to religion for their explanation. It will aid in clearing up this point if we distinguish between the active and the passive elements in religion. The passive side represents those inevitable impressions which the object of religious belief produces upon the mind. There is no one who, in the grip of the great forces of nature, does not feel his weakness and dependence, and who does not long for help. A man may despair of securing such help; or he may even interpret these forces as malign, and so meriting his hatred; or he may regard them as indifferent to his personal appeal, requiring nothing at his hands and giving nothing in return. But even in such cases there is a conscious re-action to the influence of forces which are the very root of religion. The active side of religion, on the other hand, finds expression in man's efforts to bring his whole life into con-scious harmony with the true meaning of the world-order. This effort, it is, which yields the religious values of self-surrender and resignation, of harmony and coöperation, of faith and hope in the outcome of things. Or if we find that it is impossible to harmonize the meaning of human life with the world-order as a whole, we should then regard positive religion as the loyal effort to fulfill the spiritual destiny that has been assigned to man. Not all men win the true values of religion, but all men have experiences, which, under any adequate definition of its meaning, must be referred to this source. The religious interest is universal and ineradicable, waiting only to be called into conscious life.

The answer which would be made by different persons to the question as to the breadth of meaning that should be given to religion, will depend largely upon the extent to which they have studied the religions of different races and times, as also upon the extent to which they have been able sympathetically to enter into the deeper experiences of their fellows. To many people religion always means their own religion, which is of course for them the one and only true faith. But a few test cases may aid the reader to define his own thought on the subject. Shall we, for example, regard as religious, the experience of the poet who may not recog-nize the God of the theologians, but who finds in the universe a power and beauty which thrill him with wonder and awe? In like manner, one may ask, is a scientist like Huxley religious, when, leaving his own special field of investigation, he contemplates the whole of nature with its system of discoverable laws, and recognizes his own dependence upon it, not only for his existence, but also for certain principles which should guide his conduct? Is he religious who, despairing of conventional faith, worships the ideal of goodness which has been wrought out in the spiritual struggles of humanity?

Whatever the answer which different persons would give to these questions, it is important to remember that a definition of religion can, of necessity, describe only the universal form of the religious consciousness. Its content varies almost endlessly. As soon as a particular content of ideas, emotions, and activities fills out this formula with concrete life, variety at once begins. We then have to do with religions rather than with religion. It is also true that any one of the historical religions will, according to sect and creed, display differences for every individual believer. As religion attempts an ultimate interpretation of the meaning of experience, including both the realm of nature and of human life, the actual processes of the religious life will depend upon the precise stage of culture reached, and will be influenced by every scientific, philosophical, æsthetic, and ethical view which the individual has accepted. In the last resort each human spirit will mirror the universe in a way that is unique. No two are capable of reflecting the religious life with the same shades of thought, feeling, and action. This is true even of those who sit side by side in church, repeating unquestioningly the same creed, and joining without reserve in the same worship. We must accustom ourselves, therefore, to the necessity of recognizing different types of religion, and through a genuine moral discipline learn to give to all religious experience a sympathetic understanding, and to guarantee to it its spiritual freedom.

If, now, in view of these essential features of religion, it is asked how we may distinguish between the ethical and the religious elements of experience, our answer would be that the distinction is always to be found in the point of view from which we consider the tasks and values of life. Both religion and morality are all-inclusive, each from its own stand-point. Morality, as we have insisted, aims to discover and develop all the values of human life, and to organize them into the richest possible content of earthly civilization. The spiritual activities represented by science, art, and religion form important parts of this content, and so are all criticized and evaluated by ethics. But it is equally true that this whole content may be taken up into the religious life, where it is viewed as a divinely appointed task, a business dictated by a super-human order. Morality always views the values of life as directly dependent upon our human choices and actions; religion places them in their cosmic setting, and regards them as dependent upon some power beyond man's control. Even the very willing of our moral choices is brought by religion within this setting; morality now becomes a function of the divine order. Thus the constant struggle of men to transmute personal power into forms of value may be viewed as both moral and religious. As moral, this struggle places man for the moment at the centre; destiny is now in human hands; the choice of better or worse is man's own choice. But as religious, the point of view shifts to a wider arena; the struggle is part of a super-human process; destiny is not ultimately of man's own choosing; the individual represents the cause of his God. If one desires to distinguish between the ethical and the religious motive, in their practical operation, it may be said that, when one labors for a better personal life or social order with conscious appeal to immediate human needs and relations, the motive is ethical; but the motive is religious when one labors for the same end with a conscious appeal to some principle or ideal which is regarded as transcending human purposes, and as deriving its validity from an all-inclusive meaning. It is obvious that the attitudes and motives which we have described respectively as ethical and religious will constantly unite and overlap. Now we are moved by one, now by another. Both play in and out through the experiences of life as the shuttle flies in and out through the warp.

IV. The Interaction of Morality and Religion

We now pass to consider some of the more important ways in which morality and religion react upon each other. Religion, in its social and institutional development, necessarily incorporates ethical elements. The very conception of the deity which any religion offers, represents the ethical standards of its adherents. The history of religion makes it clear that all the moral attributes of deity are drawn from the moral ideals prevailing among the chief worshippers, and that they have first been constructed in human relations before being ascribed to the gods. Morality has thus grown up from the earth towards heaven; historically it has not proceeded the other way. Man has projected upon the Infinite the highest excellence he has known, bringing his best as tribute to religion. What is true of moral attributes is also true of all others, physical, æsthetic, and intellectual. There is, therefore, a half-truth in the paradox of Feuerbach, that "instead of God creating man, man has created God." Man has certainly created his idea of God, including its moral elements. As Goethe has expressed it:

"Im Innern ist ein Universum auch,
Daher der Völker loblicher Gebrauch,
Dass jeglicher das Beste, was er kennt,
Er Gott, ja seinen Gott benennt,
Ihm Himmel und Erden übergibt,
Ihn fürchtet, und womöglich liebt." [1]

[1] Proemium to *Gott und Welt*.

As man advances to higher stages of morality his earlier
conceptions of the moral character of the deity no longer
satisfy him, and are accordingly criticized and reconstructed
to meet the demands of his new ideals. "So wie die Völker
sich bessern, bessern sich auch ihre Götter." [1] Among the
many illustrations of this principle may be mentioned the
history of the religious thought of the Greeks and of the Hebrews. Greek literature, from Homer to Plato, displays
in the clearest manner the gradual transformation of the
ethical elements in Greek religion. From the crude thought
of the gods as possessing human appetites and passions,
which give rise to constant intrigues, jealousies, and strife,
there slowly emerges a more worthy view, until in Plato
and Aristotle the conception of the deity is made to express
the highest spiritual perfection which thought had attained,
and is, at the same time, the ideal of what humanity should
be in its ethical life. The evolution of the religious thought
of the Hebrews followed a similar course. Yahweh is at
first a tribal deity, and is viewed as the partial defender of
his own worshippers, caring nothing for the fortunes or the
fate of other peoples. But, gradually, with the attainment
of a higher ideal on the part of their leaders, and especially
with the appearance of the prophets, who make a ringing
appeal for moral reform, a change is effected. Morality
is seen to require a regard for those outside of Israel; justice
and mercy as universal principles of conduct are emphasized; and in keeping with this change Yahweh becomes the
God of all mankind, dealing with all in justice, and requiring
rightness of heart and life as the condition of his favor.
The prophets declare that he will even cast off his chosen
people if they fail to meet these ethical requirements. Illustrations lying close to our own time are found in the modification of religious conceptions in the past century through
the influence of ethical ideals. Among many examples of

[1] Lichtenberg; quoted by Höffding, "*The Philosophy of Religion*," p. 322.

such transformation may be mentioned the change from
the view of God which emphasized his imperial sovereignty,
to that which emphasized his fatherhood. So, too, even
in popular thought, the Christian atonement is no longer
regarded as a *quid pro quo*, or the balancing of a ledger
account. The period of missionary enterprise has also
witnessed a radical change, due chiefly to ethical criticism,
in the attitude of the Christian world towards non-Christian
peoples.

The significant outcome of this ethical criticism of religion is that men have come to see that no one could be
called morally good, who in human relations should display
the spirit which religious thought had freely ascribed to the
deity. Accordingly a demand, springing from man's moral
nature, is made for the reconstruction of the religious view.
It was this ethical motive that prompted the remark of one
of the Wesleys when he said to a Calvinist, "Your God is
my devil." The entire history of religion bears clear and
emphatic testimony to the fact that all the ethical elements
which it contains have been transferred from the human
sphere to the divine; they are of earthly warp and woof;
they contain man's imperfect but ever growing ideal of
what he ought himself to do and to be. In other words, the
ethical elements in religion are due to an immanent, not a
transcendent, process of development. Nor could it have
been otherwise in the case of beings like ourselves. "If a
man love not his brother whom he hath seen, how can he
love God whom he hath not seen?" Were not man so constituted as to discern and love truth, beauty, and benevolence of character, it would be idle to bid him strive for
their attainment. Only as his own inner nature impels him
towards them, does it become possible for him to respond
to the call of duty to realize them in his own life. A motive
which finds no response within us is no motive at all; it is
simply powerless to move us. In the words of Martineau:

"If a Creator, in projecting a moral world, should omit to render this appreciation [of goodness] immanent in the nature of its people, no repairing message could overtake the defect." [1]

Two remarks may here be added by way of further explanation. In the first place, it is possible to see why ethical thought has slowly transformed religious conceptions, why it has criticized with freer hand than has religion itself. For religion not only strikes root deeply into the past, and, being bound up with the life of one's forefathers, is hallowed in the memory of the individual, but it is also linked to sacred usages on the part of the family and the community, and is closely connected with those doctrines of a future life which have always aroused the strongest hopes and fears of the race. About all its rites and beliefs an atmosphere of awe, of mystery, and sacredness, inevitably gathers; whereas problems of conduct, which have to do primarily with temporal and human relations, are not so hedged about with sacred and awe-inspiring sentiments—here criticism moves more freely and advances more boldly to new positions. It was but natural, then, that religious and theological beliefs should be purified and reconstructed largely through the influence of ethical insights.

Again, the fact that the ethical elements in religion appear to most minds to be transcendent, to have been let down from heaven to earth as a special revelation, is readily explicable. When once an ethical ideal has been reached by the leaders of thought, and, in accordance with the principle already examined, has been taken up into religion as a part of its content, it is then taught as a religious truth. In this new association it carries with it the sacredness and mystery of religion itself. Impressed upon children with all the weight of religious authority, and always retaining this connection in the minds of the people, it necessarily appears

[1] *The Relation between Ethics and Religion, on Address*, p. 7.

to them to be a transcendently given truth, a revelation. But its real origin and history are traceable to man's growing comprehension of his own nature, its meaning and worth, its dignity and ideal perfection.

All religions have developed, as has been seen, some more or less detailed code of morals which they have imposed upon their adherents as an element in religious obligation. Morality has often been regarded almost exclusively from a religious point of view, and it is important, accordingly, to distinguish between a theological and a scientific treatment of the problem of ethics. A theological system of ethics involves certain presuppositions concerning a superhuman order and man's relation to it. In such a system, the accepted ethical principles appear as commands, or laws, of the deity or deities. Thus the rites of hospitality which the ancient Greeks observed, were viewed as the requirements of Zeus, the protector of the stranger and guest. The ethical laws embodied in the ten commandments appear as the direct expression of the will of Yahweh. And in the Brahmanic religion the entire life of the higher castes, from birth to death, was subjected to the control of religious rules. The sanctions of conduct in such a theological system are viewed as residing in the will of the deity, who, it is believed, either directly or indirectly rewards right conduct and punishes evil doing. But a scientific, in distinction from a theological, treatment of ethics seeks to discover and explain the facts of human conduct as facts of the existing order. It seeks to find the sanctions of morality in the natural and inevitable results of the conduct itself, and to establish morality on a rational basis by exhibiting the inescapable consequences of right and wrong action, of good and evil character, as in themselves sufficient grounds for the choice of the one and the avoidance of the other.

In the historical evolution of religion there may be distinguished three general stages, which, if not phases of every religion, have at least been moments in the development of religious thought as a whole, and may well serve as criteria of its progress.   The first may be described as a stage of magic and of sacrificial rites.   The deity is thought to be propitiated by certain formal and external acts, when duly performed.   The second stage is that at which emphasis is placed upon creed and dogma, upon a right intellectual attitude towards the deity.   Less external and formal than the preceding stage, it still represents the divine favor as depending upon something else than the heart and will. The third stage is that in which the emphasis is shifted to morality, to conduct and character.   The earlier stages may of course still be represented in the final stage; the real character of a religion, however, is determined by the emphasis which is given to the different elements.   In a deeply ethical religion like Christianity, the whole of conduct is viewed as a matter of religious service, and there results a unification and harmony of the moral and religious life.   In such a view morality is warmed and brightened by faith in a Supreme Spirit, who is reverenced as the author and guarantor of the moral order.   Possessed of such a faith, the individual feels that he does not enter upon the moral conflict at his own charges, but that behind the known order, where often we see the good overborne and the evil triumphant, there is an Infinite Champion and Defender of right.

Religion may, therefore, render to morality an important service in enforcing its requirements by an appeal to supernatural sanctions.   Although we insist that, with clearer vision and more adequate knowledge, the natural sanctions would prove a sufficient support of morality, we still freely admit that, in the case of many individuals, and even of whole peoples, the supernatural sanctions—the fear of future punishment and the hope of future reward—have been strong supports of the social order.   It is easy to overestimate the moral worth of conduct induced by such hopes and fears.

But one must not forget that there are higher phases of religious experience than those in which these motives operate. The human spirit, touched with pure love and reverence for that beauty and goodness which its faith sees enthroned at the heart of the universe, may be drawn upward, even as Plato taught, by the force of this divine affection.

The powerful and varied influences which religious beliefs have exercised upon conduct in the various periods of human history cannot receive discussion here. It is clear, however, that these influences have been of a dual nature, partly beneficial and partly baneful. For though heroic and saintly souls have again and again quickened their moral life at the altar of religion, the fanatic and the inhuman persecutor have no less surely drawn inspiration from the same source. Some of the saddest pages of history are those which recount the dominance of religious motives. The zeal which is begotten by the belief that the heavenly powers are lending their sanction and support to man, has not always been a zeal according to morality. An "age of faith" is not necessarily an age of morality, nor an "age of doubt" necessarily one of immorality. It all depends upon the kind of faith and doubt in question. One should surely be cautious about measuring moral conviction by dogmatic faith, or moral enthusiasm by religious emotion. Examples are never wanting of those who "believe and tremble," and yet boldly play the devil's part in the business of life.

V. Non-ethical, Ethical, and Anti-ethical Elements of Religion

The most vital relations between morality and religion may be summarized by describing various elements of religion as respectively non-ethical, ethical, and anti-ethical, according to their actual influence upon the realization of values. The non-ethical elements in any religion may be defined as those which do not affect, for better or for worse, man's conduct in human relations. Such elements will naturally most often be found in a religion that is predominantly ritualistic or legalistic. He who believes that the gods simply require a libation or sacrifice, and that he has discharged his whole religious duty when this claim has been satisfied, will not be perceptibly better or worse in his conduct because of his recognition of such a religious obligation. Little ethical significance attaches to the lowest forms of religion. The gods are conceived as powers upon which man is dependent, but they are not thought of as ideal examples or as controlling forces in the moral order. The natural development of religion is doubtless from this non-ethical form to that in which the deities are regarded as moral powers. It is safer, however, to speak of the non-ethical elements in a religion than to describe any religion as non-ethical without qualification. Even the religion of the ancient Romans, which was so formal and legalistic as to be a good example of a religion predominantly non-ethical, cannot be adequately described by this term. For it is perhaps never the case that a religion has not exercised some influence upon men's ideas of personal character or social justice. Even where the gods are regarded simply as powers whose favor the worshipper desires to win, because, wanting their favor or incurring their hostility, he will suffer in his worldly fortunes, it would be hard to exclude all influence, positive or negative, upon the values realized in the life of daily conduct. It may well be urged, therefore, that the elements of religion which we have described as non-ethical are so only relatively. With a nicer discrimination their influence might be traced in the field of values, just as the acts which men call morally neutral may be believed, in the last resort, to fall by fine shades of difference into acts that are either good or bad.

To be ethical, religion does not, of necessity, cast off its credal, or even its ritualistic character. What is essential for an ethical religion is that these elements should minister to inspiration and strength for moral tasks. If by the performance of a rite or sacrifice, or if by the submissive acceptance of a creed, it is thought that merit is gained by which past moral delinquencies are offset, or a balance of credit laid up from which drafts may be drawn for future license, the influence is anti-ethical.

The anti-ethical elements in any religion are clearly definable, for in the case of these the gods are thought to require, or to permit, acts destructive of the true values of life. Human sacrifice and the rites of phallic worship are among the more striking examples of such aspects of religion. But the forms of anti-ethical influence in religion are exceedingly numerous and subtle. Even though the religion in which they appear may be on the whole an ethical religion, that is, one exercising in general a favorable influence upon the worth of life, it is difficult to purge completely any religion of all elements which work, in some way and to some degree, against the development of the highest values. So important is this matter that it is necessary to examine somewhat more in detail the actual requirements of a truly ethical religion. Ethics is far more exigent in its demands upon religion than is commonly thought. Indeed, the claims of ethics in this respect possess, for reasons that we shall see, a priority which we cannot ignore.

Perhaps the most frequent lapse of the great religions of the world into an attitude hostile to ethical interests has been the result of dualistic theories of value. This dualism has naturally been most prominent in connection with the belief in another world, varying forms of which belief have been widely held by historical religions. A future and superterrestrial existence has often been assumed to possess values fundamentally different from those which morality recognizes in the present life. Religious wars and persecutions have resulted largely from this error. For in these wars

it has usually been assumed by one or both parties that certain values of a supernatural order warranted, or even demanded, the overriding of all temporal and earthly values.
To win possession of an empty sepulchre by bloody wars
seemed to the crusading Christians more important than the
cultivation of the Christian virtues of peace and good will.
Often, too, religion has made the surrender of the values of
this life a condition of the possession of those of the future.
Again and again, in the history of religion, a system of conduct has been imposed upon men, not in the interests of life
as we know it, but in the supposed interest of an imagined
life of a different kind. A dualism between the values of the
present and the future order is always and everywhere the
theoretical support of asceticism and other-worldliness.
Such dualism is deeply ingrained in much of the religion of
the Orient, and appears prominently in primitive and mediæval Christianity. Many a saint of the early church and
many a mediæval monk felt that he actually possessed a
more exact and complete knowledge of another life than of
the present. This higher world cast a deep shadow upon the
world below. The engrossing interest in heavenly things
left but scant time and attention for the things of earth.
But obviously tremendous and unwarranted assumptions
underlie this dualism. Not only is it assumed as certain
that there is another life, and that its interests are, in many
ways, different from those which exist within the field of
earthly experience, but it is also assumed that the interests
and values of this other world are so clearly and fully known
that, for the sake of them, one is justified in a course of conduct opposed to that which is dictated by a just regard for
the present life alone. Such a procedure involves reasoning
from the unknown to the known in its most flagrant form.

This dualism in ideas of value is not merely of the past;
traces of it still appear in popular religion. It is often assumed that the real interests of this life, considered by it-

self, would dictate one mode of conduct, the interests of the future life, considered by itself, quite another. But in the absence of all direct knowledge of any other existence, the presumption is wholly in favor of a continuity of values with those of the present order. Nowhere do we find evidence of discontinuity in developing life. As all possible knowledge of values is derived from the experiences of the present life, no other world can prescribe standards of value to this world. In our highest endeavors after a truly spiritual life it still holds good that we must "live by realities." Dualism in values ignores the fact that every attempt to represent to ourselves the values of another sphere of life is based upon actual experience here and now. What the imagination pictures is always an extension and idealization of just those values which are discovered and appreciated in our actual experience. It is a psychological impossibility to construct such representations out of other material than that offered in our present existence. One can even say that the assured knowledge that there is no existence beyond the present life could not change a good man's estimate of what is right and wrong, good and evil. Our standards would remain the same, for we have not a particle of evidence to show that what is truly best for this life is inimical to the interests of the future, any more than we have evidence that anything inimical to our present interests, taken as a whole, can in the slightest degree serve the interests of the future. From the point of view of a sound morality and an enlightened religion our moral tasks, as far as standards of good and evil are concerned, are unaffected by belief on this question. To seek an extrinsic test for moral values is to take refuge in a flight from reality. Religion is, in fact, concerned with the relations which human values sustain to reality, rather than with the determination of these values themselves.

Many elements of historical religion have been in their

popular influence anti-ethical. Such we must without doubt pronounce the stimulation of the fear of death. The natural shrinking from the physical experience of death, which appears as a deep-seated instinct even in the animal kingdom, has often been intensified by the possibility of hideous torture in a future world. This fear has sometimes been defended as helpful in moral ways by restraining men from wrong-doing. Even when so used, it is a crude and unworthy instrument which all higher spiritual culture will surely reject. Such use of the thought of death is no better than the effort of the ignorant nurse to frighten a naughty child into submission by appealing to the terrors of the dark. The thought of death is a moral evil just in so far as it tends to detract from the worth of life; and it must be confessed, alas! that in the past it has had this effect upon the lives of countless numbers. How often the thought of death has sapped the vigor of life, or even paralyzed for a time its activity! How often it has cast over life not only the gloom of deep melancholy, but also the blackness of despair! One almost blushes with shame when one thinks of the foolish and wicked terrors with which the crude theologies of the world have surrounded the inevitable event. It is sad that the teaching of the Christian world has succeeded no better in liberating men from such terrors.

Quite different, however, must be our estimate of the thought of death when it brings to mind beautiful and heroic examples that quicken us to worthier living, or when the thought of our own death admonishes us to make good use of the present opportunity and the present joy. In the interests of life we need to cultivate a more fearless attitude towards death. Admiration must be kindled in the young for those lofty souls who have not counted their lives dear when the call of duty or the course of nature has led them into the great darkness. Such an attitude it is the task of both ethics and religion to inspire. We cannot, however, obscure the fact that death is morally destructive. It is primarily a tragic negation of values; it blots out much that we hold precious; it brings to an end experiences that we seek to conserve; and it takes from the moral struggle many who can ill be spared, while it leaves others who are comparatively useless or who have ranged themselves on the wrong side in the conflict between good and evil. It is our moral task, therefore, to fight against disease and death as we fight against other natural forces that work destructively to human interests. But when all that is possible to human powers has been done, death still remains inescapable and inexorable, not to be cajoled or cheated of its dues. And yet there is clearly a better and a worse way of meeting the fact of death; therefore, a moral and an immoral way. Our duty, then, is to moralize even this tragic event as far as possible, that is to make it serve, as far as it is in our power, the uses of life. Living and dying, our moral task is always a *meditatio vitæ*. Even in the hour of death we cannot cease to be concerned for those persons and causes that we have loved in life. The will so to act, both in life and in the very article of death, that the highest possible well-being shall come to those he leaves behind him, is no small part of a good man's concern. He will seek to make his moral effort significant to his fellows when he no longer consciously carries it on, or watches the fortunes of its progress. The meaning of a noble life is revealed in death with a clarity of perspective often obscured in the crowded days of the actual struggle. Then it is that the thought of the departed may no longer serve merely to chill the warm currents of life, but may speak to us of a brave resignation to the inevitable lot, of heroic endurance of suffering, and of unselfish devotion to ideals of truth, beauty, and love. We ought to think of those who in life have willed to serve the highest values as still united with us in a common earthly task. In very truth they are with us in the fight, not indeed

by our side as the gods in the old myths are represented,
but in an even more intimate way. They are within us,
forming a part of our deepest consciousness, fashioning our
loves and hates, determining our choices and our refusals,
rebuking our weakness and quickening our courage for the
encounter. This is no fable or figure of speech, but indubi-
table fact. To precisely that degree to which the departed
are effectively present in memory, they are still active in
the moral community. In the ethical life we do well to
strengthen our wills and comfort our hearts by these sure
realities, which neither doubt can obscure nor unknown destiny put in hazard. He who finds no comfort in the continuity and permanence of moral influence may well ask
himself whether he has deserved other comfort, and whether
it were not wise, before taking refuge in imaginative pictures of the unknown, to exercise his spirit in the fuller mastery of the possibilities of actual experience.

There are other moods frequently begotten by religious
sentiment which are also at strife with the interests of life.
Such we must pronounce to be an undue absorption in the
thought of the future or a concentration of the imagination upon the unknown. Among the things "not in
our power" is the destiny of the future, and we do well
to leave its unknown fortunes for the cultivation of those
spiritual values which are now within our reach. Unethical,
too, are those moods, however subtle and ingratiating,
which produce in idealistic temperaments a sense of home-
sickness and despair in the presence of the imperfection of
earthly existence. All forms of religious pessimism which
beget a sense of human helplessness and of the illusory and
worthless character of earthly experience are also, on ethical
grounds, to be vigorously combated. All these moods and
tendencies lead in greater or less degree to the negation of
the worth of life, and this is always in principle a destruction
of life, a partial suicide. Suicide itself is, like homicide, a

supreme moral wrong because it is the negation of all the
possibilities of value, not because man does not possess the
right to control the ending of life, as well as its beginning,
when a real ground for such control is present. A deep and
universal conviction approves the offering up of life for a
worthy cause. But suicide, save in exceptional cases, is
the disregard of the values of life, and a cowardly flight
from the struggle which these values impose.

In the past, men have too readily assumed that the moods
of disparagement or scorn of earthly values are of nobler
spiritual rank than those which impel to ends of immediate
worth. But instead of taking higher rank in the hierarchy
of spiritual impulses, they are almost always of a lower
order. Traced to their sources, they are usually found to
spring from disease, weakness, weariness, or a desire for
personal ease. It has also been assumed that the sources
of such tendencies are rooted so deeply in human nature
that it is hopeless, or almost impious, to seek to control
them. Against such a view, one may well place the words
of Höffding: "We must set to work so to modify physical,
physiological, psychological and racial conditions that the
melancholy, the relaxation of mind, the want of courage to
live, which so often underlie a depreciatory judgment of the
value of life, will disappear, or at any rate will no longer be
able to overspread and overwhelm a man's entire inner
life." [1]

But while one must reject the dualism of values into which
the historical religions have so often fallen, and must insist
upon the principle of continuity, it is still possible to recognize that this dualism has not been meaningless, but has
rendered, however imperfectly, its own measure of service.
This service has consisted in deepening the channels of the
spiritual life. It has forbidden man to content himself
with the things of sense, with surface experiences, and shal-

[1] *The Philosophy of Religion*, p. 349.

low views of the world. By it he has often been driven from the outer to the inner life, from the material to the spiritual, from the transient to the enduring. It has rebuked vulgar pleasure-seeking in the practical life and superficial cleverness in the theoretical. Its radical defects have been that it has allowed to an unbridled imagination too large a measure of influence in its doctrines, and has made the triumph of the spiritual life too remote.

VI. THE PROBLEM OF EVIL

But there is another and far more baffling conflict between morality and prevailing theological beliefs. The existence of evil, the presence in the world of many forces clearly destructive of human values, compels one to go deeper in the discussion of our problem, or to abandon oneself to a merely blind acquiescence in the doctrine that whatever is, is good. Religion, as we have seen, always attempts to interpret the universe as a whole, to construe for us the meaning of the entire process, including both nature and our own conscious life. These two elements not only stand in unceasing and complex interaction, but they also often break out into open hostility in the field of values. The order of nature again and again flagrantly disregards and ruthlessly destroys precious values—the very values which it is the task of morality to produce and conserve. And no less surely is there a dualism within the kingdom of man's inner experience, where good and evil contend for the mastery. Here, too, there is much failure and defeat. If we apply the measuring rod of our standard of worth to ourselves, to our fellow-men, and to the social order, there can be but one result. From such a survey we must return with the verdict that human life is not what it should be, that all is *not* well with the world.

The difficulties of the situation appear in familiar historical form in all anthropocentric theories of the universe, and in all anthropomorphic conceptions of God. If the universe has as its central purpose the realization of worth in human lives, its success appears to have been far from brilliant; a host of damaging facts confront us. And, similarly, if God is possessed of our human ideals of value, the question why they are so imperfectly realized in the world, admits of no answer as long as His power is regarded as unlimited. On this view, everything surely ought to be beautiful and good, yes, perfect; nothing in the scheme of things could be changed for the better. But this interpretation clashes too violently with our surest and sanest judgments of value. Morality, it must be remembered, is essentially militant; it takes men into the heat and dust of life. It involves a deep and abiding conviction that it is our duty to labor for the betterment of an imperfect order. And it is accompanied by the insight that, after all our labor, unnumbered evils will remain, that in truth scarcely one of a thousand existing plague spots can be touched. There can be, therefore, no cessation of the conflict while there is strength remaining, no "moral holiday" while life lasts. How different is the view necessarily involved in the assumptions of traditional theology! When taken in earnest, these assumptions mean nothing less than that, from the foundation of the world, all is essentially perfect, that nothing could be changed for the better. From this standpoint our efforts must seem but petty tinkering or puerile interference; even the plague spots are really good, and all the tragedy and desolation a chosen part of the scheme.

VII. Dualistic and Pluralistic Solutions

The sharp contradiction that thus arises between our judgments of value and the actual order of the world, forces religious thought to a choice of alternative views. It must either accept the idea of a limited Deity, struggling against heavy odds for the realization of a moral order launched under difficulties and carried forward against opposition, or it must frankly acknowledge that the universe is realizing other ends as well as those of our human ideals; must admit, in other words, that our human system of values is not one with the divine system. The first of these alternatives involves some kind of religious dualism or pluralism. The second, naturally allies itself with a monistic, or absolutistic, theory of the universe.

James, as is well known, was an ardent advocate of the theory of a limited and finite God. "When John Mill said that the notion of God's omnipotence must be given up, if God is to be kept as a religious object, he was surely accurately right; yet so prevalent is the lazy monism that idly haunts the region of God's name, that so simple and truthful a saying was generally treated as a paradox: God, it was said, could not be finite. I believe that the only God worthy the name *must* be finite." [1] To think God in this way makes it possible to attribute to him our ideals, to regard our values as his values. James himself described the resulting feeling as a sense of "intimacy" between ourselves and the universe, whereas monism meant to him "foreignness." Elsewhere he describes the difference as that between a "thick" and a "thin" interpretation of things.

James by no means stands alone in this view. Mr. Rashdall, in his *Theory of Good and Evil*, holds to the conception of a limited Deity. Against those who profess an optimism which declares the universe to be perfect, his utterance is most emphatic. "I confess I feel strongly tempted," he exclaims, "to adopt the words of Schopenhauer: 'I can not here avoid the statement that to me *optimism*, when it is not merely the thoughtless talk of such as harbour nothing but words under their low foreheads, appears not merely as an absurd, but also as a really *wicked* way of thinking, as a bitter mockery of the unspeakable suffering of

---

[1] *A Pluralistic Universe*, p. 124.

humanity.'" [1] Of the necessity of recognizing limitation in
the divine power he says: "The end which we must suppose
to be the end of the Universe must be the greatest good on
the whole, the greatest good that is possible; that is to say,
the good that necessarily flows from a Will of perfect goodness but limited power." [2]

Another among many representatives of the same view
was Professor Laurie, long a stout champion of theism. It is
significant that near the end of his career we find him saying,
"I find that I must modify my inherited conception of God."[3]
He insists upon the fact of "superfluous pain," i. e. pain
which does not further human good. "Much of the misery
and sorrow of life," he says, "might have been withheld
without detriment, nay with positive advantage, to the purpose of man's existence as a rational and ethical being
charged with his own destiny." "All creation travaileth.
There is something amiss." And he adds, "God is a Spirit
but a Spirit in Difficulty. . . . His life is, in truth, a strenu-
ous life." [4]

Such are the views of some of those who would settle the
account between our judgments of value and the real order
by the first of the alternatives presented above, that of a
finite Deity. It is clear that such a view answers to certain
cravings of the heart. We do unquestionably desire the
assurance of kinship, of "intimacy" with the universe in
which we live. But it by no means follows that all our
spontaneous and unchastened longings are to be satisfied.
And, more serious still, this view enormously increases the
difficulty of any kind of proof or intellectual vindication of
the existence of God—of a God, at least, who is more than
a subjective ideal. What is gained in immediate satisfaction
concerning the nature of God is purchased at the price of

[1] *Theory of Good and Evil*, vol. II, p. 243, note.
[2] *Ibid.*, p. 290.
[3] *Synthetica*, vol. 2, p. 336.
[4] *Ibid*, pp. 328, 336.

making his very existence problematical. It is impossible to enter upon the question here, but most of the arguments employed would also lead, if accepted, straight to the conception of a spirit of evil, a devil, coexistent with the Deity.

In justification of his idea of a finite God, James appealed chiefly to the evidence furnished by certain abnormal or super-normal facts of consciousness. Few can be satisfied with evidence of this kind, depending, as it does, upon such slender threads of experience. One cannot forget, too, that there are difficulties in stopping, as well as in beginning, the play of the spiritual forces which he invokes. If we are to believe in the existence of one finite Deity, why may we not equally well believe in the existence of several? The evil in the world would find one of the most plausible explanations in the lack of harmony and coöperation among numerous spiritual agents presiding over it. But if we once accept the belief in a realm of finite, encompassing spirits, such as James suggested, what bar exists to the revival of primitive and mediæval views which peopled space with innumerable spirits, good and bad, angelic and impish? That conception of things was surely "thick", not "thin"; it provided amply for "intimacy," but an intimacy, alas! from which most of us would pray to be delivered. We should prefer the "foreignness" of the Absolute to such intimacy.

The difficulties of dualism or pluralism in religion will to many seem not only grave, but altogether insurmountable. The practical solution of the religious problem which this alternative offers is purchased at a high price. But the practical solution is certainly clear. If one believes that a limited Deity is struggling under difficulties to realize ideals of worth, even weak human effort may in some measure turn the fortunes of the fight. The conflict must appeal to all that is chivalrous in human nature. Who can hesitate on which side to draw the sword? The choice of one's cause will not depend upon a calculating estimate of the

strength of the contending forces, nor upon the prospect
of victory, but solely upon the intrinsic worth of the cause.
Every true-hearted soldier of the good must go forward,

"Though marching under orders ever sealed,
And battling ever on a doubtful field." [1]

VIII. MONISTIC SOLUTIONS

But many find themselves driven by an inescapable necessity of thought to a genuinely monistic view of religion.
To them God is the all-encompassing Life, outside of whom
nothing exists. To his Being all the finite parts are truly
organic. In Him, therefore, is the evil as well as the good,
the darkness as well as the light, the sorrow as well as the
joy of existence. At once, then, the clash between our
human ideas of value and the ends realized in the universe
appears again in all its sharpness. One must admit either
that our judgments of good and evil are in some way illusory
and untrue, or must frankly acknowledge that our values,
even at their best, are simply human and relative, not one
with those of the divine order.

Attempts at compromise are indeed frequent among the
monists. Some strive to maintain the perfection of the
Universe, and at the same time the reality of evil. Thus
Royce asserts that while evil is a reality, and no illusion, of
our finite experience, yet in the whole of things, in the Absolute, there is no abiding evil, no unredeemed failure, no
ultimate imperfection. He expresses this view in almost
impassioned words. "I sorrow", he says, "but the sorrow
is not only mine. This same sorrow, just as it is for me, is
God's sorrow. And yet, since my will is here also, and consciously, one with the Divine will, God who here, in me,
aims at what I now temporally miss, not only possesses,
in the eternal world, the goal after which I strive, but

---

[1] From an unpublished poem by Harry Lyman Koopman.

comes to possess it even through and because of my sorrow. Through this my tribulation the Absolute triumph, then, is won. Moreover, this triumph is also eternally mine. In the Absolute I am fulfilled. Yet my very fulfilment, and God's, implies, includes, demands, and therefore can transcend, this very sorrow." [1] "When once this comfort comes home to us," he adds, "we can run and not be weary and walk and not faint. For our temporal life is the very expression of the eternal triumph." [2]

However strong our sympathy for this exalted mood of faith, we cannot accept it blindly. The assertion that the whole is perfect, and that there is nothing but triumph in the Absolute, will seem to most thinkers a piece of pure dogmatism. How a whole of spiritual experience can be good when the parts are evil, is indeed a puzzle. The word puzzle is here suggestive. For it is sometimes said that the relation of the parts of reality to the whole is like the relation of the pieces of a picture puzzle to the completed picture, meaningless when taken by themselves. But all such analogies fail at the vital point. All conscious individuals are themselves centers of value, and their failure as individuals cannot be made good by any assumed success of their united experience. The error of explaining away the evil of finite beings through the triumph of the Absolute is similar to that which often finds currency under the figure of the social organism, where the meaning and worth of the individual is merged in the whole. But, as we have maintained throughout, individuals are themselves genuine centers of value. The triumph of the Absolute is, in this view, purchased at the price of defeat and suffering on the part of finite beings. Any bit of unrequited suffering is surely evil, even though it occur in the brute creation. Suffering on the part of a lower order of life may be justified

---

[1] *The World and the Individual*, Vol. II, p. 409.
[2] *Ibid*, p. 411.

as the necessary condition of the good of a higher order, but the system that requires it is, at best, a very imperfect system. The attempt at the same time to justify and to refute our human standards of valuation breaks down from inherent contradictions; a fatal flaw vitiates the whole process of reasoning. This flaw is the attempt to refute what we do know by what we do not know. We do know the existence of evil as an assured fact of human experience. The complete transformation of this into good, we do not know. Such assumed knowledge is only the dubious affirmation of imaginative metaphysics or of unquestioning faith. It would be easy to sit at one's desk and draw checks for an unlimited amount, if the question of their being honored at the bank were never to be raised. And it is similarly easy to refute our experiences of good and evil by reference to an Absolute experience as long as the supreme test of the truth of the view can never be applied.

In Mr. Bradley's statement of the problem we meet the same dogma of the perfection of the Universe. In keeping with his general method, he reduces our judgments of good and evil, along with the rest of our ordinary judgments about the world, to the plane of appearance. These judgments are not wholly false or illusory, but possess a lesser degree of reality. "Goodness is," he says, "appearance, and but a one-sided aspect of the Real." [1] Mr. Bradley's logic leads directly to the idea of a "super-moral" realm, in which the distinctions of good and evil, as they exist in us, are entirely transcended. In the Absolute, the partial, the one-sided, and the imperfect are done away in completeness, unity, perfectness. And it is the characteristic of religious faith, we are told, to grasp here and now this insight, and to realize that, despite all failure, the individual is already perfect in the one perfect Life. For is it not clear that in the last resort the vessels of dishonor are as neces-

[1] See *Appearance and Reality*, Chap. XXV.

sary as the vessels of honor, and the children of wrath as truly justified as the children of light? All must be serving the ends of the Universe, whether they aim to do so or not. The difference between saints and sinners is in the rôle they are called on to play, and the consciousness with which they play it.

To such a view, which would reduce moral distinctions, together with all our other ideals of value, to a kind of *quasi* reality, or phenomenal existence, it may be retorted that we are much surer of the truth of these same judgments of good and evil than we can be of those judgments which would establish the existence of that kind of an Absolute described by Mr. Bradley. To abandon the one for the other is like leaving the solid earth and attempting to find foot-hold in the air. Certain idealists and mystics have never consented to take seriously the world we know. To be consistent, they should not take all too seriously the world which they construct out of such materials.

The mystics, in their treatment of this problem, belong with the absolute idealists. All the great mystics, Christian, Neo-Platonic, and Hindu, have been pronounced monists. On this point they have been in full agreement, however sharp the differences that may have separated them elsewhere. One Life pulses through all things; beyond it nothing is or can be.

> "They reckon ill who leave me out;
> When me they fly, I am the wings;
> I am the doubter and the doubt,
> And I the hymn the Brahmin sings."

Those familiar with the history of thought will remember how emphatic the mystics are as regards the relative and partial character of all our human ideas of value. None of them, not even love or goodness, can apply to God. He is above all such predicates. If, in their desire to describe God, they use any of these terms, they are compelled at once to deny them. "God is in Himself," says Erigena, "loving, seeing, moving, yet he is not in himself loving, seeing, moving, because He is more than loving, seeing, moving." "If I say God is good," exclaims Meister Eckhart, "it is not true. Rather I am good. God is not good. . . . Therefore be still and prate not of God, for with whatsoever speech you prate concerning Him you do lie and commit sin." Hence the negative element in the theology of the Christian mystics, who could describe God only as the "All and the Nothing." To the mystic, all our earthly life is in the land of shadows. Hence too the tendency implicit in the doctrine—it does not always become explicit—to a disregard of distinctions of good and evil; for it cannot greatly matter how things go in a shadow world. One value alone is for them outside of this relative and temporal order. This transcendent value is the mystic sense of union with the All; but it entirely defies description; it can only be experienced—the rest is silence.

Not essentially different in its interpretation of human values is the mysticism of India, save that it is avowedly pessimistic. To Hindu mysticism the idea of any positive good to be realized by individuals is part of the illusion from which mortals suffer. Good and ill—and both are ill in different degrees—are a part of the troubled dream of human consciousness, one phase of the illusion produced by the blinding veil of Mâya, through which our perception and understanding are condemned to see all things. From this illusion only the saint and sage are delivered. Their deliverance is found in turning resolutely away from human joys and sorrows, and walking the lonely and rugged way that leads at last to Nirvana, the negation of all desires, the end of all earthly striving.

In such ways have forms of monism, influential in religious thought, dealt with our ideals of human value when viewed in their relation to the Universe. They have all denied the identity of our estimates of good and evil with those of God. In this respect, the monists have divided sharply from the pluralists and dualists. Sometimes indeed the two modes of thought have contended for the mastery in the same thinker. So they contended long ago in St. Augustine. The reason that he was inconsistent, and was drawn now towards dualism and now towards monism, was because of this very problem of good and evil, the problem of human values. When the burden of evil weighed upon his mind he inclined to dualism. The Manichaean heresy always had a degree of attraction for him. In his interpretation of history he was an out-and-out dualist, as witness his dramatic presentation of the theme in his *City of God*. But when this problem is not in his mind and he works freely as a speculative thinker, he is undoubtedly monistic. Only when one approaches the study of St. Augustine with this key, will one find that the conflicting tendencies and contradictions of his thought can be explained.

The results of this part of the discussion may now be summarized as follows. If the evil of the world is willed by God, His will is not wholly good according to our human ideals; if evil is not willed by God, His will is of limited power. Such is the dilemma. If we accept finiteness in God, the resulting view is dualism or pluralism. On the other hand if we pronounce for monism, and at the same time affirm the perfection of the Whole, we must regard our human judgments of good and evil as tainted with error or illusion of some kind. We cannot take seriously our estimates of value. And further, if we believe in a finite, struggling Deity, we may regard our task as that of soldiers who enlist under his banner to fight the same enemy against whom He is contending. But if we believe in the ever triumphant Absolute of the religious monists, then our human life, just as it is, with all its evil and imperfection, must be illumined by the transcendent insight of the seer, or the unquestioning faith of the saint. So illumined, every human life will appear as somehow perfect in the perfect Whole.

IX. Evil No Illusion

But there is an ever increasing number who find neither of these views satisfying, and who are compelled to take a different attitude towards the problem. Forced to reject dualism, they are also forced to give to our known ideals of worth a validity denied them by most forms of monism current in religious thought. In any thorough reconstruction, the dogma of the perfection of the Universe must be abandoned. It is in no way essential to monism, even to an idealistic monism. Idealism, we must remember, does not change the actual values of the world. It only describes in general terms the form of reality. A world reducible to terms of conscious process might conceivably be a very bad world or a very good one. Just how good or how bad the universe actually is, remains an empirical question, a question of fact which we can at present determine only to a limited degree. At all events, mire and mud and dirt do not cease, on the idealistic hypothesis, to be sources of pollution. They soil the hands of the idealist as readily as they do those of the realist. The same is true of moral pollution; it is still evil. And, similarly, intellectual and æsthetic quagmires of error and ugliness do not, at this word, become gardens of truth and beauty.

The entire problem of the existence of evil, in the form in which the problem is commonly stated, is, I am convinced, gratuitous and artificial, a problem which we ourselves create. To ask why evil should exist in the world, is just as meaningless as to ask why there should be a world at all, why reality should exist. And to speak of this as "the best possible world," means just as little and just as much as to call it the worst possible world. In fact it is both, for it is the only possible world. Reality *is*—a given fact; good and evil are both parts of it, one as natural and as necessary as the other. Observe the inconsequent and puerile character of our ordinary procedure. In the very act of discovering that there is a world at all, we discover evil as an essential part of it. In childish dissatisfaction and caprice we then demand a different kind of world; as if the universe could be made and unmade at our bidding! But why, in Heaven's name, should there not be evil in the world? Apart from certain naïve assumptions about the universe, it would never occur to anyone to raise this question. These assumptions, born of primitive thought, have become so deeply rooted in traditional teaching that they die hard. But it is, in truth, no more strange that there should be death than birth, sickness than health, decay than growth. We should no more wonder that nerves throb with pain than that they thrill with joy. It should occasion no more surprise that men experience sorrow and anguish of spirit than that they experience satisfaction and delight. Such a view is not necessarily pessimistic. It simply recognizes that evil is an element, and, for all we can see, a permanent element in the actual order of things. It does not forbid the hope that it may be diminished. That again is a question of historical fact and of future trial. The real problem of evil, then, is the practical one, the problem of how best to meet existing evil so as to overcome it where we may, and to endure it nobly where we cannot overcome. Right endurance of evil is indeed often, in its own measure, an overcoming. But we must not therefore hastily assume that evil is eliminated, that the surd disappears. For we are unfortunately confronted with countless cases of endurance that are passive, unrequited, and without the spiritual victory which alone could justify them.

The assumptions about the nature of things which have led men to ask why evil should exist have come to us from a distant past. Foremost among these assumptions was the dogma that the world had been planned and constructed by a Being apart from it, perfect alike in the possession of all values and in the power to realize them through a creative act.[1] Such a Being, it was naturally assumed, must have been able to produce a perfect work. How did evil enter into it? Here was indeed a problem which might well weary the heads and break the hearts of sensitive mortals when in the grip of the world's sorrow and tragedy. Linked with this assumption, were naïve conceptions of the physical universe which had been constructed and launched upon the strong current of European tradition long centuries before the dawn of the new astronomy with its transforming insight. The old astronomy had placed man at the center of the physical universe, and the old theology had found the meaning of the entire cosmos on this tiny planet. All the myriad suns and stars were but candles for the stage setting of the drama of human existence. This idea, firmly imbedded in the mediæval philosophy of history, still unconsciously colors religious thought. Men still demand that the universe shall turn about them, and that their interests shall constitute the center of its meaning. But the universe is now acknowledged to be infinitely larger than the ancient astronomy had thought, and the life of God vaster than the old theology had dreamed.

Religion, however, requires that our human interests shall not be thrust outside the scheme of things nor lost in the wide content of the universe. Expressing man's place in the cosmos in the language of religion, we may say: In God's empire are many kingdoms. The life of humanity constitutes one of these kingdoms. Bounding this and in

[1] If we should reverse the commonly accepted presupposition and assume a Creator all-powerful, but malign in his purposes towards mankind, we should then have "the problem" of good. Every experience of good would be a mystery. Apologists for the existing order would then seek to show that good is a mere illusion. or at least evil "in the making."

constant interaction with it, are the kingdoms of animal and plant life, and of inorganic nature. And, beyond the known, stretches in unmeasured sweep of imagination the unknown. How many and great may be the kingdoms of ends that other worlds support, or how rich may be the values realized there, we do not know. It still remains true, however, that our human kingdom is a kingdom of the empire, not an independent state. The great imperial law of interaction holds for all the kingdoms, and involves significant relations between them. In fact we can see how man levies tribute at the boundaries of his state upon animal, plant, and mineral, and how these in turn often levy costly tribute upon man. Science has revealed the tremendous influence upon the human body for weal or woe, for life or death, of microorganisms. And man's dependence at every instant of his existence upon a vast and complex system of physical forces, which, if they further, also often defeat his ends, is too familiar to need recounting.

Our conclusion, then, concerning the cosmic meaning of human values is that they constitute a part of the real ends of the universe. Doubtless they are not all the ends, nor can we affirm that they are the most important of them, though unquestionably they are the most important we know. The central insight, however, which is vital for all religion and morality, is that the laws of spiritual life which hold within the kingdom of human values are no less valid because they are not laws of the whole empire. With presumptuous egotism men have often declared that love and righteousness have no meaning or worth unless it can be shown that they are principles which govern the entire scheme of existence. But this they can never be shown to do. Rather is it clear that they have their *raison d'être* and their full justification as elements of value within our human experience. The same is true of all our other ideals. Their sufficient vindication lies in the fact that they enrich and ennoble man's life. Their validity is established in and through our experience of them. Happily it does not fall because we are unable to show that they determine every part of the universe. That would indeed be a precarious position for the ideal. But if we give to all elements of ideal worth their rightful place in the life of man, we need not fear that they will ever be refuted by any discovery concerning the physical universe. Even though our little planet, with all its life, were to become uninhabitable, or to be swept entirely out of existence, it would still be true that these ideals had been no fiction or illusion of the fleeting moment, but genuine realities organic to the whole of Being.

It must be freely admitted that the assurance of the universal extension and complete triumph of the values we hold dear would be a source of the deepest joy. But we must remember that, because a subjective feeling of comfort does actually enhance the immediate values of the individual, the cherishing of the feeling is not on that account justified. It would be vastly comforting to believe that a thousand hard facts are not what they are. And it is also important to ask what ultimate effects comforting illusions will bring in their train. Often far-reaching social consequences are involved. It is incontestable that, despite the pain of readjustment, the result of philosophic and scientific criticism has been a great enrichment of human living. Such enrichment could not have been won without costly struggles. The deepest and most precious faith, the faith none can afford to lose, is the faith that to discover the truth about reality and to follow this truth loyally, will in the end lead to the highest good. To live by error or illusion is costly. It is like living on credit—in the end the reckoning must be paid.

The conclusion to which we are driven is that there is a measure of conflict between the processes by which human values are realized and certain other processes that are going

on in the universe. We are not justified in saying that the
one process is real and the other a mere appearance. All
are real parts of the real universe, though differing in extent and in value. This view does not forbid us to believe
that the world process as a whole is worth while, that it
contains more good than evil. It is also entirely consistent
with the belief that there has been progress, however slow,
in the historical life of the race. And how much the evil
of the world may be further reduced, how far the spiritual
process may succeed in eliminating it, just this remains the
ever fresh problem and alluring adventure of human life.
But from every speculative journey in which one seeks
to get a glimpse of the vast empire of existence, and of the
relation of our kingdom to this vaster whole, one must return to the humble duties of citizenship in the kingdom.
Here is our task, here we must find the meaning of life.
To discover and obey the laws of this kingdom, to further
the good and to thwart the evil within it, is at once our
highest duty and our deepest joy. The individual who
asks for his special place in the kingdom of ends may be
reminded that he can at least cultivate his own garden. If
he recognizes, as he must, that all that blossoms and grows
there is watered by streams from the eternal hills and
nourished by the all-pervading Life, he may undertake his
work in a genuinely religious spirit. To such a spirit it is
not essential to be assured of perfection either within the
tiny garden or in the unmeasured universe.

X. The Future of Religion

A further question still awaits our inquiry. Will religion
be a permanent element in man's life, or, having done its
work, will it at last be cast aside like a worn-out garment?
It has frequently been said that in the development of religion its value has consisted more and more in the ethical
content which it has taken up, and that it will finally be so

merged in morality that the specifically religious will cease
to exist. But this, we are sure, can never be the case. In
asserting the permanency of religion, one may point with
no little confidence to the fact that religion has a source
in man's nature and in his experience of the world quite
distinct from that of morality. Its root strikes deep into
the soil of life and will not perish. We cannot rid ourselves
of the necessity of interpreting in some way the universe
that encompasses us and determines our fortunes. For the
realization of all values we are directly dependent upon the
cosmic Power. However far human knowledge may extend
its control, we shall not gain full mastery. We must "still
acknowledge our complete dependence upon the power that
brought us hither and will conduct us hence."

Nature seems indeed at times a genial foster-mother,
satisfying us like children with the bounties she provides.
But she is not always gentle. And when, with irresistible
might, she crushes all our earthly hopes in the final tragedy
of death, we are rudely shaken out of an easy-going contentment with sense experience, and compelled to seek with
all our might for a more inward and enduring good. Life
itself is the great teacher; by differing and often strange
paths are men led at last to the Father's house. Not forever
is the spirit of man content to wander abroad; it turns home-
ward at last to seek its own and to claim its heritage.

What we must look for, then, is not the passing of religion into other forms of value, but its continued inner
growth and transformation. This process of change is not
merely of the present, but has been going on ever since
the dawn of the most primitive animism. Change is, indeed, the indispensable condition of permanence. The very
idea of religion attaining finality at any given stage of
civilization involves also the idea of its speedy dissolution.
It would cease to be a thing of life. It would no longer
adjust itself to the other growing elements of spiritual ex-

perience, but would inevitably be strangled by them. The
old order does not wholly perish but stamps itself upon the
new, so that there is no absolute break. "Impossible as it
seems, the mumbling medicine man is the far-off precursor
of St. Francis and Savonarola, of Wesley and Luther. And
the same change goes on in other parts. Sacrifice, which at
first is intended to satisfy the animal needs of the wor-
shipped, and later gratifies them rather by the mere pleasures of taste and smell, becomes finally a symbolic utterance to God of submission and faithful reverence." [1] The
course of development, however, will not be backward.
The classical age of religion, when it was the single interest
of life, has passed and can never return. Other spiritual
interests have been developed. We must not suppose that
our age could find satisfaction for its religious longing by
returning to mediævalism or primitive Christianity. This
would be possible only by surrendering all that has been
won in the intervening centuries, and returning with the
utmost literalness to the stage of culture then existing.
Only by giving up the very essence of modern life could we
enter again into the shadowy realm of mediæval faith.
Equally impossible is it for the modern man to realize his
spiritual life in the form which it assumed for a simple
Palestinian folk. Centuries of growing experience separate
us from this age. Deep racial differences are also here involved.

The result is an inner conflict between the actual life
of the western world and much of its professed faith. Were
not this opposition so largely unconscious, the result would
often be a moral dualism, and even hypocrisy. In the business of life we find men devoted to the acquisiton of wealth
and power, developing the strength and beauty of the body,
creating arts and institutions, pursuing the truth of science
wherever it may lead them—and all this, while professing to

[1] Stratton, *The Psychology of the Religious Life*, p. 339.

accept as final a faith which found little place for any of these values. In truth, those values which have given to modern life its characteristic form and its special problems are the very ones which lay beyond the horizon of early Christian thought; in origin and nature they are extra-Christian values.

It is not because the values won by modern civilization embellish life in its outward aspects that they are chiefly to be prized. It is rather because they transform life from within, giving to humanity worthier interests, deeper aspirations, and purer joys. Thus all the manifold scientific, historical, literary, philosophical, and artistic interests, to which thousands now give the service of their lives, are elements of spiritual worth. They belong to the spirit, not to the flesh. Every act and every moment of life is different because of their presence. Religion is not the same when lighted by all the insights of intelligence and warmed by æsthetic appreciation, as when deprived of these influences. Every added element of culture makes a difference in man's spiritual outlook. As the result of a mathematical problem changes with every change in the value of the factors, so the problem of human life changes with every change in its content.

The meaning for religion of this change in the content of values has, in the past, been largely ignored. Thought must be awakened to a full consciousness of the divergencies between the spiritual outlook of the modern and of the primitive Christian world. The very idea of civilization as an effort to embody, in just proportion, all human values in the growing customs, laws, institutions, and ideals of the race, was foreign to the thought of the early disciples. The kingdom, the vision of which filled with expectant longing the hearts of the early Christians, was not primarily the spiritual ordering of earthly life. It was rather a transcendent kingdom, destined to come from without, suddenly to be realized in a new heaven and a new earth wherein should dwell perfect righteousness. This new order was not to rest upon the wretched structure of existing society. Human institutions, whether of government, of education, of literature, or of art, had for them no part in the regeneration of humanity. Least of all did they dream that science, with its exact methods of observation and its attitude of doubt towards popular and traditional explanations, was to be a mighty instrument in the process of spiritual development. Little, too, did they think that the gentile Greeks had already sown the seeds of progress, and that in the course of the centuries unknown peoples and distant lands were to be the chief centers of their unfolding.

XI. THE WORLD-DENYING AND THE WORLD-AFFIRMING SPIRIT

We may here briefly characterize two important and opposing interpretations of the spiritual life of man. One has regarded the material world, the bodily life, and all the stuff of earthly experience as foreign to man's true end. For it, the embodiment of ideal values in the historical life of the race is not significant, or even possible, to any important degree. It feels little interest in the slow and painful effort to secure the triumph of knowledge and beauty, of freedom, justice, and well-being in the present world. It has turned its gaze wistfully towards another existence, transported by the vision of a perfect life to be realized under very different conditions. This view, essentially oriental in spirit, dominated for centuries the religious life of Europe. Not till the Renaissance, did the opposing interpretation gain a secure foot-hold. The latter view, Greek in origin and modern in spirit, represents one contrast of Occident and Orient. The world-affirming spirit clings bravely to the values it can discover in our actual experience. While insisting upon the true inwardness of life, it still regards all the elements of the present order as material out of which is to be fashioned a genuinely spiritual kingdom. Consenting to take one world at a time, this interpretation of life regards it as the task of humanity to realize the richest possible content of values through a slow process of development.

We have thus the active, practical, world-affirming spirit, in opposition to the passive, dreamy, world-denying spirit. It is the demand of a pulsing, expanding life, bent upon realizing its meaning in the forms of earthly civilization, in conflict with a spirit that had little interest in the development of mundane culture. It is the will to found stable government, to organize social life, to establish institutions, to accumulate wealth, to improve the physical and mental quality of the race, to develop science, to create literature, to enjoy the beauty of nature and of art—in a word, it is the will to possess a full human existence, in conflict with an other-worldly temper to which all these things are of trifling worth because "the fashion of this world passeth away."

In this opposition it is clear to which side primitive Christianity inclined. But it is also clear that Christianity contributed truths of profound import for the deeper life of the race. In its almost unconscious submission to the *Zeitgeist*, with its imperious demand for action in new fields of interest, even the so-called Christian world seems in danger of losing these truths and of keeping only the husk of an intellectual formula. Against this, every lover of morality and religion cannot fail to raise a protest. All the elements of universal worth which it contained must be taken up into the new order and conserved as integral factors of life. These elements had, it is true, found various expression elsewhere. Other voices there were which had bidden men to love their neighbor, to share their bread with the hungry, to lift the burden of the weak and sorrowing, to seek for purity of heart and redemption from the evil of the world. But no voice has had for us such compelling power as that which gave to Christianity its impulse and its ideals. Launched upon the tide of European thought and preserved in a continuous religious tradition, this teaching has never ceased to utter its protest against a shallow and external view of the meaning of life. Frequently obscured, and often flagrantly disregarded even by its professed followers, it still lives, and will continue to be a power as long as men contend with good and evil. Only superficial or prosaic minds will deny to many dogmas of historical Christianity a profound symbolic truth, even when these dogmas are not statements of scientific or historical fact.

The longing for a more perfect realization of values than is possible under the conditions of earthly life has again and again driven men to picture an ideal world, a world apart from this and moulded to the heart's desire. In such an ideal order the spirit has found refuge from the sordid and painful experiences of actual life. Historically, at least, Goethe's words are true:

> "So löst sich jene grosse Frage
> Nach unserem zweiten Vaterland."

The doctrine of two worlds has appeared in so many lands and among so many peoples that it may be said to offer, in typical form, the final solution of the problem of good and evil. In Pythagoreanism, Platonism, Neo-Platonism, Christianity, Mohammedanism, and in many other cults, the doctrine has found expression. Much of the history of religion might be written in terms of this dualism. But, as we have insisted, the dualism so created must not be allowed to break the continuity of developing values. If it does this, confusion and contradiction result. Without prejudice to any legitimate hopes of a future life, it can be said that, out of the spiritual travail of the centuries, has come with increasing clearness the insight that the two worlds of value are here and now—that they are with us in each hour, nay in each moment of choice, as we consciously will to dwell in the world of knowledge or ignorance, of love or hate, of beauty or ugliness, of generous aims or ignoble passions. By such choices we determine the place of our citizenship. The elevation of man's soul to a world of love and truth and beauty is the goal of both morality and religion. Morality views this realization of a kingdom of values as our human task; religion sees in it also the Divine Order, the meaning and fulfillment of at least one part of the Universe. The feeling that what is won in this process is unspeakably precious is the true basis of religious reverence, and confidence in the extension and growth of these values the true ground of religious faith and hope.

XII. TRUE AND FALSE OPTIMISM

How far, it may be asked, can the interpretation of the problem of evil which we have suggested yield an optimistic view? Does not such frank admission of the place of evil in the world commit one rather to an heroic pessimism? On what terms can we still maintain the worth of life?

The kind of optimism, and the only kind, consistent with the facts of experience must be both critical and creative. A critical optimism faces fearlessly the facts of nature and of human life, and does not ask to have bitter truths concealed, nor does it desire to be led by illusions or encouraged by promises that may not be fulfilled. Such an optimism rejects the idea that evil is an error of our finite thought. If the evil of the world is illusory, the good, we must insist, is equally so. As against such a view the old theology, in its doctrine of the devil, had, as at many other points, a sure hold upon the facts of human experience. The devil represented in a bold and virile way the reality of evil. If a belief in the existence of a personal devil has gone the way of many other outgrown beliefs, the facts for which the devil stood have not ceased to exist; they have still to be reckoned with. A true optimism, then, can never be easy-going or over-confident. It must rather be sober, teachable, and heroic. If it finds truth in the saying that "evil is good in the making," it recognizes that the process is a costly one, that it involves waste and suffering, and that waste and suffering are in themselves evil. From the standpoint of an ideal system of values the surd remains unrationalized. We cannot deny that the birth-pangs in which life begins, or the death-agonies in which it ends, or a thousand things that lie between, are evil. What a true optimism contends for is that life may be made good enough to pay these heavy charges, that it may indeed celebrate a spiritual triumph,

> "Spite of despondence, of the inhuman dearth
> Of noble natures, of the gloomy days,
> Of all the unhealthy and o'ershadowed ways
> Made for our searching."

A creative optimism which may hope to achieve this end must be grounded in the spiritual forces of man's nature, and in the will to create values. The belief in values, and in the power which works in and through us to produce them, is indeed the chief condition of their realization. It is here that we need clearly to discern a parting of the ways in religious beliefs. Conceptions that are true to man's spiritual life may be untrue to external nature; they may correctly interpret the world of human values, but falsify other parts of reality. If we insist that the cosmic order must correspond to the inner order—if, in other words, we make a cosmology out of our psychology—we are always in danger of illusion and disappointment, for the world is neither my idea nor my ideal. It is essential, too, that we have correct beliefs concerning man's spiritual capacities, because these beliefs assure to us firm ground on which to contend for the realization of a better order. But it is not essential, as it is obviously impossible, to have equally exact and complete ideas about the universe as a whole.

These two spheres may be further described, in familiar phrase, as "the things in our power" and "the things not in our power." In the one, destiny depends in part upon the human intelligence and will; here our effort to create the good largely decides what good there shall be. But with no less certainty we must acknowledge another realm in which docile recognition of an order beyond the control of our wills is the beginning of wisdom, and resignation the first law of life. In this realm, it makes no difference whether we will to have things as they are or otherwise. To this fixed and resistless order we vainly oppose our wills. It were a mockery of sorrow to attempt to believe that we are not left in desolation when a loved one has died. But it is no mockery to will the belief that this tragic event may prove something better for our inner life than a bitter and rebellious fact. To try to cling to a disproved theory of science or a discredited article of religious belief is to yield to the spirit of obscurantism. But to strive to adjust ourselves to the new truth with positive gain to thought and action is genuine faith and optimism.

When religion truly learns to place the Kingdom of Heaven within us, and to admit that the placing of it elsewhere is at best an hypothesis or an act of faith, it will have won a sure fortress from which it can never be dislodged. Such security it cannot possess so long as it rests upon assumptions that are open to challenge by every fresh advance of scientific knowledge. To build the spiritual life without falsifying reality—this is "the victory that overcometh the world."

For the future, if religion is to assert its rightful power over serious and thoughtful minds, it must be ready to take up all that the long experience of humanity has won. It must recognize how largely its own nature has been transformed, and it must be prepared to face further changes without fear or shrinking. Only by such a temper can religion maintain the sincerity that begets confidence. Further, if religion is deeply to pervade our lives, even the most humble acts by which we seek to create the world of values must be viewed as an expression of the Divine Order. Thus what morality requires, religion reinterprets and inspires with its own quickening spirit. So every moment of delight in nature and of joy in fellowship with our kind, every triumph of the higher over the lower impulse, every insight of the intelligence, and every forward struggle of the race, is a part of the meaning of religion. These are expressions of the all-pervading Power. He who does not find God here is in danger of finding Him nowhere.

INDEX

Democritus, 62

Descartes, 30

Desires, distinction between the desired and the desirable, 120–121; nature of disinterested, 109–110; organization of, 219–220; relation of, to the moral life, 181–182

Determinism, and practice, 353–356; and the problem of evil, 366–369; consistent with freedom, 356–360; distinguished from fatalism, 363–365; in relation to punishment and responsibility, 369–374; points of agreement with indeterminism, 343–345; some objections answered, 360–363, 365–369; statement of the problem of, 335–338

Determinist, attitude towards life of the, 374–376

Dewey, J., quoted, 101; and Tufts, quoted, 161

Dickinson, G. L., quoted, 200–201

Diderot, 30

Diogenes, 78

Dualism, in problem of evil, 406–410, 427–428; in theories of value, 398–400; of Kant, 338–339; of Plato, 82

Duns Scotus, 40n

Duty, and Virtue, 301–302; concrete nature of, 313–314; dependent on value, 250–253; limits of, 251–255

E

Eckhart, quoted, 414

Economics, relation of, to other sciences, 21–22

Economic Values, dependence of other values upon, 190–192; instrumental, 190; relation of, to moral problems, 188–193

Egoism, and altruism, 232–235. See Desires, Individualism

Ehrenfels, quoted, 121n

Eliot, George, 28; quoted, 227

Emerson, quoted, 413

Empiricism, and intuitionalism, 256–262

End, in relation to means, 57–58. See Teleology

Energism, 102

Epictetus, 89, 90

Epicureanism, 61–64

Epicurus, 61–63

Erigena, quoted, 414

Ethics, a science of values, 6–9; both normative and descriptive, 14–20; constructive in aim, 30–35; definition of, 7; etymology of, 5; field of, 1–6; practical value of the study of, 25–30; reason for study of, 26–27, 34–35; relation of, to Philosophy, 9–14; the attempt to evaluate all values, 24, 187

Euripides, quoted, 321

Everett, C. C., quoted, 304

Evil, dualistic and pluralistic solutions of the problem of, 406–410; monistic solutions of, 410–416; on the deterministic hypothesis, 366–368; problem of, 405–421; reality of, 416–421

Experience, modern desire for, 329; value, a function of, 115–117; variety of religious, 386–388

F

Fatalism, distinguished from determinism, 363–365; view of self of, 364–365

Feeling, and intellect, 208–209; as an element of religion, 382–385; psychology of, 118–120; related to function, 154–161; relation of, to value, 117–128

Feuerbach, quoted, 390

Fichte, quoted, 42

Fiske, J., quoted, 139

Fite, W., quoted, 230

Form, relation of, to content, 42–45, 47n

Formalism, and Teleology, 38–40; inadequacy of, 45–49; Kantian, 40–45; truth of, 290–295

Fouillée, 262n; quoted, 30–31, 226

Freedom, consistent with determinism, 356–360; degrees of, 358–359; meanings of the word, 356–357; statement of the problem of, 335–338; through knowledge, 359–360

INDEX

conception of, 287; Sidgwick's definition of, 287n; the essence of character values, 290; use of the term, 287–288

Virtues, of intrinsic and instrumental worth, 203; teleological character of the, 54–57; unity of the, 299–302; varying estimates of the, 300

Wealth, as exchange value, 188; moralization of, 192–193, 248. See Economic Values.

Westermarck, E., 1n, 3n, 238n

Wordsworth, quoted, 307

Work, definition of, 197–198; moralization of, 198

Wundt, quoted, 119n, 287n, 303–304

W

Wallace, W., 63n

X

Xenophon, 60

ve L